When It Was Worth Playing For

My Experiences Writing About the TV Show
"Survivor"

By Mario Lanza

First Printing, May 2015. Second Printing, June 2015. Third Printing, August 2015.

ISBN 9-781512-069884

www.funny115.com

Dedicated with love to the Survivor franchise, and to all the amazing characters over the years who have made it what it is. Oh, and also Amanda.

Foreword
By Rob Cesternino

In the summer of 2000, what we knew as television was dramatically changed forever with the premiere of the reality TV show, "Survivor." During those 13 weeks when the show originally aired, "Survivor" became the biggest cultural phenomenon of its time. Everybody was watching it and everybody was talking about it. Over the course of the following 15 years, the show would continue to evolve and age with more and more players trying to outwit, outplay and outlast each other for a million dollar prize. During that time, there has been one man who was eyewitness to the extensive history of Survivor... Mario Lanza.

I first learned of Mario during my frantic preparation to cram for my imminent departure on "Survivor: The Amazon." I had always been a Survivor superfan myself but I didn't read a lot about the show on the internet prior to my own 39-day adventure. It turns out that Mario had been writing about the show pretty much since the very first season. Mario's articles were not just about the inner workings of the game, he also included pop culture references and humor that made his writing so addictive. I tried to absorb as much of his writing as I could before leaving my computer behind to play "Survivor."

After my season of "Survivor" had ended in May of 2002, I finally had the courage to reach out to Mario. After we began a friendship that summer, I solicited Mario's help before my next Survivor adventure. I would soon be leaving for Survivor All-Stars, and I considered Mario to be the world's foremost expert on what a potential Survivor All-Star game would look like.

Mario had written the epic fan fiction pieces, "All-Star Survivor: Hawaii" and "All-Star Survivor: Alaska." These incredibly detailed stories were works of fiction but they played out as if they were real seasons of the show, cast with players from the first 5 seasons. Mario sent me paper copies of his works and I enjoyed them immensely. I didn't end up enjoying the real Survivor All-Stars nearly as much.

Over the course of the years, Mario has become an amazing resource in the Survivor community. While anybody can go back and watch the older episodes of the show, nobody quite remembers what the response to those shows was like Mario Lanza. Mario has encountered many of the key figures in Survivor history over the years and he never forgets any of the great and unbelievable stories that my fellow former-Survivor castmates are capable of.

If you're reading this, I already know you are an incredible Survivor fan. If the pages following this foreword are anything like the writing that Mario has been doing for over a decade, you are certainly in the same way Big Tom would be after Ethan gets a big plate of ham.

·

Contents:

Introduction

First off, why am I writing a book about a TV show? And why do I think that people will actually be interested in reading it? Just who the hell do I think I am?

These are all excellent questions.

For starters, I never really set out to write "a Survivor book." This really just started out as an essay on my website, funny115.com, where I talked about how I got involved with the TV show Survivor, and how I wound up becoming a commentator and columnist. And how I eventually became sort of a "Survivor Insider." And how, between the years 2001 through 2005 (and maybe even beyond), I was pretty much the most widely read Survivor columnist on the entire internet.

Again though, I never really planned for this to turn into a book. I just saw it as a fun little essay project that I was writing for my website. Every couple of weeks I would write up a new chapter about my experiences as a Survivor writer. And then I would write up another chapter. After about a year, my essays had grown into what would be considered a fairly sizable project. And it was at this point that people started coming to me and telling me that they thought I should turn it into a book.

"Me? Write a book?" I remember thinking. Who would want to read a book by a guy who writes about a TV show? And again, I like to come back to this question, but who the hell am I to warrant even having a book in the first place? I am certainly no one of any importance. I'm just some guy who likes to write about Survivor. Also, I haven't written about Survivor full time for nearly a decade.

"But your stories!" people would tell me. "You have such funny stories!" I would hear from my readers that a lot. Or I would hear, "You have such a different perspective on the show. Most people never saw Survivor from the perspective that you saw it from. You should write it up and share it with people who might have gotten into the show later and who never experienced all that."

And so, well, there you go. That is why you have my Survivor book in your hands. That is the only reason why it exists. It was just a simple little essay that I was writing on my webpage, and it slowly but surely (with the help of a lot of people along the way) grew into something much bigger. And only because I have a lot of readers out there who believed in me and who encouraged me to always keep my Experiences essay going. I dedicate this book to them. I especially owe a great deal of thanks to the gang over at the Facebook group, POS (Previously on Survivor). You guys make way too many unfunny Willard jokes, but you guys are the best.

I would also like to thank my lovely wife Diana, who for years has found the internet Survivor world to be "obsessive", "strange", and "kind of creepy." And who is amazed that I love them and that I continue to hang out with them after more than fifteen years. And, you know, I can't necessarily say that she is wrong about any of that. The online Survivor world is weird. And it is obsessive. And as you will see from this book, I am probably the most obsessive one of them all. But hey, what can I say, I love Survivor. And also, I am a masochist. I love the pain that caring so much about this franchise has always brought me. That helps.

Special thanks also to my editor, Mike Bloom, who not only read this book and helped me iron out all of the technical issues, but who is also one of the co-hosts of my Survivor podcast, "The Survivor Historians." Mike and I have only know each other for a couple of years, but he is already one of my best friends in the Survivor community, and I can think of no one else who I would rather have yell at me just because I threw too many sticks in the fire.

And I would be remiss if I didn't finally thank George Hanns, who not only came up with the title for my book, but who also provided me with some last minute formatting advice right before I sent this off to the publisher. Thank you George. Unless, of course, you aren't the one who actually came up with the title, and then in that case I will thank Gary Dreslinski instead. I don't actually know who came up with the title of the book, if you want my honest answer. But I'm sure it was one of the two of you, so you both get partial credit for it. And I guess I better also thank Sam Geesey for catching a couple of typos in the first printing of the book, and for ~~nagging~~ inspiring me to fix them and to put out a second printing where all the typos would be fixed. Thank you Sam. I promise to send you an advance copy if I ever put out a second book.

Oh yeah, one last thing, if I can ask you for a favor. After you read this book, please email me at MLanza1974@aol.com or contact me at funny115.com and let me know what you thought of it. Did you like it? Did you not like it? What did you like or not like about it? I would really like to know, because my plans are to turn this into a series of books about the overall history of the Survivor franchise. But I will really need some feedback first about what you, the Survivor fan, would like to see in a Survivor history book series.

In any case, thank you for buying my book. It was a very personal experience writing all my experiences down on paper, and I'm not the most outwardly expressive person in the world, so that "sharing everything" part was kind of difficult for me. But it is all done now, and I am very proud of the way it turned out. I hope you enjoy it.

-Mario

"Sometimes I think that Mario does not even watch the same show. What a tool!"

-Survivor: Gabon contestant Randy Bailey

1. Blame Howard

Oddly enough, it all started with Howard Stern.

It was January in the year 2000, and I was listening to the Howard Stern Radio Show one morning. I used to listen to him in my car every day on the way to work, Howard has always been one of my comedy heroes. And that morning, I heard him talk about something that was eventually going to change my life.

"Hey, did you hear about this new game show?" he said to his newscaster, Robin Quivers. "They're going to strand sixteen people on an island. And the last person standing at the end of the game wins a million dollars."

Huh?

"Yeah, no kidding," Howard explained to his skeptical crew, "They are actually going to kill people on network TV. Can you believe it? Somebody is going to die on national TV."

This was the first mention I ever heard of the show Survivor. I heard about it from Howard Stern. And I heard that people were going to die. From this point on, I was officially interested.

I went home that evening and I searched the internet for this new island game show that Howard had been talking about. Of course, this being 2000, not 2015, it was a lot more difficult to find info about new TV shows back then. All I found on Google were some vague summaries of "survival of the fittest" and "this controversial new TV show that is being developed over at CBS."

Since the internet wasn't helping me much, I went back to my original Survivor information source, Howard Stern. Every single morning that month, I tuned into his show to hear if he was going to talk about it some more. And sure enough, usually he would. Howard was absolutely fascinated by the fact that a mainstream American TV network would put a show like this onto its airwaves. He was amazed that we had come to a point in history where a programming executive would actually allow something like this to happen.

"Can you imagine the lawsuits?" he loved to point out. "Just think of all the contracts and waivers the players are going to have to sign. This is crazy.

And what if somebody actually does die out there? What then?"

Howard was fascinated by the "Wow, they are finally going too far" aspect of this new show, which was the exact same thing that was already fascinating me. There was literally nothing like this that had ever been done before on American TV. You can't just throw everyday people onto an island and film them until their bodies shut down and they can't take it anymore. Seriously? You can't do that on TV. This isn't a Stephen King novel. Are you kidding me?

When Howard Stern (Howard Stern!) is saying that a TV show might be in poor taste, you know you are talking about something with the potential to be memorable. I mean, come on, this is a guy (Stern) whose listeners made prank joke phone calls to CBS in the middle of the 1993 World Trade Center attack. And then he played them on his show. This is a guy whose radio show probably pushed troubled former child star Dana Plato over the edge in 1999. She appeared on his show to talk about her failing career, and Stern's listeners made fun of her and were so brutal to her on the air for several hours that it is probably part of the reason why she went home after the show and she overdosed. THIS is the guy who is saying that Survivor sounds like it is might be in poor taste. And so right there I knew it. I knew it, and anyone listening knew it, because Howard Stern knew it. This was either going to be the greatest train wreck in the history of TV, or it was going to be something spectacular. Even back in January of 2000 you could already see it.

Whether it turned out to be good (20% chance) or it turned out to be bad (80% chance), Survivor was already on my radar because it was going to be memorable.

2. The Big Letdown

After weeks and weeks of hype by Stern (and soon, other more mainstream media outlets), Survivor premiered on CBS on May 31, 2000.

What is significant about this date to me (and which later becomes part of the story) is that my daughter Vanessa was born two months prior to this, on March 9, 2000. Which means that the night Survivor premiered, my wife Diana and I-- like all parents of newborns-- were pretty much stuck at home, smack dab in the hell that I like to call "Baby Boot Camp."

If you have never been through Baby Boot Camp before, here is how I like to describe it.

Baby Boot Camp is the first three months of a baby's life. Nobody in the house is sleeping. Nobody in the house is happy. Everybody in the house literally hates one another. The two first-time parents (who generally have never done anything like this before) are absolutely starved for sleep, they are absolutely starved for normalcy, they are absolutely starved for ANYTHING that will help them escape from their new sleepless, friendless, funless, hellish existence.

In other words, Baby Boot Camp is a punishment I really wouldn't wish upon anyone. There is no other way to describe it, Baby Boot Camp SUCKS.

So anyway, Diana and I were smack dab in the middle of Baby Boot Camp. And here comes premiere night of Survivor. Everyone was excited.

At the time, there was really only one other show we were regularly watching on TV. The only show we watched regularly prior to Survivor was MTV's The Real World. Which, as history will show, was the original "first reality show!" before Survivor came in, stole its title, and rebooted the genre.

We went from watching the one big influential reality show to watching the new big influential reality show. Life is funny like that.

So here comes premiere night of Survivor. CBS. Wednesday night. May 31st. Everyone was excited.

I am sure that anyone who was there in the summer of 2000 can remember that first Survivor episode like they just watched it last night. That opening.

Jeff Probst's first speech. The credits. The contestants' names. The players being forced to jump in the water. That badass theme song. It was completely unique. There had never been anything like this before on American TV.

By the way, here is something I will admit about that opening episode of Survivor. I have never admitted this before, but I will now since I guess I am being honest with you. When the show started, and we got past the opening credits, my very first reaction to Survivor was disappointment. I was disappointed (and honestly a little pissed off) when Jeff Probst explained the rules of the game and he explained what the players were going to go through.

"I didn't know they were going to vote each other out," I said to my wife. "That's not how it was advertised at all. I thought they were supposed to stay out there on the island until they dropped. This sucks."

Yep. For the first time ever, I will finally admit it. I thought the concept of Survivor was terrible, and I was completely let down by it at first. I mean, my God, what a cowardly way for the producers to wimp out and soften it up for TV. They just vote each other out. How lame. So much for this awesomely harsh TV experiment of Darwinian survival.

The only thing I wasn't let down by at first, of course, were some of the players, who I thought were interesting. Hmm, this Gervase guy seems pretty funny. I bet I will like him. And what's with this guy Richard, who claims he is the winner? What an annoying fat blowhard this guy is. It will be fun to see him have some sort of a downfall.

As turned off as I was by the concept of Survivor (and some of the execution-- let's face it, by later standards the first episode of Borneo is practically unwatchable), I was interested enough in the people to want to stay and see what was going to happen.

"Okay, let's see here," I tried to predict in my head. Clearly this is going to be a survival of the fittest type of situation. You are going to want to keep the people around who will make your tribe stronger. So clearly the old people are going to go first (BB, Rudy, Sonja). And then after that probably the young people (Dirk, Colleen, etc.) are going to be next. And then the middle aged people are going to win because they are more or less the only ones who will be able to fit in with everyone else. With what I knew about psychology and sociology, I could see it just as clear as crystal in my head. I mean, come on, what is Survivor really but just basic sociology? They are building a civilization out there. You cut out the weak, the strong survive, and that is the only way that the foundation of a society can work.

To me this was the biggest no brainer in the history of TV. No one over 50 or under 30 could ever win Survivor. They simply couldn't. Basic sociology and basic social structure just wouldn't allow it.

"Watch this," I said to my wife after the end of the first episode (and after the predictable dismissal of Sonja, aka Souna). "The first three episodes will be the old people going home, and then it will finally get interesting. Then the young people have to start turning on themselves. Wake me up when we get to episode four."

It's funny. Thinking back on it now, just imagine if the first season really had played out like that. Imagine what would have happened if eventual cultural icon Rudy Boesch wouldn't have made it to the final four. Imagine if the show really had turned out to be that predictable. If that had been the case, I really do think the entire Survivor phenomenon would have played out a lot differently.

Oh yeah, two things I specifically remember about watching that first episode with my wife. I specifically remember hearing that Gretchen was a pre-school teacher and laughing about it. "Don't laugh at her," my wife (who works with little kids) scolded me, "She's probably the best organizer out there. Pre-school teachers are generally on top of stuff." I apologized, but I couldn't help it. Yeah, the pre-school teacher is going to win Survivor. Sure. Good luck with that. Let's see how that works out for her.

> **Side note:** If you aren't familiar with Gretchen Cordy, let's just say she was a lot more than just a simple pre-school teacher. She had formerly been employed by the U.S. Air Force. Gretchen was a trained survivalist, which meant that out of all the Borneo players, she was by far the most comfortable of any of them living in the outdoors. Oh yeah, and what did she do when she worked for the Air Force? Well her job was to **train soldiers how to withstand torture if they were ever captured by the enemy**. Yeah, I think it's safe to say I kind of underestimated her. Gretchen Cordy was kind of a badass.

The other thing I remember saying about that first episode was, "Am I crazy? Or did that BB guy just say warsh instead of wash?"

3. It's Like Watching Pure Evil

As I said before, I was initially disappointed with the first episode of Survivor. I felt I had been taken in by CBS' classic "bait and switch" advertising technique, and I remember not being very happy about the way it had all been presented to us. You can't promise a TV show where people are going to die on an island, and then have it turn out to be some lame old game show where the players are just voted out. Voted out? You mean there's nothing Darwinian about it at all? Why would I waste my time getting all emotionally invested in this garbage? This game isn't supposed to be about popularity, it is supposed to be about survival of the fittest. It is supposed to be about surviving the elements, the cream is supposed to rise to the top. Voting the other players out of the game is dumb.

Yes. I hated Survivor after the first episode.

But then... you know... a funny thing sort of happened.

In the seven days between episode one and episode two, I started to think about the "concept" of Survivor. I started to think about what the show was really about. I started to think about it a lot. And it started to dawn on me that the entire concept of Survivor was a lot deeper than it appeared to be the first time you looked at it. For some reason, between episode one and episode two, the whole thing started to click for me.

"Do you realize how nasty this game is going to get?" I remember writing in a television forum on one of my favorite internet message boards at the time. "Do you realize that all but one of these people are going to have their friends systematically turn on them? Do you realize that fifteen out of these sixteen people are going to be humiliated on national TV and it is going to be very painful to watch? Does anyone get that this show has nothing to do with outdoorsmen having some grand old adventure on an island? That it is really about greed and personal ethics and selfishness?"

"No matter how nice and fun and light-hearted it seems now," I pointed out, "This game is going to get incredibly evil at some point in the future. Mark my words. At a certain point down the road, it is going to get ugly out there."

This was the aspect of Survivor that I don't think clicked with a lot of the audience right off the bat. When most people watched the first few episodes, they might have fallen in love with the show. They might have fallen in love with the adventure. They might have loved this new TV game show with all of their hearts. But I think they fell in love with an entirely different aspect of the whole Survivor concept than I did.

I think what drew most of the audience in at first was the same thing that drew someone like Greg Buis in at first. I think most people were attracted to the show by the promise of adventure on a remote tropical island. I think they were drawn to it because they wanted to see what it was like to play Swiss Family Robinson when you were living on an island. They wanted to see interesting people on TV, and they wanted to see survival.

Not me.

What finally sucked me in to Survivor was the fact that this was going to be the cruelest and most gut wrenching TV show we were ever going to see in our lives. Fifteen of these people (94% of the cast!) were going to have their hearts ripped out and stomped on by their friends on national TV. All you had to do was do the math. Fifteen of them had to go, only one of them could win. And the ones who were going to go were going to be eliminated in the most degrading way possible, their peer group would shun them through a simple popularity vote. That is just nasty. If you looked down the road, you could already see where this game show was going to go. It was going to get ugly out there.

Once I realized how cruel Survivor was bound to become, I knew that I had to watch it. I knew it, there was no way to get around it now. Because this was now no longer just a television show. For me, once I realized what Survivor was "really" about, I now viewed the whole thing as one big evil televised psychological experiment.

What was the test of ethics that somebody compared Survivor to during one of the first few seasons? "F--k Over Your Buddy"? Yep. This was now F Over Your Buddy on a completely different scale. This was now F Over Your Buddy on a nationally televised scale. I caught on right away, but I don't think that most of the audience would for a couple more episodes (namely the Gretchen episode).

By the way, at this point I should probably point out that I was a psychology/sociology major in college. This is the only stuff that I ever studied when I was in school. And once I realized what Survivor was really all about, well of course I realized that it was right up my alley. This show was wandering into the exact same territory that I had been studying just about every day for the past eight years.

7

Side note: My specific interest in college was criminal psychopathology. I studied why some people turn into sociopaths and why other people don't. In 1996, I wrote my senior thesis on serial killer Ted Bundy.

What was interesting to me about Survivor was, well now here is a new game show that encourages the players to shun the needs of the group, and to only think of their own personal needs instead. To always put their own benefit above the benefit of the others. To associate with other people simply because they need them and because they need their vote. And then, at the end, the players are encouraged to discard their friends simply because, at this point, their friends are now getting in the way.

Well hey, if that isn't a good layperson definition of "sociopathy", I don't know what is!

Sociopath:
"Someone whose social behavior is extremely abnormal. Sociopaths are interested only in their personal needs and desires, without concern for the effects of their behavior on others."

Right there, THAT is what really sucked me in to the concept of Survivor. Now I could watch the cruelty of a really horrible and unethical psychology experiment on TV, and I could see it combined with the fascination of watching strangers try to form a brand new society from scratch on a tropical deserted island. This was everything I was looking for in a TV game show and more! It was like if they took Gilligan's Island, they disguised it as a gripping melodrama, and then they underscored it with the subtle evil viciousness of the Stanford Prison Experiment. Yay! Who needs the Real World after that? Who wants to watch people dying on a desert island after that? This evil psychology experiment was going to be far more interesting than both of those!

So that was my mindset as we transitioned from episode one (the Souna boot) to episode two (the BB boot). In seven days I went from "watching it as a game show" to "watching it as an evil psychology experiment." An experiment which was a lot nastier and a lot more evil than most people realized at first glance.

Oh yeah, but first things first. Before we got to the cruelty, before people could turn into self-centered sociopaths on national TV, first we had to get past the first three predictable old person boot episodes.

This show was going to become great. Absolutely. But first we had to trudge through the first three episodes, which I was already referring to as The Old Person Death March. It was obvious to me that Survivor wouldn't truly hit its stride until they got rid of all the inevitable over-50 cannon fodder.

BB (the crotchety old gumpypants of Pagong) was voted out in episode two. Completely predictable. Nobody liked BB. He was toast the minute he set foot on that beach.

And, of course, Rudy (the last remaining old guy) was expected to be next.

All along, I kept saying to my wife, "Just wait until episode four. Episode four is when it will get interesting. Episode four is when they will finally have to turn on the young people. Just wait." I said that to her over and over.

But it turned out I was wrong.

For the first time ever, Survivor turned out to be way more unpredictable than I ever expected it would be.

4. The Stacey Stillman Incident

Episode three of Survivor will forever go down as one of the most important moments in reality TV history.

Why?

Well that's easy. The reason episode three was so important was not because of the fact that a young person (Stacey) finally went home over an old person (Rudy). No, it wasn't that at all. The reason it was so important is because in my opinion (and a lot of peoples' opinions), it was the first episode of Survivor that was completely manipulated and influenced by the producers.

Most old school fans already know this story, but if you are new to Survivor the last few years, you will probably find this interesting. And no I am not making this up.

There is a great deal of evidence out there that Mark Burnett and company didn't want Rudy to leave at the end of episode three. They didn't want the three old people to be picked off "one, two, three" in the first three episodes of Survivor. They didn't want it to happen for advertising purposes, and they didn't want it to happen for just plain old fairness purposes. So there is a lot of evidence out there that the producers sort of... well, we'll say "influenced"... the way the vote went down in that particular episode.

The general story most people are familiar with is that Rudy was supposed to be the target at the end of episode three. The Tagis had him in their sights as "the cranky old guy that nobody wants to live with", and that was that. He was going to be toast. But the producers (knowing that Rudy was going to be a breakout character, not to mention the last remaining savior of the over 50 viewership, and a marketing goldmine) pulled a few key players aside before the vote and asked them if they would reconsider their choice.

"Wouldn't you rather vote with your conscience?" the producers allegedly asked. "Instead of all ganging up to vote off the old guy? Wouldn't you rather vote for one of the other players instead?"

Now, obviously, I wasn't there at the time. I have no idea exactly what the producers did, or what they said, or what they didn't do or didn't say that particular day on the island. All I know is that Stacey (the 20-something female lawyer) was suddenly voted out over Rudy. It marked an enormous shift in the way the game of Survivor was being played (strategic voting as a bloc instead of just knee-jerk picking off of the weak), and to this day there is an enormous amount of speculation out there that the producers sort of "tinkered" with the way the game was playing out at that moment.

Oh yeah, and I should add that Stacey Stillman later sued the producers over this incident. And that her lawsuit was covered by an enormous amount of national publicity. And she reportedly got a nice cash settlement out of the deal, which likely included some agreement that she never publicly discuss this in the media ever again. Which she never has.

And so there you have it. The story behind the infamous Stacey Stillman incident.

For years, I refused to accept the idea that episode three of Survivor: Borneo might have been fixed. For years I would simply refuse to acknowledge that. Any time somebody brought up the idea that Survivor was "fixed" or that "the producers rigged the Stacey vote in episode three", I would simply put my hands over my ears and make la-la-la noises. Because I didn't want to hear it. No way, Survivor is too pure, it is too awesome, and you're not gonna start talking smack about my favorite TV show. Stacey was voted out legitimately, her vote was not fixed, and she only sued the show because she is a baby and because she sucks. I can't hear you, you are rubber and I am glue, Survivor is awesome, la-la-la-la-la.

But over the years I have finally started to soften on that stance.

Actually, soften? Screw that. By this point, fifteen years later, I have completely thawed.

In my opinion, YES the producers fudged the third episode of Survivor. Absolutely. I don't think there is any doubt about it in my mind, there is just way too much evidence out there to support it. In fact, in my opinion, I think there are several things about that first season that were more than likely manipulated in some way.

But at the same time, do you know what? I really don't have a problem with that.

Seriously, if you were the producer of Survivor, think about it. What would you do? You have this golden god of a potential new TV franchise, and you know it is going to be this huge major hit when it gets back to America. There is no doubt about it. The concept is so original, and the story is so compelling, and the whole thing is so well-designed and produced, you know

11

that viewers are just going to eat it up when they start to get all wrapped up in it. This is one of the biggest no-brainers in the history of television. Survivor is going to be a hit. You know it because you can feel it. Case closed.

Ah, but here is the catch.

In the first three episodes, the three old people are going to be picked off. Bam, bam, bam. One, two, three, they will be picked off like flies. They have no chance out there because the show is completely Darwinian (survival of the fittest), and there is really very little they can do about it. The three old people on Survivor are going to be toast. Especially the cranky old Navy Seal (Rudy), who is already criticizing everyone, and is throwing around nicknames for people like "Perry Homo."

As a producer, here is what you know. You know that Rudy is a potential breakout character. You also know that you can build an entire marketing campaign around him, simply because he is a celebrity and because he is a freaking American hero (seriously, look it up, in real life Rudy is practically a legend in the American military community.) You also know that one of the show's main sponsors is going to be the U.S. Army. Oh yeah, and you also know that you would really like a viewing audience that actually includes people over the age of fifty. Especially when your TV show is going to air on CBS, which at the time had the reputation of being "the old person's network."

In other words, if Rudy Boesch goes home in episode three, for no reason other than "he's old", you will lose a LOT of your potential viewing audience. You will lose the elderly AND the military (which just so happens to be your major sponsor.) And if you lose a huge chunk of your audience so early in the season? Well say goodbye to Survivor ever becoming a CBS mega franchise.

When you look at the whole situation this way (which I am sure Burnett and company did at the time), I can see exactly why the producers sort of "influenced" the players to change their Rudy vote to Stacey. I mean, hell, we are talking a lot of money here if this show becomes a hit. We are talking money for CBS, money for the sponsors, money for Mark Burnett. Heck, for Mark Burnett, if this show becomes a hit, he probably has a new career as a reality TV show producer. There is a LOT more at stake here than simply "making sure the game is played fairly and correctly." For the producers, this Rudy episode could easily be the make or break point of the entire franchise. There could be actual careers at stake.

The Rudy/Stacey incident becomes even more important when you realize that there are rumblings that the Tagis are thinking of putting together some sort of a four person "voting alliance." And that one of the four people in that alliance is supposed to be Rudy. Rudy! If Rudy Boesch makes it past this vote (which is going to be close), your 72-year old Navy Seal legend and sound byte machine has a very good chance of making it to the final four. The final four! How do you think that will look on a future Survivor marketing campaign?!?

In any case, when you look at it that way, I have no doubt in my mind that the producers had some influence on the Stacey vote in episode three. Oh, they weren't able to manipulate the game directly (after all, the players are the only ones who cast votes), but there is no doubt in my mind that the producers had a hand in what went down in that episode. In fact, at this point in time, I don't believe there is any way that anyone who knows their Survivor can deny it anymore. Because the evidence is out there. The court depositions are available all over the internet, just Google them. You can read them for yourself. The producers absolutely stepped in in an attempt to save Rudy.

And again, do you know what I say about that? Do you know what this hardcore old school Survivor purist says about the producers influencing the game just to save Rudy?

I am freaking glad that they did!

Do you realize how much worse the first season would have been if Rudy hadn't stuck around to the final three? Do you realize how much less interesting it would have been if all the old people had been picked off three in a row? And do you realize there might not have been a Survivor 2 if America hadn't fallen in love with the show, and hadn't fallen in love with Rudy himself (who I will always argue was the single most popular Borneo contestant)?

If I could meet the producers who helped save Rudy that day, I would go up to them and I would shake their hands. Because to me, that is exactly what a TV producer should have done in that particular scenario.

Fairness? Integrity? Game show neutrality? Screw that. We're not putting together a charity event here. We're trying to build up a potential new television franchise. If Rudy stays, the show will be a hit, and right now that is all that's important to us.

So anyway, when I say that episode three of Survivor was one of the most important moments in reality show history, now you know what I am talking about. It was important to the viewers because it showed that--- OMG!--- a young person actually got voted out over an old person. And--- OMG!--- the concept of "alliances" was actually thrown around for the first time as well-- not an insignificant thing in the development of Survivor. But it wasn't just important to the audience. It was also important to the producers, to the players, and to the crew members, because it showed that yes, the producers actually <u>can</u> step in and fudge the direction of the show a little bit if they feel like it. No, they can't do it directly. But there sure is a lot of gray "wiggle room" in the middle they can play around with if they know how to get away with it.

The only problem with the Stacey incident was that the producers didn't really know how to get away with it yet. They were way too obvious about their manipulations in that particular episode, and they got caught with their hands in the cookie jar. Hence the Stacey Stillman lawsuit, not to mention a subsequent book written about the lawsuit that I could not recommend more, which was called "The Stingray."

The producers did okay this time, but in the future, they would have to become a lot more careful about things if they wanted to manipulate the game in a certain direction. Which, of course, they did. They actually got a lot better at it.

And no, I am not talking about them basically handing Russell a "hidden" immunity idol every episode in Samoa. We're not up to Samoa yet. Just wait, we'll get there.

By the way, if you are curious why Mark Burnett will never refer to Survivor as "reality TV", well now you know why. In the early days of Survivor he would go out of his way to never ever EVER utter that phrase. Ever. In fact any time somebody WOULD call Survivor "reality TV", Burnett would quickly correct them.

"Survivor isn't reality TV", he would say with a smile, "it is an unscripted drama."

If Stacey were legally allowed to talk about this, I am sure she would agree with him.

5. Australians Love B.B.

At this point in the first season, Survivor was starting to get some actual buzz behind it. We were three episodes into Borneo, the media and the internet were starting to talk about it, and it was quickly becoming the new hit show of the summer of 2000.

What was awesome about this point in the show's history was the fact that, although Survivor was cool, it hadn't yet become "too cool." It wasn't quite up to point where EVERYONE was talking about it. That would come later, of course, but at this point in time the only people who were really truly hardcore discussing it were the people on the internet message boards.

Survivor Sucks (the most popular Survivor fan site, which still exists to this day) was already around, of course, but I hadn't wandered over there and set up a membership yet. In 2000, most of my time was spent on the television forum on ISCA BBS (a popular text based message board hosted by the University of Iowa). Or, if I got really ambitious, I would wander over to my favorite TV review website, Television Without Pity (which was known as Mighty Big TV at the time.) TWOP was one of the few websites where you would find some pretty good hardcore Survivor discussion. But for the most part, to everyone else on the internet, Survivor was still just "that show on the island that most people had wanted to watch, but hadn't really gotten around to tuning into yet."

In other words, Survivor at this point just felt like that little cult TV show that only you and your cool friends had discovered. It hadn't quite taken over mainstream America yet. When you found somebody else who actually watched the show and who wanted to talk about it, it felt like you were both members of some kind of a secret club.

This was easily one of my favorite points in Survivor history. Because it was our show and the rest of you hadn't found it yet. It was like Mystery Science Theater 3000, only it was better and it was on every cable package. And it was still ours, it didn't belong to the rest of the country yet. So there, mainstream America, nyah nyah.

Like I said in chapter two, the timing of Survivor was particularly important to me because it came out in the middle of what my wife and I like to call "Baby Boot Camp." We were literally stuck in the house with a baby for three months during the spring of 2000. We had nothing to do. We had no friends we could visit. We had no relatives nearby to help out. We were too tired to go out and ever actually do anything. All we could do that spring was stay home, watch TV, and every once in a while maybe catch 15 or 20 minutes of sleep if the baby would allow it.

So, really, this fascinating new cult TV show became this symbol of greater importance to us.

Once a week, on Wednesday night, we had this show that we both loved. Then the rest of the week sucked. Then on Wednesday night, for an hour each week, we could escape and enjoy our lives again. Then it was right back to sucking. If you have been through Baby Boot Camp before, can you relate to this? Well that was the story of our lives. We had Survivor, and then we had the next 167 hours that sucked. Some weeks Survivor was pretty much the only thing that was keeping us sane.

We got through episode four (the Ramona boot), and we got through episode five (the Dirk boot). Both episodes were awesome.

And what happened next is something I will always remember.

Diana's parents decided to take us on a vacation in July of 2000. They knew we were stuck at home and that it was driving us crazy, so they decided to take us to Australia on a two week vacation. Which was awfully nice of them. The two of us certainly couldn't have afforded that.

This was a super nice gesture of them, of course, but it also meant that-- GASP-- we were going to miss the next two episodes of Survivor!

Holy crap. I mean, this was the year 2000. Most people didn't have any sort of a DVR yet. In fact, we wouldn't own a DVR for another six years. At this point, if we wanted to watch episodes six and seven of Borneo, we were going to have to rely on our crappy old unreliable VCR timer. But... but... what if the timer doesn't work? What if the power goes out while we are away? What if our VCR forgets to tape those two episodes? What if we miss the Survivor merge? Holy crap, if something goes wrong while we are away, how will we know how the rest of Survivor plays out??

I know it sounds silly now but this was a terrifying moment for me at the time. What if I didn't get to see episodes six and seven of Survivor? How would I be able to recover from that? What if Rudy got voted out next? What about Richard? Would I honestly be able to live with myself if I missed the Richard Hatch boot episode??

In any case, remember, the number one rule of Fight Club is you don't turn down a free trip that somebody else is paying for. So we flew to Australia in July of 2000 and we had a nice vacation. It wasn't the greatest vacation in the world (I mean, we still had a three month old baby with us, and she slept exactly zero hours during the entire trip), but it was a nice distraction. If nothing else it was just nice to escape the daily monotony of Baby Boot Camp for a while.

And it was in Australia, oddly enough, that I finally realized how big Survivor was going to get.

Remember when I said that Survivor still felt like some little cult show that only you and your cool friends were watching? Well screw that. I had been dead wrong. Survivor was HUGE. I just hadn't been out there enough because I had been stuck at home during Baby Boot Camp. I had taken a few months off from following mainstream pop culture after my daughter was born, and I hadn't realized that Survivor was the TV show that was already sweeping the world.

Yes, not just sweeping America. It was already sweeping the world.

> **Side Note:** Yes, I am aware that Survivor didn't actually start in America. It started in Europe, a couple of years before we ever made an American one. We just took what they did in Europe and we managed to ~~perfect it~~ rip it off. But I don't care. Americans are known around the globe for being ugly and smug and self-important and for taking credit for everything, and in this case I guess I am no exception. So let's just go with the story that Survivor started in America, if for no other reason than it works better with my essay and it makes me feel better. Thank you for your understanding about this. Also, yay soccer.

In any case, yes, it was in Australia (on a remote little island on the Gold Coast called Heron Island) that I finally caught on to how many people out there were into Survivor.

We were in a tour group one day on Heron Island, and we were doing a reef walk. And I remember I made some offhand remark that it was like walking around Pulau Tiga. I made a joke that maybe I should go get a spear so I could go spear fishing, just like Richard.

Almost immediately, some ten year old Australian kid's ears perked up behind me.

"You watch Survivor?" he asked me.

"Oh yeah," I said, "It's my favorite show."

"Did you see the episode last night?" he asked me.

"No," I said, "But please don't tell me what happened. I'm taping it at home. I'll watch it when I get back."

As you can see, I have always hated spoilers. I still hate spoilers to this day. If you know what is going to happen on Survivor, please don't ever tell me. Ever! I have honestly lost friends over this policy.

Well unfortunately for me, the kid's friend standing next to him didn't have any problem with dropping a spoiler on me.

"They voted out BB last night," he said.

I looked at the kid like he had moss growing out of his ears. BB? BB Andersen? Um, wasn't he voted out like three weeks ago? What's the deal? Is this kid an idiot?

As it turned out, the Australian episodes of Survivor were four weeks behind our episodes in the U.S. They had just seen the BB episode. Meanwhile, back in the states, in last night's episode (episode six), Joel Klug had been voted out.

Once I realized that I knew things about Survivor that these kids didn't, I decided it was time to start messing with them.

"Hey did you know that we're already on episode six in America?" I teased them, smiling. "Do you want to know what is going to happen the next three weeks?"

All of a sudden, I was surrounded by about ten other kids. One by one they came over and they crowded around me. Suddenly I was freaking Jesus Christ with an army of disciples. I quickly became the most popular person on Heron Island.

"You really know the next three episodes?" one of them asked.

"Does Richard go?" somebody else asked.

"What about Rudy?" some kid asked. "I like Rudy."

"I don't like the Pagongs," some kid said, "They're lazy."

What fascinated me the most about talking to these little Australian kids (not to mention a lot of their parents) was the fact that EVERYBODY here watched Survivor. It was apparently the #1 TV show in all of Australia. It was so big, in fact, that they were only two episodes in and they were already planning their own Australian version for next summer. This show was freaking ENORMOUS in Australia.

What also fascinated me was the fact that Australians tended to view the show a lot differently than the Americans did.

Do you know the number one comment that I heard from those kids that day on Heron Island?

"I liked BB," they all told me. "The Pagongs shouldn't have voted him out. That tribe is lazy and ungrateful."

Well as Kyle's mom would have said on South Park, "What what WHAT???" You liked BB? Back in America I bet you couldn't have found one Survivor fan who would have said anything nice about BB. The general consensus back in America (at least on all the message boards that I ever saw) was that the Pagongs were "the good guys", the Tagis were "the bad guys", and BB was a loud clueless asshole who wanted to quit because nobody would listen to him. Back in America I don't think I saw even one person under the age of sixty who ever would have said something as crazy as, "BB was the good guy. The Pagongs suck for voting him out."

But here in Australia? Man, it was like they were watching a whole different show.

EVERYBODY I talked to that day loved BB. The kids. The parents. The casual viewers. Every single person I talked to that day was pissed off that the "lazy Pagongs" had voted out such a nice old man. I didn't even know what to say. Is Australian culture really that different from American culture? These comments were just boggling my mind. There wasn't a single person here who had anything nice to say about the Pagongs. Heck, they didn't even like Gervase or Colleen! Who doesn't like Colleen?!?

19

We wound up staying on Heron Island for three days, and I swear to God I had kids following me around all three days. They just followed me around, and they would ask me for hints on what was going to happen on Survivor. I was like the goddamn Pied Piper. Everyone followed me around, and everyone wanted to know if the Pagongs would get their comeuppance for voting out that kindly old gentleman, BB.

I didn't want to drop any major spoilers on these kids (because, again, spoilers suck, and people who share spoilers suck), but I have to say, there was one little Australian kid who eventually wore me down. He was about twelve years old, and he was such a big fan of the show that it was killing him-- it was KILLING him-- that episodes had already aired and he hadn't seen them yet. He told me he wouldn't be able to sleep at night unless I told him who was going to go home in the next three episodes.

So finally, on our last day on Heron Island, I finally told him. Stacey. Then Ramona. Then Dirk.

"So the Pagongs have six people to Tagi's five?" he asked. "The Pagongs are ahead going into the merge?"

"It depends on what happens in episode six," I told him. "I haven't seen that one yet. I won't be able to see it until I get home."

"Well that's a shame," he said, shaking his head, "I really don't like Pagong."

Yeah, you and every other person in Australia. Pagong sucks. I got it.

Finally, after two weeks in Australia (and three days on Heron Island), we finally said our good byes. I bid adieu to my fan club of what must have been by this time about sixty rabid starving-for-information young Survivor fans in Australia, and I told them that the next three episodes were good. I told them they were going to enjoy them.

"Does BB get to come back?" someone asked.

Um, no. No he doesn't.

So we left Australia. We flew back to America. We came back home. And the first thing I did when I walked in my living room was I looked at our VCR timer.

Whew.

Sure enough, there they were. Survivor episodes 6 and 7 were sitting right there on my VHS tape, waiting for us. Just like we had hoped. Thank you, Panasonic Model V2-180. You did your job. You are the greatest VCR in the world, you complete me.

And you know, I thought I had loved Survivor up to this point. Up to this point, I thought it had been my favorite show in the history of TV. But I had been wrong. Because I had NO idea that the show was about to get even better than the show I had known.

Yes, we were just about to watch Episode Seven. The big one. The Gretchen episode. Which could easily be called the first truly great episode in Survivor history. In fact, some would even call Borneo episode seven the single most important episode in Survivor history.

I thought I had known what Survivor was through the first six episodes. I thought that I loved it, but I had no idea. The Gretchen episode was such a big deal at the time, and it still is a big deal today, that I consider it the point where Survivor officially left its pupa stage, and it transformed into a butterfly.

The Gretchen episode. The big one. It was sitting right there on my tape.

Yeah, it's safe to say that I'm really glad the VCR timer worked.

6. Spoilers Burn in Hell

Before I talk about episodes six (Joel) and seven (Gretchen) of Borneo--
which were both extremely significant to the franchise, of course-- I should
probably write about two enormous issues that were starting to rear their ugly
heads around this point in the first season. In fact, not only were they just
now rearing their ugly heads, they would become so big that they would
dominate just about every discussion about Survivor for the next, oh, I would
say about ten years.

The first issue I want to talk about is the spoilers.

What was amazing about the first season of Survivor (seriously, this is
completely mind-blowing if you stop and think about it) is that there wasn't a
single spoiler out there that gave away who the winner was going to be.
There wasn't one person outside of the cast and crew and network and
people who actually filmed the show who knew that Richard Hatch was
going to be crowned the Sole Survivor. It was one of the best kept secrets in
the history of television.

And why weren't there any spoilers out there? Well in Mark Burnett's book
about the first season, he specifically discusses this. He said that the cast and
crew felt so strongly about this project, they were so 100% behind the
product that they were putting together, and how good it was going to be,
that everyone inherently knew that "the big secret" had to be kept until the
end. Above all else, if Survivor was to succeed, if there was ever going to be
a Survivor 2, the winner absolutely <u>had</u> to be a surprise to the viewing
audience. If a single spoiler had come out or had been leaked to the public, it
would have ruined everything.

This sort of thinking probably sounds hopelessly naive to people who weren't
there during the first season, and who are used to Survivor's boot order being
spoiled on the internet one or two episodes into every new season. But I'm
serious, there really were no spoilers out there during Borneo. NOBODY
knew who the winner was going to be. EVERYBODY on the crew did their
part to keep the results a secret. It was amazing. To this day I have no idea
how CBS and Burnett were able to do that.

The coolest thing about there being no spoilers floating around during
Borneo was the fact that you could go online and you could safely read any
article out there on the internet that was written about Survivor. Believe me,
there were a lot of them. And it was nice, because there was never any

chance you would accidentally stumble onto who the winner was going to be.

It was around this point in the season (episode six) that I really started to turn into an online Survivor junkie. After every episode aired on TV, I would immediately log on to the internet and I would see what everyone was saying about it. I would go onto any television BBS (bulletin board to you youngsters) I could find, I would check out Television Without Pity, I would go onto CBS.com. Heck, sometimes I would even venture into that cesspool of internet anarchy itself, Survivor Sucks. And every week, it seemed like there were more and more people that were writing about it. This was literally the first show I had ever seen that seemed to double its viewing audience pretty much every week.

And because of my obsession, this was the first time in my Survivor experience that I really started to worry about running across some kind of a winner spoiler.

Ah yes, Survivor spoilers. The bane of my existence.

I have hated spoilers since day one. I hated them in seasons one through thirty. And I hate them just as much today. If you so much as drop a Survivor spoiler on me, not only will I hate you, I will probably hate you for life. I don't mean to sound melodramatic about this, but it's true. I have written about this subject many many times over the years. Survivor spoilers and the dicks who post them are the main reason I eventually had to retire as a Survivor columnist.

So yes, I really started to troll the internet for Survivor articles around episode six of the first season. And I also started to become concerned about Survivor spoilers around episode six of the first season. Because I knew they had to be out there. Somebody HAD to know what was going to happen. The info had to be out there, somewhere, and I knew that I was going to accidentally run into it. No matter how careful I was, no matter how good I was at just "skimming" the first sentence of every article as sort of a recon mission, I knew it was bound to happen eventually because I was reading so many Survivor articles. There was just no way this huge network TV secret was going to be kept for all thirteen episodes.

And then, alas, it happened.

My first Survivor winner spoiler.

BAM.

I know nobody is going believe this, but I swear it is true. This absolutely happened to me. Although to this day I have no idea what the newspaper was or what the article was. I have been searching for this incriminating bit of Survivor spoiler evidence for more than fifteen years now, and not once have I ever been able to dig it up or figure out where I originally read it. All I know is that I DID run across it one day in the summer of 2000, and it completely pissed me off.

I was skimming through an East Coast newspaper article one day around episode six of Borneo, and I happened to run across this carelessly thrown together description of somebody:

"Survivor winner Richard Hatch."

Uh, what?

Sure enough, I skimmed back through the article and there it was again. "Survivor winner Richard Hatch." I couldn't believe it. So wait, that chunky blowhard with the beard is going to win Survivor? And you just casually spring it on us like that, with no accompanying info to back it up? The hell? Thank you, random newspaper.

Unfortunately for me, the problem when I read stuff like that is that I sort of have a photographic memory. Maybe it is part of having OCD, maybe it is just because I am a visual learner, I don't know. All I know is that I never forget anything I have ever read on the internet about Survivor.

So I read my very first Survivor spoiler, and I tried to dismiss it.

"No way, that can't be true," I told myself. "There is no way Richard wins Survivor. He's too unlikable. The author is just guessing. Either that or he is just reporting his opinion as fact. There is no way that is a real spoiler."

I tried to write it off as gossip. I tried to forget it. I tried to just keep watching the show the way I had been watching it up to this point, completely unspoiled, like all was right in the world.

And then, thank goodness, blessed relief.

Within about two days of reading the infamous Richard Hatch wins "spoiler", I ran across two other articles from different newspapers that also gave away the Survivor winner. Only... well look at this... they both named somebody other than Richard.

One article I read talked about "Survivor winner Rudy Boesch." Another talked about "Survivor champion Gretchen Cordy."

Ha ha. Suck on that, Richard spoiler. So now who is giving away the winner?

So that was my first experience with Survivor "spoilers." And in my opinion, I don't think that first spoiler was really even a spoiler at all. I think the author was just guessing who the winner was going to be, and in this case he just happened to guess right. Just like the Rudy author was guessing, and just like the Gretchen author was guessing. And just like half of America was guessing when Ramona caused a near riot by referring to Gretchen as "a survivor" in her exit interview right after the fourth episode on the CBS Early Show.

I remember when Ramona made that comment on TV. I remember seeing it and I was like, "What??" Ramona said bad things about everyone else in the cast. She was no fan of most of the Pagongs. But when she was asked to describe Gretchen, she referred to the Pagong leader as "a survivor"? And of course because the online Survivor audience is obsessive like I am, the only question that was on everybody's mind after Ramona's comment was, "Does this mean that Gretchen wins the show?????"

This was seriously the mentality of the Survivor audience as Survivor went into its fifth and sixth episodes. People were DYING to know how the show was going to play out. But at the same time they really didn't WANT to know because everybody wanted to remain unspoiled. It was a really interesting time to be a Survivor fan. You really didn't know WHAT you wanted to know about the rest of the season. All you knew was that you were hooked.

But man, when that Ramona comment came out, it sent a shock wave through the entire Survivor community. Everybody at the time thought that was a legitimate spoiler.

Well, everybody but me anyway. After all, by this point I had heard the Richard "spoiler." I had heard the Rudy "spoiler." And now I was hearing the latest one, the Gretchen "spoiler."

Personally, after seeing it play out with three different names, I didn't think that any of them were true.

I thought that the winner was going to be somebody else. I thought it was going to be a surprise to us all. Turns out that wasn't entirely correct (although Richard winning was a complete shock to most people, including me. I never saw that win coming at all, not even towards the end.)

Seriously, if there is one thing you should admire and respect about that first season of Survivor, it is the fact that it was completely spoiler free. There wasn't one legitimate verified spoiler about the winner out there. Ever. From anyone. And for a show like this, with a crew this big, and with such enormous interest from the American public surrounding it, well that has got to be one of the most impressive and amazing things that has ever happened in TV. I don't know how they were able to pull that off. Unless, well, as Mark Burnett said in his book, unless the cast and crew really did believe in this thing. Burnett tends to exaggerate about a lot of things, but he might not have been exaggerating about that.

Even though I would grow to hate spoilers (and people who post spoilers) with a passion in future seasons, in that first season, man, everybody did what they were supposed to do. Nobody gave anything away. Even Stacey Stillman didn't give anything away. How did that happen?

Of course there WAS the infamous "Gervase wins/Gervase X" spoiler that would pop up on the internet in a couple of weeks, but just wait. That was important too, but the truth behind that one was a little bit different. Don't worry, we'll get there soon enough.

P.S. Oh yeah, here is another funny spoiler anecdote about that first season. Like I said, the television site that I frequented the most at that time was called Television Without Pity (aka Mighty Big TV). Well, on the header for every Survivor article at TWOP, they had a picture of Kelly Wiglesworth plastered up at the top. Her face was posted at the top of every Survivor article all summer.

Now, I don't know why they decided to put Kelly up there. Maybe they just picked her because they liked her face from the Survivor bios. Who knows? All I know is that Kelly's face was plastered up there at the top of every single article beginning with episode one. She sat up there all season, she never went away. She became the symbol of the franchise. And as the episodes went along, as Kelly got further and further in the game, I know I wasn't the only one to notice that her face up there actually could have been a spoiler from the beginning.

"Aw, man," I remember thinking, "Did Television Without Pity really know who the winner was all along? Was the winner that obvious and we just didn't realize it?"

Suffice it to say, I was heavily invested in Kelly not winning Survivor. HEAVILY invested. Seriously, if Kelly had won, I might not have ever watched Survivor again. If that really had been a spoiler, and it had been that obvious, this show and that website would have been dead to me.

Well, you can pretty much guess what happened. Richard Hatch won in the end. And Kelly Wiglesworth lost. Bah effing hah. It turned out that the Survivor editor at TWOP had just picked Kelly at random at the start of the season, and she had been as amazed (not to mention a little worried) as everyone else when Kelly came closer and closer to winning Survivor each week. And no, I wasn't the only one who had been paying attention to this. Apparently the TWOP editors had been bombarded by hate mail as the season went along, with people demanding to know every week if Kelly's picture up there had been some sort of a spoiler.

When Kelly turned out not to be a winner, I am guessing the TWOP editors were probably more relieved than anyone.

7. The A-Word

Remember when I said that there were two big issues that started rearing their ugly heads at this point in the first season? Spoilers were one of them.

And the other one?

Yep, you guessed it. The A-word. The dreaded "alliance."

To this day, I have no idea what Mark Burnett expected when it came to the concept of alliances on Survivor. In some interviews he has claimed that he never expected them to form at all. In some interviews he will claim that the idea that people would band together and vote as a group was "a complete shock" to him. Yet in other interviews throughout the years, he has completely contradicted this. In some of his interviews he has claimed that alliances were natural, and that they were the only smart way to ever win Survivor, and that they were inevitable.

Like I said, I have no idea where he really stands/stood on the concept of alliances.

All I do know is that they were a BIG topic of discussion in Borneo. They were a major major talking point around this point in the season, among the players, the host, the producers, and the viewing audience. In fact, it is no exaggeration to say that, around episode five, the word "alliance" quickly became the single most hotly debated concept among Survivor fans. There was simply no way to have a discussion with another Survivor fan without mentioning them.

I know it sounds weird to people who just started watching the show in the last couple of years, and who are used to seeing alliances on Survivor, but in those early days of Borneo, the "a-word" really was sort of a curse word. You just didn't want to use it in mixed company. Because if you were pro-alliance (which was really a minority of the Survivor fan base at the time), it really sort of said bad things about you. To most people at the time, the idea of forming an alliance on Survivor was basically just seen as cheating.

I wish I could fully describe how different the fan mentality was back then, compared to what it is now. I wish I could do that. But unfortunately I'm just not a good enough writer to be able to pull that off. There is no way I could put into words how much different "Borneo audiences" are from "Season 30 Audiences."

All I can say about the subject is this. When Richard Hatch won Survivor, he was hated. He was absolutely HATED. Don't let retroactive history tell you anything else. In the summer of 2000, I would say that maybe 5% of the mainstream Survivor audience wanted Richard Hatch to win Survivor. And I think that 5% is probably even being generous.

And why did people not want him to win Survivor?

Well for a lot of people, I'm sure it was because he was cocky. For a lot of viewers out there (like my wife), they will never root for the cocky guy on Survivor. From Richard Hatch, to Silas Gaither, from John Carroll, to Jonny Fairplay, from Boston Rob, to you name it. For a lot of viewers, cocky and self-confident equals unlikable. And they will never root for the players like that.

And then there were probably some viewers who just didn't like him because he was gay. Or because he walked around naked all the time on the island. Who knows? I don't know what the exact percentages are, but I would be a fool not to list those two reasons as being possible factors in his (lack of) popularity.

But for the vast majority of America in 2000? It was simple. They didn't want to Richard to win because Richard had put together the a-word. Richard was the guy who had put together the alliance.

Which, in 2000 opinion, meant he had cheated.

Like I said, there is no way for me to really get into how "alliance" equals "cheating", other than to say that that was definitely the reality back in 2000. Most viewers (in America at least) were pro-Pagong. They were very much pro-Pagong. They loved the plucky leader pre-school teacher Gretchen. They loved Greg and his wacky eccentricities and his coconut phone. They loved Gervase and his charming laziness. And boy oh boy did America love Colleen Haskell.

Heck, they even loved Jenna Lewis. America loved her even before she released a video of herself giving oral sex on her honeymoon. They loved her even before she went full Kardashian!

America (and most of the Survivor fan base) was pro-Pagong. Period, end of sentence. Don't let anyone tell you otherwise. Oh, not everyone loved them, of course. My favorite was Rudy, so I was always pro Tagi. But if you took a poll in the summer of 2000, I would guess it would have turned out something like 80% in favor of Pagong, 20% in favor of Tagi. And that 20% was probably only because of Rudy.

> **Side Note:** Obviously polls taken in Australia would have been flip flopped. What is it with you Australians?

Okay and now we come to the bigger question. Why was Pagong so beloved by the audience, while Tagi wasn't?

Well that's easy.

The reason the Pagongs were the audience favorites at the time was because THEY PLAYED THE GAME CORRECTLY and THEY DIDN'T CHEAT BY USING ALLIANCES!

There was a HUGE wave of sympathy for the Pagongs among the viewing audience the minute that talk of "a Tagi Alliance" first started popping up in the episodes. Seriously, as hard as that is to believe now, as abhorrent as it might seem that Survivor fans once respected the Pagongs, I am telling the truth. The Pagongs chose not to use alliances, the Tagis did choose to use them, and the audience reacted. They reacted very strongly to that.

And their main reaction was something along the lines of "Holy crap, if Richard or Sue wins this game, I am never watching again. Alliances should be illegal. The producers should step in and do something about them."

If I ever get a chance to sit down and conduct an interview with Jeff Probst or Mark Burnett, I have always said that this is the first question I would ask them. Because to me, this was probably the single most fascinating moment in Survivor history.

I would ask them, "What were your thoughts about Borneo the minute it was evident that a Tagi Four member was going to win the game? And that the audience was probably going to reject that winner? What was the first thing that went through your mind when you realized that was going to happen?"

I mean, think about this for a second. You know the producers were thinking about that. You know they weren't happy about alliances at the time. Hell, if you pay attention to the middle episodes of Borneo, you can see that Jeff Probst wasn't happy about the Tagi Alliance at all. He isn't even trying to hide it, nearly every single Tribal Council question in those middle episodes of Borneo is some variant of "Hey, I heard there's an alliance. Want to tell me about it?" Probst was determined to expose what the Tagis were doing, because he wanted to make it a little more difficult for them, and he wanted to throw a wrench in their plans. In fact, he was probably being instructed to do that every week upstairs by the producers.

Personally, for me as a viewer, I never really had a problem with the alliance. The minute Richard started talking about putting one together, I remember thinking, "Hey, that's really smart. I like that guy, he really wants to win this game." In fact it is safe to say that Richard eventually became my favorite player in Borneo specifically BECAUSE he was the head of the Tagi Alliance.

But believe me, I was definitely in the minority. The tiny tiny tiny minority.

The minute Richard opened his mouth and started talking about that alliance, man, he was dead. He was dead to the audience. He was dead because the audience in 2000 didn't want to see a Tagi member win the game. And they sure as hell didn't want to see THIS guy win using THIS tactic. No way. There was no way they wanted to see Richard Hatch "cheat" and use alliances to get rid of their favorites like Gervase, Gretchen, Greg, and Colleen.

Colleen Haskell? America's Sweetheart? The victim of an alliance?

To quote Darth Vader at the end of Revenge of the Sith, *falling to knees* "Nooooooooooooooooooooooooooo!"

So anyway, there you go. Episodes five and six of Borneo were really "the birth of an alliance." This was a very important moment in Survivor history. And I would be lying to you if I said that the audience was in any way, shape, or form behind this development. Alliances were wrong, alliances were cheating, alliances were unsportsmanlike, they were a completely unethical and cowardly way to win the game. In fact, I remember one prominent TV columnist at the time (I forget his name) summed up America's feelings about alliances quite nicely: "How can you support a game where the weak, the cowardly, the out of shape, and the wholly unethical can just team up to vote out the strong?"

Now, if you ask me, I always loved Richard Hatch's response whenever people would ask him about alliances. Richard always claimed that they weren't unethical in the slightest. He never felt guilty about being a part of the Tagi Alliance at all. Whenever this question would come up in an interview after the season, he would just look amused and say, "Alliances aren't unethical, they're just smart!"

And he's right, of course. There was absolutely nothing wrong with the concept of a voting alliance. Nothing wrong with it at all. There never has been. The only problem was that Richard was about a year ahead of most of the Survivor audience. It took a LONG time before most fans started to come around on him and his opinion of alliances. In fact, it was probably the first episode of Australia before most fans made peace with the idea of "a voting alliance" at all. And that was probably only because, this time, "the good guys" had formed one.

Of course, now if the Pagongs had formed the first alliance, and not the Tagis, well then that might have been a whole different story.

What if Gervase had won Borneo because of "The Pagong Alliance"? What if Colleen had won? What does the audience think of a voting bloc then?

I think that is an interesting discussion question.

Side Note: Okay, let's dish out a little bit of the truth tea here. Richard Hatch did NOT invent the Survivor voting alliance. I know it has become trendy to say that over the years, heck I believe I even inferred it here in this very chapter. But he did not put together the first alliance. He didn't even put together the first Tagi alliance. If you have read Mark Burnett's book, you will know that Stacey Stillman was actually the person who came up with the idea for the Survivor voting alliance. Yes, Stacey. Banished, forgotten, pariah Stacey, who has never really received her rightful credit.

In the first couple days of the game, Stacey came up with plan that the four Tagi women should all vote together, and that way the men could never vote them out. It was a genius maneuver. And it should have worked. Stacey's only problems were that A) Sonja Christopher was incredibly weak, and the other women might not want to keep her around after she cost them the first immunity challenge, and B) Sue Hawk thought that Stacey was a rich spoiled brat and was a pain in the ass, and she wanted nothing to do with her. So Sue broke away from the Tagi Women's Alliance at the first vote and became a

32

free agent, and eventually she wound up hooked up with Richard. And just between you and me, I have always suspected that Sue was probably the one who came up with the idea of the famous Tagi Alliance in the first place. I think she was probably more instrumental in the whole thing in the first place than Richard was.

In summary, there are lots of things to love about Richard Hatch, but let's not give him credit for being "the guy who invented the Survivor alliance" anymore. Let's give that title back to Stacey, where it has always belonged. Or, you could even give it to Ramona and B.B., who were talking about being a voting bloc because only they know where the watering hole was on the first day at Pagong. Depending on how you define "an alliance", you could even say that *they* were the ones who invented the concept. In any case, it certainly wasn't Richard.

8. Joel Got Screwed

Like I said earlier, I came back from my Australian vacation in July of 2000, and I sat down to watch episodes six and seven of Survivor. Which, as it turned out, was an interesting combination of episodes to watch back to back. Why? Well only because they contained two of what I consider the most significant moments of the entire season.

Episode six featured what I will lovingly refer to as "the cow joke." And it ended with Joel Klug being voted out over it, despite having absolutely nothing to do with the cow joke or the cow joke issue whatsoever.

Okay, let's just cut right to it. This episode pissed me off. It still pisses me off. It pisses me off so much, in fact, that it inspired me to write a column for Rob Cesternino's old website, The Fishbowl, a couple of years ago. I titled it "Mario's 10 Most Troubling Reality Show Moments", and I included what happened to Joel as #9 on the list.

The reason Joel's boot episode pissed me off so much was twofold. First off, like I said, he had absolutely nothing to do with that cow joke whatsoever. He didn't tell the joke, he didn't bring up the joke, and he certainly wasn't the one who pissed off all of the women by telling it. He could not have been a more innocent bystander in the entire thing. So right there, there was the fairness issue. That was what bothered me. It was the first time in Survivor history that a player was voted out through no fault of their own. Unlike Souna, BB, Stacey, Ramona, or Dirk, Joel wasn't voted out because of something he did, or because of his physical condition, or because he was dragging down the tribe. He was voted out specifically because of events around camp that he had nothing to do with.

Side Note: There is no way to prove this, but I have always believed that Joel wasn't actually voted out because of the cow joke. The more I watch Borneo, the more I have learned about it, the more I learn about Pagong and its dynamics, the more I have always suspected that there was a lot more going on in that tribe that the editors didn't show us. Specifically, I think that there was a power struggle developing between the girls and the guys. I think it had been developing for a while. And the girls were probably led by Gretchen "Girl Power" Cordy, who wanted nothing to do with a man taking over that tribe once the Pagongs made it to the merge.

34

Again, there is no way to prove this, but here is my theory. I think the girls were lining up on one side of that Final 6 vote, and the only person they would vote for was a guy. And I think the guys were lining up on the other side, and they were only going to vote for a girl. And then here in the middle is Greg Buis, who the guys think is on their side, but who really isn't, because Greg doesn't play that way. And because he thinks that Joel is a turd. So THAT is what I think really happened in that episode. I think Greg got Joel out more than anything, because Greg wasn't interested in playing the males vs. females game. And because he didn't respect Joel. And I think the editors only used the cow joke as an excuse (quite unfairly, I might add) because they didn't want to ruin the Pagong image by showing them as having "pseudo" alliances.

Again, this is just a theory. But I do believe it. And because I believe it, now I think it is even MORE unfair that they portrayed Joel as a sexist on TV on his way out, despite the fact that he didn't even tell the joke, and the joke had nothing to do with why he was voted out in the first place!

Keep in mind that, to a Survivor viewer in the summer of 2000, the fact that Joel Klug (alpha male Joel Klug, I might add) was voted out this early in the game was pretty revolutionary stuff. Wait, what? He was voted out despite the fact that he was the leader of the tribe? He was voted out despite the fact that he was the best one in the challenges? He was voted out despite the fact that he was the only player on Pagong who truly understood that they needed alliances, and he was the only one on Pagong who truly understood where the game was going to go once they got to the merge?

The Pagongs voted that guy out of the game, this early? The hell?

And of course then we come to the second reason why this episode pisses me off.

The reason this episode REALLY pisses me off (and I'm talking even more so than the fairness issue), is because it totally ruined a guy who could (maybe even should) have been the first breakout star of Survivor.

Yeah, I know what you are saying. Joel Klug? The first Survivor breakout star?

But I'm serious. Go with me here.

If you go back and you watch Borneo, pay attention to Joel Klug. Pay attention to his storyline. You will notice that he was the only person on Pagong who had any idea how powerful an alliance would become later in this game. Seriously, he was the only one! Very early on in the season, Joel comments that the Pagongs will need to stick together once they get to the merge. He freaking tells them this right to their faces!

But do they listen to him? Do they listen to the only guy in the tribe who had any idea how one of them would make it to the end? Of course not. They just blow him off and ignore most of what he says. In fact some of them (Greg especially) will later go so far as to mock him and make fun his entire "Captain America, I'm the leader, I'm the strongest person in America" persona any chance that he can.

I remember in Mark Burnett's book about the first season, he was very critical towards the Pagongs about how they had no respect for authority. They had no respect for BB, they had no respect for Joel, they had no respect for anyone. And Burnett went on for page after page about how he and the crew all hated the Pagongs, and how the producers hated having to deal with them from a production standpoint. The Pagongs just really didn't seem to have any respect for anyone. Hey, you know, now that I think about it, maybe those little kids I met in Australia were right. Maybe the Pagongs really were all spoiled little brats.

So anyway, if you are wondering why episode six of Survivor pisses me off more than just about any other episode of Survivor (at least until Marquesas), well now you know. Joel Klug easily could have been the Colby Donaldson of the first season. Hell, he easily could have been the Richard Hatch of the first season. He was the only player on Pagong who could have given the Tagis a challenge once they got to the merge.

But no. The Pagongs thought it would be more fun to make fun of the guy. And to ignore his advice about alliances. And to humiliate him right when they needed him the most.

I remember in Burnett's book, he talked about how glad he was that a Pagong didn't win the game. And when writing about Joel, he simply wrote, "I felt bad for the guy."

Well I felt bad for him too.

Had the Pagongs been a little bit smarter, Joel Klug could have easily become the show's first breakout character. He very easily could have become the original Colby Donaldson.

The fact that he nearly cries when he gets his torch snuffed pisses me off every single time that I watch it.

Postscript: Okay I should probably add a little anecdote that I have never written about before. I posted that essay about "Troubling Reality TV Show Moments" at the Fishbowl back in December of 2005. And I swear, within about two days, I got an email from Joel Klug's girlfriend. She emailed to tell me how incredibly grateful she was that somebody was finally telling Joel's story. She said that he had always sort of been the "forgotten" cast member from Borneo, and he felt bad about it. And she knew how happy it would make him that there was a fan out there who had actually been bothered by the way he had been voted out. She went on to say that Joel still didn't really understand why he had been voted out to this very day.

I exchanged emails with Joel's girlfriend for a couple of days, and then one day Joel himself wrote me out of the blue to basically say the exact same thing. He said yeah it sucked how he had been voted out, but what sucked even more was that no one had ever really explained to him why it had happened. He never knew why he had been voted out until he saw the episode on TV.

It was clear from our conversation that Joel had sort of moved on from Survivor. He didn't really want to talk about the show anymore since five years had passed, and he had more or less moved on with his life, so I didn't get into it much or ask him too many questions about it. Basically all he wanted to say was that he agreed with my essay, and that he was glad that somebody finally came out and wrote something about it. He thanked me for remembering him, and for writing about the show, and that was the only email contact I have ever had with a Survivor from the first season.

Good guy. Nice guy. I still think he should have been the first Colby.

9. The Vote That Changed Everything

Now if I thought that the Joel episode was a significant moment in Survivor history, well apparently I hadn't seen nothin' yet. Because the next one, the Gretchen episode.

Wow.

This was the one that changed everything.

Seriously, if you have ever wondered when Survivor went from "an addictive little niche viewing experience" to "a worldwide global TV phenomenon", you need look no further than episode seven of Survivor: Borneo. To me, this will always be the Survivor moment that changed EVERYTHING.

As I mentioned before, at this point in its history, Survivor already had a pretty strong and active online fan base. There weren't really any full time Survivor "writers" around yet (like I would later become), but there was definitely a group of regulars on most TV message boards, who would go on for page after page writing and talking about the latest episode of Survivor.

It was around this time I that I finally joined two of the biggest TV message boards that existed at the time. I finally registered at Television Without Pity (which was known as Mighty Big TV at the time). My username there was "Sandwich Artist." This, of course, was a tribute to my former career of working at Subway, which I did for two years back when I was in college. No matter what else I will ever accomplish in life, I will always be proud of the fact that I was a Subway Sandwich Artist between the years 1993 and 1995.

> **Special Subway Trivia Note:** Don't listen to them when they say they can only fit eight meatballs in a foot long sub. You can fit up to nineteen meatballs in a foot long sub. Trust me, I have done the research. Oh, and Jared is an f'ing liar, you will never lose weight eating at Subway. Don't believe the hype.

After I registered at TWOP, I went over to Survivor Sucks and I finally registered with a username there. Although I should point out that I didn't particularly LIKE Survivor Sucks. Even back in 2000 I thought it was a little too mean spirited and a little too snarky for what I was looking for from a

Survivor site. I didn't particularly want to be registered there, but since it was the biggest Survivor fan site at the time (and it still is to this day), I decided I needed to be a part of it. We were only six episodes into the season, but Survivor Sucks was already well on its way to becoming a well-known online phenomenon. So I registered there as "Super Mario" and that was that.

By the way, I should point out that what I saw as "mean spirited" in 2000 was entirely different from what I would call "mean spirited" in 2015. Back then the meanest Sucks ever got was when they would refer to Richard as "Dicque" or "Machiabelly." Meanwhile in 2015, Sucks is famous for comparing unattractive female contestants to post-op transsexuals, or Danielle DiLorenzo to a horse. Again, that's not really my style, but hey that's Survivor Sucks. Sucks can be a cesspool. It is what it is.

It is just amusing to me to think that people were considered so horrible in 2000 when they referred to Richard as "Machiabelly." My, how the internet has changed.

Okay, so with six episodes of Survivor under my belt, and my newly registered accounts on both TWOP and Sucks, I was finally ready to take part in most of the mainstream discussion of the show. I was ready to be a part of the big boys. I was finally being allowed to sit at the grownups table.

And then-- BAM-- came episode seven. The one that sent shockwaves.

Now, if I am correct in my assumptions, I am guessing that most people who are reading this book weren't watching Survivor in the summer of 2000. I am guessing that most of you probably caught up with and started following the show much later in its run.

If you are one of those latecomers to Survivor, I will do my best to describe the impact of the Gretchen boot in a manner that will make sense to you.

I know that modern viewers of Survivor will look back at the Gretchen episode of Borneo and they will think, "Yeah, so what's the big deal? The Tagis had an alliance and they picked off the Pagong leader at the merge. What was the big deal about that? That is the way that Survivor has always worked."

But no. You are wrong. That is NOT the way that Survivor has always worked.

The way Survivor worked up to that point in history (Borneo, episode seven) was that if you went home, there was generally a pretty good reason for it. If you were Souna, you were voted out because you were old and weak. If you were B.B, you were voted out because you were bossy. If you were Stacey, you were voted out because you had a big mouth (or, if Richard is to be believed, because you were putting together an alliance and you were the most dangerous to him.) If you were Ramona or Dirk, you were voted out because you were sick and because people were worried about you.

If you were Joel, it might not have been fair why you got voted out, but yes, even you were voted out for a reason. You were voted out because the women weren't a fan of yours.

But with Gretchen-- and here is the important difference-- there WAS NO REASON for her to be voted out.

Okay I know what you're thinking. A cynical modern Survivor fan will just roll his eyes at that sentence and think, "No reason? My ass. There was a great reason she was voted out. It was called strategy."

And see, this is where the difference between a 2000 Survivor fan and a 2015 Survivor fan shows up. Because in 2000, there simply was no "strategy" when it came to voting people out of the game yet. Up to this point in the season it was complete Darwinian sociology. Up until Gretchen, when a person was voted out of the game, it was because they were either weak, or because somebody didn't like them. And that was it. There was no other reason to get rid of another player. Prior to the Gretchen vote, there was no way you would ever be voted out on Survivor if you were valuable and if people liked you.

When the hammer fell on Gretchen-- who was easily the single most respected player in the cast, heck even the Tagis loved her-- man, the impact of that moment was just chilling. It was like the Scooby Doo villain mask had suddenly been pulled off of the face of Survivor. Our eyes had been opened. We finally saw Survivor for what it was. We finally realized that the game we thought we were watching was not the game we were actually watching.

Simply put, being likable and competent no longer meant anything. The game had just bastardized. It was the moment that changed everything.

Again, there is no way I can capture this moment to people who weren't there when it happened. I am just not a good enough writer to be able to do that. The Gretchen vote literally changed everything. The Pagongs went

40

from "We're the happy-go-lucky group of castaways who America loves" to "Holy shit, we're fucked" in about five seconds. The look on Colleen and Jenna's face was just devastating. Meanwhile, Richard and his little "alliance" immediately went from "this cute little group of four older people working together" to "the most hated cheating bastards in all of America" in the span of about two seconds. And I'm serious, it was just like that. BAM. Like the flip of a switch. Over the span of about thirty seconds, the entire game of Survivor was altered irreparably.

Every time I sit down to write about the fateful Gretchen episode, all I can do is go back to what Burnett wrote in his book about the first season. Because it is obvious from his book that the producers of Survivor were shocked. They were SHOCKED! They had no idea that a player like Gretchen (a likable mom and pre-school teacher who was a kickass outdoorsman and who had once taught U.S. Air Force survival tactics) could ever be taken out of the game that easily. In fact, if I recall, Burnett compared the mood in the Survivor production camp the night after Gretchen was eliminated to that of a funeral. The entire production crew immediately went into mourning that night. Gretchen was by far everyone's favorite player among the crew, and they couldn't believe she had been voted out of the game that early. After all, she was the "good guy" that the production crew had been rooting for. Aside from Colleen, she was one of the only real "good guys" in the cast.

I remember watching the Gretchen episode at home with my wife that night (back to back with the Joel episode), and I remember my jaw nearly hitting the floor after that vote reveal. I wasn't quite in mourning like Burnett said the Survivor production crew had been, but, like most of America, I was completely shocked. I mean, sure, the Tagi alliance had been talking about "severing the head" of Pagong. Sure, Rudy had been joking about it all episode. But no one thought they would actually go through with it. Not against Gretchen. Not like that. Not without her having a chance to be able to defend herself.

Just like that, with one swift chop of the knife, the Pagong Tribe was toast.

Oh man, I remember reading the Survivor message boards that night. I logged on right after I watched the Gretchen episode and you should have seen it. The message boards were humming. EVERYONE was suddenly talking about Survivor. I swear, Survivor Sucks must have doubled its number of registered users that day just because of that episode alone.

Everything you read that night online was "Fuck this" and "Fuck that" and

41

"Fuck the Tagis" and "Fuck Richard" and "I'm never watching this show again." It was crazy.

Meanwhile there was a very small minority of people (like me) who were secretly thinking "My God, that was the greatest thing I have ever seen in my life!" Yes, I will admit it. There were a few of us out there. But no one would really log onto a message board and come right out and say it. No way, not at that moment. There was just way too much heat directed at the Tagis. You would have had to have been nuts to write something under your own name saying that you admired the Tagis and that you thought it had been a good strategy move. If I had logged on to a message board and written something in defense of the Tagis that night, there is a very real chance I would have been permanently banned from the TWOP message boards. I am kidding you not. People were really worked up about this.

For better or worse, if there is anything you need to know about that first season, you just need to know this. The Gretchen vote changed everything about Survivor. It changed EVERYTHING. You had pre-Gretchen Survivor. And then you had post-Gretchen Survivor. The two eras were completely different, the fan bases (and message board posts) were completely different, and there is almost no way you can realistically compare the two eras. It just became a completely different TV show.

Survivor pre-Gretchen was nice and happy. It was about people trying to survive and live together on a desert island. Like Gabriel Cade would say three seasons later, it was about "building a society."

Survivor post-Gretchen was about cold-hearted strategy. And it was also now completely predictable. There was now zero chance that anyone but a Tagi Four member was ever going to win this game.

From this point on, we were now in for the ride of our lives.

For better or worse, Survivor had now officially become what it was going to become.

Postscript: Oh yeah, and the most ironic part of the whole "Gretchen's vote completely changed Survivor" moment? The fact that she wasn't even supposed to be the target that night in the first place! According to Burnett's book, Greg Buis was supposed to be the one voted out that night, not Gretchen. Greg was spared at the last minute, however, because he got lucky and he won immunity. So the vote switched to Gretchen.

Okay, so let's do the math in our head now. What happens if Greg goes home that night instead of Gretchen? How does that impact the rest of the season?

Are the Tagis still the #1 hated alliance in all of America? Probably not. I mean, America wasn't going to like them regardless. That is just the nature of the beast. But if they had taken Greg out instead of Gretchen, I doubt it would have had quite the same impact. After all, Greg wasn't the spunky pre-school teacher that the people on the production crew had been rooting for. Greg was simply the weird guy. Greg was the oddball who spoke into a coconut and who liked to make jokes about having sex with his sister.

Okay so now Greg doesn't make the jury, but Gretchen does. How does that impact the final jury vote? Keep in mind that Greg's vote is the one that broke the 3-3 tie and, technically, is the vote that won Richard the game. So how does that change? Do you think Gretchen also votes for Richard to win over Kelly in the end?

To me, this will always be one of the most fascinating "what if" questions in the history of Survivor. What if Greg goes home first instead of Gretchen? Do you think Richard still wins? And if he doesn't win, would Survivor have had quite the same impact on America? Would the franchise have developed in quite the same way? I know for damn sure that episode seven wouldn't have been as memorable if Greg had gone home instead of Gretchen. And if episode seven doesn't resonate so strongly with the audience (seriously, for most fans I know who were watching that first season, episode seven was one of those "where were you when you first saw it?" types of deals), if episode seven doesn't generate an insane amount of buzz, do you think Survivor gets the same amount of press that it would later wind up getting? Do you think 500 billion people wind up watching the finale?

Just think, all of this could have changed if Sean Kenniff had been a faster swimmer. If Sean had won immunity that day over Greg, we could have wound up with an entirely different alternate Survivor universe. One where Kelly Wiglesworth wins Survivor. One in which the entire franchise plays out a little bit differently. Ick. I feel like Doc Brown. I feel like I just invented the flux capacitor.

This is exhausting.

I might have to take a little nap after this chapter. This is too complicated.

10. Gervase X

Once Gretchen was voted out of Borneo, and a member of the Tagi Four was probably going to win the game, the producers officially now had a very serious problem on their hands. In fact, in many ways, this was the biggest problem they were ever going to face in the history of Survivor. This was the first dilemma they ever encountered as producers of a weekly reality TV show, and it was definitely the big one.

What do you do when the ending of your show is now completely obvious?

Seriously, the minute that Gretchen Cordy's torch was snuffed, that was the minute that a member of the Tagi Alliance had officially wrapped up the million dollar prize. That was it. There was no way the Pagongs were going to recover, there was no way the Tagis were going to fall apart, and there was no way that Dr. Sean (who was far more interested in coming off as "the good guy" than he was in actually winning) was going to do anything to stop them. Either Rudy, Richard, Kelly or Sue was going to win Survivor. Case closed. At this point now it was inevitable.

Like I said, once it was obvious who was going to win, the producers now had a very serious problem on their hands.

Well… they had two problems actually.

The first problem they faced now was the fact that the audience probably wasn't going to be very happy with the eventual winner. Yeah, I know, it is fashionable now to say that the Tagis were "the good players", and that the Pagongs were "the bad players", but at the time the producers were well aware that it wasn't going to come off that way to the audience. The Pagongs were going to be seen as the sweet lovable underdogs and the Tagis were going to see as the cocky smug cheating bullying assholes. Like it or not, that was an issue that was going to become a problem down the road. And I am sure that the producers were aware of it.

But the BIGGER problem the producers faced, the one that threatened the entire future of Survivor the franchise, was now the one of inevitability.

How on earth were they supposed to keep the audience interested when the next five episodes of the show were now completely predictable? This was a HUGE problem. It was an especially huge problem for a show like Survivor, which depended so much on unpredictability and the all-important question of "what will happen next???" If the viewers suddenly figured out that the next five weeks were irrelevant, they might turn the channel and they might lose interest in the show and they might watch something else. And if they lose interest in the show, there might not ever be a Survivor 2. And then Mark Burnett might not get to roll around on a giant pile of money in his 80-room mansion made entirely of diamonds.

For obvious reasons, I think a lot of people very high up were quite concerned about this part of the season.

So what did the producers decide to do about it?

Well, for me, this will always go down as the biggest genius move in Survivor history. I mean, forget player moves, forget Richard Hatch, forget Brian Heidik, forget the Dead Grandma lie, forget anything Sandra ever did. THIS was the single greatest strategy in Survivor history. The only reason Survivor is still around today is because of what the producers decided to do right after the Gretchen vote.

Ready for this?

What the producers did next is they decided to lie to us.

I know. It sounds so easy on the surface. Duh. Well of course the producers were going to lie to us. That's what producers are supposed to do. You make up fake drama and fake cliffhangers, and you try to throw off the audience. You try to hide the ending so that no one can guess it.

But what surprised everyone was the lengths the producers would go to actually accomplish this.

The first thing the producers did was to start a completely bogus and fabricated storyline called "When will the Tagi Alliance fall apart?" Well here is a spoiler for you. It wasn't gonna fall apart. The Tagi Four were in it to the end. But you wouldn't have known that if you watched the previews and the commercials for Survivor right around this time period. Nope. Every single preview or promo around this time period was some variant of "Kelly and Sue are having a blowout? This is the end of the Tagi Alliance!" Or "Richard is getting too cocky for his own good, and the other players are ready to take him down!" Seriously, EVERY single promo around this time period was based around the mythical fall of the Tagi Alliance. In fact, the promos were particularly focused on the upcoming fall of Richard Hatch. The producers knew that the audience was going to be rooting for Richard to fall at this point, so they pretty much led us all over in the promos like a donkey with a carrot in front of his face.

Like I said, all of this is pretty much television producing 101. This tactic was really nothing special. I mean, it was well done, and many people fell for it, sure, but I don't think it was particularly revolutionary or a particularly out of the box strategy. That is just what you do when you are producing a TV show. You hide the inevitable. You throw out red herrings.

No, what was REALLY out of the box is what the producers did next.

Remember when I said there wasn't a single spoiler out there at any point during Survivor: Borneo? Well keep in mind that it certainly wasn't because people weren't looking for them. People on the internet were CONSTANTLY trolling and digging for spoilers. All season long. Anywhere you could look. Any little hint, any little clue, any little spoiler about Survivor that people could find was immediately posted onto every single TV message board on the internet, where every Survivor fan on the face of the earth could talk about it and discuss it and throw out theories about it.

And since Survivor-- by this point-- was easily the most talked about TV show of the past ten years, it meant that the internet fan base was particularly aggressive about digging around for things.

Combine a rabid fan base + the internet (which was still relatively new at the time) + people digging around everywhere, looking for spoilers, and you have a perfect recipe for what happened next.

At some point around the Gretchen episode, the producers (or somebody at CBS) decided to set a little trap for people who were looking for spoilers. Just kind of a little "gotcha" for people who were digging around the CBS website, snooping for clues.

Somewhere deep down in the files on the CBS website server, there were sixteen pictures.

These sixteen pictures were the faces of the sixteen Survivor contestants. Only next to each face they had a small red X. These were the pictures that went up on CBS.com whenever a contestant was voted out of the game. After each episode, the eliminated player's face was replaced with one of these x "voted out" pictures. It happened every week.

Well just to have fun with everyone who was digging for spoilers, the producers decided to remove one of these pictures from the CBS server. They decided to remove the Gervase picture. He was the only one of the sixteen contestants who had no longer had any "voted out" photo anywhere in their database.

The producers (or like I said, somebody at the CBS website) laid this trap, and they sat back and waited.

And they smiled.

Because they knew that it wouldn't take long.

11. You Bastards Got Everyone

Okay, I'll be honest. I don't really know if the famous "Gervase X" spoiler was intentionally planted by CBS. It could have been intentional, or it simply could have been an honest mix-up on the website. Maybe somebody just forgot to upload a file. I don't know. In fact, nobody has ever known. Well okay, maybe a few people know, but at this point in time, they sure aint talkin'.

In Peter Lance's book "The Stingray", he says there is evidence that all that happened was that somebody at the CBS website simply screwed up. He claims there was no producer involvement at all. He thinks somebody just forgot to upload one of the .jpg files.

Fine.

But you know what? It doesn't matter. Because the minute one of the spoiler hunters discovered the missing Gervase picture on the CBS website, all of a sudden fan involvement in the show amped up to a whole new level. Because word around the internet quickly spread that somebody had cracked the code. One of the many many online Survivor fans out there had finally beaten CBS at the "hiding the secrets" game. And word spread like wildfire all over the internet.

Gervase Peterson was the winner of Survivor.

What you have to keep in mind here is that there was no such thing as a line between "The Survivor World" and "The Survivor Spoiler World" back in 2000. That hadn't happened yet. Interest in Survivor was so high, and people were so rabid about following this new TV show, that any so-called spoiler was inevitably posted on every single website, on every single message board, anywhere people were interested in talking about it. By the end of the week pretty much every single person on the internet who followed Survivor had heard about this new "Gervase X" spoiler.

Again, was this a planted red herring? Or was it just fans digging too deep and finding an honest CBS website screw up? You decide.

All I know is that two things happened immediately after the Gervase X spoiler came out.

The first thing that happened is that fan interest in Survivor quickly surged to a new all-time high. Holy crap, Gervase is going to win Survivor? GERVASE?? The Tagi Alliance is going to fall apart and a Pagong member is going to win the game?

Since this was the outcome that approximately 110% of the Survivor fan community was hoping for at the time, this discovery was of no small significance.

"Holy crap. The cocky Tagis are going to fall? Well now I have to see this."

Again, even if CBS didn't plant the Gervase X spoiler intentionally, this was a Survivor producer's wet dream. This was EXACTLY what they were hoping for at this point in the season. This was the only reason a lot of fans were even going to stay invested in the show at all. They were going to stick around because they wanted to see the fall of the Tagis.

And then came the second big thing that happened.

Mark Burnett, knowing that the audience was digging around all over the place, looking for clues, decided to plant an actual red herring fake Survivor spoiler. And this one most definitely WAS planted by the Survivor producers. This one was so good that it got me too.

At the start of the 8th episode of Survivor (the Greg boot), Mark Burnett inserted a quick insert shot of the final four Tribal Council. It was quick, and you might not have noticed it if you weren't looking for it, but there it was, right there in the opening credits. In fact, if you go back and you watch the episode on DVD, it is still there today.

A shot of Gervase, Colleen, Rudy, and Sean. The Final Four Survivors of Borneo. In the finale Tribal Council. It stayed on the screen for approximately two seconds.

What Mark Burnett (or somebody very high up at CBS) did was he took a shot of the actual final seven Tribal Council, and he digitally removed three of the players. He digitally removed Kelly, Richard, and Sue. Then he slipped the fake "Final Four" shot into the opening credits of that week's episode, because he knew that people would notice it.

And oh man, did the shit hit the fan after that happened.

With the discovery of the "Gervase X" spoiler, and then the fake final four image that was missing three of the Tagi members, internet chatter about

Survivor suddenly went through the roof. Now suddenly EVERYBODY was excitedly talking about the show.

People quickly realized that this was now a cat and mouse game between the fans hunting for spoilers and the producers. Mark Burnett was either trying to give away the winner through his clues, or he was trying to mess with us. It could not have been more obvious. With the discovery of that fake Final Four shot in the opening credits, a line had now been drawn in the sand between the producers and the spoiler hunters.

And I will always say this was a key reason why Survivor remained so popular for so long.

The reason Survivor stayed more popular than so many other shows for so long was because, after the Gervase X/fake final four shot spoilers, many people now viewed the show (for good reason) as some sort of an interactive detective experience.

Even though I hate spoilers with a passion (and I was already dreading them, even back then), I was intrigued by the discoveries of the Gervase X and the fake final four image. Because to me these weren't spoilers, they were clues. It seemed obvious to me that somebody at CBS was trying to mess with us. And the reason I didn't see them as spoilers is because, to me, it just didn't make logical sense that Gervase could win seven straight immunities and win the game. Sorry, I love the guy, but he aint winning. That logic just didn't ring true to me. Lots of people were fooled by the Gervase X spoiler, but I wasn't.

Now the fake final four image... well that was something different altogether.

The minute I saw that fake final four shot at the start of the Greg episode (and immediately wished I hadn't seen it), it was seared into my brain that the producers were trying to tell us something. But unfortunately, what I thought they were telling us wasn't what they were actually telling us.

When I saw that, I immediately started trying to outsmart the producers. And what happened is I wound up outsmarting myself.

"Okay," I thought, "So here is a shot of Colleen, Gervase, Sean, and Rudy. And it has obviously been inserted there so we would notice it. Why is that there?"

In truth all the producers were doing was hiding the fact that the Tagis were going to march to the end. Unopposed. Duh. Unfortunately, in the summer of 2000, I just didn't see that yet.

In my eyes, what the producers were doing was trying to both fool us and give away the winner in the exact same clue. They were telling us that the Tagis were going to fall apart (because that would keep the audience interested), but they weren't going to fall apart in the way that we expected. Because there is no logical way that Gervase and Colleen were going to make it to the final four. I just couldn't see that happening.

But the fact that they left Rudy in that shot... well HE was the guy who immediately jumped out at me.

In my mind, because of that clue, here was what was going to happen. The Tagis were going to make it to the finals, but in the end the two cocky masterminds (Richard and Sue) were going to fall. I didn't see any way around it. Both the Gervase X spoiler and the fake final four image were telling us that. Richard or Sue were not going to win this game. Sue because she wasn't all that smart, and Richard because he was way too cocky and because everybody else was gunning for him. All the hints and the foreshadowing were there.

So I started to go back and look at all the clues that had been in the episodes so far. Because now that I knew the producers were throwing out clues for us, I figured they must have been doing that all along.

And sure enough, there it was in the very first episode. Richard tells us he is the winner. Yeah, whatever. Classic cocky overthinking. This douchebag can't win. No way.

Then in either that same episode or the next episode, Rudy tells us that "I have to change, they don't." He tells us he would only fit in with the Tagis if he learned to adapt.

Bam. That sounds exactly what a winner would say.

Then I started thinking about the fact that the U.S. Army sponsored the season, and that so many of the challenges so far had a military theme. And the fact that Rudy had been so heavily featured in the promos, etc. And that he (along with Colleen) was by far the most popular of the castaways left in the game.

He was also the least threatening of the four Tagis remaining. Which meant he was the least dangerous player of the most powerful alliance. There was no way that anybody would ever vote him out.

By this point it was now becoming completely obvious to me.

Rudy Boesch was going to win.

Oh my God. Rudy Boesch was going to win. The clues have been there all along. The 72 year old Navy Seal is going to win Survivor. There is no way a bad guy wins this show, there is no way the Army would sponsor this show if a bad guy had won in it the end. That means the winner has to be Rudy.

I know, I know. In the spring of 2015 this all sounds so ridiculous. I can see you sitting there, thinking, Mario, you dumbass. There were a billion clues that Richard Hatch was going to win. Burnett even gave it away in the opening credits ("Only one will remain" - superimposed over a very obvious shot of Richard). But I am telling you, nobody thought it was that obvious in the summer of 2000. NOBODY saw the Richard win coming. He was way too cocky, it was way too obvious, and it just didn't make logical sense that someone that disliked could win such an amazingly popular show like Survivor. Are you kidding me? 50 million viewers and the bad guy wins? That fat cocky bad guy? Like hell _that_ would ever happen on TV.

No, from this point on, I was fully invested in my belief that Rudy was going to win.

Actually, let me put a small asterisk next to that. I knew that Rudy was going to win, but I _wanted_ Richard to win.

Why Richard?

Well like I said before, it's because he was the guy who wanted to win the most. Unlike most viewers, I never really bought into the belief that Richard Hatch was "a bad guy" who played "unethically." I personally didn't see anything unethical about his behavior at all. I just saw him as a guy who wanted to win Survivor really really really really badly, but who didn't seem to realize that the others didn't want it as much he wanted it. I also felt kind of bad for Richard because I didn't think he had any idea he would come off as a bad guy when the episodes aired on TV. I figured that the public response he was getting from Survivor fans was probably a bit of a letdown for him. I think he expected to be a lot more admired and respected than he actually was.

So around this time I finally made my predictions for the end of Survivor.

Rudy is going to win, and I am going to be really sad when Richard is voted out.

I am going to be really sad because the producers are clearly setting him up to take a fall, and that will be a shame when it happens. Because he is clearly the best player out there. He also clearly wants it the most.

See, I was already bracing myself for the very sad "Richard comes this close to winning but he gets voted out at the end" episode that I knew was coming. I just <u>knew</u> it was coming.

Sigh.

Screw you producers.

You got me.

You bastards got everyone.

12. The Death of Pagong

Once Greg was voted out, and once every single fan on the internet was now tuned in to the whole "Fall of Tagi" and "Gervase X" spoiler drama, what happened next is exactly what the producers were dreading was going to happen: What happened was that we got a trio of three Survivor episodes that were extremely predictable.

Jenna went home. Then Gervase went home. And then Colleen went home.

Bam, bam, bam.

It was the death of the Pagongs.

Now, even though Jenna's boot was completely obvious if you were following the pattern, what saved it from being a meh moment in the season was the fact that (in my opinion) it is still one of the Top 20 all-time best Survivor episodes. Seriously, if you are an editor working on Survivor, and you want a good dramatic storyline you can play around with in your episode, you aren't going to get much better than the storyline in "J for Jenna." It is an almost perfect Survivor episode. In fact, in my opinion, "J for Jenna" is an even better episode than the Borneo finale, and that is saying something.

What made "J for Jenna" fun, of course, was the fact that it completely pissed off every single Survivor fan on the face of the Earth who wanted Richard to be voted out of the game (which, as I have mentioned, was just about everyone). Richard comes thiiiiiis close to being voted out, he probably should have been voted out (and on his birthday too!), and then he is spared at the last minute because of Doctor Dumbass and his ridiculous alphabet voting strategy. I mean, tell me that isn't a compelling Survivor episode. That is the type of TV you will be talking about with your friends for a week. Survivor would kill for that kind of an episode in most seasons.

So Jenna went home (seriously, screw you Sean, and that is even coming from a Richard fan), and then Gervase went home, and bam there went the myth of the entire "Gervase X/Gervase Wins" spoiler.

Oops, guess Gervase isn't going to win after all. Never mind. Sorry guys, that was our bad.

Personally I wasn't all that surprised when Gervase was voted out. I mean, who else was going to be voted out? He was the next Pagong. Never in a million years did I think he was ever going to make it past the final seven. So for me, no, Gervase being voted out wasn't all that big a deal. .

Now, for the millions of people who really DID buy into the whole Gervase X spoiler, and who really DID think he was going to win... well that was a whole different story. Old timers on Sucks and other Survivor websites still talk about the Gervase boot in the same somber terms that music fans once talked about Ritchie Valens, Buddy Holly, and the Big Bopper. They talk about that episode because it was the one that just destroyed everyone. After all, that was the first episode in Survivor history that proved all the spoilers were wrong.

But for me? Nah. I knew the winner was going to be Rudy. In fact, at this point, I probably would have put money on it.

So Gervase went, and then Colleen went. No biggie. While most of the world was in complete love with Colleen Haskell at the time (seriously, no other player will ever top her as America's Sweetheart), I was never really all that enamored with her. I never really saw Colleen's appeal at the same time that everyone else did. For me, most of the season I just thought of her as Greg's annoying little sidekick. The one who had that weird pseudo-French accent despite the fact that she lived in Miami. Yeah, you know. The one with all the bug bites. Her.

Personally, most of the season I was rooting for Greg to snap his little kitten's neck.

By the way, I should probably point out that when I went back to rewatch Borneo a couple of months later, I became a huge Colleen fan. And I mean HUGE. The more I watched her, the more I caught her sly little sense of humor and her intelligence. The more I watched her, the more I realized she was much closer to being a female Greg Buis than she was to being an Elisabeth Filarski. After a while, it totally clicked with me and I realized she was a really cool person. So yes, in time I eventually did get pulled into the cult of Colleen Haskell like everyone else. But I certainly wasn't there at the time. At the time I couldn't get past that weird little fake accent that she had.

Oh yeah, and I also think that Colleen was really good in the movie "The Animal." I think that was what eventually made me appreciate her. If you have never seen "The Animal" before, you should. It is not a great movie by any stretch of the imagination, but hey at least you get to see Colleen at her peak of being adorable.

So anyway, no more Greg, no more Jenna, no more Gervase, no more

Colleen. No more Pagongs. Colleen even left with her memorable little admonishment to the Tagis to, "Be nice, play fair," which I think should definitely go down as one of the top 10 most underrated Survivor quotes ever. If you have ever wanted a Survivor quote that summed up what 99% of the audience was thinking at any particular point in the franchise, all you have to do is go back to that quote that Colleen dropped right before her torch was snuffed. "Be nice, play fair" to the Tagis. She perfectly summed up what the vast majority of the Survivor audience was feeling at that particular time. And that is why America loved her.

After Colleen was gone, that meant it was time for Doctor Dumbass to be voted off. And of course he was. In perhaps the least suspenseful Tribal Council in 30 seasons of Survivor, Sean Kenniff was voted out at the final five. He became the last Borneo juror right before the finale.

> **Side Note:** I know I like to refer to him as Doctor Dumbass, but Sean Kenniff actually had a pretty good strategy if you stop and you look at it. In his mind, he found a way to vote along with the alliance every single time while not actually being a part of the alliance. Since all the Pagongs were last in the alphabet, he technically found a way to vote with the majority every time, but never take any of the political hit for it. On paper, it was actually a really good strategy. There was no way anyone could ever accuse him of being an "evil" alliance member. What he was really doing was being political and playing for jury votes.
>
> Oh yeah, but here was the problem. Sean didn't seem to realize that he wasn't the only person out there who had figured this out. He didn't seem to grasp that everyone else on the island might have actually been smart too, and that you didn't have to be a neurologist to figure out what he was doing.
>
> So here comes Dr. Sean with his great alphabet strategy that only a brilliant neurologist like him could have come up with, and he is completely oblivious to the fact that even a person like Sue can see right through what he is doing, and that they all think he is a tool. So the rest of the players would just sit around all day and they would openly make fun of him, and he didn't even realize it.
>
> In any case, that is the problem that did in Dr. Sean more than anything. On paper, the Alphabet strategy was actually a really good

strategy. He just never seemed to realize that laypeople might actually be smart too, and that they would see what he was doing.

After Sean left, the cast was down to four. And all that remained in the season at that point was one last amazing, fantastic, memorable Survivor episode.

The finale.

Four players.

Three tribal councils.

One... Survivor.

And all this was going to happen in an episode that Jeff Probst (in a promo) hyped as being so amazing, so incredible, so top secret, that they couldn't even show us ONE SECOND OF FOOTAGE in the previews. Wow. Not even one second? You talk about overhype.

Hey, who knew he wasn't actually joking about that?

While I was definitely excited that we would finally see ~~Rudy~~ the Survivor winner being crowned (who wasn't?), I will admit that I was a little bit sad those last couple of days leading up to the Survivor finale. The reason I had such mixed emotions over the finale was because I was sad that Survivor was about to be over. This show that had been so revolutionary, this show that had been so amazing, this show that had had such incredible word of mouth and momentum as it went along (seriously, to this day I have never seen a more talked about TV show than Survivor in the summer of 2000) was going to be over in less than a week. And after that, then what? There would be no more Tribal Councils. There would be no more internet detective games. There would be no more Richard, Rudy, Gervase, Colleen, or Sue. Never again in my life would I ever hear a 72 year old Navy Seal call somebody a "bare-ass queer."

Yeah, it was awesome, absolutely. Survivor was crowning its winner. How awesome is that? But for me it was also a little bit sad. Because at the time I honestly didn't think there would ever be another TV show like this again. Sure, there was talk that a sequel was being planned for next spring, and it would be set in Australia. But at this point everyone was pretty much sure that it would never be as compelling as the original. I mean, come on, how compelling could Survivor be if it didn't have Rudy? Or Richard? Or even Greg? The belief among most people at this point was that Survivor was going to be a once in a lifetime phenomenon.

Sure, Survivor 2 might be fun, but it just wasn't going to be the same because it didn't have the characters we loved. It was going to be like if they took Seinfeld and they remade it starring Seth Green and Helen Hunt. Sure, it might be close. But it just wouldn't be what we were used to.

I figured that, like pretty much every sequel, Survivor: The Australian Outback would just be a bigger budget (and much more hyped) ripoff of the show we had already seen. And a lot of Survivor fans I knew didn't really see the point. I mean, why do we need sixteen new people all doing Richard impressions when we already have a Richard? Why do we need a new old guy who is just going to try to be Rudy? What is the point of that?

So yes, as Survivor wound down to its final days, I was definitely a little bit sad. This was the show that I had lived and breathed the past three months of my life. It was the show that had pulled my wife and me out of the weekly hell that we knew as Baby Boot Camp. Hell, it was the first TV show my daughter had essentially grown up on (okay, she was only three months old at the time, but hey, it counted in my head.)

In one week's time, it would all be over. And then I would be sad.

In fact, I would be doubly sad because I was sure that Richard Hatch wasn't going to win. And that guy was my favorite. That part of the finale (which I just knew was going to happen) was going to suck.

You see, I was still 100% certain in my mind that the winner was going to be Rudy. And I don't think I was alone in this.

I don't have the data to back this up, but I think most of America probably thought the winner was going to be Rudy.

13. 51.7 Million Viewers

Before I sat down to write this chapter, I spent about a day trying to get my mindset back to where it was the week of the Survivor finale. I spent an entire day just trying to reminisce, and think back, and remember what I was thinking and what I was doing those last few days before one of the biggest events in television history.

By the way, when I call it one of the biggest events in television history, that is really not an exaggeration. To put into perspective how many people watched that Borneo finale, I would really have to compare it to... um... uh... well, crap. Okay, I can't really put it into perspective. All you have to know is that the audience for Survivor grew steadily all throughout the first season. The momentum just grew. It became the #1 show in America sometime around the fourth or fifth episode, and the ratings pretty much went up every single week after that. And then when it came to the finale, forget about it. All of a sudden everybody who loved Survivor and everybody who hated Survivor and everybody who was just curious "what this show everyone is talking about is all about" came together into one perfect storm combination of a viewing audience.

In Howard Stern's movie "Private Parts", there is a great scene where an NBC radio executive is baffled by the unbelievable ratings that Howard is getting on his morning radio show. According to the astonished executive, people who love Stern are listening to his show for something like two hours a day. Meanwhile, people who hate Stern are listening to his show for something like FIVE hours a day.

Why?

Well because people who hate him "just want to hear what he is going to say next."

This is pretty much exactly what happened with the Survivor finale. Everybody who loved Survivor and who was completely obsessed with it (like me) tuned in, of course. We tuned in because we were brainwashed and because that was what we did. We tuned in because we had to tune in, we needed our crack fix. But everybody who hated Survivor and all the people who were completely sick of it (which was also a sizable chunk of the world at the time) also tuned in. The Survivor haters also piled on to watch the finale that night. Not because they loved the show, of course, but because they were sick of it, and they wanted to see how this trainwreck of a reality TV abortion was finally going to end.

60

And then of course there were people like the Amish and people who had never heard of television before, who somehow stumbled upon a TV set in the Sears Audiovisual department that week and thought it would be fun to watch this Survivor thing that everybody else in the world was talking about.

So anyway, that is what the climate was like going into the Survivor finale. People who loved the show were throwing tiki parties and having luaus in their backyards, and they were watching the finale with their friends in big fun loud groups. And people who hated the show and thought it was a stain on the human race were watching it so they could tear it apart the next day in the media, and they could write on the internet about how a dark time in television history had finally come to an end.

I remember reading somewhere that half the television sets in America that were turned on that night were tuned to Survivor, which is something that is nearly impossible to accomplish in the world of television after the post-1990's cable age. Once cable took over television in the late 90's, there were so many more channels available now than there were before that it was almost impossible for a network TV show to pull in half of the viewing audience like shows used to be able to do in the old days. Yet the Survivor finale pretty much did it. That is astounding that a show could still pull off an audience like that in the year 2000, when it was up against cable.

The only TV event I can think of in my lifetime that would compare to the Survivor finale would be the Seinfeld finale back in 1998. That was another event that nearly everyone in America was talking about at the time (even non Seinfeld fans were talking about it.) I know that the Seinfeld finale got something like 70 million viewers. But without looking at the numbers, I am guessing that the Survivor finale was right behind it, and I am guessing it was probably the #2 highest rated TV finale of the past 20 years.

Side Note: Okay I was wrong. I looked it up on Wikipedia right before I published this book. If you discount the Super Bowls, the Survivor finale is actually the 4th highest rated TV episode of the past 20 years. And, surprisingly, the Seinfeld finale isn't even #1. According to Wikipedia, the Cheers finale was #1 (80.4 million), then the Seinfeld finale (76 million), then the Friends finale (52.5 million), and then the Survivor finale (51.7 million). Although I am a little surprised about Cheers and Friends being so high, because in my memory the Seinfeld and Survivor finales were a much bigger

61

deal. Of course, Cheers was also nearly 20 years ago, so my memory could be a little bit fuzzy on that one. And also Friends just sucks, so fuck Friends.

And so there you go. On August 23, 2000, the Survivor finale drew 51.7 million viewers. It was enormous. It was also nearly double the amount of viewers that watched the Dr. Sean boot episode (28.7 million) the week before.

It also delivered what is probably the single most famous episode in Survivor history.

The show would never again be this huge.*

* Although it came close. The Australia premiere episode drew 45.4 million.

Postscript #1: I know this will sound like little more than the sour grapes whining of a Survivor fan, but honestly, I have always felt that Survivor drawing 51 million viewers is way more impressive than Cheers drawing 80 million or Seinfeld drawing 76 million.

For starters, Cheers was on during a time when there were still only three mainstream TV channels in America. Fox (the fourth network) didn't really show up as a serious competitor until the early 90's, and even then a good chunk of Americans still didn't have cable. So Cheers was great, sure, and Cheers was a big deal, sure. But it also came out at a time when there was a lot less competition. And then the Seinfeld and Friends finales were huge, absolutely, but they also both had seven plus years to build up a loyal audience and to get people to care about the characters. Of COURSE people were going to tune in for their final episodes. Those shows were on so long that their finales essentially marked the end of an era for a lot of people.

Survivor, on the other hand, was only on the air for thirteen weeks. It went from 15 something million viewers in its premiere episode, and it more than tripled that viewership in less than three months. When is the next time you will ever see a television event like that in your lifetime? You aren't just talking a popular TV show here, you are talking a legitimate summer phenomenon. This was the Rubik's Cube of the 21st century. It came out of nowhere and it just took over everything.

Again, nothing against Cheers, Seinfeld or Friends, but I think Survivor's accomplishment was way more impressive than any of theirs were.

Oh yeah, and Survivor totally killed Friends' impact on American culture by the summer of 2001. But we will get to that when we come to season two. Although again, in any case, ha ha screw you Friends.

Postscript #2: Okay here is something that can actually put the Survivor finale into perspective for you. The Survivor finale in 2000 drew 51.7 million viewers. Remember the Lost finale from 2010? Remember the biggest television event in a decade? Well the Lost finale only drew 13.5 million. Multiply that by four and then you have the Survivor finale.

14. God is a Survivor Fan

What I remember the most about the Survivor finale is the fact that nobody on the face of the Earth wanted Richard to win.

Well okay. There were definitely a few closet Richard fans out there (including me, and from what I have been told, most of Rhode Island.) But nobody really wanted to come right out and say that. The general consensus both on the internet and in the rest of the world was that Richard couldn't win Survivor, otherwise everyone would be pissed off. If he won, then the whole season would have just been an enormous infuriating waste of time for everyone.

Believe me, you think I am making this up, but people were very adamant about this. They were saying it on every single Survivor message board at the time. They were saying it on every single entertainment website at the time. If Richard Hatch won Survivor, something like 50% of the audience was vowing that they would never watch the show again.

I always wonder what Mark Burnett thought about that.

Hell, I always wonder what Richard Hatch thought about that.

Like I said, I never really thought that Richard stood a chance, so I didn't really care what the audience thought about him. I mean, I wanted Richard to win, sure. But to me it seemed like he was dead meat. I just didn't see how a jury would ever reward a guy that nobody liked. So to me it was kind of a moot point that everyone in the world seemed to hate him. Yeah Richard's cocky, Richard sucks, Richard is a blowhard, blah blah blah. But he is never gonna win, not on a show like this. So who cares?

I'm sure that everyone who is reading this book is quite familiar with the Borneo finale, so I am not going to recap it blow by blow. However I will say that the thing that *I* personally remember the most about the finale was the moment where Richard took his hand off of the idol during the final three immunity challenge. That was such a great underrated TV moment. Richard won Survivor while simultaneously screwing his best friend Rudy in the process. Oh yeah, and he did it in the one way that didn't technically "break" his final two deal with Rudy, which meant that Rudy wouldn't come back and slit his throat in the middle of the night with all his SEAL buddies two months down the road.

Again, you think I am kidding, but go back and watch Rudy's final words in All-Stars. Go read Burnett's book, and read some of the things Rudy would threaten to do to people in Borneo if they were planning to backstab him. I honestly think that if Richard had broken his deal with Rudy in the wrong way, Richard Hatch might not be with us today. Rudy might have literally murdered him.

Am I exaggerating? I don't know. Probably. All I know is that I am not the only one who likes to make jokes about this. Like I said, Mark Burnett commented on this several times during his book about Borneo. He wrote that Rudy was CONSTANTLY threatening people that something bad would happen to them if they ever went back on a deal with him. And, as the game went along, he didn't think that Rudy was joking.

Have I mentioned before that I love Rudy? This is just reason number ninety-five why. I love 72 year old white guys who issue fatwas on people.

Of course "Richard screws Rudy and essentially wins the game" isn't the way that most people saw Richard's decision to take his hand off of the idol at the time. No way. Most of us watching at home were always about two steps behind Richard when it came to the strategy department.

I swear, the minute Richard took his hand off of that idol, the minute he volunteered to go immunity-less into the final three, my jaw just about dropped to the floor. Because all across America, I could practically hear 51 million people screaming at their televisions all at once, "HE'S VULNERABLE!!!!! VOTE HIM OUT!!!!! VOTE THIS DICKHEAD OUT NOW!!!!!!!!!!!" And that is the one moment I will always remember about the Borneo finale. That was the first time that I ever watched something happen on TV, and I instinctively knew what nearly every other Survivor fan was thinking at that exact same moment. That one scene, where Richard pulled his hand off of the idol, will always be the defining moment of Borneo for me.

So anyway, Richard screwed Rudy on national TV (in the most polite way possible, of course), Rudy was voted out of the game in third place, and I was legitimately shocked.

Shocked!

I wasn't shocked because Richard had managed to make it to the end. No, what shocked me was that Rudy Boesch wasn't going to be the Sole Survivor. The hell? Nearly every single scenario I had gone over in my head the past two weeks before the finale had wound up with Rudy winning Survivor. Nearly every single one. The only ones that didn't end with Rudy winning had ended with Sue winning.

And now this? Richard and Kelly? The snake against the rat?

Who saw that ending coming??

I am not joking about this, I was legitimately flabbergasted when I realized that Rudy wasn't going to win Survivor. And what happened is that I had to quickly think back in my head and backtrack over everything that had happened throughout the season. Was there some clue I had somehow missed along the way? Was there some hint all along that Kelly was going to win?

Even at this point, I still didn't think that Richard was going to win. No way. That just wouldn't go over well at all. Seriously, NO ONE wanted Richard to win. Richard winning would be the most infuriating thing that had ever happened on TV.

But Kelly winning?

Hmm.

I had to think about this.

I wasn't quite sure what I would think about Survivor if Kelly won. Because honestly, that wasn't a scenario that had ever crossed my mind all season. Not even once. Kelly Wiglesworth, the Sole Survivor? That just seemed wrong. I mean, even if you didn't like Richard, a "Kelly wins" ending just didn't seem to fit. That wasn't the ending that this narrative we had been watching all season had been pointing towards.

In my opinion, the story of Survivor all season long had been "Richard Hatch." That was it. Even in 2000, even if the middle of "We Hate Richard!" mania, I can't think of one person who would have disagreed with that. Even if you hated Richard, you had to admit that he had been the main character in just about every episode. Even if you hated Richard, you had to admit that he had been the central character in just about every moment. Every episode, every scene, all summer long, had been all about Richard, and how Richard was either going to win, or Richard was going to go down in an enormous fireball of humiliation.

To me, Kelly winning-- in the manner she was about to win-- well that just didn't make sense.

The problem I was trying to reconcile in my head, I quickly realized, was that Richard hadn't had his majestic downfall yet. That was the aspect of this ending that was starting to bother me. Because honestly, when you have a character who is this big, who is this arrogant, and who is this hated by your audience, why else does he exist except to have a majestic downfall at some point down the road? Seriously, that is just Storytelling 101. You don't build up a villain and then have him just fizzle out in a boring lame old jury vote. That wouldn't make sense at all. To me, a villain has to either die a spectacular death, or he has to be humiliated in the most embarrassing way possible. Otherwise why would he have been your villain?

And in my mind, I just didn't see either of those fates awaiting Richard. This jury simply wasn't angry enough at him.

And it was at this point-- for this very reason-- that I started to think that maybe he could actually win this thing.

"Could it be that Richard is actually going to win?" I remember asking my wife. "Do you think he could actually pull this thing off now?"

"No way. He's Richard."

On one level, I had to agree with her. On a pure gut instinct level, I knew there was no way that Richard was ever going to win a jury vote. No way. Survivor was now down to the final two, which meant that it was essentially now a popularity contest. And nobody liked him. How much more black and white could it get than that?

But then I brainstormed and I started going over the individual jury votes.

Rudy, of course, well he was probably going to vote for Richard. Those two had been tight since day one. Plus Rudy was so old school that he would probably never ever vote for a girl. Not in a game like this he wouldn't. His vote for Richard was going to be easy.

Sean will probably vote for Richard too, I thought. Those guys were buddies. So now that is two votes.

I knew that Richard needed four votes to win. And the more I thought about it, I started to think that he might not have been as "hated" as the editing had tried to lead us to believe. In fact, I could now see an entirely realistic scenario where Sue or Greg or even Gervase might vote for him to win, simply because they respected him and they didn't respect Kelly.

And wow. I suddenly realized that all Richard needed were two of those three votes.

Richard Hatch could actually win Survivor.

Holy crap.

As I sat there, and I did the math in my head, I suddenly realized that this season had a chance to become even more buzzworthy and talked about than it had been up to this point. Because if Richard Hatch won, well that would pretty much just be the icing on the cake. That would REALLY make this Must See TV. That would be the ending that this season should have had since day one, but that just about nobody on the face of the Earth wanted to see. Yet maybe it was possible. In fact maybe it was probable. And all along maybe the producers had been trying to hide it from us.

Wow.

If you thought that people had been talking about this show before, just wait until you see what happens when the bad guy wins!

Even though I had been rooting for Richard all along, I suddenly realized that that really hadn't been "true" rooting at all. What I had been doing up to this point was just sort of "cute" rooting, where you pick a guy who can't possibly win, but you think he is fun to watch, so you root for him like he is a mascot. Kind of like how everybody cheers for the 5'3" white benchwarmer who comes in and plays the last two minutes of any blowout college basketball game. Up to this point Richard had been my Survivor equivalent of Rudy Ruettiger.

But now? Now I was legitimately rooting for him.

I wasn't rooting for him because it was the correct outcome for the season (which it was.) And I wasn't rooting for him because Kelly winning would be the equivalent of this huge season ending as a fizzled little fart (which it would have been.) No, I was rooting for him because if Richard won, holy crap. If "Darth Gaydar" won... man oh man was the entertainment world going to be buzzing and talking about this episode tomorrow.

If Richard won, every single TV columnist on the face of the Earth was going to write a column tomorrow about how awful this show was, and how Survivor was the single worst thing that had ever happened on television. And how the Survivor finale was the first sign of evidence that we were doomed as a species. The haters were all going to come screaming and clawing out of the woodwork tomorrow, and everybody was going to be completely pissed off about everything. Richard Hatch winning Survivor wasn't just going to be a big deal. It was going to be front page news that everyone was going to be outraged about for the next six weeks. It was going to be glorious.

And this is where I said a little prayer to God. Please let Richard win. Look, I know that I am an atheist, but please have Richard win, just for the reaction alone. Please? For me? Just this once? Ohpleaseohpleaseohplease?

I said a little prayer and, yep, I got my wish. God listened. It happened.

Richard won Survivor.

And that was when the fireworks began.

P.S. Okay we need to talk about Greg's jury vote at the end of the game. You know, the one where he asked Richard and Kelly to pick a number between one and ten, and because Richard's number was closer, Greg voted for Richard to win. Greg's vote was the one vote that cost Kelly the win in the end, and it has also been one of the biggest Survivor controversies since the night that Borneo finale aired on TV. So I guess this would be a good place to talk about it.

First off, let me point out that in the days following the Borneo reunion, news came out that Greg's little pick a number game had really been a sham. It turned out that he had ALWAYS intended to vote for Richard. He just decided to make up the "pick a number" game on the spot because he wanted to mess with the producers.

I don't remember where I first heard this story, all I remember is that it came out right after the season ended and that everybody heard about it. And that within a couple of months, pretty much everyone in the fanbase was now on the same page that, oh yeah, Greg was going to vote for Richard no matter

69

what. That vote wasn't random at all. Richard had four votes lined up as a slam dunk going into that finale (Greg's, Sue's, Rudy's, and Sean's), and the only reason the vote wound up being close at all was because Sue's speech was so mean that it actually caused two of the jurors (Gervase and Colleen) to switch their votes to Kelly out of sympathy. So instead of Richard winning 6-1, he only won 4-3 because Sue's "rats and snakes" speech had actually cost him two votes.

Again, this was the fan base consensus for a couple of years. Everyone knew this. This was the common wisdom that explained the ending of Borneo.

And then, suddenly, and inexplicably, things changed.

A couple of years ago, I started seeing a lot of posts show up on Survivor message boards that criticized Richard Hatch as a winner, because "he only won based on pick a number." And at first I tried to ignore them. At first I was like, well clearly these are just new fans that only started watching the show in the last couple of years. They have no idea what they are talking about when it comes to Survivor history, so it would be best just to ignore them.

But the posts kept coming. All of a sudden there were a lot of them. And all of a sudden there was this huge groundswell growing among people who wrote about Survivor that Richard "had only been lucky" and that "Kelly really should have won that season, because she was the better player." And they all bashed Richard for winning only because of "pick a number."

Well I certainly can't handle Survivor fans bashing Survivor winners, so now I took this on as a personal crusade. How dare Survivor fans turn on Richard and claim that he shouldn't have won Borneo. Didn't they realize that vote really should have been 6-1? And that Kelly very nearly got shut out?

I went on my new "save Richard's reputation" crusade for a couple of years. I defended him on Survivor Historians. I wrote about him every chance that I got. I pointed out that Kelly was a flip-flopper who no one respected because she jumped in and out of the Tagi alliance whenever it was convenient for her, and that no one respected her for it. Above all else I tried to beat it into peoples' heads that Greg's vote was NOT random, and that no Ivy League brain like him EVER would have voted for a homeless high school dropout like Kelly as his superior in a game of strategy. I'm sorry, but I know people, and people just don't do that. I don't care how much of a wild card Greg liked to play on TV. Deep down he was still probably just an elitist Ivy League kid.

I kept up the good fight defending Richard for <u>months</u>, and then, suddenly, about a year and a half ago, things dropped out from under me.

One day, Greg Buis just randomly showed up on a Survivor podcast. I don't know how that happened, but all of a sudden he was resurrected from the dead and he just showed up on some random interview. And, naturally, he was asked about his vote for Richard, and if it had really been based on pick a number.

"Oh yeah," he said happily, "It was totally random. If Kelly had picked a different number, she would have gotten my vote."

Well, poop.

In the end, was Greg's vote at the time really random? Or has he just changed his story over the years? Or does he even remember it fifteen years later at all? I have no idea.

All I DO know is that, fifteen years ago, everybody knew that Richard Hatch nearly beat Kelly Wiglesworth in a shutout. That was just common knowledge. Sue's speech got Gervase and Colleen to switch their votes to Kelly, and that was the only reason the final vote was even close in the first place. It really should have been 6-1. So whether Greg's vote really was random or not (I still don't buy that it was), in the end it shouldn't have even made that much of a difference. Richard was an infinitely more respected player than Kelly ever was, and in the end a Survivor jury will always vote for the player that they respect the most.

And I'm sorry Kelly fans, but that "most respected" player was Richard.

15. The Most Important Survivor Moment You Have Never Heard Of Before

This is going to be a short chapter, but it occurred to me as I was finishing this section that I bet there are a lot of Survivor fans out there who think they know why Richard won, but don't *really* know why he won. In fact, there is one specific scene that happened very early on in the game (and was incredibly important to the rest of the season) that most of you have probably never heard of before.

This might be review for some of you uber Survivor nerds out there, and if it is, I apologize. But for the rest of you, get ready to have your Borneo eyes opened. Because this is a really big moment that I am about to tell you about.

Okay, so we are on day two or three of Survivor. It is very early on in the game. And at this point in the game, Richard Hatch is destined to be the first player voted out of Borneo.

That's right. Through the first two days of the game, Richard Hatch was as dead as dead meat can be. There was no chance in the world he ever would have been able to make it far in this game. The rest of the Tagis (especially the girls) all thought he was pompous and annoying.

And trust me, in a social game like Survivor, that is a bad combination. Especially early on.

Richard was in very bad shape in the game early on, and he knew it. All his grand proclamations about being "the mastermind", all his big cunning plans of "forming an alliance", all his predictions that he would not only win Survivor, but he would also be the guy who would be hand-picked by CBS to host Survivor 2 (which was what Richard totally expected would happen after the season), well all those plans were going downhill fast, and he knew it. The rest of the Tagis just did not like him. They didn't want anything to do with him. Richard was such an annoying blowhard that the Tagis were going to get rid of him before they got rid of either of the old people.

And this is where we come to the scene which could arguably be called the single most important moment in Survivor history.

The Tagis are sitting around the campfire on either night two or night three (I forget which one), and Richard decides that he is going to have a little

72

"come to Jesus" meeting with the rest of his tribesmates. He decides that he is tired of them only seeing him as a big fat know it all blowhard. He wants these people to like him. If he is going to get far in this game, he needs them to start seeing him as a human being with feelings.

So he sits the Tagis down, and he comes out of the closet.

He shares his biggest secret with the rest of the Tagis, that he is actually a homosexual. And that most people in real life don't know that about him.

He tells them about all the struggles that he has faced in his life. He explains how difficult it was being gay and growing up in a conservative area. He explains how difficult it was to keep his secret when he was in the military. He explains that he was sexually abused when he was a child. He tells them that he was thrown out of the house for being gay when he was a teenager. And then, lastly, he explains how hard it is to raise a son when you are a single gay father.

He comes out of the closet and he spills all of his deep dark secrets to the rest of his tribesmates.

And do you know what? From then on out, the Tagis all rallied around him.

From then on out, Kelly Wiglesworth (in particular) was completely protective of Richard. She wanted nothing more than to align with him because she knew that she wanted to be friends with the guy.

And that is 100% the only reason why the Tagi Alliance ever happened.

Now I know what a lot of you are saying. Most of you are hearing about this for the first time and you are saying to yourself, "bullshit." Because since that scene was never actually shown in the episode, a lot of Survivor fans have no idea that it ever actually took place. In fact, I would be willing to bet that about 90% of the people who are reading this book are only hearing about the "Richard comes out of the closet" scene for the first time right now. That is how buried it has become in the pages of the Survivor history book.

But this is the God's honest truth. That scene really did happen. And Kelly really did become very protective of Richard because of it. And Sue really did start to take him seriously as a teammate after that. It was all because Richard came out of the closet that night around the campfire. That was the moment that determined the entire course of the rest of the Survivor franchise.

Now, naturally you might be saying to yourself, "Well Mario, if we never saw it on TV, then how the hell do you know about it? Do you have some sort of secret insider access when it comes to Borneo that nobody else has ever been privy to?"

Uh, no. Not really.

The reason I know about that scene (and I know how important it is) is because Mark Burnett wrote about it quite extensively in his Survivor book. Burnett flat out says that THIS is the moment that the Tagi alliance was formed, and THIS is the moment that determined the rest of the season. And that Richard only wound up winning because the other people suddenly wanted to be friends with him.

Again, his win had nothing to do with strategy.

It had nothing to do with being a villain.

It had nothing to do with "screwing people over" or "blindsides" or "taking out his enemies."

Richard only won Survivor because the other players helped him win.

<u>You can only win a game like this if the other players like you.</u>

This is by far one of the biggest lessons that has ever come out of Survivor (you can't win the game yourself, you can only win it if other people help you) and it is amazing that it has been so completely forgotten and bastardized over the years. But there it is, in plain black and white, spelled out so eloquently in Mark Burnett's book. Survivor is a social game. If the other people don't like you, you don't stand a chance. Richard Hatch had no chance to win whatsoever until he opened up and he got all the other players to start liking him.

Again, Mark Burnett wrote about this quite extensively in his book. He called that the most pivotal moment of the season. He said that was the scene that changed everything. He raved on and on about how that moment completely led to the birth of the Tagi alliance.

And then, naturally, it was completely cut out when they edited the first episode.

To me, this has always been one of the more baffling editing choices in the history of Survivor. Why cut that scene out of the episode? If it was so important to what would happen later in the season, if it was so important to Survivor history, indeed if it was THE scene that really explained everything, why edit it out? Why do you leave it up to me, fifteen years later, to explain to everyone in the fan base what a big deal it was?

These are good questions.

In the end, why do *I* think it was cut out of the episode?

If you ask me, I think it was cut out of the episode because they wanted to add to the suspense. Simple as that. Mark Burnett didn't want you to know that there was a Tagi Alliance until it benefitted the story for the audience to know that. He didn't want it to show up until the third or fourth episode. Even though, in truth, the seeds of it had already been planted. The seeds of it had been planted the minute that Kelly stopped making fun of Richard behind his back, and she finally started to have empathy for him.

And that, more than anything, is why one of the most important moments in the history of Survivor, is one that you never saw.

And no one has ever seen.

16. A Woman Can't Win Survivor

I can pinpoint the exact moment that I decided I wanted to write about Survivor. Seriously, I can pinpoint it right down to the exact second.

The day after Richard Hatch won Borneo (which was met with approximately the exact same sound as Alderaan being blown up in Star Wars - millions of voices crying out at once), every single psychology expert with an agenda to push had to get on TV the next morning and talk about their big old grand theory of what Survivor had taught us. All you saw on TV the next couple of days were psychology experts and sociology experts and relationship experts talking about Survivor and what it "meant" and why it happened, and what sort of message this TV show had delivered to the world.

The most memorable speech regarding "What was Survivor really about, and why did we watch it?" came from the host of the reunion show himself, Bryant Gumbel. Does anyone else remember that speech? Gumbel went on for like a minute at the end of the Borneo reunion show. He did a little monologue where he talked about what Survivor really meant, and why we had all been interested in it. And he wondered what it said about us as a society when 50 million people all got wrapped up so deeply in these characters and in Mark Burnett's little island game show psychology experiment.

First off, I loved that speech. I think it is one of the best things that has ever been said about the phenomenon of Survivor. Why <u>did</u> we watch it? Seriously, why were we interested in it? What exactly was so fascinating about everyday people living on an island and basically de-evolving? I think that Bryant Gumbel (as hard as it is to believe) made an excellent point in what he was trying to say at that moment. The fact that America got so wrapped up in what was basically home movie voyeur footage was both fascinating and also a little bit creepy.

But here is the second thing. As much as I loved Bryant's speech, and I really did, as much as I loved his attempt to philosophize on what this show said about us as Americans, it was completely the wrong forum for him to be doing it.

Are you kidding me, Gumbel? You are going to stand there at the end of Survivor, with 50 million rabid Survivor fanatics still reeling over Richard's win, you are going to stand there right after the ending of the most exciting thing that has happened on TV in more than a decade, and you are going to tell us that we were all creepy because we loved this show? He honestly thought that was going to go over well?

In my opinion, Bryant Gumbel should have saved his speech for the next morning on the Early Show. He should have waited for the next morning to jump on the "What was Survivor? And why did we watch it?" bandwagon just like everyone else. The fact that he chose to do it during the reunion show came off as incredibly smug and not to mention a little bit douchy. It is stuff like that that made the world hate Bryant Gumbel in the first place.

However, again, I will admit that I think he had a very good point. He just made it in the wrong place.

So anyway, Richard won, and every single psychologist on the face of the Earth crawled out of the woodwork the next morning to offer their opinion on it. Which of course you knew was going to happen. What did Survivor *mean*? *Why* did Richard win? Why did we watch it? And what real-life lessons can we learn from watching this show?

As I said before, everyone who had a psychological agenda to push came on TV to talk about Survivor over the next couple of days. Even people who had never even watched the show prior to the finale came onto TV to talk about it. And the absolute worst of them all was a feminist studies professor who appeared on the Early Show the morning after the finale. Her ridiculous appearance is the main reason I decided I wanted to become a Survivor writer.

According to Ms. Feminist Studies Professor, the reason Richard Hatch won Survivor was because no jury on the face of the earth would ever vote for a woman to win over a man. She said it had nothing to do with him being a better player, or him being a better strategist, and it had nothing to do with the fact that Kelly was a little weasel who nobody liked. No, she said that American society is so conditioned to value males over females that a woman could never possibly win Survivor because no jury would allow it.

And I'm sorry... but Bull. Fucking. Shit.

Like I said at the start of the chapter, if you want to know why I became a Survivor writer, there you go. That quote right there. "A woman can never possibly win Survivor." There were a lot of psychologists and other "experts" who pissed me off with their theories about Survivor over the next couple of weeks, but she was the absolute worst. She just sat there and talked about how Survivor illustrated the plight that women face in America, and it just drove me up the wall. Are you kidding me? Kelly lost because she was a woman? Seriously? You are going to sit there and argue that?

What drove me even crazier was the fact that nobody on the Early Show said anything to rebut this. Bryant Gumbel and whoever the hell else was hosting the show that day just sat there and nodded their heads, like what she was saying was completely obvious. Oh yeah, of course a woman could never win Survivor. Yeah we see that. Sure. Richard only won because he had a dick.

Of course the irony here is that the jury voted for a gay man to win over a woman, not a straight man, but I guess that didn't fit into her argument.

So anyway yeah, there you go. The moment I knew that I wanted to write about Survivor.

The reason I wanted to write about this show because everyone who WAS talking about it at the time had some stupid political or psychological agenda that they wanted to push. They didn't really care about the show. They only hopped onto the bandwagon at the end because there were 50 million people watching and they knew they could get some airtime or some new readers by showing how Survivor illustrated their theory. They weren't Survivor fans at all, they were all just opportunists.

And then meanwhile here's me (not to mention a lot of other people just like me). And I happen to know a lot about psychology too. And I actually AM a huge fan of the show. These douchebags shouldn't be talking about Survivor, I should be talking about Survivor! And guess what, I don't even have an agenda to push. I just want to talk about the show because I love it so much.

All I wanted to do at this point was find some forum where I could write about Survivor, and where I could talk about some of the psychological/sociological undertones that were going on with it. That's all. Because there was some pretty cool stuff going on in that first season. The show was always a lot deeper and more meaningful than it appeared on the surface (which, again, is where I agreed with Bryant Gumbel.)

By the way, want a good example of something interesting that was going on that first season that nobody really talked about? Well here is a perfect summation, written by a friend of mine named Doug Jacobson. Here is a great example of something interesting (sociologically) that came out of that first season, and which Survivor never really got enough credit for:

> I remember that Survivor ending was a really difficult time for me. I was rooting for Richard for three major reasons: 1) He played the best game and 2) I always root for the villain. The 3rd reason is very personal for me and it may sound corny. The time the first season was airing was also the time when I was coming to terms with my sexuality. It was amazing to me to see a gay man so comfortable with himself and so "accepted" by the group. The way he lived his life was an inspiration to me. He gave me hope that I could live an open and happy life. Keep in mind that this was the year 2000 and we didn't have all the reality TV with so many open gays on television yet.
>
> So, I've always had a special place in my heart for Richard. Like I said, this may sound corny to you but I wanted to let you know how the first season greatly impacted my life.

See, right there? One really cool aspect of Borneo, and one which had some definite real life societal impact.

Before Survivor, I don't think most of America had ever really seen a gay man on TV who wasn't prissy or portrayed as comic relief. And Richard, of course, wasn't portrayed comically at all. Richard was so non stereotypically gay, in fact, that Rudy Boesch, a 72 year old career military man who specifically went into the game expecting to hate anyone who was queer, didn't realize Richard was gay and soon became his best friend. How revolutionary was that for TV in the year 2000? I can think of very few moments in TV history that had as much impact as Rudy Boesch announcing to the world that "Richard is queer, but he's good. If the rest of 'em are smart, they'll listen to him."

In my opinion it was no accident that TV became a lot more gay friendly after the summer of 2000. Will and Grace became a Top 20 show. Queer Eye for the Straight Guy debuted. Ellen DeGeneres went from being a punchline (she really was at the time, look it up) to being a beloved television icon. All of that came after Survivor. All of that came after America saw that Richard Hatch was actually a pretty normal guy who was just like everyone else. Like Doug said in his comments, Richard was probably the first "real gay guy" that a lot of people in America had ever seen on TV.

I am far from the first person who has ever pointed this out, but the fact that an old-school military guy like Rudy would gave Richard a stamp of approval on national TV? And the fact that the two of them would later become friends? Rudy, who specifically went into the game with the goal of "hunting down and voting out all the queers"?? Well that friendship probably did more for gay acceptance in America than anything that had ever been seen before on TV. Heck, even in Mark Burnett's book he pointed out what a big deal that friendship was. He mentions in his book, over and over and over, that nothing like this had ever been seen on a mainstream television show before the summer of 2000. He says that Rudy and his friendship with Richard was the most amazing (and unlikely) thing he had ever seen happen in his life.

And there you go. That right there, that friendship. Between Richard and Rudy. That literally changed the way that gays would be portrayed on TV in the future. It was the heart of the season. And it is a shame that Survivor has never received enough credit for that.

So anyway, this is where I stood the first few weeks after the Borneo finale. There were a ton of people out there who were talking about Survivor, but they just weren't saying the right stuff. They didn't care about the show. They only cared about their own agendas. And they weren't writing on Survivor fan sites, they were writing in places where Survivor fans wouldn't really be, like The New York Times, or The Wall Street Journal, or Psychology Today. Simply put, they were the wrong people, and they weren't writing for the right audience.

As I saw it, the big difference between me and all these TV psychologists (aside from their numerous degrees and the fact that they were actually getting paid to do this for living) was the fact that I actually DID follow this show. I actually DID care about where it went after the first season. Survivor was all I had lived and breathed for the last two months of my life. I didn't want it to flame out and become a one season flash in the pan, like they all clearly expected it to be.

I wanted to write about this show, and I wanted to write about it as it developed. Because like I said, I knew there was a lot more going on than we saw in the episodes. And I thought that the second season had the potential to be even bigger, and even bolder, and if we were lucky, just as revolutionary as the first.

I knew that I wanted to write about Survivor. The only problem was that I didn't know where I was going to write about it yet, or what I was going to say. Or how I was going to find any sort of a readership.

At this point I was little more than just some guy on the Television Without

Pity message board who was known as "Sandwich Artist." Or, as most people knew me better, user #14412441.

This anonymity was going to be a problem for me.

Postscript #1: By the way, I am not the only one who thinks that Rudy and Richard single handedly made TV more gay friendly in the 2000's. One of my all-time favorite Survivor alums (Rob Cesternino, from Survivor: Amazon) told me the exact same thing once in an email. We were just randomly talking about Borneo one day, and he mentioned that Rudy Boesch should have gotten royalty checks for the TV show "Queer Eye for the Straight Guy." I asked why, and he said "Well because prior to Survivor nobody had heard the word "queer" in America in thirty years." Rob claimed that Rudy single handedly brought that word back into the American lexicon, and that he should have been compensated for it.

Postscript #2: Okay, I'm sorry, but this has to be said. There has been a lot of talk in recent years (especially from seasons 20 on) about how Survivor has "changed" over the years. People (Russell Hantz fans, mainly) love to go on and on about how the only reason Russell hasn't won Survivor yet is because the criteria for winning the game has changed on him. Russell fans claim that strategists simply aren't rewarded anymore. Nowadays, they claim, the only thing you need to do to win Survivor is be nice. Because over the last couple of years it has all changed into being a big popularity contest.

Oh and here is my favorite one. "If Russell had played back in the first season, he would have won. Because back then the jurors appreciated strategy."

pauses to clear my throat

pauses for dramatic effect

Well I am sure I will have plenty to say about Russell and Russell Nation much later in the book (ha ha, seriously, get ready for it), but for now let me just point out this little tidbit which I always love to bring up. Richard didn't win Borneo because he was the best strategist. Richard didn't win Borneo because he screwed people over and because the jury rewarded him for it. Richard didn't win Borneo because the jury was just way more interested in strategy back then.

No, Richard won Borneo because the jury simply liked him better than they liked Kelly. It is as simple as that. Kelly jumped in and out of the alliance, while claiming she was never actually <u>in</u> the alliance, and the jury didn't want to reward a transparent flip-flopping little weasel who wouldn't be honest with anyone about what her loyalties were. Just like they have done every season, and just like they will always do in every season, the jurors gave the money to the person that they respected the most.

In other words, I'm sorry, Russell fans, but Survivor hasn't changed one bit. It has ALWAYS been a big popularity contest. Russell sucks now and he would have sucked then.

17. The Burnett Book

So now I decided that I wanted to be a Survivor writer.

However, there were two problems if you wanted to write about Survivor in the year 2000.

The first problem was that there was no place to do it. Oh sure, there might have been message boards dedicated to the show (like CBS.com and Television Without Pity, and the granddaddy of them all, Survivor Sucks). But for the most part those weren't a very good place if you wanted to find an audience. At CBS.com there really wasn't a forum for editorials or commentary, and TWOP had so many posters that anything you wrote would immediately be buried by two hundred other anonymous posts in the next twenty minutes.

And then... there was Survivor Sucks. Yuck. I mean, I love Sucks, and I have been there in one form or another pretty much since the day it was founded. But that is NOT the place you want to go if you want intelligent discussion about the show. Oh, every once in a while it might go through a sane, rational phase. Every once in a while the smarter, more intelligent posters will actually emerge out of their gopher holes. But for the most part Sucks is where people go if they want to debate if Erin Collins (Thailand) was really a transsexual or not. That is not the type of audience a newbie writer should really be aiming for.

So this was dilemma number one. Where on Earth do you go if you want to write about Survivor? There was another website out there called Reality News Online that eventually popped up, but I don't remember if it was there for the first season or not. And even then it was more of a "reality TV" site than it was a specifically-about-Survivor site, which wasn't really what I was looking for. I am not really a fan of "reality TV" as a genre. I just like Survivor. In fact, I have gone on record before taking offense to anyone who classifies Survivor as a "reality show", because I think that is sort of an insult to how unique and how revolutionary it was. You can't compare Survivor to crap like Keeping up with the Kardashians or Hogan Knows Best or The Real Housewives. Survivor was a once in a lifetime television phenomenon with a ton of real world psychological and sociological applicability. Just because it basically invented a genre doesn't mean it should be lumped in with the rest of the shit in the genre. That is like saying that Psycho and Leprechaun 4 are the same movie because they both contained scary parts.

So anyway, no, I wasn't going to write for a "reality TV website." I personally don't even like reality TV. The only shows I do like are the ones that I think are the exceptional ones. I like the clever, unique, intelligent competition shows. Which is why I have always liked The Mole as much as I like Survivor.

And then we come to problem number two.

The second problem with writing about Survivor in the year 2000 was that, unfortunately, as the audience, we really had no clue what really went on out there in Borneo. Oh we might have *thought* we knew what went on, since we saw it on TV and we talked about it on the message boards, but in truth all we really saw was about 5% of the story. All we saw at home was what the producers wanted us to see. We saw what they could logistically fit into a sixty minute episode. In other words, we never saw the true story of Borneo at all, all we ever saw were the edited highlights.

This was a significant problem.

One thing you should probably keep in mind about Survivor at the time is that there was NO such thing as contestant/fan interaction in the summer of 2000. Zero, none, zip, zilch. Survivors were strictly forbidden from writing about the show or emailing fans, and there was no such thing as Survivor fund raisers or reality alumni get togethers like Reality Rally or Hearts of Reality. There was also no Facebook, no Twitter, no MySpace, etc. There was nothing. We were not supposed to have any interaction with the players whatsoever, and they were most definitely not supposed to have any interaction with us. It said so right there in their contracts. They were only allowed to talk about Survivor when CBS said that they could. And up to this point CBS just wasn't allowing it.

This ban on fan and player interaction was an enormous difference from the way that the show is produced today, and I think a lot of modern Survivor fans would be completely shocked if they knew how off limits the players used to be to us. Do you know that the players' last names weren't even used on the CBS Borneo website? We weren't supposed to know who they were, where they lived, what their last names were, or basically anything about them other than what it said in their CBS bio page. In fact I remember being stunned when Kelly actually used her last name in one of the first season episodes and the CBS editors allowed it to stay in the episode. At one point she yelled at Sean,"You're gonna have to deal with Wiglesworth", which if I recall is the first time any of us had ever heard any of the players' last names.

As you can imagine, this ban on the players speaking to the public was a huge problem at the time. How were we supposed to find out what "really" happened on Survivor if nobody was allowed to talk about it? Because the producers weren't talking. Jeff Probst wasn't talking. The players sure as hell weren't talking. How on Earth do you delve into Survivor if you only saw about five percent of what really happened out there in Borneo?

And this is when the portals of Valhalla opened up.

And a magnificent gift was delivered to us.

At some point later, around September of 2000, I was walking through a Barnes & Noble bookstore in Dallas one day, and I noticed a new book that had just been released. It was called "Survivor: The Ultimate Game." And it was written by Mark Burnett.

I had never heard of this book before.

Huh. Interesting.

I opened it up and I peeked through the first couple of pages.

Well now isn't this interesting. This is only THE COMPLETE INSIDER HISTORY OF EVERY SINGLE THING THAT EVER HAPPENED ON SURVIVOR. Including about three hundred pages of stuff we never saw on TV!

To me, this book was now officially the Survivor Bible. I bought that sucker and, man, I devoured it. I must have read it cover to cover five times in the first week alone. Holy crap, this book told you everything you ever wanted to know about the way Survivor was produced, the way it was filmed, what the players were really like, why they interacted the way that they did, why Richard won. This book had everything! And it was all written from the producer's point of view, not the players', so it was completely non biased or unskewed in a certain direction. There was no agenda here, there was no hype. There was no spin to try to make any one player seem like he was more important than anyone else. It was just an unemotional non-judgmental completely comprehensive insider recap of Borneo.

In other words, this book was EVERYTHING I was looking for. You could not have given me a better gift at any point in my life.

I took that book everywhere with me for a couple of months. Every time I sat down to think about Survivor, or why a certain player did a certain action at a certain point in the game, I would cross-reference that with what Burnett wrote about it. And I would try to reconcile the two different versions in my head. Why was it shown one way on TV, while Burnett wrote about it a completely different way in the book? Why do the players see things in one light, and the producers see them in another? And how does this influence the way we view the show as an audience?

What I realized very quickly was that there really isn't just one "truth" when it comes to Survivor. There isn't just one storyline. What Survivor really is is a collection of sixteen individual storylines. And this tends to get overlooked at times since each player is only capable of seeing the game from his or her own particular perspective. So what happens is you have people (like some of the Borneo cast were already doing) complaining to the media that they had been edited unfairly on TV. Or that the episodes didn't tell the whole truth of what had really happened out there.

When you hear Survivor players doing stuff like this in the media (and it happens every season, complaining about one's edit has now become a Survivor tradition), just think back to my theory of sixteen different storylines. And think back to the fact that nobody can really see the entire storyline except for the producers. In others words, OF COURSE the players are going to think that the editing is dishonest. Every player is going to think that! They see it that way because they only saw Survivor from their own particular perspective. Which is perfectly natural, it would happen to anyone who was playing in a game like this. As you are playing it, you can logistically only see the game from your own individual point of view. You can't see it from anyone else's. That is just how the human brain works.

I was fascinated by this concept of "sixteen perspectives of the exact same story", because it reminded me of a book I had once read about the Civil War, called The Killer Angels. I remember reading The Killer Angels in high school and I remember being fascinated by it, because it basically showed the exact same events from the Battle of Gettysburg over and over, only each time from the perspective of a different general. Every single chapter was completely different from the one before it, even though they might all be talking about the exact same thing. I thought this was a very cool and unique way to tell a story about something.

Well right there and then I was fascinated by the whole "producer vs. players" aspect of Survivor. I loved the fact that you could look at the exact same storyline sixteen different ways (seventeen if you count from Burnett's perspective), and even if they were all wildly different from one another you could still technically always be telling "the true story of Borneo." It would always be the truth, every single time. Even if some of the versions of the storyline weren't even all that close to one another!

I loved the fact that Richard had played the most ethical game that he knew how to play, and that he had been a good guy to everyone. But to the Pagongs he had been the biggest asshole on the face of the earth with no ethics and no qualms about cutting their throats. I loved how both sides of that story were equally correct.

This "multiple perspectives" way of looking at Survivor came in very handy a few years later, when I started writing my All-Star fiction stories. But more on that when we get there. For now I just sort of filed it away in my head as yet another cool thing to love about my favorite TV show.

This was such an interesting time to be a Survivor fan. There were so many fascinating things going on with this show at the time. So many things that nobody was talking about yet. To me, it seemed like that when it came to the phenomenon of Survivor, as fans we had really only scratched the surface of what was so interesting about it.

Yes, people loved watching Survivor, sure. But up to this point it seemed like the love for the show was very superficial. So far people just loved the idea of people being on a deserted island and voting each other out. Or they loved the characters. Oh yeah, or maybe they loved the challenges. At this point there were some people out there who only watched Survivor for the challenges.

But there was so much MORE going on here. So much more than any other TV show I had ever been a part of in my life.

The only question was, how do I figure out what I want to say about this show?

And, more importantly, where the hell was I going to say it??

Postscript #1: Please go buy the Mark Burnett book. Even now, fifteen years later, I still think it is mandatory that you need to own it. It is seriously the Holy Bible for anyone who has ever wanted to know what Survivor is like. I can't emphasize that enough, there is no way you can properly digest or understand how Survivor works unless you have read the Borneo book. Oh, and I also can't believe that Burnett never wrote another one for any other season. Seriously? He didn't even write an insider recap for Australia? As much as I admire the guy, Mark Burnett can be a bastard. An Australia book would have been killer.

Postscript #2: Okay I should probably share a funny story from this time period. Remember how I said you weren't supposed to interact with Survivors if you were a fan back in 2000? Well there was one Survivor who would actually break that rule. Not surprisingly, it was she-who-would-later-sue-the-show-and-be-blacklisted-from-it, Stacey Stillman. Stacey showed up on some random TV message board at some point in 2000, and I remember I had a little Instant Message chat with her. I didn't really ask her any questions about the show. I think I was too shell-shocked that I was actually talking to one of these mythical "Survivor contestants" and I sort of forgot where I was.

The only thing I remember about that chat is that I told Stacey I went to school in the Bay Area, which is where she lived. And we joked that people in Northern California say "hella" a lot. As in "Man it's hella hot out today." Or, alternately, you can use the slightly less profane version, "hecka", as in "Anna Kournikova is hecka fine, too bad she's still hecka underage."

Stacey was amused that people only seemed to use the phrase "hella" in Northern California, and we shared a quiet little moment over our shared insider knowledge of Bay Area linguistic quirks. Then she signed off forever and she was out of my life.

Oh yeah, and there's approximately a 0% chance that she would ever remember that.

18. SNL, The Sports Guy, and Survivor

Most people in the Survivor world don't know this, but I actually had a fairly well-known career as an internet writer before Survivor ever showed up on TV.

Between the years 1996 and 2000, I wasn't yet known as "The Survivor Guy." Most people on the internet back then knew me as "The SNL Guy." Mainly because I used to write Saturday Night Live episode reviews and commentary for the biggest SNL fan site on the internet, saturday-night-live.com.

I first started writing about SNL when I was in college in 1995. The internet was very much still in its infancy back then, and I would guess that something like 90% of internet content back in the mid 90's came from college students like me who had nothing better to do than sit around and write about TV and movies and music and other aspects of pop culture. This is how I was first introduced to the internet, in the spring of 1994 on the University of Iowa Computer Bulletin Board (ISCABBS). And it is essentially how the World Wide Web then spread to the rest of America. It started with college students, it spread to the general public through services like AOL and Compuserve and Prodigy, and then, by the end of the 90's, the internet was finally available to everyone.

Oh yeah, and most of the content on the internet back in the 90's was free, as opposed to later years when businesses would take over and you would have to start paying for websites and for subscriber content. This is a personal pet peeve of mine, by the way (everything is supposed to be free on the internet!!!), but that is an entirely different subject for an entirely different essay.

> **Side note**: A teenage friend of mine made a joke the other day, saying how it was weird that so many "old people" like me seemed to hang around the internet these days. I couldn't resist pointing out how it was people my age who invented the internet; we were the pioneers who first started providing content for it back in the mid 90's. In other words, we aren't the ones intruding on your turf, you are the ones who are intruding on ours. So show some respect!

Sorry, small digression. Please forgive. This is a sensitive subject for me.

Around 1996, I decided that my pop culture specialty was now the TV show Saturday Night Live. I hadn't missed an episode of SNL since 1984, and I figured it would be fun to write about the show for one of these newfangled things called "websites." So I posted my first SNL episode review in March of 1996. And four years later, by the summer of 2000, I was one of the most widely read SNL columnists on the entire internet.

Why do I bring this up in a Survivor essay?

Easy. Because the first thing I ever wrote about Survivor was actually on an SNL website.

In the year 2000, a friend of mine named Patrick Lonergan created a website called "Saturday Night You." The premise of this site was that there were thousands of aspiring sketch comedy writers out there on the internet, and that any one of them could write better sketches than were currently showing up on Saturday Night Live. So every week Patrick invited us to send in our best fan-created sketches, to see if we could write a better show than the actual SNL writers could.

Saturday Night You popped up right around the time that the first season of Survivor ended. It was somewhere in the summer of 2000. And of course, as an SNY sketch writer, I decided it would be fun to write a Survivor parody as my very first SNY submissions.

The very first thing I ever wrote about Survivor was a comedy sketch called "Celebrity Survivor." It was basically a takeoff of the Celebrity Jeopardy sketches that were popular on SNL at that time, only instead of Jeopardy I changed the setting to a Survivor Final Tribal Council gone horribly wrong. I had Martha Stewart and Sean Connery as my final two, and the celebrity jury was made up of people like Alex Trebek, Tom Green, Tom Cruise, and a couple of other celebrities who were all in the news at the time.

When I posted my Celebrity Survivor sketch on Saturday Night You (in September of 2000), I expected it to be a big hit. After all, Celebrity Jeopardy was popular. Survivor (which had just ended) was popular. And Saturday Night You was a well-known website that was already getting a fair amount of media attention in magazines like Entertainment Weekly. I figured, Celebrity Jeopardy + Survivor + Alex Trebek and Sean Connery jokes. How could you possibly go wrong?

Well, turns out that I had miscalculated.

I swear, I don't think I got even one comment about my Celebrity Survivor sketch. Not even one person bothered to respond to it. And this baffled me. Um, wasn't everybody on the face of the Earth watching Survivor about a month ago? Didn't that finale get something like 50 million viewers? Didn't everyone love Survivor? Why wasn't this sketch a big smash hit?

I went back and I read through my Celebrity Survivor sketch to see if maybe it just wasn't any good. Nope, that wasn't the problem. I mean, it obviously wasn't the best thing I have ever written in my life, but I had already written a bunch of comedy sketches prior to this. I knew that the jokes worked.

So I went back and I looked at the other sketches that were on SNY that week, the ones that I hadn't written. Were people just not reading this week's sketches at all? Did I just post my sketch on an episode that no one was reading or commenting on? Was that what went wrong here?

Nope. That wasn't the problem either.

The problem, I found out, was that a good chunk of the world had already developed what I would call a fairly severe case of "Survivor backlash." Survivor hadn't ended more than five weeks ago, and everybody but the diehard fans already seemed to be sick of it. They were sick of the hype, they were sick of the concept, they were sick of Rudy, Sue, Colleen and "that fat naked guy." They were sick of the media overkill. They were tired of all of it.

This was the problem that Survivor faced between Borneo and Australia. The backlash. It was huge.

I had somehow walked right into the middle of it.

> **Side note**: By the way, I'm not sure if you have been paying attention to this, but Saturday Night Live has NEVER, not one time in fifteen years, done a single Survivor parody. Never. Ever. And they are probably never going to do one either. If you want a good example of how quickly the world got tired of Survivor, and how hard most people were rooting for it to fail after that first season, this is all the evidence you will ever need. Saturday Night Live, the biggest most famous pop culture skewering TV show of the last four

91

decades, has publicly proclaimed that they are never going to do a Survivor parody. To me that is just astonishing.

The reason I bring up my failed Celebrity Survivor sketch, and the extreme backlash that Survivor faced from mainstream pop culture (like SNL) after Borneo ended, is that I realized something very quickly when it came to wanting to be a Survivor writer. I realized very quickly that if I wanted to write about this show, it would have to be on a standalone Survivor website.

I wasn't going to be able to write about this show on a mainstream television website. Or a crossover pop culture website. That just wasn't going to work. Because it was clear to me that there was going to be no crossover when it came to Survivor. After Borneo, you were either going to be a Survivor nerd like me, or you were going to be somebody who hated Survivor. That was it. The lines had been drawn. Even back in late 2000, all the warning signs were there.

This franchise, as popular as it was right now, was going to morph quickly into a nerdy little niche show.

Basically the end of this story is that I quickly had to decide which show I wanted to write about in the future. Did I want to continue to be "The SNL Guy"? Or did I want to make a run and try to become "The Survivor Guy?" Because there was no way I was going to be able to do both. People who liked SNL clearly didn't give two shits about Survivor. And people who loved Survivor tended to obsess over it so much that they didn't care about any other TV show, period.

Sometime around September of 2000 I had to make the choice. And it was easy. I decided that I wanted to write full time about Survivor.

I decided that I was now a Survivor writer.

That was fifteen years ago. I haven't written an SNL episode review or a single SNL commentary article ever since.

P.S. I know it sounds kind of dorky to say "Hey I used to write my own SNL competitor sketches on the internet!" But believe me, Saturday Night You was actually a pretty inventive website for its time. When SNY first came out in the summer of 2000, it was written up in Entertainment Weekly as one of the Top 10 New Websites of the year. It had a ton of hits that first year, and it received all sorts of creative and famous fan submissions.

The website had so much publicity, in fact, that I actually had four of my sketches eventually purchased by different TV shows. Producers that were putting together new comedy shows in 2000 and 2001 would often stop by SNY to see if there was any good material they could buy, and to this day that is the most money I have ever made as a pop culture writer. I cleared $1200 by selling the rights to four of my comedy sketches. It wasn't much, but hey at least it was something.

Hmmm, maybe I really should have stuck to writing about Saturday Night Live. Maybe I made the wrong choice. Writing about Survivor doesn't pay squat.

P.P.S. Okay here is another story that I have never really shared before, but I think a lot of people will find it interesting. When people first read my stuff, one of the comments they usually make is something along the lines of "Hey, you write just like Bill Simmons ("The Sports Guy" on grantland.com)." I can't tell you how many people have compared my style to Bill Simmons' style throughout the years.

Well there is actually a very good reason for that.

The reason my style is so similar to Bill Simmons is because we used to know each other. Back in 1998 he used to write for AOL Digital City under the name "The Boston Sports Guy." His site was kind of a niche site, and it wasn't really all that well known, but I was a big fan of his because he was one of the few internet writers who could actually make me laugh. Oh yeah and also because he was a big fan of SNL and The Karate Kid (which is my favorite movie too.)

Well basically what happened is that I became one of his most prominent readers, and he became one of my most prominent readers. He loved my SNL reviews. He would usually write me after every one I posted (usually to complain because I rated the sketches too high.) And I of course was a huge fan of his sports/pop culture website. I loved it so much that I eventually became his "link of the day" guy. Every single day I would send him a daily funny link that he could post on his website. He posted my links so often that he and his readers eventually just came to know me as "Mario from Seattle."

If you are wondering why Bill Simmons and I have a very similar writing style, well, that's why. We were both fans of each other's writing back in the late 90's, and at one point we probably had a very similar sized reader base. Then of course I stopped writing about SNL, and he was hired to write for ESPN, and our... uh... "careers" kind of diverged. Nowadays he produces documentaries and he runs Grantland.com, and he is one of the most successful writers on the internet.

Again, this really has nothing to do with how I became a Survivor writer, I just figured people would find it interesting.

EXTRA: My Celebrity Survivor Sketch

This is my comedy sketch "Celebrity Survivor", which was a complete ripoff of Saturday Night Live's Celebrity Jeopardy, and was the very first thing I ever wrote about Survivor. If it looks similar to the Survivor Fallen Comrades Parodies I would later write and become famous for, well there is a very good reason for that. This was more or less my first attempt at a Fallen Comrades Parody.

Celebrity Survivor
written by: Mario Lanza
Copyright 2001

[The scene opens to the familiar Tribal Council set. We are sitting at night around a ring of fire. Jeff Probst is our host.]

Jeff Probst: Well, here we are at the final Tribal Council for Celebrity Survivor. You guys have been through a lot. Nearly two weeks out here at the Aspen Estates Ski and Snowboard Resort. A filet mignon shortage. And no cellular telephones. You have all earned the title of Survivor, in my mind. But today we must determine a winner. Both Sean Connery and Martha Stewart have played this game flawlessly, and it is now up to you the jury to decide who is the ultimate Survivor.

[The camera slowly pans across the jurors' faces. Anne Heche, her eyes glazed open and full of crazy. Tom Cruise, looking overweight and depressed, he has really let himself go since the divorce. Rudy Boesch, who is fast asleep. Tom Green, who is playing with and talking to his left nipple. Alex Trebek, who is looking smug and well groomed and pompous. Robert Downey Jr., who is passed out in a pool of his own vomit. And Nicole Kidman, who is sitting far away from Tom Cruise and who is glaring at him]

Jeff Probst: First off, we will let the two finalists give their opening arguments as to why they should be the Sole Survivor. [he nods to Sean Connery] Mister Connery, you're up.

[Sean Connery stands up and he addresses the jury]

Sean Connery: I just wanted to take this moment to mention that Trebek looks just as bad in the morning as his mother does. Thank you.

95

[He sits down]

[The other finalist, Martha Stewart, now stands up to address the jury. She is wearing a necklace made out of bald eagle feathers and cocoa beans]

Martha Stewart: I just wanted you all to know how much I have cherished these past twelve days. From the time I crafted a tent out of pine needles. To the day I fashioned a canoe out of nothing but fish scales. This entire experience has been very cleansing to my WASP-y white soul. And that has been a very good thing.

[The two finalists sit down, and again Jeff Probst speaks to the jurors]

Jeff Probst: The jurors can now address the finalists, and can ask a question or make a statement. Anne Heche, you're up first.

[Anne Heche bounces over to the finalists like she is a sprightly little elf]

Anne Heche: Do you guys know any famous lesbians I can hook up with?

Jeff Probst: [cutting her off] Anne, no. We have gone over this before. This is not a place for you to find a date. This is Tribal Council.

Anne Heche: [angrily] Fine. **[to the jury]** Then do you know any famous straight women I can hook up with?

Jeff Probst: Anne, what did I just say? Are we going to have to take away your Evian privileges again?

[Anne hangs her head in shame]

Jeff Probst: Go back and sit down. Tom Cruise, you're up.

[A fat, bloated Tom Cruise stands up and addresses the two finalists]

Tom Cruise: Hey guys. I wanted to ask you a two part question. One, what was your favorite thing about Celebrity Survivor? And two, why is my ex-wife Nicole such a c---? [the last word is bleeped]

[Nicole Kidman yells at him from over in the juror's box]

Nicole Kidman: Impotent midget!

Tom Cruise [to Nicole]: Frigid ginger she-witch!

Jeff Probst: Okay! Enough, you two! We will not have another caviar flinging incident like we had on day four!

Martha Stewart: If I may interject, Jeff, I would like to add that my favorite moment of the season was when I made a down-lined parka from the feathered breast of a swallow. It was a day I truly cherished.

Jeff Probst: [annoyed] Jury, PLEASE disregard the comments by Mr. Cruise. That was not a legitimate question. And now, up next, we have Survivor star and ex-Navy Seal Rudy Boesch. Rudy, you're up.

[Rudy stands up to speak to the finalists]

Rudy Boesch: I just wanna say this whole group is nothin' but queers. I hate queers.

Jeff Probst: [laughing along with the rest of the jury] Oh Rudy. You are a delight.

Rudy Boesch: I'm serious, all queers should die. I hate 'em all. Queers need to roast in hell.

Jeff Probst: [laughing so hard he is crying] Rudy, stop it, you're killing us! You delightful, charming man.

[Rudy sits down]

[Jeff Probst pauses for a moment to regain his composure]

Jeff Probst: Okay. Tom Green, you're up.

[Tom Green stands up. At some point in the last two minutes, he has put on a wacky penis-shaped camel mask]

Tom Green: I would like to congratulate the two of you on a great game. GAME GAME, YOU PLAYED A GREAT GAME! GAME GAME! YOU PLAYED THE SAME GAME! GAME GAME GAME! JUST LIKE MY NAME! GAME, GAME! YOU LIGHT LIKE A FLAME!

[Sean Connery stands up and he snaps Tom Green across the face with his

97

belt. Tom Green cries out and he immediately falls to the ground. Now he lays silent in a pool of his own blood]

[The rest of the jurors start to applaud]

Jeff Probst: On behalf of Celebrity Survivor and all of America, thank you. Okay, Nicole Kidman, you're up.

[Nicole Kidman stands up and she holds herself regally. Then she turns to face the rest of the jurors]

Nicole Kidman: I would like to talk about a male's inability to perform sexually.

Jeff Probst: Okay I know where this is going, and please stop it. Your sex life with Mister Cruise is off topic at Tribal Council. Do you have any questions for the actual finalists?

Nicole Kidman: Of course I do. How can a once good looking actor gain so much weight in two months? Is it because of a flaw in his genetic structure? Is it because Scientology is completely made up?

Tom Cruise: Ice Queen!

Nicole Kidman: Fat ass!

Jeff Probst: Enough! The two of you! Sit down and respect the f---ing **[this word is bleeped]** solemnity of Tribal Council!!! Robert Downey Jr., you're up.

[He looks over at the jury box. Unfortunately Robert Downey Jr. remains passed out in a pool of vomit. He isn't going anywhere.]

Jeff Probst: Well I guess that leaves our final juror. Mister Alex Trebek.

[Alex Trebek rises to face the two finalists. He looks incredibly smug at the moment. He knows that the cameras are on him and this is finally his moment]

Alex Trebek: Well, well. Look at the situation we have here. Ms. Stewart, you are looking as effervescent as always. And Mister Connery, it is certainly no conundrum to see you being as churlish as always. I have been ebullient waiting for this moment a long time. To finally face you. [smiling] To deliver my palaver. [pausing, angrily] Because you, sir, you are a . . .

Sean Connery: [interrupting] Hey Trebek, where's the bag?

Alex Trebek: [stammering and caught off guard] ...the bag? What? I don't know what . . .

Sean Connery: The bag you put over your wife's head before you have sex with her.

[The entire group bursts into laughter. Sean Connery points at Alex Trebek and he starts snickering]

[Alex Trebek begins crying]

Martha Stewart [to Alex Trebek]: If she needed one, I could make your wife a delightful springtime bag out of the dewy wings of a grackle bird.

Jeff Probst: [pissed] Enough! Everyone, shut up!! It is time to vote. Grab a goddamn pen, write who you want to win, and sit the f down. Let's get this thing over with.

[One by one the jurors walk to the podium to vote. Well, except for Robert Downey Jr., who remains laying in a pool of his own vomit, and Tom Green, who is dead]

[As they go up to vote, the Survivor security staff ensures that Nicole Kidman and Tom Cruise don't actually get a chance to walk next to one another]

[When they are done voting, Jeff Probst walks over to the edge of the sound stage to retrieve the voting urn]

Jeff Probst: Okay, it is time to reveal the winner. Remember, you are voting FOR somebody this time. These are votes for a player to <u>win</u>.

[He reaches into the urn and pulls out the first vote. It reads "I vote for the queer."]

Jeff Probst: Um, this vote is a little bit vague. Mister Boesch, did you by any chance cast this one?

Sean Connery: The rules say ya can't vote for Trebek anyway.

99

[The entire group laughs again]

[Jeff reaches into the urn and pulls out the second vote. It reads "Tom Cruise is fat and impotent. And I hope he dies."]

[Jeff reaches into the urn and pulls out the third vote. It reads "Nicole Kidman hates America and she should be deported."]

Jeff Probst: Okay, very nice. I will just disregard both of these votes, because they are both ridiculous. Nice work.

Tom Cruise [angrily]: New Zealand is way better!

Nicole Kidman [angrily]: Brad Pitt is way hotter!:

[Jeff sighs and he pulls out the fourth vote. It reads, "How about famous men? I will hook up with any famous rich men too."]

Jeff Probst: Great. Just great. Four votes, and none of them actually pick a winner. Way to go, Anne.

Anne Heche: I will hook up with any famous gay men too. I'm flexible.

Jeff Probst: One vote left, I guess. I guess I better reveal it.

[He reaches into the urn and he pulls out Alex Trebek's vote]

Jeff Probst: And the winner. . . of Celebrity Survivor. . . is. . ..

[With a big sigh, he pulls out the last vote. It reads "Sean Connery . . ."]

Jeff Probst: Sean Connery! **[pause]** No, wait a second. . .

[He flips the vote over. One the other side Alex Trebek has written ". . . is a vurcilator."

[Alex Trebek stands there and he looks incredibly smug]

Alex Trebek: Take that, you usurbator! Revenge!!

Sean Connery: I don't even know what that word means.

Jeff Probst: Nobody knows what that means. Thank you, Mister Trebek, for ruining the game. And for those interesting contributions to our language.

Alex Trebek: But... but... I got him. I zinged him.

Jeff Probst: Nobody cares.

[Sean Connery shoots Alex Trebek the finger]

Jeff Probst: That means we have no winner here on Celebrity Survivor, and because of that, money will actually be deducted from their favorite charities. Well done. Truly a magnificent performance put in by everyone.

Rudy Boesch: You're all a bunch of homos!

Jeff Probst: That's it. I quit. Security, please remove Tom Green's corpse from the Tribal Council set.

Martha Stewart: I could make a wonderful autumn poncho out of the corpse of Tom Green and some hazelnuts.

[Scene fades out]

[end]

19. Survivor 2: A Sequel?

Okay now we start getting to the good stuff.

Between seasons one and two of Survivor, there were a lot of interesting developments.

The first thing that happened during this time frame was that there was suddenly this brand new subgenre of television. Now, almost specifically because of Survivor, there was this new genre of television called "reality TV." All of a sudden every network and every producer on the face of the Earth decided that they were going to put together their own ripoff version of Survivor.

Big Brother. The Mole. Temptation Island. The Amazing Race. Lost. Chains of Love. Murder in Small Town X. Boot Camp. The Bachelor. Joe Millionaire. All of these shows were either announced or first showed up on TV in late 2000 or early 2001. And they all existed specifically because Survivor was such a huge megahit that made a ton of money and cost almost nothing for a network to produce. Because of Survivor, every single TV network in America saw "reality" as a genre that was going to make a lot of money for them over the next decade, and they all wanted to jump onto the bandwagon as quickly as possible.

By the way, for the record (as embarrassing as this is to admit), do you know which one of those shows I was the most excited about at the time? Yep, you guessed it. Lost. Out of all those shows, out of all the grandfathers of reality TV, I was most excited about the one that was narrated by John Tesh where people were stranded in a random country and they had to find their way home. For some reason I thought that this little three episode crap-fest would be a far superior adventure reality choice than something like The Amazing Race.

Suffice it to say, just like Walter Donovan... I chose poorly.*

Meanwhile, in the interim, as every Survivor ripoff was being announced or was just starting to take off on TV, there was that minor little thing known as "The Survivor Sequel" that it was time to start getting excited about. Because as 2000 ended and 2001 began, Survivor 2 was the show that much of America was starting to buzz about. Between the people who loved Survivor and wanted more of it, and the people who hated Survivor and wanted to see it fail the second time around, "Survivor: The Australian Outback" was one of the most talked about shows in history before it ever aired.

I know I already mentioned this in an earlier chapter, but the general feeling about The Australian Outback at the time was that it was going to be fun, but it wasn't going to be as good as the original Survivor. Because, honestly, how can Survivor be good without Richard, Greg, Colleen, or Rudy? It was going to be fun to see new people try to play the game, sure, and it was going to be fun to see all the rituals and terminology ("Tribal Council", "The tribe has spoken") that we were so familiar with come back again. But it just wasn't going to be the "Survivor" that so many of us had fallen in love with.

The criticism I remember hearing the most about Australia at the time was "Everybody is just going to join an alliance on day one. They all already know how to win the game this time around, so it's not going to be any fun."

Looking back, this was actually a very valid criticism. In retrospect, I actually think the people who made this argument were making a very good point. The minute every player in the game knew that "alliances are how you win Survivor", the show ceases to be a social experiment anymore and it simply turns into an extravagant elaborate game of chess. Which is fine, I guess, if you are looking to watch a game of chess. But I don't think most of the original fans tuned in to Survivor to originally watch a strategy game. I think most people were originally intrigued by the fact that this show was a social experiment where people could make up the ethics and the rules and the storyline as they went along.

I will come back to this subject later, but I definitely think that the people who made the argument that "Survivor won't be fun anymore if everyone already knows how to play it!" were actually on to something. I think they hit the nail right on the head. Survivor really COULD only exist once. The minute the producers planned a sequel, the show lost about 75% of its validity as a social experiment. And it started the slow, painful (and I would argue quite inferior) slide into becoming a strategy game.

Of course at the time I didn't see it like that. At the time I would hear that argument and I would simply rebut, "No way! The show will be much better if everyone is already good at it! Can you imagine Richard playing against himself? Can you imagine a game with sixteen Richard Hatches? Survivor 2 is going to be awesome!!"

.

103

* That's from Indiana Jones and the Last Crusade. But you should have known that.

20. Nick

As you can imagine, the security lockdown around Survivor 2 was pretty hardcore. Just like with season one, the producers weren't going to take any chances with spoilers. No information got out of that production camp at all. There were no leaks whatsoever regarding the names of the people who were going to be in the cast, what the game was going to be like, what the tribe names were going to be, who was going to be in the final two, etc. Just like with season one, the producers (and the reality genre in general) had far too much riding on the success of this show to be playing around with anything incriminating being leaked to the public.

Survivor 2 had to be a hit. It <u>had</u> to. Everyone knew it. If Survivor 2 failed, then reality TV would fail. And there wasn't a TV executive on the face of the Earth who wanted reality TV to fail. It was simply way too profitable. Without question, Survivor 2 was going to be the make or break moment for the entire concept of "reality TV" as a big money maker.

It was around this time (and under this incredible umbrella of security and secrecy) that I received a piece of information that was going to impact my life.

Remember how I said that fans and Survivor contestants weren't supposed to have any contact with one another back in the summer of 2000? How it was explicitly forbidden that any Survivor fan site say or write anything about the show that could in any way be considered "insider information"?

Well that rule was about to fall directly in my lap.

My brother, who was a student at Harvard Law School at the time, sent me an email completely out of the blue one day. He knew I was a fan of Survivor, and he had something that he wanted to share with me.

"Hey Mario," he wrote me in an email one day, "I think I know one of the guys in the new Survivor cast."

Um. Hello. What?

"His name is Nick Brown," my brother explained. "He's from Seattle and I ran into him up there at Christmas in a bar. I asked him why he hadn't been in class [at Harvard] all semester and he said he had been away filming the new Survivor season in Australia. You might want to write to him, he is a really nice guy."

Okay now this was a little bit interesting.

So wait, you are telling me that this show, this show that I absolutely love, the show that is about to get 100 million viewers in February when it premieres, is something I suddenly have a personal connection to? I am actually going to share emails with an actual Survivor?

A Survivor who CBS has strictly forbidden that any fans are even allowed to know about??

As you can guess, I decided to send Nick an email about thirty seconds after I got that email from my brother. I didn't have his direct email, so I just asked my brother to pass it along to him since they both worked together on the Harvard Law Review.

A couple of days later, I received an email response from Nick himself.

"Hey Mario," he wrote, "Thanks for being a fan of the show. Obviously I can't say anything about what happens in Australia, but I'd love to chat more after the season ends (or I get voted out). Thank you for writing me, we will talk more later."

Okay now this was a score.

What you have to keep in mind (again) about this time period was that NOBODY in the general public was allowed to interview Survivors. No way. The only people who were allowed direct access to the Survivors at the time were CBS and approved media sites like Entertainment Weekly or US Weekly or TV Guide. There was no way a fan or a fan site was EVER going to get direct access to a Survivor in the winter of 2001. It simply wasn't going to happen.

And now here I had a very direct connection to one of them. A very nice one, who would probably be willing to do an interview with me.

An actual Survivor interview on a Survivor fan site?

Conducted by me?

This was big!

Remember when I said that I usually posted on the message board Television

Without Pity back in 2000? Well I knew that TWOP had a special feature on their website called "Extras." An Extra was where anyone could submit an article to the site. Even if you weren't an approved staff writer (which I wasn't), you could still submit something as an Extra. And if the moderators liked it, they would post it.

Well here I was, just some lowly guy on the TWOP message board named "Sandwich Artist." Or, as I said before, anonymous user #124413141. Most people had never even heard of me before. They had no idea who I was. I was just some guy who wrote random funny things on their Survivor message board every once in a while.

This Nick interview was how I was going to change that.

So I wrote to the moderators at Television Without Pity, and I told them I had some very insider access to one of the new Australia Survivors. I asked if they would be interested if I could get them an insider interview. I promised it would be an exclusive only for TWOP, and if they wanted it, I could get the ball rolling with this guy that I knew.

The moderators wrote back and asked what his name was.

Since the cast hadn't been announced yet by CBS, I knew the name "Nick Brown" wouldn't mean very much to them. But I said that was his name, and that I knew him in real life.

Sure enough, when the Australia contestants were officially announced a couple of weeks later, and there was indeed a "Nick Brown" in the cast, the TWOP moderators were suddenly a lot more interested in what I was telling them. The next email came back to me very quickly.

"Yeah absolutely, we would love an interview with him," the moderators wrote back.

Yes!

Now that Television Without Pity knew about it, I wrote back to Nick and I explained the deal. I said that I wanted to do an interview with him, if he was okay with that, only we could wait until after the season ended so he wouldn't get in trouble. I said I didn't want to get him busted for talking to anyone during the season (because CBS was very very nitpicky and vindictive about this sort of stuff-- I knew that because I had already read the book "The Stingray", or as it is alternately known, "How CBS fucked over the cast of

107

Borneo by making them sign away their life rights and not letting them make any money off the experience.")

Nick said yeah, sure, we could talk after the season ended, that wasn't a problem. He added that he hoped I enjoyed the season.

So that was that. For now.

It was very exciting.

I had no idea how much of a debacle this would later turn into.

Postscript: By the way, remember when I said that Mark Burnett's book about the first season is the book that I consider the Bible of Survivor? You know how I said that is the book that every Survivor fan on the face of the Earth should know inside and out? Well if there is a second Survivor Bible, it is The Stingray by Peter Lance. Just trust me on this one. If you are familiar with Burnett's book and The Stingray, you probably know more about the way this show works behind the scenes than 95% of any other Survivor fan out there. And the good news is that you can get both books on Amazon for less than a dollar. So let's get going on this. There is no excuse for you not to have read them anymore. "The Stingray" by Peter Lance and "Survivor: The Ultimate Game" by Mark Burnett. Write those down.

21. There Is No Elisabeth

Pre-Chapter Historical Note: By the way, I am not going to write an entire chapter about it, but if you want a few hours of fascinating reading, check out the whole Stacey Stillman vs. CBS/SEG lawsuit that started sometime in late 2000 or early 2001. I wrote a quick summary of it back in an earlier chapter (Stacey alleged that the producers coerced the players into voting for her instead of Rudy in episode three) but there was actually a lot more to the lawsuit and a lot more to the story. The case basically hung around in the legal system for about three or four years, and then CBS allegedly paid her off to go away and to keep her mouth shut. Naturally, once some sort of a payoff happened, no one has heard a peep about Stacey or Stacey's lawsuit ever since.

I am not going to write an entire chapter about the Stacey incident because I don't know all of the facts personally (most of which are sealed in court records anyway). But if you are wondering when Survivor came the closest it ever came to being canceled, it was probably right here. If the Stacey lawsuit had come out a little bit earlier, if more people had heard about it when it was going on behind the scenes, if the whole "Survivor is fixed!! Oh My God!!!" controversy had gathered a little more steam than it actually did, there very very easily could have never been a second Survivor season.

As it was, the "Survivor is rigged!" outrage did come on very strong about midway through the second season ("They use body doubles to recreate challenges!" "They reshoot scenes!" "They show confessionals and interviews out of sequence!") And in many ways it is still right here with us to this very day ("The producers told Russell where to find all the hidden idols!" "They rigged Redemption Island so that Boston Rob would win!")

As for me, I don't personally think that Survivor is fixed. Well, okay, maybe with some of the Russell stuff I do. At least to an extent. But you would have to be naive at this point to think that the producers didn't muck around a little bit at least with the first season. Especially if you read the testimony by Dirk Been, which is freely available if you go looking for it on the internet. Dirk flat out admits (in Stacey's lawsuit) that the producers told him to vote for Stacey, and he admits that they did a lot of other bad stuff that they weren't supposed to be doing too. It is fascinating reading if you can get your hands on it. Seriously, do a Google search - Dirk's testimony is freely out there and it is not hard to find.

I believe the producers got a little too cute with their manipulations in Borneo, and I believe they got caught. And then they got sued. And then I think they got smart and they backed off and they played things much more legitimately in Australia.

Now with Africa, you could make an argument that they started trying to manipulate the game again with the Twist. Only they did things a lot more cleverly this time around. But we will get to that argument when we get there, I guess.

So where was I?

Oh yeah, the beginning of Australia.

If there is one thing you need to keep in mind about Survivor: The Australian Outback, if there is absolutely one thing you need to know about Survivor the second time around, and what the show was like for Survivor fans in February of 2001, it is this:

There was no "Elisabeth" in Survivor 2.

Nope. There was no "Elisabeth." Nor was there a "Mad Dog." Nor was there a "Jeff Varner", a "Jerri", a "Mitchell", or a "Colby."

What we had in Australia, at least from a Survivor fan's point of view, was a cast full of sixteen ripoff versions of the players from Survivor 1.

You see, there was no "Elisabeth Filarski." There was only "The new Colleen."

Mad Dog wasn't "Mad Dog." She was simply "the new Rudy."

Jeff Varner wasn't "Jeff Varner." Since he was the schemer, he was obviously "the new Richard."

Goofy Mitchell was going to be the next goofy Greg.

And so on, and so on, and so on.

I remember feeling very bad when the cast list for Australia was first announced. Because the first thing that everyone did on the internet was they started comparing these people to their original counterparts. Because I'm serious, that is EXACTLY what it was like. Mad Dog was crowned "the new Rudy" about 30 seconds after her picture first showed up on the website survivornews.net (which quickly became the new go to website if you wanted to know any inside info about Survivor.) Poor Elisabeth barely had her face in the news for five minutes before she was being hailed as an inferior version of Colleen.

By the way, before I feel too guilty about the way this whole thing went down, I should point out that Survivor fans on the internet were not the only ones who were making these types of comparisons. That first season was so ingrained in all of us by this point, it had been so universally recognized and deified by Survivor fans around the world, that even the players in Australia were making these types of comparisons. According to an article written in the 2001 Entertainment Weekly Spring Television Preview issue, one of the challenges of filming Survivor: The Australian Outback was the fact that the players spent approximately eight hours a day comparing themselves to the players from the first season. Mark Burnett said that he had to <u>constantly</u> remind the players not to talk about the first season, otherwise he told him their interviews would never wind up on TV. Apparently these types of comparisons ("Hey let's build a fire with our glasses like BB did! Yeah!") were pandemic the first few couple of days of filming in Australia. It is pretty much all that the players did.

Oh yeah, just for trivia sake, there was also a pretty significant spoiler in that Entertainment Weekly 2001 Spring TV Preview issue, although no one who was reading it caught it or noticed its significance at the time.

Want to know what the spoiler was? Well here you go.

At one point in the article (which I still have a copy of on my desk), Mark Burnett mentions that the tribes in Australia are supposed to be mortal enemies. And that his number one goal as producer this season is to keep them apart at all times so that they won't be able to fraternize.

Well, according to the article, at one point early in the shooting, when the producers weren't paying attention, the two tribes sort of drifted near one another before a challenge was supposed to start filming. They walked over and they introduced themselves to one other. And they started asking questions about what life was like at the other tribe's campsite.

Well, when Burnett saw that the tribes were making small talk with one another, he flipped out. He immediately ran over and he started screaming something like, "Separate them! Get them away from each other! Keep the tribes apart!!!"

But unfortunately for him, the damage had already been done.

What happened in that one brief moment of conversation is that Kimmi (on Kucha) informed the Ogakors that Jeff Varner had received a throwaway vote at the first Kucha Tribal Council. She mentioned this little tidbit of information to Tina, who filed it away. And the Ogakors later used this information to win the 5-5 tiebreaker vote at the merge and essentially win the game. It was that one split second where the tribes fraternized and Kimmi shared a little bit of info that directly led to Tina winning Survivor: The Australian Outback.

Like I said, no one realized this was a significant spoiler at the time. But there it was, smack dab in the middle of the Entertainment Weekly 2001 Spring Television Preview issue. Just a cute little story about what life was like for a Survivor producer, and what sort of challenges Mark Burnett had to work around when he was filming a TV show.

Who knew that that little pre-reward challenge meet and greet would become a very significant moment in Survivor history?

22. A Chef and a Circus Freak

As I said before, I knew a member of the Australian Outback cast before it ever aired on TV. I knew Nick Brown. I had exchanged emails with him and one day we were going to do an interview together.

As a Survivor fan, this was a really big development for me.

The reason this was so significant for me was because it marked a HUGE change in the way I was going to watch Survivor the second time around.

The first time Survivor aired on TV, I only watched it as a neutral observer. I was just some guy out in TV land who didn't know these people, who had no personal connection to anyone, but who just thought the concept was interesting. Therefore I was allowed to watch the show and enjoy it without any sort of emotional attachment whatsoever. I had no personal ties to anyone, so I really didn't give a crap who won or who lost. Oh sure, I might have developed favorites along the way (like Richard, Rudy, and Gervase), but at the end of the day if a certain player won Survivor, or if a certain player lost Survivor, it wasn't going to ruin my day.

But with me actually knowing a player the second time around, well now that was going to change things a little.

The problem with me actually knowing a Survivor contestant (indeed, not only knowing him, but also having a stake in how well he did in the game!) was that my loyalty as a fan was now a little bit compromised. I had to root for Nick. I simply had to. Because Nick doing well meant that my interview with him was going to be that much more of a big deal. If he did well, heck if he somehow even *gulp* won, I had that much more of a chance to one day become a well-known Survivor writer.

And if I rooted for Nick, that of course meant that I also had to root for the Kuchas.

Again, it is hard to explain why this was such a significant change for me as a Survivor fan. But it definitely was. It was such an incredible difference just loving the show the first time around and being able to watch it and love it for what it was, and then with Australia me basically knowing I was going to live or die based on the success or failure of one particular person. Take it from me, that is a very difficult way to watch Survivor.

If you ever want to try an experiment, try watching a season of Survivor this way. Pretend that one of the players is your husband or your wife. Pretend that this person's happiness or sadness is directly correlated with your own. Pretend that if they get voted out, if their dreams are crushed on national TV, then your life will be ruined too. Watch how stressful that makes your Wednesdays.

Obviously my connection to Nick wasn't anywhere near this close, but you can see where I am going with it. I definitely had a lot riding on his success in Survivor 2. If he did well, I had a huge chance to become a well-known Survivor writer. Plus, you know, I also sort of liked the guy. He seemed like a really good guy in real life, not to mention a big Survivor fan. I knew this experience was going to mean a lot to him.

From day one-- because of my connection to Nick-- my experience watching Survivor the second time around was a lot different than watching it the first time.

I should probably point out, by the way, that even though I liked Nick, and even though I obviously had a huge vested interest in how well he did in the game, there were a few other players in the Australia cast that I was also sort of rooting for on the sly.

Keith Famie, for one. I thought that Keith was a fascinating casting choice.

I know it is hard to sell people on the "Keith was a fascinating player" argument here in April of 2015, but believe me, he was a media darling before he ever set foot in Australia. He was the pre-season star of the cast. Because seriously, this guy was a gourmet chef. He went into Survivor with the strategy of "I'm gonna feed these people, I'm gonna whip them up gourmet meals every single day, and they are all going to be amazed by me."

As much as we all loved the first season, there had never been anything like Keith in the first Survivor. He was a true unique. There had never been a person who could cook like this in the original cast. So from this perspective, Keith Famie wasn't just some quote-unquote "ripoff" of one of the original castaways. This guy was a complete original, and I thought he was going to be interesting.

How is a professional chef going to fare in the game of Survivor?

How is he going to feed everyone when he has to find all the ingredients every day?

114

This was something we had never seen the first time on Survivor, and I was definitely rooting for him because of it. In fact, if you go back and you read anything about the first few seasons of Survivor, you will see that the producers were all rooting for him too. Keith was actually one of the very first people cast for the first season of Survivor. He was cast for Borneo because he gave a wonderful interview and a wonderful audition where he explained to the producers all the gourmet meals he would be able to cook for people, and how he would use banana leaves and underground fire pits. He explained that he was going to win this game because nobody would ever be able to vote off the guy who was feeding everyone.

Keith completely charmed the Survivor producers because of his creativity and his general media savviness (a lot of people don't know this, but he was already a well-known celebrity TV chef prior to Survivor). And like I said, he was originally cast as one of the original sixteen castaways who would be competing in Borneo.

Of course, Keith ended up being cut from the first season because of scheduling conflicts, and he wound up being moved to the second season instead, but still. You are talking about a bona fide Survivor legend before he ever set foot in Australia. The producers were all big fans of the guy.

Besides Nick and Keith, another castaway I was pulling for in Australia was Mitchell.

Why Mitchell?

Easy. Because people who are seven feet tall are weird. I wanted to see what happened the first time an actual circus freak played Survivor.

Yes, if you are looking for the very first time Survivor ever employed the concept of "stunt casting", you need look no further than our dear friend Mitchell Olsen from Australia. Who, of course, I am hoping doesn't hunt me down and kill me now because I just called him a circus freak. Sorry Mitchell! It was only a metaphor!

Seriously though, who thought a guy with that metabolism and that little body fat would ever be able to make it on a game like Survivor? Really, producers? It was no surprise at all that Mitchell was nearly dead by the fourth episode. You put a seven foot guy with no weight to lose on one of the harshest of all the Survivor seasons? Man, the Stacey Stillman lawsuit would have looked like child's play if the producers would have actually managed to kill a guy.

So anyway, there you go. My mindset going into the premiere of Survivor 2. By the way, don't just automatically refer to it "The Australian Outback." Or "Survivor: The Australian Outback." That might be the technical title, sure, and that is what is known as now. But to most of the world, and to most of the players in the cast at the time, the second season of Survivor would have more accurately been described as "Survivor 2."

It wasn't really its own standalone season yet. That would come later, of course (probably around the time of Kel and the Beef Jerky), but at this point in time it was really little more than "the Survivor sequel."

P.S. By the way, I know this will make a lot of newer fans kind of upset, but this is the way I have always described the evolution of Survivor. There aren't really 30 "Survivors." There was only one Survivor. And then afterwards there have been 29+ different sequels or ripoffs.

This isn't to say that some of the sequels might not have been higher quality than the original (Pearl Islands, in particular, I think that season was fantastic. Marquesas and Amazon too. Among others.) But you really can't compare any of the later seasons to the first season because they are all completely different entities. The sequels were all trying to accomplish entirely different things. This is why I never include Borneo when people ask me to rank the Survivor seasons.

Again, there was really only one "Survivor." There could have only ever been one. Everything that came after that was just some sort of an homage to it.

P.P.S. There are a lot of stories out there about people who were originally cast for the first season but who were then yanked out and cast in a different season instead (like Keith.) Another prominent one I like to mention is

Gabriel Cade, who finally appeared three seasons later in Survivor: Marquesas. Gabriel was originally cast for the first season of Survivor, but the producers had reservations about how unique his background was (he was raised on a commune), and they were worried that nobody in America would be able to relate to him. So he was sort of swapped out at the last minute for Greg Buis. Greg took his place as a member of Pagong.

I love the irony of that story, by the way. The producers put Greg in the cast over Gabriel because "Greg was the more relatable one." Meanwhile here is Greg walking around talking about secret rebel alliances on a coconut phone and joking about having sex with his sister. Classic.

P.P.P.S. Another player who claims he was originally cast for the first season in Borneo, but was later replaced by somebody else, is Coach Benjamin Wade. Coach once told me that the producers actually came up for the concept of the show because of him, and that the first season only came about because it was inspired by all of his travel adventures. And that the only reason he had to pull himself out of the cast for the first season was because he was off doing some solo kayak trip.

Yes, Coach really told me this. He has actually told a lot of people about this. Of course, then this begs the question, do you believe him? Keep in mind that Coach also believes that most of Greek mythology was inspired by his soccer team. So caveat emptor, I guess.

P.P.P.P.S. By the way, I am going to get in trouble for telling this story, but what the hell. It is my Survivor book, and you came here to be entertained.

Remember how my brother told me about Nick because they were classmates together at Harvard Law School? Well Harvard used to be quite the hunting ground for reality show producers. In fact it still is to this day. Reality competition shows are always hunting around looking for law students from Harvard. In fact, the year after Australia, my brother told me about two more classmates of his who were going to be in the new cast of The Amazing Race.

"They are both really hot," he explained to me, "Two girls in my class who are drop dead gorgeous. And they are Harvard lawyers. They are super smart, everyone is going to fall in love with them."

I kept an eye out for these two Anna Kournikova sex goddess clones he was describing to me, and sure enough when the cast of the Amazing Race 3 was announced, there they were on the CBS website. Their names were Heather and Eve.

They were cute, of course, but the description I had gotten of them ahead of time was a little bit different.

"Um, yeah they're good looking," I wrote to my brother, "But I wouldn't call them supermodels or anything. Are you sure we are talking about the same people?" He had described them as both being the second coming of Helen of Troy.

"You don't think they're hot?" he asked me.

"I do," I said, "I think they're cute. But there are hotter girls on Survivor. In fact, I would say Elisabeth is cuter than they are. No offense man, but supermodels? I live in Southern California, I guess we just have a different rating system out here than you do."

My brother was crushed.

"Well what can I say?" he finally wrote back. "This is the Ivy League. This is the best we get."

Sorry Dom.

I love that story.

23. The Blair Witch Connection

Okay, I know I am supposed to be writing about the Australian Outback. But I can't resist. I saw something on TV the other night that perfectly ties in with my book about Survivor, and I think this would be the perfect place for it.

I was watching a show on AMC this weekend called "Movies that Shook the World." And it happened to be the episode about The Blair Witch Project.

You remember The Blair Witch Project, right? It was that movie in the summer of 1999 that cost like $30,000 dollars to make, and wound up becoming one of the biggest and most talked about sensations in movie and internet history. EVERYONE in America was familiar with the Blair Witch Project and the Blair Witch Website for about six months in early 1999. And then when it became a movie and it finally hit theaters, the film itself wound up grossing something like 250 million dollars. You remember all that, right?

To this day, The Blair Witch Project remains one of the biggest cost-to-profit movie phenomena in American history. In fact, if you are just looking at the ratio of how much it cost to put together, compared to how much money it eventually took in, it might be the #1 most profitable movie ever.

In other words, The Blair Witch Project could arguably be called the single most successful movie in American history.

I know, that is kind of a broad, sweeping statement to make. Especially when you are talking about a movie that about 75% of the world got tired of very quickly, and most of whom still can't stand even today. But I bring up The Blair Witch Project in my Survivor book for a very good reason.

The reason I am writing about The Blair Witch Project in my Experiences with Survivor book is because if there had been no Blair Witch Project, there probably never would have been a Survivor.

What? Blasphemy, I know. But just keep in mind that I am not the one who came up with this theory.

The person who came up with this theory (that BWP = Survivor) is none other than the creator of Survivor himself, Mark Burnett.

There, now it doesn't sound so crazy, does it? Now I've got some actual ammunition behind this argument. When Burnett talks about Survivor, it is probably best that we listen to him.

I was watching the AMC documentary about the Blair Witch Project phenomenon the other night, and sure enough up pops Mark Burnett in one of the interviews. And he started talking about how the BWP was such a big deal when it first came out in 1999. He said that because the movie made so much money, and because it had such a low-budget guerrilla type of storytelling, and because it was so revolutionary and so much different than anything else that had ever been seen in a theater up to that point, that the Blair Witch Project was pretty much the only reason that CBS ever agreed to greenlight Survivor.

Oh yeah and he then called The Blair Witch Project "the grandfather of all reality TV."

Now I have to say, when I heard this theory come out of Burnett's mouth, my jaw nearly dropped to the floor. Because I am telling you, I have studied and written about this show for years. YEARS. I have been obsessing about and studying and writing about Survivor for more than a decade and a half. And I had NEVER made the connection in my head between the Blair Witch Project and Survivor before. Never ever ever ever. And that is amazing, because I am one of the biggest Blair Witch Project fans on the face of the earth.

I love Survivor with all of my heart. And I love The Blair Witch Project with all of my heart. So how was I never able to put two and two together and see that they are basically the exact same concept?

The Blair Witch Project (for those of you who are unfamiliar with it) was a pseudo "reality" documentary from the summer of 1999. Two filmmakers basically made up a mythology about a witch who lived in the Maryland woods. And then they hired three actors to go out into the woods and pretend they were filming a documentary about her.

Only... oh yeah, sorry we forgot to warn you guys about this... every time the actors were alone in the woods in the dark, the filmmakers would basically ambush them and try to scare the shit out of them. And then whatever the actors' natural reactions were to being frightened out of their minds, the filmmakers would later edit these real reactions into a fictional movie called "The Blair Witch Project."

Again, Mark Burnett was spot on. This is the birth of reality TV. This is so

100% Survivor that it amazes me that I never saw it before.

What a lot of people don't seem to realize about Survivor (and which is something I have been saying and harping about for years) is that Survivor is NOT reality TV. Never has been, never will be. Survivor the TV show has nothing to do with reality. Mark Burnett has been saying this since day one of season one, he will go out of his way to NEVER call his show "reality TV", yet for some reason the media and the "reality TV" haters in general have never really played along with him. Survivor continues to be called "reality TV", and it continues to unfairly get lumped in with the inferior crap like Flavor of Love, Hogan Knows Best, etc., that it really has nothing in common with.

Survivor-- just like The Blair Witch Project-- is nothing more than a fictional narrative made up of actual footage.

Sixteen people go out into the wilderness. They play a game for thirty-nine days. The game part is real.

And then the editors and producers come back into the editing studio. They take about 1% of the actual footage of the game, and they do their best to create some sort of a fictional narrative out of it. They use music and foreshadowing and overdubs and selective perception to break it down into sixty minute episodes. And they basically use every editing trick in the editor's handbook to make this new fictional storyline as compelling as possible.

Bam. Game, set, match. That is Survivor. That is what it has always been. Fiction based on actual people and actual footage. That's it. Nothing "real" about it.

What kills me after all these years is that Survivor still gets routinely referred to as "reality TV." This phrase has always been a dagger to my heart. The reason it is such a dagger to my heart is because it is so demeaning and so completely inaccurate.

Yes, they are using actual footage when they make Survivor. Yes, there was an actual game that actual people played a couple of months ago. And yes it produced an actual winner. Yes, at that point, all of that footage would be considered "reality."

But here is the catch. What we see on TV generally has very little to do with what actually happened during the game. Oh we might see the highlights.

Sure, but we certainly don't get to see all of them. All we get to see are the tiny little parts that make the "storyline" better. We only see the ones that the editors and the producers have determined are the ones that are the most important to the television show.

In other words, Survivor "the game" and Survivor "the TV show" are two entirely different things.

And the only one we ever really see at home is the TV version of Survivor!

The only season that could even remotely be called "reality TV" with a straight face is maybe the first couple episodes of Borneo. Maybe. Which, as I have said before, is also the only era of Survivor that I think is also pretty much unwatchable. You go back, and you watch the first two or three episodes of Borneo now, and it is obvious how much more interested the producers were in portraying it as a documentary back then. Back in the early days of Survivor, they were definitely trying to present the whole thing as "reality."

Which was too bad. Because in my opinion, when you present Survivor as true reality, the show kind of sucks.

To me, it seems like the editors started off trying to make Survivor into sort of a pseudo-documentary based on real footage. Kind of like its admitted inspiration, The Blair Witch Project. But I think they quickly figured out that the story worked much better if they didn't have to do that. I think the editors and the producers figured out very quickly that Survivor the TV show worked way better when they could move the editing around and they could start setting up foreshadowing and story arcs and character conflicts, as if they were telling a fiction story.

Survivor might have started out as a "reality show", true. But at a certain point very early on, I think that changed. Around episode two or three of Borneo, Survivor stopped being reality at all. Around that point (with more editing and more music, more foreshadowing, etc.), it sort of morphed into (as Mark Burnett would later refer to it), "an unscripted drama" show.

And then of course-- a few months later-- there was the big backlash after the end of the first season, when America found out that their new favorite TV show probably wasn't 100% "reality" at all. At that point you had legions of people who were pissed off about this fact and who started badmouthing "reality TV" and rooting for the entire genre to fail, simply because they thought the whole thing was stupid. And because they felt that the concept of "reality TV" (which was a term Burnett never even used in the first place) was nothing more than a lie. In fact, in many ways, this backlash and this stigma against "reality TV" still exists against Survivor even today.

Oh and hey, by the way, do you know what the original Survivor backlash sort of reminded me of? It reminded me of the exact same backlash that Blair Witch faced when people found out it wasn't 100% real either! Speaking of which, do you ever see anything good written about the Blair Witch Project nowadays?

I know, this chapter is kind of rambling now. But I couldn't resist. When Mark Burnett claims that The Blair Witch is "the grandfather of reality TV" and that Survivor wouldn't have existed without it, he is telling the truth. He is also telling the truth when he claims that Survivor isn't even "reality TV" in the first place, that it is much more of an unscripted drama that is heavily dependent on editing. The two projects (Blair Witch and Survivor) could not have been more similar or more of a national phenomenon when they first came out. They both faced the exact same surge in popularity, they both faced the exact same backlash, and they both came out within about nine months of one another in 1999 and 2000. People forget that they were so close to one another on the overall timeline, but they were. It is one of those things that we like to call "riding the hot new entertainment concept." Survivor just ripped off a similar storytelling device that had already worked very well for somebody. Do the math. In TV and movies, it happens all the time.

Oh yeah, and before I end this chapter, there is one other big similarity between The Blair Witch Project and Survivor. In fact this one is probably the biggest one.

The creators of both the Blair Witch Project and Survivor probably don't give a crap what you think about their project now or what you think about the overall concept of "reality TV." All they care about is the fact that they made hundreds of millions of dollars off of their idea, that they took hundreds of millions of dollars out of other peoples' pockets, and now they can just hang around in their mansions all day and do nothing but roll around naked on a giant pile of money.

God bless America. And God bless whatever weird hybrid this is that most people like to refer to as "reality TV."

A fictional narrative based on real footage, featuring no actors, no scriptwriters, no unions or talent regulations, and best of all, no budget.

A guaranteed million dollar moneymaker.

I wish I had thought of it.

P.S. Remember the immunity challenge towards the end of the first season where the players had to run around in the jungle and videotape themselves saying the answers to trivia questions? Remember what movie that challenge was based on? That was not a coincidence.

24. Yub

Okay we are finally here. The premiere episode of Survivor: The Australian Outback. Or, as much of the world would have referred to it at the time, "Survivor again, only this time with new people we aren't going to like."

Australia debuted on Sunday, January 28, 2001, right after the Super Bowl. And (in my opinion) to this day, that episode marks the point that Survivor was the biggest it ever would be. Thanks to the lead-in from the Super Bowl, and the hype and expectations that were still lingering around from the Borneo finale only seven months before, the Australia premiere pulled in an astounding 45 million viewers. Which, to this day, remains the second most watched episode ever in Survivor history.

Of course the Borneo finale drew a slightly larger audience than the Australia premiere (51 million vs. 45 million), but I will always argue that the Australia premiere was a much more impressive accomplishment.

The reason the Borneo finale audience had been so big was because it had been made up of both Survivor fans and Survivor haters. It was made up of people who loved the show, people who despised the show, people who didn't care about the show but had heard the finale was going to be interesting, and every other slightly curious looky-loo on the face of the Earth. The Borneo finale was basically just one of those things you sort of HAD to see, whether you were even slightly interested in Survivor or not. It drew crazy ratings that night not because there were all that many diehard Survivor fans at the time, but more because it was one of those "you just had to be there" TV events that come about every once in a decade.

Now the Australia premiere, on the other hand, well that was an entirely different story.

When Survivor 2 came around, and a lot of the early media fascination and the Survivor hangers-on sort of got stripped away from the equation, basically all you had left at this point were your core group of hardcore Survivor fans. Instead of 20 million people who loved the show, and 20 million people who hated it, and 10 million people who were just there for the ride, this time around you had 45 million people who had somehow become enormous fans of the show over the past seven months. And they were now dying to watch Survivor again. To me, that was a phenomenal accomplishment.

And yes, I know you can probably question maybe 10 million of those viewers who were only there because they had been watching the Super Bowl, and they were too lazy to turn off the TV. But still, you take away 10 million and you still have 35 million rabid hardcore Survivor fans. Australia was always more consistently popular than Borneo. From start to finish, Australia is and always will be as big as Survivor would ever get.

No matter how you slice it, to me Australia will ALWAYS be the absolute apex of Survivor. Australian Outback was easily this franchise at its peak. The first time around, I think Survivor's popularity really sort of caught CBS and most of America by surprise. By season two it seemed like everyone was ready for it.

Okay, on to the premiere itself.

The first thing that I think of when I think back to the Australia premiere is the question that I think most viewers were probably thinking at the time. In fact there is no way you weren't thinking this if you watched the premiere back in January of 2001.

The first thing I think of when it comes to Australia is, "HOLY SHIT HOW DID JEFF NOT FALL OFF THE BACK OF THAT PLANE?!?!"

Ha ha. Sorry, just a little inside joke for all you Survivor nerds out there. But that is the great thing about the obsessiveness of the Survivor fan base. I know that 75% of the people who are reading this book immediately got that joke and know exactly what scene I am talking about. Yes, Paul Asleson of Montana. Yes, you and others just like you. I am talking to you.

In the opening scene of Australia there was a great shot where Jeff Probst is sitting on the back of a military transport plane, and then the plane banks hard to the right.

Seriously, I can't watch that scene (even to this day) without wanting to tell Jeff to hang on. It is the one scene in fifteen years of Survivor where I suddenly turn into Jeff Probst's mom. I watch that and I feel like maybe it is too cold out and I should ask him to put on a sweater.

Aside from Probst nearly falling off the back of a plane (hang on, Jeffy!), the other things I remember about the opening minutes of Australia are the gratuitous barfing shots of Mitchell and Elisabeth, the shot of Keith Famie praying (seriously, why was Keith considered a bad guy again??), the first shot of our beloved Harvard lawyer hero Nick Brown (yay!), and for some reason I always remember a shot at the end of the intro where Jeff Varner looks like

126

he is going to throw up. And Debb motions to him that, to help, he can have a sip of her water.

Poor Debb. Poor sweet misunderstood Debb. She really didn't deserve what happened to her.

But we'll get back to that later.

The other thing that I remember about Australia is the fact that it still featured what I have always considered to be the single most important thing you can have in a Survivor premiere. You know exactly what I am talking about, don't you? You old school hardcore Survivor nerds know exactly which long-lost segment of the show I am referring to.

The part of the premiere that I have always felt is the single most important for us as a viewer is the "introduction" scene. This is where Jeff Probst introduces each player to us and he explains what they do for a living and where they are from. And then he shows us a few clips of what they look like back in their regular life.

To me this has always been the single most important segment of a Survivor season. It is important because it immediately introduces us to every single player on a personal level, and because it allows us to pick out our favorite(s) or pick out who we think is going to be good at the game. It is also an extremely NECESSARY segment. Because if this segment doesn't exist, if we never get that personal introduction of every castaway, it is impossible to pick out our favorites. It is impossible to feel like we even know who these people are. Without this introduction, we are just watching a game show about a bunch of nameless strangers who we can never possibly care about. Without that segment, we might as well be watching The Price is Right.

Naturally, the producers stopped doing these personal introduction segments about twenty five seasons ago.

Thanks for that, by the way, producers. Yeah we don't need those player introductions anymore. We wouldn't want to root for the players on a personal level. Nice job eliminating the important part. Love you too.

By the way, I totally forgot about my favorite part of the Australia introductions until I just watched them again on YouTube a couple of minutes ago. After all these years, I still laugh that Amber grew up in a town called "Beaver."

In related news, yes, I'm twelve.

P.S. Oh yeah, one other thing I have always loved about the Australia premiere. I have always loved how the opening credits begin with a crocodile saying "yub." I'm sorry, fifteen years later and that still rocks. Unless they find a way to feature Chuck Norris or Ivan Drago in the opening montage, or maybe Rudy karate chopping Russell in the throat, or maybe Teri and Ian from the Amazing Race turning their heads towards the camera in exact sync with the music, no Survivor opening credits will ever have a moment as awesome as the Australia crocodile yub.

25. Meeting Our Hero

Remember when I said that watching Survivor is a hell of a lot different when you actually know one of the players and are rooting for them to do well?

Remember how I had already pegged Nick Brown as my horse in this particular race?

Well you can imagine the icy cold pit in my stomach when Nick immediately got labeled as "the guy who can't read the compass" in the first couple minutes of Australia.

The guy who can't read a compass? The guy who got the Kuchas lost in the woods? The guy who everyone is already annoyed with and it is only the very first day?

Nooooooooooooooooooooooooooooooooooooooooooo!

Right off the bat I had a bad feeling about my man Nick. I knew that this possibly wasn't going to end very well for me. Er, I mean him. Because there was just something about the guy, even in the opening minutes of Australia, that sort of screamed "dead meat" to me. I had no idea why, there was just something about the way that Nick was so laid back, and so even keeled, and the other characters seemed so much more over the top and dynamic than he did, that told me he probably wasn't going to be the star of Survivor this particular time around.

And then, of course, he was the first one that everyone on Kucha started bitching about because he couldn't figure out the compass.

Crap. Crap, crap, crap, crap, CRAP!!

As I have said before, I am not really a religious man. But I said a quick prayer right there and then, asking that Nick make it through the first episode. PLEASE let Nick make it through the first Tribal Council. Because I was worried about him. And by being worried about him, of course that meant I was also very selfishly worried about me. If my Nick interview turned out to be a dud, I was never going to make a name for myself as a Survivor writer. It just wasn't going to happen. And I wanted to be so much bigger than simply "Oh yeah, remember that guy who did the Souna interview?"

Luckily Nick eventually turned it around, and by the end of the first episode he was no longer being mentioned as a target. Which, between that, and the fact that he was a healthy young athletic male who the Kuchas were going to need, meant that he was probably going to stick around for at least a couple of episodes.

Phew.

Heart attack averted.

Besides Nick, there were a few other characters who also jumped out at me as being particularly interesting during the first sixty minutes of Australia. Well, okay, maybe Nick wasn't all that interesting to anyone but me, but please just go with me here. This is my book. To me, Nick Brown was basically Richard Hatch and Rudy Boesch and Colleen Haskell all rolled into one, only if they were all way more interesting. To me Nick always seemed kind of like Jesus.

One other character I really liked on the Kucha Tribe was Michael Skupin. I loved the way that Mike had such a quiet little soft spoken voice, and such a childlike little giggle. And I loved how he was also clearly a borderline psychopath. I loved his whole little innocent/likable/scary/giggly dichotomy. Yes, it is safe to say that Mike was easily one of my favorite players in Australia. And I would only love him more over the next five episodes.

That is all I have to say about Mike for now but don't worry, there will be a lot more on him later.

Another player who I thought was interesting on the Kuchas was Kimmi Kappenberg. I am not entirely sure why I liked Kimmi, since her voice would probably drive me crazy if I were ever around her in real life for more than ten minutes. But I thought she would be a fun character for a couple of episodes. Which, again, surprised me, because Jenna Lewis was somebody I hadn't appreciated at all during Borneo, and Kimmi and Jenna were almost the exact same character.

> **Side Note:** Actually no, that's not quite true. Kimmi seemed to have a sense of humor about herself, and Jenna didn't. Maybe that was the difference. I remember in his book about the first season, Mark Burnett went on and on about how the producers always expected Jenna to eventually become the "villain" of Borneo. They

could just see it in her eyes. They didn't think she was a particularly nice person. They also thought she was selfish and that she was exceptionally fame-hungry.

Well, "Jenna the Villain" never quite happened the way that the producers expected it to happen, but there was definitely something about Jenna Lewis that I was always a little wary of as well. I dunno what it was, just something maybe about her demeanor. Just like the producers, I always sort of had a bad feeling about her as a Survivor character. Which is probably why I preferred the much more goofy version of her, Kimmi. Or, as I liked to call her, Jenna Lewis version 2.0.

And yes, of course I am going to write more about Jenna when we get to All-Stars. Which is something I totally predicted, by the way, right down to the fact that she would come out fighting like an alley cat the second time she played Survivor. Again, who called the Jenna Lewis transformation from likable to evil? This guy.

When it came to the rest of the Kuchas, most of the Survivor audience at the time seemed to be in love with Jeff Varner (because he was a schemer) and Elisabeth Filarski (because she was the sweetheart.) Those two were clearly always the darlings of the Survivor internet crowd. Unfortunately I never really had much of an opinion of Jeff or Elisabeth, so neither one ever really made much of an impact on me. To me they were just two of the other random members of the Kucha tribe. The ones who weren't Nick, Mike, Rodger, or Kimmi.

Side note: Actually no, that's not quite true. I DID always have one very strong opinion of Elisabeth. My opinion of her is that I hated the fact that 95% of the Survivor fans on the internet would only refer to her as "Lis." They routinely referred to her as "Lis" despite the fact that SHE WAS NEVER CALLED THAT NAME EVEN ONE TIME AT ANY POINT DURING THE EPISODES. In fact the one time Elisabeth actually DID have a nickname on the show, it was when her mom revealed that her nickname at home was "Bessie."

131

Seriously, if you ever want to annoy me to the point that I literally might turn green and turn into the Hulk, just start casually referring to Elisabeth as "Lis." In fact, if you are an internet historian, this would be a great simulation of what the World Wide Web was like back in February of 2001. It was just twenty million Survivor fans referring to Elisabeth in every single post as Lis. I hated it. In fact, I don't mean to start conspiracies, but I truly believe that the overuse of the name "Lis" might have actually led to 9/11.

Aside from that, the only other thing I remember thinking about Elisabeth is that she was cute and that she vaguely looked like a muppet.

Over on Ogakor there were also a few characters who stood out to me in that first episode of Australia.

The big one, of course, was the Colbster. Colby Donaldson. Who, as we all know, later turned into the first big crossover star to ever come out of Survivor. And also the guy who almost converted Rosie O'Donnell back to being straight. We will talk more about that later.

Yeah I know. You are sitting there saying "Colby? A crossover star? The guy who might or might not actually be a Hershey bar?" But you might not remember. Colby was the first spokesman for the Schick Quattro. Remember the Schick Quattro? It was all the rage at the time. It was the razor that had four blades. Seriously, it was a razor in 2002, and IT HAD FOUR FUCKING BLADES!!! How cool is that?!? Do you remember where you were the first time you ever saw the Schick Quattro? I know that I do.

All kidding aside, I liked Colby because he was sort of smug, but he also seemed to have a sense of humor about himself. Kind of like Richard. I knew that he was going to be a fun character.

Of course I didn't realize how big Colby was going to get until much later, but we will get to that in the upcoming chapters.

Another Ogakor player I liked at the time was Keith Famie. I liked Keith because, well because like I said in an earlier chapter, he was something completely different we had never seen before on Survivor. Unlike so many of the other Australia players, there had been no equivalent to "a professional chef" the first time around in Borneo. So if nothing else I knew I would

132

enjoy Keith because he would bring something new to the show.

Jerri or Amber? Didn't care. Jerri wouldn't have an impact on the season at all until the second episode. Although what an impact it was! And Amber was... um... well, yeah. That's exactly what Amber was. Why was she cast on All Stars again?

Mitchell Olsen I thought was interesting. But I already talked about Mitchell in an earlier chapter. Mitchell was easily one of the most written about Survivors during those early days of Australia (all the magazines and websites absolutely loved him.) But I was pretty sure he wasn't going to be around for very long. In fact, I didn't see how he COULD possibly last very long. The guy was 7 feet tall and he weighed about 150 pounds. I didn't see how a person with that metabolism could possibly last very long in a game like Survivor. To me it seemed like the producers had legitimately risked a guy's health who probably had no business being out there, simply because they wanted to cast a guy who was seven feet tall. To me Mitchell always smacked of nothing more than gimmick stunt casting.

Of course there was also Mad Dog, who (like Mitchell) the magazines and the websites at the time were all completely enamored with. Mad Dog was easily the biggest star of Australia going into that first episode. Just from her bio and her interviews alone, people were already referring to her as "the next Rudy" before she ever spent one second on TV. Everyone loved how down to earth, how funny, how gruff, and how quotable she was.

Unfortunately I never really had much of an opinion of Mad Dog one way or the other. I thought she was kind of funny, true, but I also thought she was a little bit forced. I thought she was trying a little too hard to become the next big Survivor "character." So for me she was never quite as fascinating as people like Keith or Colby or Mike, who I thought were all very interesting, very genuine people. I have never been all that big on people playing "characters" on Survivor. Although who knows, for all I know maybe that is what Mad Dog really was like in real life too. Maybe she wasn't playing a character at all. Who knows?

By the way, I should probably point out that Mad Dog wasn't the only player who I always thought was playing "a character" in Australia. I always thought that Elisabeth was playing a character too. With Elisabeth, I always got the impression that she was playing the sweetheart in Australia because she knew how well that would come off on TV and how much everyone would fall in love with her (just ask Colleen.) In fact that is probably the number one reason why I was never really fully invested in Elisabeth Filarski as a Survivor character. I always thought there is no way anyone can be as sweet as she is all the time. I figured, a lot of that has to be calculated or it has to be editing.

When it comes to Kel, even though a lot of people remember Kel as being a dud, the thing I remember the most about him is the fact that I thought he was very good looking. In fact I remember making some comment to my wife after that first episode of Australia, about how I thought that Kel was very handsome. Only, you know, not in a homosexual way.

Yes, that's right. You had to add the "...but not in a homosexual way" punchline to any phrase you ever made about a male Survivor back in 2001. We weren't being homophobic, don't blame us, those were just the times. That was just the way that it was. Thanks to Rudy we all had "but not in a homosexual way" fever back in 2000 and 2001. It wasn't mean. It wasn't cruel. That phrase was just the hula hoop of the early 21st century. Even my grandma was using it.

Oh yeah and I also felt it was important that my wife knew I wasn't going to leave her to have sex with Kel Gleason. That was an important disclaimer.

So anyway, those were the original seven members of Ogakor. Colby, Keith, Mitchell, the dreamy Kel, Jerri, Mad Dog, and some other girl who might have been named Amber.

And then, of course, we come to the eighth member of the tribe.

My favorite.

Even though Nick was the guy I was rooting for in Australia, there was a woman on Ogakor who I was absolutely fascinated with, almost from the very first episode. In fact, even though people these days know me as "The guy who is obsessed with Chris Daugherty", Chris wasn't always my number one all-time favorite Survivor player. Nope. For years there was another player who I used to talk about almost as much as I talk about Chris. And who, for years, I used to refer to as my all-time favorite Survivor player.

My more recent readers won't know this, but anyone who was reading my columns between 2002-2005 will know that my all-time favorite Survivor used to be Tina Wesson. They will know this because I used to never shut up about her.

And why exactly was Tina my favorite?

Well, when it comes to my fascination with Tina Wesson, I am sure I will have a lot more to say in the upcoming chapters. Trust me, I will be writing a LOT about Tina in this book. Especially when we get to episodes three and four of Australia and she turns into a 95-pound little badass ("In the spirit of the Olympics, let the games begin!")

All I will say about Tina in episode one of Australia is that A) she was barely in it for more than five seconds, B) the editors deliberately hid her from us for a reason (and they later regretted it), and C) it was fun to watch her bouncing up and down when she was running.

Don't worry. I liked her for much more noble reasons very quickly. I just thought it was best to be honest with you.

P.S. Oh yeah, one other great scene I forgot to talk about from the Australia premiere. I loved the scene at Kucha where Rodger receives inspirational notes from his family back home, only they are scattered around in the pages of his Bible and he has to search for them like a scavenger hunt. I love that scene. In my opinion, it is scenes like that (non-strategy, character-building scenes) that made Survivor such a special show back during those early years. Of course, nowadays, that scene would have been cut so we could fit in five more minutes of people talking about vote splitting. Whatever.

26. The Dark Side of Survivor

Although the Borneo castaways were obviously the true "pioneers" of Survivor, in many ways the Australia cast were just as revolutionary and could just as easily be called the true Survivor trailblazers. In fact, if you want to get right down to it, I would argue that the cast of Australia actually faced a much tougher challenge than the original cast from Borneo ever did.

The downside with being on the second season of Survivor was that there were three major problems the Australia players faced that the Borneo cast simply never had to face. And all three problems had the potential to have some very serious long term consequences. In fact, I would argue that all three of the problems that the Australia cast faced were ones that very easily could have killed the entire Survivor franchise.

The first problem the Australia cast faced, of course, was the very obvious question of "how do you differentiate this season from the original season"? Because remember, Survivor had been a national phenomenon that something like 50 million people had watched, and it had only ended a couple of months ago. So that whole first season was still very fresh in America's mind. People like Colleen and Richard and Rudy and Gervase were now all legitimate media celebrities. Colleen was so big at the time that she was about to star in a movie. Rudy Boesch had just published a book.

So how are you going to do this a second time? How on earth do you do a Survivor 2, and make people forget about the original one? How do you replace a cast that was considered one of the most memorable and interesting group of characters in television history?

This was by far the most difficult problem that the cast from Australia faced, and never for one minute did I envy them for what they were going to go through. Okay, sure, maybe I was a little bit jealous that these people had been cast on my favorite TV show, and I hadn't. But that jealously went away very quickly when I realized the enormity of the task they were now going to be up against. These people were now Coy and Vance (the replacement Duke Brothers that nobody ever accepted) from the Dukes of Hazzard. They were now officially New Coke.

These people very easily could have been rejected by all of America.

For me the exact moment that "Survivor: The Australian Outback" became something more than just "Borneo Part 2" was in episode two, with Kel and the beef jerky. To me that episode will always be the one that defined Australia as being its own specific and unique entity. Because there had never been a moment in Borneo that had been anything like the way the Ogakors attacked Kel over smuggling in the beef jerky.

Actually, to be more specific, there had never been anything in Borneo quite like the audience's REACTION to the Ogakors and Kel and the beef jerky.

Seriously, you thought the Sue Hawk rats and snakes speech had enraged the Survivor audience? The Sue Hawk speech was NOTHING compared to the fan reaction to Kel and the beef jerky. That was the moment that I have always claimed turned Survivor into what it would eventually become. That was the moment that completely pissed off the entire fan base, and made the producers realize that when this show was a Jerry Springer-like melodrama-- when people in the audience were furious that one of the characters (Jerri) simply "had to go down" now -- well that was when Survivor was the most addictive to watch.

In other words, with the Kel beef jerky incident, and the creation of the first true Survivor mega villain (Jerri), the second season finally blasted off into being a full-fledged soap opera.

By the way, I should probably point out that even to this day most people involved with Australia (including Probst and Burnett) think that Kel actually did have some sort of beef jerky on him. And that the Ogakor witch hunt wasn't really a witch hunt at all. Probst and Burnett have both gone on record as saying that the Ogakor response (including going through Kel's bag) was probably justified.

But don't try telling that to the Survivor audience in January of 2001.

No way. Back in 2001 the audience reaction to the Ogakor beef jerky hunt was much different. It was more or less "Fuck you Jerri and fuck you Tina for going through Kel's bag. I hope both of you bitches burn in hell."

Think I'm exaggerating? Well I'm not. I have never seen a Survivor contestant as hated as Jerri was after the second episode of Australia.

Tina Wesson, by the way, was actually nearly as hated as Jerri for a while there, if only for the fact (like I said above) that she was the first person who actually went into Kel's bag. People tend to forget that now, but it's true. When that whole scene first aired on TV, Tina took nearly as much heat on the message boards from the fans as Jerri did. A lot of the hatred towards

Tina eventually sort of died down after a while, because people tended to forgive her when she became the star of Australia and America's new mother sweetheart strategist and all, but there are still a bunch of hardcore old school fans out there who have never forgiven her for it. They still just think of Tina Wesson as "that bitch who opened Kel's bag."

I know this whole idea of Tina hatred will sound ridiculous to some of the newer Survivor fans out there, but just trust me on this one. If there is one person in the Survivor community who has been keeping tabs on the shifting fan reaction towards Tina over the past fifteen years or so, it is me. Remember, you are talking to the original Tina Wesson obsessor here. Tina was hated by many many people before the audience ever started to root for her.

Now of course by bringing up Jerri (and the fan reaction towards Jerri) we come to the second problem that the Australia cast faced that the Borneo cast never really had to face. And this one was an especially serious one.

The second problem that the Australia cast faced (and one which had some terrible real life implications for a few of the players down the road) was the simple question, "What happens to you if your "reality TV" experience doesn't really work out the way you had expected it to work out? What if America hates you instead? What is that going to do to your life?"

You see, even though the Borneo cast had contained a few quote-unquote "villains" among their midst (like Richard and Sue), for the most part America really hadn't hated them all that much on a personal level. Nearly everyone from the Borneo cast-- like them or not-- had later become an instant media celebrity. Heck, even Richard Hatch, the guy who most of America had loved to hate at the time, seemed to be viewed after Borneo as more of a charismatic scoundrel than an actual bad guy.

I will never believe that Richard was truly "hated", by the way. I think that most people just laughed at him because he was so cocky and because he was so clearly full of himself. But actual hate? No way. If the guy ever showed up on The Weakest Link or Who Wants to be a Millionaire?, or any other celebrity game show (which he would do for a while), people would still tune in to watch him. They would tune in because they thought he was interesting, and because he was fun to watch. And... oh yeah... most of all because they knew it would be awesome to see him get his ego crushed on national TV.

Again though, I would argue that nobody ever actually "hated" him on a personal level. They just wanted to see him fail. There was a subtle difference there.

In my personal opinion, I don't think any of the original Borneo cast members were hurt in real life by the fact that they had been on Survivor. Oh sure, some of them might have regretted their Survivor experience later, after the fact. Like Colleen, who famously said later on that the show was "dangerous" and it was "a bad idea" - two statements I happen to agree with by the way. And some of the Borneo castmembers might have tried to distance themselves from the show and pretend like they had never been on it (Greg Buis, I am looking at you). And some of them might have sued CBS afterwards and gotten into a mini Holy War with them over allegations that the game might have been rigged (oh hai Stacey.) But for the most part I think that every single person who had played in Borneo had gotten exactly what they had expected to get out of Survivor. They had had a fun adventure. And they had become a mini TV celebrity. And they had made a little money along the way. For all intents and purposes, I think that is exactly what every single one of them had been hoping to get out of their Survivor experience.

And, well, do you see the problem here? The one that the players in the Australia cast might not have seen looming directly in front of them?

The problem that the Australia cast faced was the fact that they were walking into a situation where nobody had actually failed before. Seriously, they were walking into a scenario that had turned out to be 100% successful for just about every single person who had starred in Survivor the first time around. The Australia players saw this, and they probably expected that life was going to become this huge exciting whirlwind of an adventure the minute they were cast on the show. Just like the Borneo cast. And that after the episodes started airing on TV, the Australia players would all become instant beloved (or at least popular) mini celebrities. Again, just like the Borneo cast had been.

Which, as anyone who has followed "reality TV" over the past ten years or so can tell you, is not a very realistic way to go into your reality TV experience..

Especially when you are playing a game that can easily devolve into public humiliation.

I think a few members of the Australia cast were hit over the head by reality pretty early on at the start of their Survivor experience. And nobody was hit over the head any harder in the first two episodes than Debb Eaton and Jerri

139

Manthey.

Debb Eaton, as everyone knows, was the very first person voted out of Survivor: The Australian Outback. And if you remember her reaction at Tribal Council and her memorable final words afterwards, you will know that she was completely devastated by what had happened to her. When Debb was voted out first, in an episode that was watched by more than 40 million people, she was legitimately horrified.

The reason Debb was so horrified was because (in her mind) you weren't supposed to vote out a fit young worker bee so early in Survivor. No way. That simply wasn't how the game was supposed to work. In Borneo, the strong and the athletes and the worker bees (like Debb) had all lasted for a while. It wasn't the Debbs of the world who were supposed to go first, it was the weak old people like Sonja and BB and Rodger who were supposed to go first. In Debb's experience there had never been a precedent for something like this happening before. She thought she had known what she was walking into when she signed up for Survivor, yet she had been completely blindsided by reality.

In other words, Debb Eaton was the first "first boot" ever who had been voted out purely because of social reasons-- not because she was weak, but because people just didn't like her. And I think the realization of this logic when she finally figured it out must have just absolutely hammered her.

Remember how I said that Survivor had the potential to easily devolve into public humiliation? Remember how so many sociologists and psychologists had been against the concept of this show right from the start? Ever hear the story about how the first guy voted off of the Swedish version of Survivor (1997) eventually committed suicide?

Remember how Colleen Haskell famously referred to Survivor as "a really bad idea"?

Well now you know why.

Debb Eaton was the first person voted off in Australia. She was publicly humiliated on national TV because the rest of the tribe just didn't want her around. And I think she was absolutely mortified by this. Because as she herself said in her final words, this was her worst nightmare. Short of actually dying out there, this was the single worst thing that ever could have happened to a person in their Survivor experience.

Or so she had thought.

Sadly, for Debb the worst part actually hadn't happened to her yet.

To add insult to injury, the minute Debb Eaton came home from Australia, she found out that the press had dug up the fact that in real life, she was technically engaged to her stepson. The media dug up the details, they ran with the story on every single media site on the internet for a couple of days, they painted her as some sort of a sick child molesting sexual deviant, and they absolutely tore her life apart before she ever even got the chance to become any sort of a mini celebrity.

All of this humiliation, of course, came BEFORE the episode where she was actually voted out of the game. Her reputation was destroyed before her boot episode even aired on TV. So Debb basically got to be humiliated by her peers in the game of Survivor, she got to be humiliated by the media when she returned home, she got to be made fun of by the press and by millions of people who didn't actually know her on the internet... and then she got to go through it all over again a couple of weeks later when her episode actually aired on TV. Then she got to be humiliated again, only this time in front of 45 million people.

To say that Debb's life was ruined because she appeared on Survivor is probably an understatement.

I mean, you've seen the Australia reunion show. Right? You saw her crying over this. In my opinion no one has ever been destroyed as completely by becoming a "reality TV star" as Debb Eaton was. Her old anonymous happy quiet life was literally taken away from her, just because she wanted to be a contestant on a game show.

Debb Eaton definitely saw the dark side of becoming a "reality star." She fell prey to the nastiest problem that the Australia cast was going to run into -- the problem of having unrealistic celebrity expectations after what had happened to the players in Borneo. And, unfortunately, she wasn't the only one. Because what happened to Debb was just a drop in the bucket compared to what happened to Jerri.

Jerri was so hated in the middle of Australia-- and I am being totally serious here-- that I wouldn't be surprised at all if she was receiving death threats.

P.S. By the way, the Debb story reminds me of a Richard anecdote that I forgot to mention in my Borneo chapters. I just realized that Debb was

NOT the first instance where a player came home, and the media more or less tore their life apart. Richard Hatch actually went through a very similar experience when he came home from Borneo.

This is a story that was very well publicized at the time, but for some reason (actually, probably a very good reason), it has sort of been forgotten over the years. What happened was, when Richard came home from filming Borneo, he discovered that his son hadn't been eating healthy or exercising while dad was away. The kid had gained a little bit of extra weight over the past two months. Well, as a former "fat kid" himself, Richard was concerned about what this was going to do to his son's image and self-esteem once September came, and the kid went back to school. So Richard immediately put his son on an exercise program so that he would be able to work all the weight off.

Long story short, here is what happened. A neighbor saw Richard making his son jog every morning in the street, and he noticed that Richard was yelling at him like he was a drill sergeant. So the neighbor reported Richard Hatch to the police for child abuse. And once it became known that this was RICHARD HATCH and THIS GUY IS A SURVIVOR CONTESTANT (and because this was the year 2000, let's be honest, there was probably also a little OH MY GOD, CREEPY, A GAY GUY ADOPTED A KID), naturally the newspapers and the media jumped all over it. Within about two days, it was reported all over the news that "One of the contestants on CBS's new Survivor show was recently arrested for child abuse." And this misrepresentation of the news haunted Richard all season, to the point that I honestly believe it had something to do with why CBS tried to distance themselves from their winner as the season went along.

In any case, a couple of months later, the child abuse allegations against Richard were dropped, but naturally the media didn't make as big a deal about that part as they had about the first part. Because the media is always sooooo helpful that way. So the vast majority of America still considered Richard to be a scummy old child abuser, even though the police had long since cleared him of any charges and had claimed there had been no wrongdoing. Yet the allegation still hung over Richard's head all season, to the point that I really do believe it tainted his reputation as a Survivor legend.

Wow. I hadn't thought about that whole Richard "child abuse" bullshit for a long time. In fact, I hadn't thought of it for about fifteen years until I was just reminded of it right now. And, again, I am reminded what a raw deal he got in that whole thing, simply because he was on Survivor, and because so many people in the media wanted Survivor to fail. Because I am not kidding, it really was a big deal at the time. That story was all over the place.

It was such a big deal at the time that it pretty much derailed any chance Richard might have had to become any sort of a media celebrity. In fact, in many ways, Richard Hatch's experience with the dark side of Survivor was just as nasty as Debb Eaton's was. Only, because Richard's story sort of went away after a couple of months, and Debb's story didn't, most people who weren't there at the time aren't aware of that.

Seriously, what a crazy year those first two seasons of Survivor were. I am glad that I got to experience it as a fan, sure, but at the same time I am also glad that it is never going to happen again. Because there was some really messed up stuff those first twelve months of the Survivor franchise. Richard's and Debb's stories are the prime examples of that.

27. In Defense of Jerri

Jerri Manthey. Ah, yes. The original Survivor villain.

In fact, I believe it would be safe to say that, prior to Jonny Fairplay in Pearl Islands, she was really the <u>only</u> Survivor villain. In my fifteen plus year history of following this show, I have never seen a player who was more hated at their peak than Jerri was.

Now, what is ironic about the fact that Jerri was so hated at the time is that if you go back and you watch Australia now, you will see that she really wasn't even all that bad. She really doesn't do anything that you would say was "villain-like." The only criticisms you can really make of Jerri if you go back and you watch Australia now is that she was probably a little too smug when she was in power and things were going her way, and she was probably a little annoying to have to live with on a daily basis. Oh, and she was probably a little bit mean in the way she belittled Keith for no particular (at least that we ever saw) reason.

But honestly, you watch Australia now, and it is obvious that Jerri really didn't do anything that was all that bad. I mean, hell, players like Clay (from Thailand) and Jean-Robert (from China) were just as smug as she ever was, and they were probably just as annoying to live with around camp on a daily basis. But were they singled out as the single most hated villain in Survivor history?

Nope. Only Jerri was.

Like I said before, the big problem that the Australia cast faced at the time was that they needed to show in some way that their season was going to be different than the first season. And this problem wasn't only specific to the players. It was also very much the editors' and the producers' problem. Every single person involved with Australia, from top to bottom, had to demonstrate very early on that the Australia season was going to be a completely different product than the Borneo season had been. They had to make sure the audience knew that this wasn't going to be just some quickie knockoff that CBS had thrown together in a couple of weeks. No, in many ways, it was imperative that Australia had to be bigger and badder and way more memorable than the first season had ever been.

And, most importantly, it had to distinguish itself as being bigger and badder and more memorable than Borneo very quickly.

Like I pointed out in the last chapter, I have always pinpointed episode two as the exact moment where Australia sort of became its own distinct entity. And it did so because it contained the infamous "beef jerky incident", which to me marked an incredibly different version of Survivor than we had ever seen before.

The reason the beef jerky incident seemed so different to me (and the reason it enraged so many Survivor fans at the time) was because for the first time in Survivor history, a tribe had turned on one of their own. And they had turned on one of their own because of 100% personal reasons. In fact, not only had the Kel feeding frenzy come off as being personal (as opposed to being strategic), on TV it had come off as being a little bit mean.

This wasn't Sonja being voted out just because she was old.

This wasn't Dirk being voted out just because he had lost too much weight and he was getting too skinny.

This wasn't Gretchen being voted out just because she was on the other side of an alliance.

Heck, this really wasn't even Debb being voted out just because the other Kuchas thought she was annoying.

No, the way the Kel vote was portrayed on TV, and the reason Jerri took such an incredible amount of abuse from Survivor fans for it later down the road, was because it looked like the Ogakors had ganged up on him and they had made up a beef jerky lie about him, simply so they could smear his character on TV and they would have a reason to vote him out. On TV it came off like the Ogakors took nice, quiet Kel out of the game out simply because there were seven of them, because they were more cutthroat than he was, and because they were bullies. Oh, and also because there was no rule that said that they couldn't do that.

As I like to refer to it, the Kel vote in Australia episode two was the very first gangbang vote in Survivor history. Seven people ganged up on and tore apart the one military guy just because he was quiet and because he was sweet and because he wouldn't defend himself.

Now, of course, this probably wasn't the way that the Kel vote actually went down in real life. In real life there is evidence that Kel actually did have beef jerky stashed away somewhere, and that the whole outraged reaction from the Ogakors was perfectly justified. In fact, in real life, I wouldn't be surprised if Colby had actually spearheaded the Kel vote himself (behind the guise of Beef Jerkygate) simply so he could get rid of a potential rival alpha male very early in the game. In real life neither one of those scenarios would surprise me at all.

But that certainly wasn't the way the Kel vote was portrayed on TV. And that certainly wasn't the way that the audience reacted to it.

No way.

In February of 2001 all we saw on TV were seven Ogakors ganging up on a guy who was quiet and who seemed kind of aloof. They accused him of having beef jerky. They (Tina and Jerri) searched through his bag. They laughed at him and they mocked him when he came back and he tried to defend himself. They voted him out.

And then we got the infamous shot of Jerri smirking about it afterwards.

Seriously, if you were not a Survivor watcher in the early days, if you weren't there for the whole beef jerky incident when it first aired on TV, it would be impossible for me to describe to you how hated Jerri became because of this episode. Because I am not kidding. The fury of the entire Survivor fan base came down on her with a vengeance. And it came down on her HARD. This was nothing like what Richard or Sue had ever faced. When Survivor nation came down on Jerri Manthey, it came down on her so completely that it totally went medieval on her ass.

And hey, what do you know? Just like that, the editors and producers now had EXACTLY what they had been hoping for. They now had their first uber-villain. They also now had a season that was never going to be confused with Borneo. Australia (which was only two episodes in!) was apparently going to be the first really vicious Survivor season.

Now, of course, this leads us into the next logical question. Do you think the editors threw Jerri under the bus on purpose?

To be honest, I have always had mixed feelings about that.

On one hand, I think they did sell her out. I think they intentionally made Jerri look like the villain in that scene, and I think they did it for a reason. I think they realized that for Australia to succeed, it needed to be meaner and way more personal than Borneo had ever been. I think the producers knew that if you made Australia a very personal season (which is something that

146

Borneo had never been, other than of course the Sue-Kelly speech at the very end), it would come off as less of a documentary and as more of a soap opera. Which meant that it would be way more compelling to watch. Soap operas, by definition, are just about the single most addictive type of television you can possibly produce, since they rely so heavily on storylines and foreshadowing and things like retribution and vengeance and comeuppance. This is exactly why, if I were ever a Survivor producer, I would try to make my season into a soap opera as quickly as I could. The quicker you turn your season into a soap opera, the more guaranteed you are that your audience will get hooked and they will want to keep coming back. In fact, quite frankly, I think it should be the goal of every Survivor season to turn it into a soap opera as quickly as possible. That is just what a good TV producer is supposed to do.

So anyway, there is one reason why it was important to turn Jerri into a villain. It was important to turn her into a villain because every good soap opera needs a good soap opera villain. It is as simple as that. Jerri just happened to be in the right place at the right time, and she became the anointed one.

The second reason it was so helpful to turn Jerri into a villain was, well, because for storyline purposes, later down the road she was organically going to BECOME the villain.

Look at it this way. As an editor, you know that Jerri is going to become the "villain" a couple of episodes into the season. By the middle episodes of Australia, nearly every single other player in the game is going to be routinely referring to her as the person they would like to get rid of. And that ISN'T going to just be editing. By the middle episodes of Australia, it is obvious that the other players in the game are just sort of getting tired of her.

When you look at it this way (Jerri = natural antagonist), you can see what the logical thought process must have been for the editors. Since Jerri is going to become the "villain" in the middle episodes anyway, since her boot in episode eight is going to be a moment we are going to want to exploit for as much drama as possible, why not just get the viewers to dislike her a couple of episodes earlier? Why not? Let's do whatever we can to build the "Jerri falls" episode (episode eight) into something amazing. Let's show her as the sole person behind Beef Jerkygate in episode two. Let's get America to hate her for what she did to Kel. And let's see what it does for her story arc down the road. After all, we have a very long boring Pagonging coming later in the season, and we are aware of it. Let's try to break up that monotony by having

147

something (Jerri's downfall) that is amazing in the middle.

> **Side Note:** I'm not sure if I spelled this out in my Borneo chapters, but "Pagonging" was very much a word in the fan base at the time, and it is still a common word in the fan base today. If you have never heard the phrase before, a "Pagonging" is where one alliance picks off the other members of an alliance, one after another. It is very predictable, and it can really be quite boring. If you are a TV producer a Pagonging needs to be avoided at all costs.

When you look at Jerri's story arc from this point of view, I think it is obvious. I think the producers totally knew what they were doing with her in episode two. And I think that they did it intentionally.

I think they totally backdated her as a major Survivor villain.

Now as for "was this an ethical thing to do to one of your players?" I really don't have much of a problem with it. After all, the Survivor editors have been doing stuff like this for years. They are constantly taking minor scenes, and minor interactions, and manipulating them in order to create Survivor villains. It has been happening every single season since Borneo (think of all the Stacey Stillman eye rolls). So from an ethical point of view, no, I don't see a problem with what they did to Jerri at all.

The problem, of course, is that I don't think the producers could have predicted how vicious the hatred towards Jerri was going to get. I think they knew she was going to be hated (I mean, duh, that was sort of the point), but I certainly don't think they knew that she was going to be THAT hated. But I wouldn't really call that their fault either. I would chalk what happened to Jerri up more to Survivor just not having a very sophisticated fan base back then. Back in the early days of the show, the audience hadn't really developed the ability yet to identify a storyline for what it was. In the early days we all tended to view the show as a completely accurate portrayal of real life events that were happening on an island (aka, it was still being seen as a documentary.) I don't think most viewers would figure out how important things like "editing" and "foreshadowing" and "story arcs" were to Survivor for a couple more seasons. Most viewers wouldn't put the pieces together that Survivor was much closer to the WWE than it was to a nature documentary for a couple more years. And unfortunately I think that Jerri paid the price for that ignorance.

148

Oh yeah, and I guess I also better address this giant white elephant in the room. Yes, I also think there was a lot of plain old fashioned sexism involved in what happened to Jerri.

Richard had been a big horrible villain, sure. Yet for some reason that had been okay because Richard had been a middle aged man. But when a young self-centered wannabe actress starts being portrayed as the next big Survivor villain? Uh oh. At that point now all bets are off. That is what I think essentially happened to Jerri more than anything. She got screwed because for some reason a lot of people in the fanbase just have a problem with a really good female villain (see also Richter, Lindsey or Strobel, Heidi.)

The audience always reacts differently to a female villain on Survivor. Always. That has been a constant since day one.

Jerri, bless her heart, just happened to be the first of them.

> **Side note:** By the way, when I talk about "unsophisticated viewers", I am certainly not trying to sound like a snob. I am definitely including myself in that group as well. I was certainly no more sophisticated a viewer than anyone else was back in the spring of 2001 (no one was, we were all newbies.) I HATED Jerri during Australia. Her boot episode (when it happened) was one of the best Survivor moments of my life. But even back then I also felt sort of bad for her. No matter how much I disliked Jerri as a Survivor character, I could tell that in real life this whole Survivor experience just wasn't going to end all that well for her. There was no way you could be that hated by all of America and still turn into a TV celebrity. No way, it just wasn't going to happen. Even as an unsophisticated newbie TV watcher back in 2001, I knew that Jerri's life was going to be affected by Survivor, and it was probably not going to be affected in a good way. Like Debb, I knew she was going to regret for a long time that she had ever signed up for this.

In any case, if you are wondering why Jerri became so hated, and why she is still referred to today as "the original Survivor villain", well now you know why. She is called that because she really WAS the first big Survivor villain. And ever since then, I would say that no one-- not Fairplay, not Russell, not Phillip, not Colton, no one-- has ever really even come close. In the spring of

2001, I would guess that something like 95% of Survivor fans across America wanted Jerri out of the game. In fact, I would guess that probably half of those Survivor fans would have been perfectly happy if she had just been dragged outside and had been beaten to death with a bat. I mean, it was scary how rabid the hatred towards her was back during Australia. I had never seen anything like it. I STILL haven't seen anything like it.

The most ironic thing about the way Jerri came across to America at the time was that, to my dying day, I will never believe that she actually went into Australia actually intending to be "the villain." In fact, I would guess that she was probably so completely shocked by the way she was portrayed on TV, and by America's reaction to her, that it probably caused a pretty jarring case of cognitive dissonance in her brain. Based on her final words, and based on some of the interviews she gave immediately after the season, in real life I don't think she saw her villain edit coming at all.

Side note: What makes Jerri's TV portrayal doubly ironic is the fact that not only do I think she wasn't intending to be the villain of Australia, I don't think ANYONE was trying to be the villain of Australia. I think the Australia cast on a whole was so polite, and was so well behaved, and was so civil to one another, that it was practically the only season in Survivor history where there wasn't a single actual villain to be found. Seriously, watch how civilized and even tempered the final Tribal Council in Australia was. It is the most emotionless final Tribal Council ever. It is quite obvious that nobody in that season really hated each other.

I think the players in Australia were trying so hard not to be seen as the equivalent of the Borneo cast (who most of America still thought of as being fun at first, before they had all turned mean and nasty), that it created one of the rare moments in Survivor history where there really wasn't a villain at all. EVERYONE that season was on their best behavior. EVERYONE was trying to be seen as "the good guy." Which, like I said, makes Jerri's fate and legacy even all the more sad and ironic. Like everyone else in Australia, she was trying her best NOT to be a Survivor villain!

Side note #2: Oh yeah, and the whole "every player in Australia was trying to be nice" theory and the "nobody wanted to be seen as the bad guy the second time around" theory? Just keep those in mind when we get to the end of Australia. Because they sure explain Colby's decision a lot better than simply saying "Colby was an idiot." Look, Colby wasn't an idiot. He chose to take Tina to the end for a reason. And Australia is the only season in Survivor history where it ever would have gone down like that. Remember, Australia was almost a direct contrast to the way that the first season had played out. It was a direct response to Borneo. Nearly every person involved with Survivor (the players, the audience, the producers, the media, the fans, everyone) was rooting for "the good guy" to win the second time around. And Colby would have been perfectly aware of that. Just keep that in mind before you say that Colby was an idiot.

To me, the saddest thing about the whole Jerri situation is that, prior to Australia, I don't think she ever realized that she came off as being annoying to people. Absolutely not. I mean, I have never met Jerri, I have never exchanged a single email with her. But from everything I have ever read in interviews, or everything I have ever read about the Survivor: The Australian Outback, I can say with pretty good certainty that she did not expect to become the big villain of season two. No way. She had no idea that she annoyed people. She couldn't have seen that "greatest villain in Survivor history" legacy coming at all. Not even for one second.

From everything I have ever read, it sounds like Jerri expected that she and Colby were going to be portrayed as the "power couple" of the Ogakors. I know it is kind of a weird parallel, but think of Richard and Sue. In her mind, Colby and Jerri were going to be the main two good guys of the season, Keith was going to be the arrogant sneaky cocky villain who they had to deal with, and then-- BAM-- Jerri was going to be taken out when her ally Colby turned on her midway through the season and he became the bad guy.

In other words, I think Jerri totally expected to be portrayed as the screwed over power player who had an easy win taken away from her when her partner got greedy and he stabbed her in the back. Think Rudy in Borneo. Think of his fate. That is EXACTLY how I think Jerri expected to be portrayed on TV. She expected that because that was exactly how she saw the game when she had been playing it. She and Colby were the young cute power couple, and they were the good guys.

Honestly, can you imagine sitting down to watch the first couple episodes of Australia, and realizing that your portrayal on TV was going to be 100% completely different from how you saw it in your head when you were playing the game? Can you imagine what it would have felt like to see that Keith was now the hero, and that YOU were going to be the villain? Can you imagine what that portrayal flip flop would have emotionally done to you?

Especially so soon after Borneo, when virtually all of the castmembers had become respected media celebrities?

And now you were the first player that every Survivor fan on the internet was loudly screaming should die???

Look, like I said before, I have never met Jerri Manthey. I have never exchanged an email with her. She is one of the few Survivors from the early seasons that I have never had any contact with whatsoever. So I don't have any particular agenda behind writing this. In fact I specifically keep my distance from most Survivors just so that I <u>can</u> write chapters like this. By keeping my distance, I can write whatever I feel like, and nobody can ever accuse me of saying things just because I am writing about a friend of mine.

All I am saying (in my completely unbiased way) is that what happened to Jerri was a dark, dark moment in Survivor history. She didn't deserve the fan treatment that she got. She didn't deserve the edit that she got. And she sure as hell certainly didn't deserve the reputation as "the biggest bitch in Survivor history who I hope dies" that she got. From everything I have ever read about her, she sounds like she is actually a very nice person.

Again, what it really comes down to is the fact that Survivor: The Australian Outback had three very large problems facing it the day that it premiered:

> **A)** It needed to be different than Borneo
> **B)** The players were all trying to be much nicer than the Borneo players had been
> **C)** And the players might not have realized yet that "reality TV" could actually turn out to be a very painful experience for them.

Jerri Manthey, unfortunately, got screwed by a combination of all three of those.

P.S. Some people will argue that Australia actually faced a fourth problem too. Some people will argue that "Should I actually join an alliance?" would have been the fourth big ethical dilemma that all the Australia players faced. But I don't believe that was really much of a dilemma at all. The moment Borneo ended, I think that every single Survivor fan in America kind of accepted that alliances were going to be a part of this game (yes it was now a game) whether they liked it or not. So I would say that "alliance or not?" was not really the big question for the players at the time. I think the mindset was more "Well everyone else is gonna join an alliance, so I might as well protect myself and join one too." In other words, I don't think "alliances" were considered a big ethical problem anymore the moment that Borneo ended. Starting with Australia they were basically seen as inevitable.

28. Nick is Very Lazy

There are a handful of Survivor episodes where I can still remember exactly where I was and exactly what I was doing the first time that I saw them.

Episode three of Australia (which I still consider one of the all-time best Survivor episodes) is definitely one of them.

You will see why in a minute.

In February of 2001 I was employed as a programmer for a company based out of Boston. I didn't actually work IN Boston, 99% of my time was spent writing computer programs from my house across the country in Los Angeles. But every so often my manager would want me to actually be in the Boston office to attend a meeting or a conference or to meet with a client or whatever, so then I had to get on a plane and fly back to the East Coast. This only happened maybe three or four times a year, but it happened to occur to me the first week of February in 2001.

The thing that sucked about flying back to Boston was the fact that I had to leave my family for a week. I have always hated leaving my family.

However the good thing about flying back to Boston was the fact that I actually had family there too. At least, at that moment I did. Remember how I said that my brother was a student at Harvard Law School at the time? Well, if I flew back to Boston that meant I got to visit my brother at Harvard, and it was always fun to hang out with him for a week. Especially because of the fact that he was a college student, and I was a former college student, and if there is one thing that former college students enjoy doing it is pretending that they are still college students. For a week it was fun to pretend that I wasn't an actual grownup yet.

So anyway, I flew to Boston in February of 2001 (between episodes two and three of Australia) and the first thing I told my brother when I got to Harvard was that I wanted to know if I could meet Nick Brown. You know, the guy who I had already emailed a couple of times. The guy I was supposed to do an interview with after the season. I hadn't ever actually met Nick in person up to this point, so I figured that maybe Dom could introduce me to him.

My brother didn't know where Nick lived on campus, so he just took me over to the Harvard Law Review (an on campus scholarly journal) and said

154

that maybe we would run into him there. Since Dom worked with Nick on the Law Review he said this was as good a place to run into him as any.

We went over to the Harvard Law Review offices. Dom let me inside. And, unfortunately, no Nick.

But what I did find there was almost as good.

I don't know if you have ever been in the offices of a student newspaper, or the offices of a scholarly journal, but basically what happens is there is usually some sort of a running tally posted on the wall. It keeps track of which student has contributed the most articles to the journal that semester, or which student has contributed the least, etc. And of course plastered all over the wall were tiny little pictures of Nick's face.

Every time a Harvard student had published an article in the Law Review, a tiny little icon representing them had been posted on the chart. For some people this icon was something funny, like a sun, or a can of beer, or a Cobra Kai logo, or a picture of Yoda, whatever. But for Nick they had decided to use his picture from his Survivor bio at cbs.com. So all over the wall there were tiny little pictures of Nick Brown's Survivor headshot smiling at me.

It was actually kind of cute.

I never actually did meet Nick in person that day (and in fact, I still have never met him). But when I went back to my brother's apartment to watch Survivor that night, we were in for a treat. This is exactly why I will always remember where I was and what I was doing when I was watching that particular Survivor episode.

That episode (episode three) happened to be the infamous "Nick is very lazy" episode.

Do you remember the "Nick is very lazy" episode? Do you remember where you were the first time you saw it?

No, of course you don't. I am well aware that I am the only person on the face of the Earth who even remembers who Nick Brown was, let alone is weird enough to sit down and actually write a 400 page book about him. So no I am quite sure you probably have no idea what the hell I am talking about.

The scene that I am talking about happens about 1/3 of the way into episode

3 of Australia. Jeff Varner is talking about the other members of Kucha that he likes, and which ones he trusts, and then he decides to go on a nice little mini rant about Nick. Because according to Jeff, Nick is "a total player" who Jeff "wouldn't trust as far as I can throw him."

And then we get to the money quote.

We cut to a shot of Nick sitting on a bench at the Kucha camp. And then, in a very jarring overdub, Jeff's voice opens the scene by telling us "Nick is very lazy."

Ha ha. I know, I know, it is more of an inside joke because Dom and I had an actual connection to Nick at the time, but for some reason this quote has always KILLED me. It is just so blunt, and it comes completely out of nowhere, and it is such a jarring shift in the tone of that confessional ("Nick is a player! Nick is dangerous! No, Nick is LAZY!") that I have always remembered it.

I know. I know what you are thinking. You are probably reading this and saying, "But Mario. Nick was just another young black man on Survivor who Mark Burnett decided to portray as lazy. Why would you even laugh about that? It was awful." I know, I know, you're right. It was horrible. It was offensive. It was racist. Handwring handwring handwring. Nick being called lazy was a dark moment in reality TV history. I admit that. It is horrible that I have even decided to joke about it.

But still, here is what was so awesome about that particular moment.

The minute my brother heard that quote ("Nick is very lazy") he just about fell off his chair laughing. I asked him why and he said that he was going to totally use that if he was ever up against Nick in a mock trial. He said, "Mario, you don't understand. This is going to be the single greatest objection in legal history. I am going to use it any chance I get. It will never not be funny."

Some examples:

Nick: Your honor, I would like to submit this piece of evidence.
Dom: Objection, your honor.
Judge: Grounds for objection?
Dom: I object because Nick is very lazy.

Nick: I object to this line of questioning!

Dom: I feel this argument is necessary, your honor.

Judge: Why?

Dom: Because it establishes motive. And it also establishes that Nick is very lazy.

Judge: Does the defense have any opening statements?

Dom: Yes your honor. My client is not guilty. And Nick is very lazy.

My brother and I must have joked about this for at least twenty minutes, just thinking of all the ways he could bust his friend's balls for the fact that he had just been called lazy on national TV. Because seriously, if you are a guy, and if you joke around and bag on your friends as much as Dom and I both tend to do? If that is the case then you can't possibly pass up an opportunity like this.

A good friend of yours just got called lazy in front of 30 million people. So what do you do? Well forget sympathy. Sympathy is for girls. As a guy, it is your duty now to find some way to take advantage of this.

Honestly, just imagine if you were ever on Survivor, and if somebody bagged on you in a particularly memorable soundbyte. Imagine if somebody said something like "Hey that Mario, he's a great guy and all, but his face looks like a blocked kick." Do you think I would ever be able to live that down? Or what about "Hey that Mario's a great player. I bet he has a tiny penis." Do you think that could possibly end well for me? I think not. I mean, just ask Robert "Little Sausage" DeCanio about that some time. Ask him how well his Survivor legacy turned out for him.

"I should send a Christmas Card to the Harvard Review this year," my brother joked. "They can post it on the wall. It could be something like:

Roses are red
Violets are blue
Merry Christmas to you all
Nick is very lazy."

In any case, when I say that I always remember where I was and what I was doing during Australia episode three, now you know. I was laughing at the "Nick is very lazy" quote while I was crashing at Harvard. To this day it is still one of my all-time favorite Survivor moments. In fact, I don't think I have ever laughed harder at a Survivor scene that didn't involve Russell getting his hat burned or Jonny Fairplay lying about his dead grandmother. Or Coach. Of course we mustn't forget about Coach.

Oh yeah and there were other reasons I thought episode three of Australia was so awesome too. Most of those involved Mike Skupin and Tina. Or, as I like to refer to her, Tina the 95 pound little badass.

Don't worry. We will finally get to my Tina worship in the next chapter.

P.S. Want to know the best thing about the "Nick is very lazy" quote? The best thing is the fact that there is really no comeback for it. There is no way you can bust out a reality TV quote to demean a guy in the middle of a legal argument, and have him reply with anything that could remotely be called a comeback. It is sort of like a kryptonite insult. Seriously, what is Nick going to say in response to that? "Fuck you"? "Go to hell"? Where do you go when somebody goes all Jeff Varner on you? As a comedian I could not have been more delighted by this Survivor development.

I wonder if my brother ever did bag on Nick in the middle of a legal argument. I wonder if he even remembers that scene. I don't know. I should probably ask him.

29. Tina the Badass

Okay, onto Tina. That's what he said.

Sorry, I couldn't resist. I just watched the Office last night.

In episode three of Australia we were introduced to a player who I feel is one of the baddest mothers in 30+ seasons of Survivor. And yes, I mean that in a very literal way. Because Tina Wesson was not only an incredible badass, she also happened to be a mother of two. And she set an incredibly bad example for her kids because she was unable to eat rice if it wasn't cooked to her exact princessly standards. There could not have been a player to whom the term "one bad mother" applies better than it does to her.

Oh, I know what you're thinking. You are reading this and you are probably thinking, "Tina Wesson a badass? Um, wasn't she the nice sweet mom who made everyone forget about Richard? And now she is suddenly a badass? What the hell show were you watching, Mario?"

Well, allow me to rebut that.

In episode three of Australia (again, which I still say is a top 20 episode), we were introduced to one of my all-time favorite Survivor episode arcs. This was the episode where Mad Dog and Tina were best friends, where Mad Dog gushed profusely about how much she loved Tina, and how Tina was awesome, and how Tina was "a constellation." And then at the end of the episode Tina cold-heartedly slit Mad Dog's throat and she voted her out.

And we ended with a shot of icy cold Tina just staring out into the nothingness, with blackness in her eyes, completely unmoved by what she had just done to her best friend.

Oh my GOD did I love that episode.

I will never forget episode three of Australia for as long as I live, because to me, at the time, that was the coldest and most heartless thing that I had ever seen on TV. I mean, forget Gretchen. Forget Jenna not getting a video from home. Forget Jenna Lewis voting out her first ever black friend. This was way more cold hearted than that. This was a person who deliberately voted out her very best friend in the game. And who afterwards didn't look like she felt even the slightest bit sad about it.

For something like that to happen so early in season 2, when it was still very much understood that "Survivor was a social game" and "you didn't vote out your friends"?

Wow. This was pretty revolutionary.

I will never forget the moment that Tina voted out her friend Mad Dog. I was sitting there watching it in my brother's apartment in Cambridge and my jaw practically dropped to the floor. Because this sort of stuff just didn't happen on Survivor. Not this early in the game it didn't. And it sure as hell didn't come from people like Tina, who was the tiny sweet little Christian mom who was the heart of the Ogakors.

Holy shit, and is Tina now just staring off into space, like she is Michael Myers and she is staring through a wall? She is not even the slightest bit guilty over this???

I remember watching that episode (the Mad Dog episode), and I immediately called my wife across the country in Los Angeles. Since California is three time zones behind Boston, I knew she hadn't seen the Tina betrayal yet. And I knew that she was going to be as shocked about it as I was.

"Wait until you see this episode," I promised her. "Holy crap, it just ended about two minutes ago and I am absolutely speechless. You are about to see the most cold hearted thing you will ever see in your life."

I didn't want to spoil it for her, but I wanted her to know that this episode was going to be special. This was a new type of player we had ever seen before on Survivor.

Again, Australia was only three episodes in, and it was already creating a legacy for itself.

After the episode ended, I went back and I thought about what Tina had done to Mad Dog. And I started thinking back to why I had never noticed her as a player before. How can you have a player who is this much of a badass (in that tiny little unassuming package!), and how could I have never noticed her prior to now? What had I missed up to this point when it came to Tina Wesson as a Survivor player?

Unfortunately, Tina really hadn't had much of a presence in the first two episodes of Australia. In episode one the editors had deliberately not shown her at all. She was the only player in episode one who didn't get an interview

160

or a confessional - which is something I know Mark Burnett later admitted was probably a mistake. By hiding Tina so blatantly they had sort of made it obvious that they were doing it for a reason. Because players weren't routinely hidden back in the early days of Survivor. That just wasn't the way that the producers treated their characters back then. Nearly everybody got camera time for the most part.

In episode two, the only things we learned about Tina were that A) she had a very thick accent, B) she was one of the... um, we'll say "disliked"... people who went searching through Kel's bag, and C) she couldn't eat gross food to save her life. Her squeamishness had single handedly cost the Ogakors that second immunity challenge.

Unfortunately that was all we knew about Tina through the first two episodes of Australia. She wasn't a particularly strong player, or even a particularly memorable player. She was just some tiny little blonde lady from Tennessee with a thick accent and almost zero survival skills. Oh yeah, and she also had those massive implants. We can't forget about the implants.

And then episode three came around and BAM. We got our first glimpse of Tina the badass.

I was so enamored by Tina the badass that she instantly became my new favorite Survivor player. Forget Nick. Forget Richard. Even... may God forgive me... forget Rudy. When I see a player who is this much of a badass, and who is obviously going to be good at this game, and who wants to win it so bad, and who is in this deceptive of an innocent little package, I'm sorry. That's my new favorite player. From a fan point of view, it is fair to say that right there and then I completely fell in love with Tina Wesson as a Survivor player. She would remain my favorite player for a very long time.

And do you know what happened next?

This is the part that I love the most.

Not only was Tina a huge badass in episode three, not only did she completely slit her own best friend's throat and not even feel guilty about it afterwards, she turned out to be even MORE of a badass in episode four! Because episode four was the one where Tina led an overthrow to take out Mitchell (Jerri's best ally) and completely destroy Jerri's alliance before it ever had a chance to get started.

Episode four was the one where Tina held up her ballot for Mitchell, she smiled sweetly into the camera, and then she gave one of my all-time favorite Survivor quotes. Because this one was perfect. This quote really did encapsulate everything that was about to happen the rest of the season:

Tina (voting for Mitchell): "This was not my original intended vote. However, on the way here to Tribal Council, a new scheme was developed. So in the spirit of the Olympics, let the games begin!"

> **Side note:** I have heard a lot of behind the scenes info about how Tina was never really part of the Jerri alliance, and how she was <u>always</u> aligned with Colby and Keith. And how the whole "overthrow" was nothing more than creative storytelling and editing to get the audience to root against Jerri. But whatever, I don't care. All we can really care about when it comes to Survivor is the edited version that we see on TV at home. And as an edited storyline, this one was fantastic. Right down to the way they edited Tina to be the last one to cast her vote. You talk about a two episode story arc (Australia 3 and 4) that deserved a reality TV Emmy.

So anyway, Tina turned on Mitchell. Mitchell was forced out of the game after a second revote (including the particularly bitchy Tina voting comment, "This game isn't easy. I didn't come out here to starve myself and to face the elements to keep the weakest person.") And just like that, all of Jerri's power in the game was officially destroyed. Her #1 ally (Mitchell) was gone, Tina was now officially in control of the Ogakors, and Jerri was never a power player again at any point during Australia.

By the way, if you have episode four of Australia on DVD, go back and watch the look on Jerri's face at the end of that episode.

If you are wondering why they built Jerri up as such a big bad villain during the first two episodes of the season, well now you know. They did that just so they could get the money shot of "Jerri takes a fall and she looks crushed" at the end of episode four.

And all of that (according to the episode) was at the hands of Tina.

Tina Wesson.

The badass.

My new hero.

Even though Australia was still very much the story of "How Kucha is kicking Ogakor's ass" through the first four episodes of the season, it is safe to say that I was rooting for Tina to win from here on out. I was rooting for her to win for the exact same reason that I always rooted for Richard to win. I was rooting for her simply because she wanted it the most.

I rooted for her because she weighed 95 pounds, she was scared of eating pasty rice, she probably couldn't scarf down a piece of seafood to save her life, yet she was still the biggest badass in the first two seasons of Survivor.

Oh yeah and anyone who still thinks that Tina was "just some sweet little mom" who "only won by accident" because "Colby screwed up" clearly hasn't watched Australia in a while. This woman wasn't a pushover. This woman wasn't a goody goody little Christian choir girl. This woman was a gamebot who you wouldn't want to play checkers against.

Tina Wesson, although tiny, was a cold blooded Survivor assassin.

P.S. I am really not exaggerating when I say this. Go back and watch episodes three and four of Australia again, and tell me that isn't one of the best two part Survivor episodes ever. Because it really is just like a two-parter. Every setup in episode three (The Kuchas make fun of Mike for wanting to kill a pig, Jerri naming her best friends at Tribal Council, Keith doesn't want to be pushed around by Jerri anymore, Tina becomes a huge badass) has a perfect resolution in episode four. The Kuchas make fun of Mike, then Mike kills a pig. Jerri names all her friends at Tribal Council and excludes Tina, so Tina destroys her. Tina cuts her best friend Mad Dog's throat, then she cuts her other friends Mitchell's and Jerri's throats just as easily.

I like episodes three and four of Australia so much that it has always been nearly impossible for me to think of them as just "individual episodes." I have always thought of them as a nearly perfect two episode story arc. One that shows just how much more effort and detail the editors put into the show back then compared to the crap that they try to shovel onto us now.

163

Oh, and if your heart doesn't break when Rodger and Mad Dog keep falling down during the episode three immunity challenge race, then your heart is as cold as Tina's is.

P.P.S. Oh yeah, another reason why I say the editors put way more effort into the show back then than they do now. Go back and watch the episode three reward challenge, where Mike and Colby square off and they try to carry the most water weight. Watch how much the editors tried to build up Mike and Colby as being the two strongest men on Earth right before that challenge. Watch how epic the editors tried to make that particular showdown, like it was life and death and it wasn't just "two guys holding up buckets on a reality show."

That challenge in particular is a great example of how important what I like to call "loving editors" are to a show like Survivor. If the editors try to sell something as epic, it is going to come off on TV as epic. Right down to the music, the slow motion intro, the pacing, and afterwards, Elisabeth's little victory war whoop.

I know this is sort of a weird comparison, but it fits in this particular context. A few years ago the Seattle Mariners lost their longtime radio announcer, Dave Niehaus. He had been the voice of the Mariners on the radio for 34 years, before he finally passed away in 2010 after a heart attack.

When a few former Mariners players (including Ken Griffey Jr.) were asked about the passing of Mr. Niehaus, and what their thoughts were about the man, more than one of them said something along the lines of "Without Dave Niehaus I never would been anything more than just another ballplayer. When he described me, I wasn't just some guy with a bat. In his words I was always a hero. A good radio announcer can turn a player into a god whenever he wants to."

This, to me, is a great parallel to what the Survivor editors have always tried to do (or at least what they should be doing.) If you are an editor, you don't just gloss over big moments on your show like an immunity challenge. You don't just write off a big Colby vs. Mike showdown like it is something that happens every day. No, if you are a Survivor editor, you effing SELL that thing. You build this showdown up into the biggest and most amazing thing in the history of the world, featuring the two strongest men in the history of the world. You turn that thing into a Rocky Balboa movie.

164

Is that type of overblown melodrama corny when you see it on TV? Sure. Is it kind of cheesy? Of course. But I would argue that Survivor has always worked best when it is epic and cheesy and corny. Go back and watch the opening immunity challenge (the flaming carts) in Africa, and watch how epic they tried to make that thing. Between the music and the editing, they treated that challenge like you were watching the original Greek Olympiad.

To me, this is why the early years of Survivor are the golden years, and why they will always be the golden years.

The editors just don't try to make the show as cheesy and as corny and as epic as they used to.

30. Taking Down Friends

Dangit, there is one thing I completely forgot to write about when I started writing about Australia. And this was a pretty big omission too, because if there is one thing that I will always remember about Australia, and how big it was when it originally aired on TV, I will always remember that Survivor: The Australian Outback was the TV show that essentially killed Friends.

If you aren't familiar with the whole Survivor vs. Friends bloodbath, or if you weren't a TV watcher in the spring of 2001, don't worry. Here is some backstory on one of the single greatest showdowns in the history of network television.

For anyone who watched TV in 1999 and 2000, Friends was the big one. It was by far the most popular sitcom on TV. And it basically dwarfed any other comedy show that dared to challenge it. It had taken over the title of "the most popular sitcom on TV" from Seinfeld when Seinfeld went off the air about two years earlier, and by 1999 Friends was cruising along as one of the single most successful shows in the history of television. No other show would dare go up against it. No other show would dare even go near it. It was basically the American Idol of its day, cruising along, pulling in millions and millions of viewers, and destroying any lesser show that wound up in its path.

I was a big Friends fan at the time (who wasn't?), so obviously I was kind of right there in the middle of all of this. Before reality shows, sitcoms were the only types of shows I would ever watch on TV. And Friends was by far my favorite. Sure, Frasier would go on to win the Emmy for best sitcom every year, but to me it always seemed like only old people watched Frasier. In my opinion, if you wanted to be a part of hip young popular culture in the late 90's, you had to watch Friends. It was the center of everything.

Remember, Friends was popular for a reason its first couple of years. It was the epicenter of pop culture because it was good.

Now, when Survivor came along in the summer of 2000, this signaled an interesting shift in the TV viewing habits of one Mario J. Lanza. Because all of a sudden there was this new show that was different from ANYTHING that had ever been seen before on American TV. In fact, not only was it different, it actually had a lot of real life psychological and sociological applicability, which is something that a show like Friends could never possibly have.

I mean, as much as I loved Friends, it was still only a sitcom. A well written sitcom, sure. But it could never possibly be as fascinating as this new kid on the block called Survivor. Survivor was so much more interesting, and was so much deeper, and was so incredibly new and unique, that Friends... as much as I loved it... well it dropped down very quickly to now being my second favorite TV show.

By the way, I should probably point out that Survivor became the first ever non comedy show in my life that I ever really obsessed over. And, if you know me, you will know that that was no small feat. Normally I get bored very easily by anything that isn't a comedy.

This is why I could never really get into a show like J.J. Abrams' Lost. I was completely zoned out of Lost by the second episode. And I never really could get back into it either. That has always happened with anything I have ever watched on TV that isn't a comedy. No matter how good a show might be, no matter how well written it might be, if I am not laughing on a consistent basis I am usually not all that interested in it.

> **Side note**: This is the exact same way I make friends too. Make me laugh and I will find you interesting. Ever since I was a kid, I have always been like that. I have always interpreted "sense of humor" to equal "personality." This is 100% consistent among pretty much anyone I have ever been friends with.

Now, normally, having two shows that I loved so much (Friends and Survivor) wouldn't necessarily be a problem. After all, Survivor was on Wednesdays, and Friends was on Thursdays. At this point they didn't really invade upon one another's turf. At this point I could still tell <u>both</u> of my girlfriends that they were the prettiest.

Sure, Friends might have been the #1 sitcom juggernaut on TV. And sure, Survivor might have been the single most watched new phenomenon in television history. But you could still watch both of them and still claim to be a fan of both of them because they were on different nights. You didn't have to choose between the two best shows on TV yet. No problem.

Well, as you can imagine, this soon did become a problem. At least for me it did.

Because a few weeks after Survivor became the biggest freaking cultural event in American television history (seriously, I can't possibly overstate how huge that Borneo finale was), Mark Burnett and CBS decided to play hardball with American's beloved #1 sitcom.

Survivor Borneo ended. The Survivor sequel (Australia) was announced. 50 million people rejoiced.

And then Mark Burnett pointed his crooked finger at Thursday night and he made a proclamation. He said, "Give me Thursdays at 8:00. I am taking down Friends."

And wow.

This was a very bold move.

I will never forget where I was when I first heard that Survivor was moving to Thursdays at 8:00. In fact, the phrase "Holy shiiiitttttttt" probably wouldn't be quite strong enough.

Are you kidding me? Survivor had been a huge smash hit, sure. Yes, it had drawn 50 million viewers for its finale, of course. But taking on Friends? The #1 sitcom in America?? The show that was not only more beloved than Seinfeld, but that got about twice the ratings of Seinfeld??? Um, are you sure you really want to be doing that?

Of course, most people in the media assumed that Survivor was just going to be a flash in the pan. The common wisdom at the time (among magazines, websites, basically just about everyone) was that Burnett and CBS had had one good season, true, and Survivor had had a good run while it was new and it was popular. But a lot of that had probably just been timing and luck. Even before Australia aired in February of 2001, Survivor was already being viewed by the media as little more than just a bright shiny comet that everyone admires and oohs and aahs over for a while, but eventually just fizzles out and crashes into the ocean and everyone forgets about.

The common wisdom at the time was that Burnett and Survivor had now officially bitten off more than they could chew. Because seriously, taking on Friends? Voluntarily? In what universe was that going to work out for anyone?

For me, of course, this now became an enormous problem. Because now I was going to have to CHOOSE? Between my two favorite children? Why not just kick me in the nuts?? Because remember, this was a few years before most people had anything called a DVR. If two shows were on at the exact same time, you would only be able to watch one of them.

Of course, if you know my history, and you know how I eventually became a Survivor writer, you can probably guess which direction I went. I went with Survivor. I took my very favorite sitcom of its era, Friends, and I waved bye bye and I told it to politely go away. And I told Monica to go eat a sandwich because she was starting to look anorexic.

I mean, seriously, how could you not choose Survivor in that situation? How could you not admire the balls on a guy like Mark Burnett, who was so confident about the future of his show that he basically gave the middle finger to the #1 show on TV and he told NBC to eat him?

I don't know about you but I always thought that bravado was pretty awesome.

99% of the producers on TV never would have voluntarily gone head to head against Friends. But Burnett wasn't like that. He had the confidence (not to mention the showmanship) to take on the biggest scariest juggernaut on network TV, and I loved it. I especially loved it because it now set the stage for easily my favorite TV showdown of the past thirty years. Friends vs. Survivor. The sitcom vs. the reality show. At this point you could no longer claim to be a fan of them both. You had to pick one or the other. It was like asking a kid in the 60's to pick between The Beatles and The Rolling Stones. Go ahead, pick one. Pick your favorite, and stick with it. But pick wisely.

In the end, as much as the media expected (and probably hoped) that Survivor and reality TV would wind up being crushed by brazenly going head to head against Friends, what happened in the ratings was actually the opposite. Survivor not only did well its second season, it actually thrived. The ratings for Survivor: The Australian Outback actually went UP.

Meanwhile Friends (which had basically been unchallenged for about four years) sort of lost its hold as "the most beloved show" of its era. Survivor cut into a good chunk of its audience, Friends started a slow death spiral into becoming just another popular but gimmicky sitcom, and within about a year Friends completely changed its writing style and started having all its main characters begin to hook up with one another.

Joey started dating Rachel. Monica started dating Phoebe. Rachel had an affair with the cameraman. I think Ross might have had a four-way at some point with Tom Selleck, fat naked guy, and Marcel the monkey. It was ridiculous.

During its last season, I remember tuning into Friends for the first time in a couple of years. I watched a couple of episodes, and I remember thinking, "What the hell happened to this show that I used to love? What happened to all the comedy? Why is everyone just dating each other? Why is it all just a big dumb romance novel now?"

So anyway, now of course we come to the big question. Did Survivor single handedly kill Friends?

I have no way to prove that it did. I mean, Friends was probably on three or four seasons too long as it was. Maybe it is natural that it would have eventually turned into a parody of itself. Maybe that's just what happens to all successful non Seinfeld sitcoms. Maybe they all turn into a joke after about their fifth season.

All I know for sure is that Survivor decided to take on Friends head to head starting in Australia. And not only did Survivor have its single most successful season ever, it pretty handily trounced Friends for most of that first year. It was amazing. Even hardcore media watchers and TV bloggers were surprised that Survivor had that kind of staying power. Believe me, I just went back on the internet and I re-read some news articles from that time period. Almost no one in 2001 expected that Survivor would be able to hold its own against Friends. No one! It was just this new little reality TV fad that kept on going and going and going.

Even though Survivor usually beat it in the ratings (at least prior to 9/11 it did), Friends remained a top 10 show for the duration of its run. And it had an enormous finale that drew 50+ million viewers in 2004. But I will always say that Friends was forever tarnished the minute that Survivor started stealing its audience.

The minute the #1 sitcom in America was knocked off its beloved high perch, it got gimmicky, the humor got more forced, it totally turned into a shell of what it originally was. It also destroyed what I thought at the time was a pretty good legacy. I know this probably sounds like a stretch, but had Survivor not taken it down, I have no doubt that Friends would be considered the single most beloved sitcom of the past 30 years. And I don't think it would even be close.

Instead, most people remember Friends as a show that was great at first, but then ran out of steam its last couple of seasons. In other words, "It was good, but it wasn't quite as good as Seinfeld."

Again, was this Survivor's fault? Who knows. It's fun to think that it was, but maybe it wasn't. Maybe Friends just wasn't all that great to begin with.

All I know for sure is that there is no way you can talk about the history of Survivor without talking about its intertwined history with Friends. The two shows will always be inexorably linked because they went head to head with one another.

Oh yeah, and if you ever hear old school Survivor fans laugh at the phrase, "Move Survivor back to its original night on Thursdays!" well now you know why they think that's funny. Survivor didn't start on Thursdays. It started on Wednesdays. It only moved to Thursdays because CBS and Mark Burnett wanted to lay the smackdown on Friends.

31. That Crocodile Promo

If you were to ask me at what point in history do I think Survivor was the biggest it ever got, I would say it was around episode six of Australia. To me I have always considered that to be "the peak" of Survivor. And I say that, of course, because I will always remember that week as being the single most talked about time period in the history of Survivor. Well, okay, except for maybe the twist episode in Africa. But we will get to that later.

Do you have any guesses why Australia episode six had so many people talking about it?

Well here is a little backstory for you.

At the end of episode five of Australia (which featured one of the all-time most underrated Survivor moments, Ogakor coming back to win immunity in the maze), we got a preview of episode six during the "Next time on Survivor..." segment. It featured a crocodile sliding off a branch into the water. And a man screaming in pain. And then Elisabeth crying as somebody on Kucha was medevaced in a helicopter.

And... wow.

Holy crap.

I suppose it goes without saying that there had never been ANYTHING like this promo on Survivor up to this point. Hell, through the first season and a half of this show no one had gotten so much as an injury. And then this? A mysterious promo for episode six, where somebody apparently gets attacked by a crocodile and is forced to leave the game? Featuring ominous music and a crying Elisabeth?

Again, yikes. Survivor just pulled an Emeril Lagasse. Survivor just decided to kick things up a notch.

I will always remember where I was when I saw that crocodile promo for the first time. It just hit you like a punch in the gut. I mean, the entire thing was all just so ominous. And there had been no hint during episode five that anything bad was about to happen to one of the players, that was the worst part. There had been no warning that this was coming at all. We were just the same old happy Survivor fan base that we had always been, and we were happily enjoying the second season of our favorite TV show. And then BAM, out of nowhere comes this scary ass promo. And that was it. No warning. No names. No details. No faces. Nothing. Just a quick shot of a crocodile and then a man screaming. That was all you got. Like I said before, it was one of those moments in your life that if you were really into Survivor like I was, you will always remember where you were the first time you saw it.

Again, keep in mind that this was a period in time when there were still very few spoilers floating around out there on the internet. Survivor wasn't yet the bootlist-happy internet joke that it would later turn into. In March of 2001 most viewers really didn't know what was going to happen on the show. All we knew was what CBS told us in the promos, and that was about it.

As you can guess, most people had no idea that something ominous was about to happen in Australia. There had been no lead ups to this in the first five episodes. There had been no foreshadowing, there had been no warnings, there had been no weird sad story arcs. There had been nothing. Survivor had just been chugging along like it always had, and Kucha had been kicking Ogakor's ass, and everything had been right in the world.

And then this. That damn crocodile promo.

That scream.

The crying.

Survivor would never really be the same after this.

I remember basically running onto the internet after that stupid crocodile promo aired for the first time, and trying to see if anyone out there had any more details they could share. Because what the hell was about to happen on Survivor? What the hell did I just see? Was somebody going to actually die out there? Why hadn't we been warned this was coming ahead of time?

And who was it going to happen to? Who was that scream? Was it Mike?

As you can imagine, the message boards were FLOODED with people posting their theories about the promo that night. Just absolutely flooded. Like I said, I don't think there has ever been another episode of Survivor that has ever had that kind of a buzz behind it. All you saw all over the internet that night were people asking about that promo. And discussing which player they thought was going to be eaten by a crocodile.

Side note: I know this whole thing sounds silly now, since Survivor viewers are so much more editing savvy now than they were fifteen years ago. But there really WAS a crocodile in that promo, and that is exactly the one thing that everyone latched onto. Now, as to why CBS decided to put a crocodile at the beginning of that clip (despite a crocodile having nothing to do with the accident at all), well you can take your best guess. All that promo really did for me in the end was drive home the fact that editing is something like 90% of your perception if you are a Survivor viewer. After all, if the editors want you to think that somebody was attacked by a crocodile, it isn't that hard to do. All you need to do is insert a quick random jump cut. Let everyone's imagination take over from there.

By the way, this is a very important lesson to learn if you are a Survivor fan. The show has always been about 90% editing. Learn it. Live it. Accept it. Love it. It took me a long time to accept that fact for myself, but believe me, things are a heck of a lot easier when you finally admit it. The editors have always been the true MVPs of the Survivor franchise.

When I got onto the internet that night, and I checked out the fan "chatter", of course the most popular theory among most people was that somebody on Kucha was going to be attacked by a crocodile. And, naturally, since Mike Skupin was a known psychopath who had already had an encounter with a feral pig, he seemed like he would be the obvious choice. The pieces and the editing all fit. Mike was about to be ripped apart by a crocodile in the sixth episode of Survivor.

And then, of course, I heard an alternate theory.

"I heard...," which is the way that all great rumors start, by the way, "...that Rodger had to be evacuated from the game. I heard he was riding a horse during a challenge and he fell off and he broke his collarbone."

I don't remember who first posted the "Rodger breaks his collarbone" rumor, but the minute that one hit the internet, man, now it was all over the place too. Somebody apparently heard from a friend of a friend that the old guy on Kucha was medevaced after breaking his collarbone.

Then someone else posted that they had heard it too.

Then of course the ever-popular game of "telephone" started up.

174

Now it seemed like everyone had heard it.

Within about two days, that stupid Rodger rumor was all over the place. Suddenly everyone on the internet was talking about the Rodger collarbone injury as if it were fact.

"Why else would they show Elisabeth crying?" somebody wrote. "It is obviously Rodger. Did you notice he wasn't even in the promo? Elisabeth is crying because she is the closest to him."

"Yeah but why would they have Mike screaming in the promo?" somebody else would rebut. "That is obviously Mike's voice. Why would they include that if it wasn't Mike who gets hurt?"

The "Mike gets attacked by a crocodile" versus "Rodger falls off a horse and breaks his collarbone" debate raged on for an entire week. And I am not kidding, it was everywhere. EVERYONE on the Survivor message boards was dying to know what was going to happen in episode six of Australia. And CBS didn't help matters at all because they weren't giving anything away. They didn't show us any promos that week that gave away any information. Everything was a mystery. And because of this incredible secrecy, Australia episode six wound up easily being the least spoiled-- and the most anticipated-- Survivor episode after the Borneo finale. I can't imagine there were more than a handful of people out there who knew exactly what was going to happen and who exactly it was going to happen to.

Like I said, to me, this will always be the "biggest" that Survivor ever got. It was literally more than just a TV show for about a week. Even non Survivor fans were sort of interested in this episode.

By the way, since I know you are curious, yes there were several other theories that were being thrown around on the internet before episode six of Australia aired on TV (including one about Nick being the one who was injured, which obviously worried me a lot.) But almost all of these alternate theories involved Mike. He just seemed like the most logical choice to get hurt. And almost all of the theories involved that stupid crocodile.

The crocodile theory made so much sense, in fact, and it seemed to fit Mike's overall storyline so well, that I probably would have bet money at the time that he was going to go out due to a crocodile injury. To me, that just seemed like the most logical outcome.

As for the Rodger/collarbone theory? Well I never believed in that particular rumor. I mean come on, riding a horse? Since when do they ride horses on Survivor? Why would they have people riding horses during a challenge? That just sounded stupid. To me, that rumor (no matter how many people claimed it was true) was as dumb as the other big one at the time, which was that Steve Irwin, "The Crocodile Hunter", was going to make a cameo in a couple of episode of Australia. TONS of people seemed to believe that stupid rumor at the time too, but I never did. Why would Survivor need Steve Irwin? And why would Steve Irwin even care?

You know, thinking back, I specifically remember the "Steve Irwin will appear on Survivor" story being reported on several mainstream media outlets. I remember USA Today even writing about it. People really did believe that he was going to be a major part of Survivor: The Australian Outback. Hard to believe in retrospect, isn't it?

Oh yeah, there was one other theory that was floating around that week about the injury in episode six. This one wasn't as widely discussed as some of the other ones, but I do remember hearing about it.

Apparently some Survivor fan on the internet had run across a picture of Mike Skupin that had just been taken a couple of weeks ago. It had been posted on the internet in somebody's private photo album, and this random Survivor fan (whoever he was) had just stumbled across it.

In the picture, Mike had his arm slung around a friend's shoulder.

And Mike's left hand was wrapped up in a burn glove

Somebody from the Survivor fan community found this picture, of course, and they posted it on Survivor Sucks. And then they asked, "Hey, what about this picture? What if Mike hurts his hands? What if his hands get burned or something?"

I have to admit, I heard the "Mike burns his hands" theory once or twice before episode six aired. I even saw the picture. But I never thought in a million years that it would actually be true. Because seriously, burned hands? Who would get medevaced for burned hands? And if you burned your hands why would everyone be crying about it?

The famous "Mike with his hand in a burn glove" picture would eventually go down in history as the first really big unintentional internet spoiler. But most of us didn't realize that at the time. Like I said, even though I saw the picture, I still didn't think it really meant anything. All it showed to me was that Mike didn't die (which, of course, was at least some good news.) He wasn't dead, and he probably hurt his hand back home when he was trying to slaughter a deer or something. With Mike that always seemed like a pretty good possibility.

At the time, I was still willing to bet that Mike was going to be attacked by a crocodile. And that it was going to be ugly. And that it was going to culminate in one of the most jaw dropping memorable episodes of Survivor.

Okay, so I was wrong about the crocodile part. Mike didn't get attacked by a crocodile. Obviously. At least not on that day. And not that we ever saw on camera.

But as for episode six being "jaw dropping" and "memorable", well yeah, I was pretty damn close.

32. Do The Dew, Baby!

I have been sitting here for about a week, thinking about how I wanted to write about the Mike falls into the fire episode of Australia.

The reason I have been holding off writing this chapter for so long is because I wanted to make sure I had an outline in my head before I actually sat down to write it. I wanted my recap to be perfect. Because to me, the Mike episode has always deserved that kind of reverence. To me, I would probably call Australia episode six the single greatest episode in Survivor history.

Yeah, I know. I'm sitting here calling an episode where a guy falls into the fire and almost dies "amazing TV." Way to be thoughtful and sensitive, douchebag. But I am being totally serious. If the world ended today, and future historians came back in 200 years and dug up a time capsule of all our television shows from the 2000's, I think the Mike/fire episode is the Survivor episode that they would be the most impressed by. They would probably even start quoting Nick's amazing catchphrase of "He's burned. He's burned pretty bad, Terry" like 99% of America was doing back in March of 2001.

Okay I'm joking. No one was actually quoting Nick back in 2001. That is more of an inside Survivor Sucks joke. I have no idea why, but people on Sucks have been referencing Nick's weird little "He's burned pretty bad, Terry" quote for more than a decade and a half now. Probably because, aside from me, that is the only thing that most Survivor fans actually remember about Nick. They remember that he saw Mike getting burned, and that he correctly identified that Mike was "burned pretty bad." Oh, and that somebody named "Terry" may or may not have been involved.

Side note: Most people also forget that Nick was the person who helped Mike on his infamous pig hunt. Nick was the guy who cornered the pig so Mike could get his knife and he could go all stabby on it. Yeah, guess Nick wasn't so invisible after all, now was he? Nick Brown had a direct part in arguably the two most memorable moments in Australia.

It's just a shame that Alicia couldn't have wagged her finger in Nick's face instead of Kimmi's face, because then he would have participated in all three incidents in the Holy Kucha Trifecta.

Where was I? Oh yeah, back to Mike.

Like I said, I know it is kind of disrespectful to say that the Mike episode was amazing TV. I know that, and I fully admit it. But if you are a Survivor fan, what else do you want to see on this show? You want to see gripping drama, you want to see memorable events, and you want to see things you have never seen before on TV. Oh, and you also want to see something that every Survivor fan in the world will be talking about later that night on the internet.

And I have to say, the Mike episode definitely fits all four of those criteria. It is the one episode in Survivor history that I can watch over and over and over, and I will never get tired of.

Which is nice, because I have probably already watched it more than fifty times in my life.

I am not going to sit here and recap the entire Mike falls into the fire episode, because I know that everyone who is reading this book probably already knows that episode inside and out. But what I WOULD like to talk about is something that most people probably DON'T remember about that episode. Because there is one aspect of Australia episode six that I think most Survivor fans (even the most obsessive ones) tend to forget about.

Okay, you ready? Just put aside the whole ending of episode six for now. Just forget about Mike falling into the fire and forget about the whole Kucha love/sob fest afterwards. Forget about Bizarro Amber dropping an "Oh my god, it's sooooo bad" when she reads about what happened to Mike (one of the great underrated Australia moments, by the way.) Don't worry, there will be time for all that. We will get back to all of those later.

What I would like to talk about is the episode six reward challenge.

Yes that's right. In an episode where a guy almost died, I would first like to focus on the reward challenge. I would like you to focus your attention on something that actually happened BEFORE Mike fell into the fire.

Why?

Well the reason I ask you to think about the episode six reward challenge is because, to me, this could be the single greatest challenge in Survivor history. Seriously, if you sat me down in a room and put a gun to my head, and told me to come up with the single most exciting challenge in Survivor history, I wouldn't even have to sit there for more than five seconds. I already know the answer. I would pick either Australia episode six (the blindfolded Doritos challenge), or the reward challenge in Marquesas where Kathy and Gina come back to out row John and the General (episode six, I think?).

As you may have just noticed, the Australia episode six reward challenge is the one that I like to call the "blindfolded Doritos challenge." This was the challenge where Nick and Jerri had to lead their blindfolded tribesmates through a series of obstacles. And then at the end of the challenge the winning tribe got a picnic of Mountain Dew and Doritos.

First of all, this was a horrible reward. Chips and soda, are you kidding me? For starving castaways? What about hot dogs on this particular picnic? What about hamburgers? Who goes on a picnic and just eats Doritos??

Secondly, I always love how Jerri immediately gets in a plug for Mountain Dew the minute that Jeff announces what the reward is going to be. Jeff says "Mountain Dew" and Jerri immediately screams out "Do the dew, baby!!!" I love the fact that if there was one person in the cast who immediately knew her response was going to be shown on TV (because she blatantly plugged the sponsor), it would be Jerri. Yes, no one on Survivor was ever more media savvy than our dear young friend Ms. Jerri Manthey.

Oh yeah and thirdly, since Tina was involved, I really shouldn't be calling it the blindfolded Doritos challenge. I really should just call it "Blindfolded DurEEEEtose." Again, just one more reason why I love Tina. Her random and quirky worship of DurEEEEtose.

So anyway, here you have this challenge with a simple premise, and a stupid reward, yet it somehow turns out to be the single most exciting challenge in Survivor history.

The Ogakors surge ahead at first. They lead for the entire challenge. But then... inexplicably... and unexpectedly... Amber totally chokes at the end and the Kuchas come back out of nowhere to steal the win. And then Colby gets pissed at Jerri for losing the challenge and he tosses a bucket of water in her face.

Awesome. What more could you ask for?

Seriously, I could watch this challenge a hundred times and I will never get tired of it. Ever. I will also think that Ogakor is going to win every single damn time. You could watch this challenge over and over and over and STILL never see that Kucha win coming, even on the 101st viewing. The ending is that sudden and it is that exciting.

Oh and then you have Rodger's awesome tagline at the end of the scene. He walks over to his screaming teammates, who are now celebrating their victory and doing war whoops, and he calmly (I don't know how he stayed calm) observes, "You all have no idea how close that was."

God bless Rodger. I love Rodger.

And so there you go. Lost in all the greatness of Australia episode six (because the ending really is great) is the fact that it also has probably my all-time favorite Survivor challenge. The Kucha blindfolded DurEEEEtose challenge has got to be one of the ten most exciting moments in Survivor history. Like I said earlier, among challenges, only the Marquesas Kathy/Gina rowing comeback probably even comes close.

What I guess I am trying to say here is please don't overlook this awesome moment in an already awesome episode when you sit down and you think about Australia. I know that it has become fashionable nowadays to trash Australia, and to call it "a boring season." And to say it was dull because "it was a boring Pagonging" and "it just had a bunch of smug self-righteous ultra-religious dull people left at the end."

I get that, and I don't necessarily disagree with any of it.

What I AM saying is that the first six Australia episodes are not like that at all. The first six Australia episodes prior to the merge are all AWESOME. In fact Australia is the one Survivor season, more so than any of the other ones, that it is as if the first half and the second half are almost entirely different seasons. The first six Australia episodes are awesome, and then the last eight Australia episodes are a snoozefest. And it's a shame too, because if Australia had had any sort of momentum down the stretch, just any little momentum at all, I would have no problem calling it probably the all-time greatest Survivor season. The first six episodes are that good.

Unfortunately, as great as episode six was (and we will get to Mike falling into the fire in a second), it also marked the turning point of the season.

Sadly what was the best moment of the season also turned out to be the worst moment of the season.

Yep, you guessed it.   We're here.

It is finally time to talk about Mike's accident.

P.S. Oh yeah and look what we have here   Nick Brown was the caller
leading the Kuchas in the single best challenge in Survivor history (by the end
of the challenge he had been yelling so much that he even lost his voice.)
That is now THREE huge Australia moments that he had a significant part
in.   So suck on that, all you Nick haters. Nick Brown wasn't invisible. Nick
Brown was everywhere!

33. We Are One, We Are Kucha

Over the past fifteen years, there have really been about three different distinct types of Survivor episodes.

The first type of episode is the mundane episode. There are the episodes where Survivor is really basically just going through the motions (i.e., pretty much seasons 21-28). This sort of Survivor episode can be fun, sure, but in general nothing really memorable ever happens in a mundane episode. This would just be your typical sixty minutes of Survivor on a Wednesday. Nothing less. Nothing more.

Then there is the second type of episode - the exciting episode. These are the episodes where Survivor is really exciting and unpredictable and memorable and good. Think the Rupert boot episode in Pearl Islands, or the first episode of Amazon. Or the episode that I think is the funniest Survivor episode of all time, the Heroes vs. Villains premiere. These episodes are very fun to watch, they can be particularly memorable or noteworthy or exciting, and they are often (and very rightfully) categorized as being among the all-time best Survivor episodes.

And then, finally, there is the third type of episode. The special one. These are those hallowed Survivor episodes that rise above everything else and are just completely transcendent. This is that special category of episodes in Survivor history that are so memorable, and are so emotional, and are just so much larger than life (to the point that you often remember where you were the first time that you saw them) that I have always called these special episodes the "holy shit!" episodes.

These are the episodes that when you watch them on TV, they are so outstanding that you immediately hop onto the internet afterwards to see what everyone is saying about them.

What I have always loved about Survivor (as well as good unscripted TV in general - think The Amazing Race when it is really working well) is that it is one of the few shows on television that can actually produce "holy shit!" moments on a fairly regular basis.

Seriously, say what you want to say about how reality TV sucks, and how it is all manufactured and artificial, and how it is ruining network TV by killing actors' and writers' careers, blah blah blah. I don't care. All I care about is that the highs on Survivor are REALLY high. In fact, I would say that Survivor's highs are much higher than just about any other show I have ever watched on TV, with the exception of maybe something like Mystery Science Theater 3000 or Saturday Night Live. Those are two other shows where you often have to wade through a lot of crap just to get to the good stuff. But people will do that (they still do it with SNL and Survivor), because every so often a show like that will pull off an unbelievably transcendent moment that no other traditional show on TV ever would have been able to pull off.

This has always been the magic behind Saturday Night Live, and this has also always been the magic behind Survivor. There is a reason that both shows have now been on TV for longer than 30+ seasons and both of them still have a very loyal and forgiving audience. They survive because-- no matter how much crap you have to wade through when the show is bad -- they both have the ability to still amaze you every once in a while. And because of their unique formats, and the way they always have cast turnover, they always will.

When I think back to Survivor over the years, the most fitting thing I can say about it as a TV show is that when Survivor is good, it is AMAZING. When it is clicking right it is easily the best show on TV. But when it isn't so good (aka the going through the motions seasons) it still isn't actually even all that bad. Even the weakest Survivor season is still more interesting than 75% of the rest of the crap on TV. And the reason it is always interesting is because the general setup of Survivor is just inherently interesting.

Unfortunately (and now we come to the downside of Survivor's success) this interesting format (people being voted out, backstabbing, lying, social politics) is both Survivor's blessing as well as its curse. Because no matter how lazy the Survivor producers tend to get (and they do get lazy), no matter how obviously they are just going through the motions at times, it doesn't really matter in the end because the show still works and they will still always manage to pull in top 20 ratings. In other words, even though they still manage to produce "holy shit!" episodes every once in a while, there is really very little incentive for a Survivor producer to actually try to do this. They don't have to put in the extra effort like other shows do because they will still pull in the ratings and the fans and the ad revenue no matter what. And they know this. No matter how much the producers tweak the game, or change the casting process, or make changes to the format, or piss off the audience, they know that the audience is always going to be there for them and they will always be loyal to the show, no questions asked.

Again, what works for Survivor is also what has always hindered it. The producers can basically do whatever they want (like ignoring applicants and only casting friends of the casting department, or adding nonsense to the game like The Medallion of Power or five hundred different hidden immunity idols, or casting Russell Hantz three out of every four seasons) and they know that we are sheep and we are still all going to tune in to watch no matter what.

By the way, I have always believed that this lack of a critical fanbase is what is going to eventually lead to the end of Survivor. Obviously it hasn't happened yet, but I suspect that it probably will happen one of these days. After all, no show can go on forever. At some point in time the producers will get bored, the players will stop caring, and the audience will eventually switch over to a newer, trendier, less intelligent show like Wipeout.

Relax, it hasn't happened yet. Survivor is still here. But the writing is on the wall. The warning signs are there. Better get ready for it one of these days, it is going to happen.

Side note: Comedian Sam Kinison used to have a joke about McDonald's that I have always thought also applied pretty well to the Survivor producers.

Kinison used to joke that McDonald's was so successful, and their audience was so loyal, that whenever McDonald's was bored they would just mess with everyone and do experiments to see what America would pay to eat.

"I love this new thing they just came up with, the McRib," Kinison joked in 1990. "Have you seen this piece of shit? Yeah, now you can tell that McDonald's is just fucking with us. Now you can tell that they're bored. You can see them up in their boardrooms, just laughing at us: "Hey, I know. How about we take shit, and we put it on a fucking bun? How about that, the McShit. Let's see if people will pay to eat that."

To me this is a very apt parallel (albeit exaggerated) to what has happened to Survivor over the past fifteen years. It is still a good and watchable show, of course. But man has the focus of this show changed over the past 15+ years. It is really not even the same product anymore. Basically what happened is that too much success + a completely uncritical and undemanding audience + massive ratings no matter what the producers do = Survivor basically became McDonald's.

185

In other words, from time to time now it seems like they are just messing with us. Now they really have nothing better to do. A season based around "Hey I know, let's have Boston Rob fight Russell!" is basically just the Survivor equivalent of "Hey let's see if people will eat the McShit!"

Sorry, got stuck on a little tangent there.

The reason I bring up the three different types of Survivor episodes (going through the motions, exciting TV, and holy crap transcendent bigger-than-TV life moments) is because the Mike episode definitely falls into that third category. In fact not only does it fall into the third category, in my opinion it is pretty much the KING of the third category. To me the Mike falling into the fire episode was even more transcendent than the finale of Borneo. In my opinion Survivor never really got any better than this.

Like most of the great Survivor episodes over the years, I will always remember where I was and what I was doing when I first saw the infamous Mike episode. I was sitting in my living room and my twelve month old daughter was throwing a temper tantrum on the floor.

The only reason I remember that is because, to this day, my wife is still annoyed about the fact that I chose to watch Mike fall into the fire that night over helping her out with the baby. Which I feel bad about, of course. But I'm sorry. This was an important episode. Kucha needed Mike to stay in the majority!

Man, I remember every little detail about the Mike accident. In particular, I remember the reactions of the Kuchas afterwards, and just how shell-shocked they all were. I mean, you can talk about reality TV being fake all you want, and you can talk about how artificial it is. But the whole second half of the Mike episode was most definitely NOT fake. Some guy fell face first into a fire, his hands were almost burned completely off, and then his friends went into shock on national TV.

Seriously, if you ever want to see what a shock victim looks like in real life, go back and watch Elisabeth the last twenty minutes of episode six. THAT is what somebody in shock looks like. The poor girl was essentially shell-shocked.

In fact, this episode was so real and so gritty that it almost makes me feel guilty even writing about it.

186

So many memories of being a Survivor fan are locked into my mind from this episode. They are just seared in there permanently, as if I only watched it for the first time today. But I didn't. In fact, I haven't watched this episode in more than four years. Everything I am saying right now is just right off the top of my head.

I remember how 95% of the internet hated Jerri even more after Mike's accident than they had already hated her before (which was hard to do.) And the reason for that was because most fans on the internet felt that "Jerri didn't seem sad enough when she got the news about Mike." All around the internet the next day, you saw things like "I don't believe Jerri was sad for a minute, it seemed she was only acting sad for the cameras." It was ridiculous. Most people already hated Jerri prior to the Mike incident, and then they seemed to hate her even MORE after the Mike incident. And Jerri didn't even have anything to do with it!

I remember how everyone on Ogakor assumed that something bad had happened to Rodger. I remember that the note they received from the producers had been almost cruelly vague, it didn't tell them anything. So the Ogakors all assumed that something bad had happened to Rodger because of his age. In fact, I can still hear the gasp that Tina let out when somebody suggested that Rodger might have suffered a heart attack.

I remember the haters of reality TV, and the haters of Survivor in general, who insisted at the time that "a producer must have pushed" Mike into the fire. You think I am making that up, but I'm not. Even back in 2001 there was a belief (especially among the vocal anti-Survivor people in the media) that the producers would have actually pushed a guy into the fire and filmed it instead of rescuing him. In fact, I remember Mark Burnett took a lot of flak over this because the cameraman actually DID film footage of Mike after the accident. A lot of people felt that CBS never should have filmed the incident at all, and that they certainly never should have shown any of the footage on TV. In fact I bet a lot of people still think that.

I remember Elisabeth's really good and really long speech about what Mike looked like and what he was saying to the Kuchas as he was being loaded into the helicopter. I love that speech. In fact, to this day, that might be my all-time favorite Survivor confessional that doesn't involve Coach. If Elisabeth wasn't yet "the new America's Sweetheart" (and she wasn't really; to me she was always just a more manufactured version of Colleen), she came awfully close to becoming America's New Sweetheart after that particular confessional. That was the speech that made a lot of people fall in love with her. If you haven't seen it in a while, go find it on YouTube.

I remember Jeff Varner's speech about how the Kuchas were going to win this game now in Mike's honor. And how the five of them were going to chew Ogakor up and spit 'em out, "because that's what Mike what would have wanted." Like Elisabeth's, that was just another great speech. For at least five minutes of his life, Jeff Varner actually became one of the Survivor good guys.

I remember the scene where Rodger gathered the Kuchas around in a circle and they all said a prayer. And they made a promise to stick together to the end in honor of Mike. Great moment.

And this, of course, leads me into what I will always remember the most about Australia episode six.

What I will always remember the most about the Mike falls into the fire episode, which unfortunately is something that I don't think anyone will understand unless they were there and they actually "lived through it" at the time like I did, was how unbelievably unified everyone in the Survivor fan community was at that particular moment.

For the first time in Survivor history-- indeed, probably the ONLY time in Survivor history-- nearly every single person who either watched the show, who was a contestant on the show, who wrote about the show, or who was a fan of the show, was on the exact same page. Every single person who loved and cared about this show (except for probably the five members of Ogakor) was probably thinking the exact same thing as the credits started to roll at the end of the episode.

Something like 99.99% of the Survivor fan base at that moment was thinking, "Win this, Kucha. One of you has to win this thing for Mike now."

It was chilling to experience that. I have never seen any other point in Survivor history where the show and the players and the fans and the editing were all aligned so perfectly in the exact same direction. It was like it was a sign from God that we were all supposed to be rooting for Kucha now. And keep in mind, this is coming from a guy who isn't even the slightest bit religious. This is coming from an atheist. This was one of those special almost spiritual moments in my life that I will never forget.

And yes, this means that for some of us, Survivor can actually be more than a TV show.

Of course you know what happened next. This weird "aligning of the stars" at the end of episode six (where everyone and their mother was pretty much rooting for the Kuchas) is precisely why Australia is such a frustrating season if you are an old school Survivor fan. Because the producers and the editors and the Kuchas had a picture perfect storyline for what probably would have been the greatest single Survivor season of all time. Everything was aligned exactly the way it should have been for a Kucha to win. And then, of course, it all fell apart the very next episode and the Ogakors took over the game.

sigh

Just another reason why reality TV is interesting, I guess.

The highs are very high. The lows aren't very low.

And it never works out exactly the way the producers hope it will work out.

P.S. Remember when I said that there is almost no doubt that some of the first season of Survivor was manipulated? Well here is some pretty good evidence that the second season in Australia was most definitely NOT manipulated.

If you can, try to convince me why the producers would have built up episode six as such a big Kucha lovefest, and then had Kucha lose and been systematically dismantled over the next five episodes. Go ahead, try to tell me how they would have wanted that to happen. I double dog dare you.

Actually never mind. You can't convince me of that, because it's impossible. There is no way you can convince me in any way, shape, or form that what happened in Australia was what the producers wanted to happen. Especially after watching the Mike episode.

What I think happened is this. My guess is that the producers... well we will say they "fudged"... some of the rules in the first season, and they got busted for it. They got caught. So they tried not to fudge anything in Australia, out of fear of being caught again, and look what happened. You wound up with a picture perfect Kucha win storyline being yanked away because the producers screwed up. Remember what happened behind the scenes in

189

episode two? The producers forgot to keep the tribes separated and they forgot to keep the players from mingling before the waterfall challenge. And because of that little producer screw up, because the people in charge had simply forgotten to pay attention for a couple of minutes, the Ogakors knew that Kucha's Jeff Varner had received a stray vote at the end of episode one. And they later used that information to their advantage. Which was the main reason that the Kuchas lost.

Think the producers were very happy that the season played out that way? I don't.

I think they were pissed.

After the second season ended, I think the producers thought long and hard about how they wanted to handle this. I think they sat down as a group and they said to themselves, hmmm, okay, so after Australia ends, then now what? How do we get around this little problem once we get to the third season? Because it really was a problem. How could the producers manage to push the game in a certain direction if they really needed to (which you know they would have loved to do with the Kuchas)? And, more importantly, if they wanted to push the game in a certain direction, and they needed to do so, how could they do it effectively without being busted for it like they had been in Borneo?

And that was when I think the answer finally came to them.

Hey I know! We will introduce a "twist!" Yeah, and we will start using it in season three!

And hey, guess what. The great thing about a twist is that we will be able to use it whenever we feel like it. We can just throw one in whenever we don't like the direction that a particular storyline is headed. Yeah, and best of all, nobody will ever be able to call us on it! If anybody ever tries to bust us for throwing in a twist, we will just be able to say sorry man, it was planned. It was always planned to happen that day. My God, this new twist plan is foolproof! It is ironclad! It is going to be perfect!

Don't worry, we will be talking more about this soon. The introduction of (and the meaning behind) the first twist is a big moment in Survivor history.

I know we are going to have fun with it.

34. Blabbermouth

In my last chapter I talked about how Survivor: The Australian Outback was a great example of how unscripted TV can be awesome, and how it can also suck at the exact same time.

At no point in Survivor history was this more evident than in episode seven of Australia.

Remember, because of the awesomeness of the last episode, what you had going into the merge was basically an entire fan base solidified behind the idea that the Kuchas were going to come back now and they were going to "win it for their leader." Seriously, if I invented a time machine and I went back to March of 2001, I doubt I could find one hardcore fan or even one casual Survivor fan at the time who was rooting for the Ogakors at this point. Up and down the fan base, all over the internet, everything you heard from anyone now was "rally for Mike" or "win it for Mike." Or "The Kuchas are going to stick together and they are going to kick the Ogakors' asses."

I doubt there has ever been any other point in Survivor history where the audience had all been on the exact same page like that.

Hell, even I was hardcore on the "win it for Mike" bandwagon after episode six. And you are talking to maybe the biggest Tina Wesson fan on the face of the Earth! After the Mike accident, and especially after the spectacular ending to episode six, my main focus at this point was just rooting for Tina to be the last standing Ogakor. That was really all I was hoping for out of the rest of the season. I wanted Nick to win (obviously). I wanted Tina to put up a good show and make me proud and get far. And of course-- like most of America at the time-- I would have been very happy if somebody were to slap Jerri in the face somewhere along the way too. No real reason for that. Just because.

Oh, and I also wanted Amber to shut up with all the fricking "Oh my Godddddddd"s already. Are you kidding me? Just shut up for a second, would you?

And anyway, like I said at the start of the chapter, this is where unscripted TV reveals itself to be so awesome yet at the same time so incredibly frustrating.

So what happened in episode seven of Australia, anyway? Did the Kuchas come back and rally behind their fallen leader, and take control of the game, like they had promised to do? Did the awesomeness of episode six translate well into an equally awesome episode seven? Are the lame, bickering Ogakors made bitches of by their superior and much smarter Kucha overlords?

Um, no.

About five minutes into the merge episode, we find out that the Ogakors know that Jeff Varner already has a previous vote against him. So they just ride that knowledge to a 5-5 tie. And then they use the tiebreaker rule to basically knock Jeff Varner and the Kuchas right out of the game.

Well okay then. Guess that's it. So much for that storyline.

Sorry Kucha. I guess it sucks to be you.

I can't even begin to tell you what a fizzled fart of momentum episode seven of Australia turned out to be. It just took everything that had built up through the first six episodes of the season, it took all the awesomeness of the Mike falls into the fire episode, it took all the audience support and love that had built up behind the beloved Kuchas, and it just threw them all away. Just like that, in about fifteen minutes, the entire "win it for Mike" storyline was completely thrown into the garbage.

Ah yes, reality TV, my friends. Unpredictable. Awesome. Unscripted. And frustrating enough to make you throw your remote through the window.

I will always believe that it was the death of the "Win it for Mike!" storyline in Australia that convinced the producers to start introducing twists the following season. Because good lord, if you were the producer of a TV show, and if you had a storyline that was this good, if you had a storyline that the audience was practically begging to see pay off, wouldn't you be pissed if it just fizzled out into nothingness? I know that I would be. Hell, if I was a Survivor producer, I would have been furious now that I could see how the rest of the season was going to play out.

I mean, come on. Impartial shmimpartial. As a producer I don't want the Ogakors to win. The audience doesn't want to see the Ogakors win. 99% of America wants to see an effing Kucha win! We are producers here, why aren't we able to do anything about this???

Combine the fact that episode seven completely killed Australia, with the knowledge that Survivor has one true inherent flaw and there is no real way around it (Pagongings are inevitable and boring), and I have no doubt in my mind that the producers started planning twists specifically because of the Australia merge episode. I believe they wanted to find a way to ruin Pagongings (which just suck no matter which tribe is ahead), and they wanted a way to keep the show somewhat under their control if they ever needed to change something. And they wanted a way to do it covertly where nobody could ever call them on it.

Of course, I doubt the producers are ever going to word it quite like that if you asked one of them about it. "Oh yeah, sure, we needed a way to manipulate who was winning because the wrong people were winning." But if you cornered a producer about ten years after the show ended, and you asked him off the record why Survivor started using twists in season three, I have no doubt he would hint that it was because Richard, and then the ~~Ogakors~~ not-Kuchas, and then the Samburu Mallrats, started dominating the game.

A show that draws in a bazillion dollars in revenue per year, yet the producers have absolutely no say in how it plays out or how it gets presented to the audience? Yeah right. My guess is that Australia is the only time they tried letting a season play out completely without producer influence, and I think they got screwed by it.

Starting with the third season, they just weren't going to take a chance like that anymore. Especially when they saw that either Silas or Lindsey was likely going to be the winner of Survivor: Africa.

Uh, Silas Gaither winning Survivor? Silas aka Chip?? Or, even worse, Lindsey????

Not gonna happen.

> **Side note:** A few people have mentioned to me over the years that Australia was actually the first season that was supposed to have a twist. But when it came time to implement it into the game, the producers "didn't feel that the time was right." So they scrapped it and they decided to save it for the next season. Now, I don't know how much truth there is to this particular rumor (it could very well be 100% true), but either way it doesn't negate my theory that Africa was the season that really galvanized them into action. I mean, Kucha losing Survivor was one thing. That might have sucked, but

at least some of the Ogakors were likable. But Silas or Lindsey winning? Well that was a whole other thing. So yes I think what happened in Africa definitely had something to do with when that very first Survivor twist showed up. I think the producers were just sitting on it until they reached a point where it would have the maximum impact.

By the way, there have been many explanations over the years as to exactly WHO was responsible for the Ogakors knowing that Jeff Varner already had a prior vote against him in Australia. I have never heard a 100% verified answer as to how that whole interaction went down, so all I can do is speculate. All I can do is tell you that the story that I have heard the most over the years is that Tina was the one who got the info out of Kimmi. The two tribes were talking and introducing themselves the day of the Butch Cassidy waterfall challenge (episode two), and supposedly Tina asked Kimmi what the voting had been like at the first Kucha Tribal Council.

Kimmi, of course, because she is Kimmi, told her it had been 7-1. Seven votes for Debb, and then Debb's lone vote for Jeff.

Tina filed that info away for later.

And this, of course, led to the beginning of badass Tina.

Now... is all of this true? Or is this me believing one version of the story over the others simply because it makes my favorite player look good? I don't know. I have heard so many random explanations over the years as to how the Ogakors knew about that vote ("Varner told them!", "A producer tipped them off!", "The Ogakors read about it on a cameraman's note sheets!") that I really don't know what to believe anymore.

What I DO know for a fact is that I have heard the Tina version the most frequently over the years. That is the version of the story that people whose opinions I trust tend to repeat the most often. And to me it makes sense. It totally fits Tina's character because she is sneaky and because she is such a devious little mind gamer. I can totally see her talking circles around Kimmi before Kimmi even realizes what she is doing. So to me I can totally buy the Tina/Kimmi story as being "what really happened" that day about the Varner vote.

By the way, to further back up this argument, Jeff Varner even kind of confirms the Tina/Kimmi version of the story in his final words. After he is voted out, he explains to us that some "blabbermouth" gave away the fact that he had a prior vote to the Ogakors, and that is what cost him the game. He doesn't specifically name Kimmi as the blabbermouth, but I would be willing to bet that if you looked up the word "blabbermouth" in the dictionary, I am pretty sure you would find a picture of Kimmi there.

Again, I don't know this as a fact. But "Kimmi = blabbermouth" sure makes a lot of sense. I mean, come on, who else spilled the beans to the Ogakors? Alicia? Rodger? Elisabeth? Nick, the Harvard Law Student? I don't think so.

Oh yeah, I should probably point out that I actually had a chance to ask Tina this question a couple of years ago. Well, indirectly, anyway. Tina was a guest on Rob Cesternino's "Rob Has a Podcast" show in December of 2010. And before the show Rob asked if there were any questions that the fans wanted to ask her.

As you can guess, this has always been the #1 question that I have wanted to ask Tina. "Were you the person who got the info about Varner's previous vote out of Kimmi?" I wanted to know the answer to this question because, to me, this backs up a lot of my theories about how Tina was underrated and how she was a very sneaky player. I also wanted to know the answer because, well... let's be honest here... because I think about Survivor way too much and because I have way too much time on my hands.

So anyway, I submitted my question to Rob. And he asked Tina if she had been the one who got the info out of Kimmi. And how did Miss Tina Wesson, who is maybe my all-time favorite player, not to mention the person who I think is arguably the single greatest Survivor player in history, answer this particular question?

"I don't remember."

Damnit!

That was so not the answer I was hoping for. Tina, you're killing me!

P.S. Since I guess this book is basically now a love sonnet about Tina at this point, I suppose I should point out that my favorite moment of the entire "Tina is a badass" storyline takes place during episode seven of Australia.

I thought it was awesome how Tina managed to ferret the info about Varner's vote out of Kimmi in episode two (yes, we will just treat this as fact for now - clearly Tina can't dispute it at this point, ten years later, so forget her.) And I thought it was badass how Tina cut Mad Dog's throat without a regret in the world at the end of episode three. And I thought it was fantastic how Tina turned on Jerri, as well as her own good friend Mitchell, in episode four, and how she did it through those memorably snarky little voting comments. And how, by doing so, Tina more or less invented the idea of a Survivor power shift.

And of course I thought it was impressive how Tina swam across the river and saved the canister of rice later during the flood. Nobody else would have tried to swim across that current in the dark. Not even Colby would have dared to swim across a moving current during a flood with basically zero visibility. But badass Tina would. And she did. Because Tina is awesome like that.

Absolutely, I loved all of those moments.

But to me, Tina's most badass moment came in Australia episode seven. Yes, the much maligned episode seven, the one that pretty much killed the entire season and that I absolutely hate.

Tina's most badass moment in Survivor history came when she stood there on that pole in that immunity challenge. And there wasn't a chance on God's green Earth that she was ever going to get down and give up. Ever.

Seriously, go back and watch the episode seven immunity challenge in Australia. Watch the defiant little look on Tina's face throughout that challenge. She wasn't going ANYWHERE. Ever. She was NEVER going to step down. In fact, if the Kuchas hadn't all stepped down from their poles first, and Keith hadn't begged her to give him immunity (for the good of the team) I am guessing that Tina would STILL be standing up there. It is now nearly fifteen years later, it is the spring of the year 2015, and I bet Tina would still be standing there with her hands on her hips, and swinging back and forth slightly, and hoping that Probst wouldn't come out and tempt her with a bag of DurEEEtose. Because that was the only way short of a lightning strike she was ever going to get down from that pole.

Badass Tina, my friends.

History will show that Keith Famie won immunity in Australia that night.

But history will also show that even Keith would tell you he only won because Tina stepped down so that the Kuchas wouldn't be able to target him. She only handed him immunity that night because it was the smart strategic team thing to do. In essence, Tina actually refusing to be a badass was the most badass thing she ever could have done.

Because that was the move that clinched the win for the Ogakors.

35. The Flaw in the Show

Now that the game was over for the Kuchas, and now that all the suspense was officially gone for the rest of the season (seriously, I can't overemphasize how big a flaw there was in Survivor prior to twists - Pagongings were a complete season killer), that meant that for me personally, it was now time to shift modes as a Survivor fan.

Since we all knew how the season was going to end now, it was time for me to stop thinking about Survivor as a TV show, as start thinking about my interview with Nick and how I was going to conduct it. After all, since he was a Kucha, that meant he was toast. I had to decide what I was going to ask him after he was voted out at some point in the next three episodes.

By the way, I know a lot of people are reading this and are thinking it is kind of silly that I keep saying "Nick Brown interview" and "my entry into the Survivor writing world", but I would like to point out that if you have read any of my other interviews, you will see that I generally ask some fairly interesting questions. When I interview a player like Chris Daugherty or Coach (I have done both), I don't just stand there and ask how they got on the show, or what it was like to be on Survivor, or what their strategy was, etc. When I talk to a Survivor player I actually ask them something interesting.

> **Side Note:** For example, when I interviewed Chris a couple of years ago, I got him to drop the bombshell that Ami wasn't really the brains behind the women's alliance in Vanuatu. He told me that Leann was. And the way they showed it on TV was completely backwards. He also told me that Scout was by far the most dangerous player in Vanuatu (he was scared to death of her), and that for years he was so unpopular among the fan base that people would come up to him at charity events just so they could curse him out. This was important stuff that explained a lot about Vanuatu, and Chris had never ever mentioned it in any other interview.

Here is the thing about me and interviews. I have always been pretty good when it comes to following what the internet Survivor fan base is talking about at any particular moment. And the reason for this is because I have always been a voracious website reader. I read pretty much everything. So I have always had a pretty good finger on the pulse of what people are saying and thinking about a particular Survivor season at any given moment.

Because of my knowledge of what the fan base was thinking at the time, the questions I was planning to ask Nick weren't your usual generic interview questions like "Why did you bring your luxury item?" or "How many times did you apply?"

For my interview, I had questions planned for him like "When Mike fell into the fire, what was the first reaction around camp and how long did it take the medics to get there? And did you have to scream for them to come over and help?" Because I know Nick had been there when it happened, he was the first one who reacted to it. I also planned to ask Nick what he would say about the widespread belief among fans that the cameramen had probably filmed Mike falling into fire, and they just hadn't done anything to help him because it would look better on TV.

These were the kinds of questions that people were very much talking about on the internet at the time. And I was curious how somebody who was actually there would answer them.

I also planned to ask Nick what would have happened if Kucha had gone into the merge 6-4. Would the theorized Mike-Nick-Elisabeth-Rodger alliance have made it all the way to the end? And what exactly were his endgame plans? Who was his final two partner? Which Kucha was he plotting with that we just never saw?

It was a common belief on the internet at the time that Jeff Varner probably would have won the game if Kucha had been up in numbers going into the merge. Most fans at the time believed (and in fact most Survivor fans STILL believe) that Varner would have won because he was the sneakiest. But according to Mike and some of Mike's comments after the game, the REAL power core on Kucha had nothing to do with Jeff Varner. The real power trio had been Mike, Rodger, and Elisabeth. The three that were known as "The Christian Coalition." So I was curious where Nick himself had fit into that threesome. Or if there was some sub alliance on Kucha that nobody on TV had ever seen.

Even though it seems silly to call a Nick Brown interview a big deal now, fifteen years later, if you go back and you look at Australia you will see that he was a crucial part of just about everything important that ever happened on Kucha. He was right smack dab in the middle of everything. Strategy, memorable moments, big scenes, you name it, he was in the middle of all of it. I could not have possibly had a better subject for my interview.

199

So this was what I spent all my time now focusing on. Now that an Ogakor was going to win Australia for sure, I just started focusing all my energy on my interview with Nick and what we were going to talk about.

The first thing I did to prepare for the interview was I went over to the message board at Television Without Pity (or Mighty Big TV, as it was called in 2001), and I posted a thread announcing what I was going to do. I said, "Hey guys, Nick Brown is a friend of mine, and I am going to be interviewing him for MBTV after the season ends. If you guys have any questions you would like me to ask him about Australia, just let me know and I will try to work them in."

I figured, okay, well if nothing else at least this will get people interested in my interview ahead of time. A little pre-project publicity can't hurt, right? After all, remember, there really was no such thing as a Survivor interview on a fan website back in 2001. Back then CBS controlled ALL access to the Survivors, and they enforced that law with the proverbial iron fist. Any interview done the first two seasons of Survivor either went through the approved media filters and CBS channels, or it didn't happen. And that was the law.

Some random fan announcing that he was going to interview a Survivor on a message board? Um, that didn't happen very often.

So I posted my interview announcement on the TWOP message board (and I think I also mentioned it on Survivor Sucks, even though this was a project that was supposed to be exclusive to TWOP), and I waited for the questions to come trickling in. And sure enough, they did. People started asking me very good questions that they wanted me to pass along to Nick. Stuff like "How come we never see Survivors wearing sunscreen or getting sunburns? Are you guys under shade or does the network provide you with stuff?" Somebody else wanted me to ask Nick "How many retakes do you have to do of shots that are obviously redos? How long does production stuff like that take?"

I sat back and I let the questions for Nick slowly filter in.

And then I turned my attention back to the show.

And I watched as the once outstanding Australia season slowly and unfortunately fizzled out into tedium.

I wish I could say that it didn't. I wish I could sit here and tell you that the second half of Australia was just as great and just as amazing as the first half. But unfortunately it just wasn't. And no it had nothing to do with the fact that I was 100% rooting for the Kuchas (although I am sure that didn't help).

The problem with the second half of Australia is that it is just boring. I'm sorry, as much as I am a Survivor purist, as much as I love the early seasons of this show with all of my heart, the inherent Pagonging flaw in Survivor back in the early days was just brutal. The minute a tribe went up 5-4 back in the early days of Survivor, you might as well have just turned off your TV and watched Friends for the next four weeks. Because nothing interesting was going to happen. The boot order was going to be very predictable.

The biggest problem with Survivor back in those early days is that the players just weren't very ballsy yet. I mean, I hate to say that, but it's true. Nobody would EVER break out of a dominant alliance the first couple seasons of Survivor. And the reason they wouldn't break out was because they had all seen how well alliances had worked in the first season. I mean, think back to some historical precedence here, think back to what would have been in everyone's mind as they filmed Australian Outback. At this point in time (early 2001), the formula for being a good Survivor player had already been established. It had been established by the Tagis. And nobody (especially in the second season) wanted to be the person who went against that. Nobody in Australia wanted to be the first idiot in Survivor history who was dumb enough to go against what had worked for the Tagis.

If you were a player in the early seasons of Survivor, and if you were up 6-4, or 4-3, or 5-4, or whatever, even if you were the fifth man on the totem pole you wouldn't have had the balls to break away from your alliance. You would have just stayed there. You would have just ridden that alliance all the way to the fifth place finish that everybody (except for you) would have seen coming a mile away. I hate to say it was that predictable, but it was. It happened every single time. We saw it all the way up to Marquesas.

Most people (especially new school fans) will watch stuff like this in the early seasons and they will say, "Well the players were just stupid back then." Or the popular "People are just better players now, they all sucked in the early seasons." Or my favorite, "Nobody knew what they were doing on Survivor until about the sixth season."

No!

None of those are true at all!

Just because the players played differently back then doesn't mean they were idiots. It doesn't mean they weren't playing to win. What they were doing was following a precedent that had worked very well in Borneo. They were following a template that had been watched and studied by 600 bazillion people, and was considered "the playbook" of how you were supposed to win this game.

Remember. Keep this in mind. At this point in time, **NO ONE HAD EVER SEEN ANY OTHER WAY TO WIN SURVIVOR!**

The players weren't dumb. The players weren't weak. The players were simply following a precedent.

I used to have a friend named Thomas who would write me emails after every single episode of Survivor. He knew I was a big fan of the show, and he would constantly send me emails with strategy comments like, "Hey if Amber wanted to win, she should just team up with Rodger, Elisabeth and Nick. She should put together a cross tribe alliance and they can be the final four." Or "Hey, if Kim Powers and Brandon teamed up with the Borans, they could knock off Lex."

Thomas was CONSTANTLY sending me emails like this back in the early years of Survivor. After every single episode. And I would always write back and say something like, "Well yeah it sounds good on paper. I doubt it will happen though. Survivors don't do that, nobody every switches tribes or leaves their alliance."

Thomas was about two years ahead of the game when it came to talking Survivor strategy. But you have to keep this next part in mind. When he wrote me that stuff, when he explained to me what I used to call his "fanciful Survivor theory of the week", I was never impressed by them. I wasn't looking at him like "Wow, this guy is a strategic mastermind. I should look into his strategies more closely."

No, when Thomas wrote me this stuff, I would usually just write him off as a joke. Nearly ANYONE in 2001 would have written theories like that off as a joke. Because back in the early days of Survivor you just didn't. Jump. Out of a. Dominant. Alliance. Ever. No one would have EVER done it. Had Rob Cesternino been a player in season two I doubt that even HE would have done it.

This refusal to jump out of a dominant alliance was very much a hallmark of the first few seasons of Survivor. And it goes a long way towards explaining why the second half of Australia (with a couple exceptions) is just one giant pile of suck. The Ogakors had a 5-4 lead, no Ogakor was ever going to jump out of that alliance to improve their chances in the game, ever, and basically it just played out exactly how you could have predicted it was going to play out. The minute that Jeff Varner went home, that boot list was set.

Yeah, I know, there was a Jerri blindside in the middle there. I know, and yes it was awesome TV (the first alliance shift ever??? Oh my God!!!) But the Jerri vote didn't really change anything. The Ogakors were up so handily by that point that they could easily dump a member of their alliance that they were sick of living with, and they could STILL waltz to the end. So the Jerri vote-- as awesome as it was at the time—well, it really didn't affect anything.

Well, okay, it did affect one thing. It made 99% of America scream with delight. The audience LOVED the Jerri blindside, as you can probably imagine. In fact, since I was the guy with the finger on the pulse of the Survivor fan base at the time, if you want to know what the fan base was saying all throughout the second half of Australia, here is what they were saying:

"I don't care if any of the other Ogakors win. I just don't want fucking Jerri to win. I will never watch this show again if Jerri wins."

Needless to say, the Jerri blindside episode was, yeah. It was very popular.

So anyway, this is what happened in the second half of Australia. The Kuchas were picked off one by one. None of the Ogakors were foolhardy enough to change their position because you just didn't do that back then. The game was predictable. Then there was a flood. Then everyone got all tired and lethargic because they ran out of food and they didn't have any more energy. After around the eighth episode, no one in Barramundi had the strength to expend any effort around camp anymore because they weren't eating any food. So they just sat around the campfire all day and they did nothing for two weeks.

Just wonderful.

Even though the critics claimed that nothing new would ever happen on Survivor, even though they called Australia a retread and a ripoff of Borneo before episode one even aired on TV, even though they said we had already seen everything in Survivor that could ever possibly happen on Survivor, and that the second one would simply be a pale imitation of the first, in the long run it turned out that the critics were wrong. Yep, they were all wrong. It turned out we actually COULD see something new and unique when it came to Survivor the second time around.

For the first time in two seasons-- thanks to a combination of elements that the producers couldn't control (the flood, lack of food) and elements that they probably could have controlled (Pagongings are boring)-- Survivor was now officially becoming boring TV.

I don't care how much you liked the Ogakors, or how much you liked Colby or Tina, or how much you loved Rodger or Elisabeth or America's Sweetheart himself, Nick Brown. Survivor just wasn't a very fun show to watch at the moment. It was simply becoming way too predictable. The flaw in the game (and the only flaw) had officially been exposed. When Pagongings happened, they wound up destroying the season.

Oh yeah, and they were also going to happen every single season now because of the way the game was designed.

If you were a Survivor producer, this was not good.

P.S. Yes, Russell Hantz, there IS a flaw in Survivor. But it's not the one that you and your brainless minions keep yammering on about. The only flaw in Survivor is what happens with Pagongings. That's it. Aside from that? Sorry man, the best player always wins.

36. The Kucha Traitor

Remember how I said that the producers leaked fake spoilers and fake screencaps during the second half of Borneo, in an attempt to keep the audience interested in what was going on, and to distract them from the obvious Pagonging that was about to take place? Well the same thing happened during Australia too. Right around the time of the Alicia boot in Australia, a few "spoilers" started leaking out onto the internet. And naturally, they all claimed that, despite all evidence to the contrary, a player from Kucha was still going to win the game.

Now, I am guessing that most people who are reading this book have never heard of these particular spoilers before. We are now getting into some hardcore old school obscure minutiae. But hey, that's why you are reading my Survivor book, right? You came here because you want to hear all the juicy stuff.

It was right around the time of the Alicia boot (or maybe even as early as the Jeff boot) that the first big Australia endgame spoiler came out. And this spoiler claimed that one of the Kuchas was going to become a traitor. In fact, not only was one player going to turn on the Kuchas and become a traitor, the spoiler claimed that they were going to ride this treachery all the way to the end of the game.

Well, needless to say, this was a pretty interesting rumor.

Now, again, I don't know how this rumor started. I don't know if the producers leaked it, or if it was just some overzealous fan who started it. Hell, maybe somebody like Jeff Varner started it just to mess with everyone. I don't know. All I know is that for a few weeks there, it was everywhere. This was THE Australia spoiler floating around about midway through the season. It was the famous Kucha Traitor Spoiler.

And of course I was overjoyed when people started theorizing that the traitor was probably going to be Nick.

Yes I know. Admittedly, this all sounds kind of silly fifteen years later. In fact it is downright laughable that people back then thought that Nick (maybe the most forgettable Survivor player ever) might actually turn out to be the major villain of the season. But that is exactly what started to happen. The Kucha Traitor spoiler gathered so much steam, and so many people started to believe it would actually happen (probably because they all really <u>wanted</u> it to happen), that of course it completely distracted us from the fact that this was just going to be a boring old Pagonging. And that is why I have always believed that the producers must have leaked this particular rumor. I mean, seriously, if you were the producer of a TV show like Survivor, and if you knew what was coming down the road, and you knew how bored the audience would be watching it all play out, wouldn't YOU want to stir things up a little bit? Of course you would. If you were the producer of Survivor you would want to completely disguise this Pagonging any way that you could.

By the way, I should point out that there was one specific piece of visual evidence that a lot of people believed backed up the whole Kucha Traitor/Kucha comeback storyline. There was a scene in the middle of one of the episodes that a lot of people felt "confirmed" that the "A Kucha Still Wins" spoiler was going to come true.

There is a scene in episode eleven (titled "No Longer Just A Game") which shows a kangaroo stuck in a river. He is just standing there, waist deep in raging flood water, and he is trying to jump out. But he can't jump out, because the riverbank is too high. So he starts jumping, and jumping, and jumping. And panicking. And meanwhile the floodwater is getting stronger and faster, and it is trying to pull him downstream to his death.

We get about thirty seconds of this kangaroo frantically trying to jump out of the river. And then finally, when all hope appears to be lost, he finally makes it. He gets out of the water just in the nick of time. Had he stayed there in the water just a couple more seconds, he probably would have drowned.

Now, I will tell you, a few people on the message boards focused on this scene in episode eleven and they absolutely flipped. I mean, they completely freaked out. Because why would a shot like that have been included in the episode? Seriously, there is no reason on God's green Earth that Mark Burnett should have dedicated a full minute of a Survivor episode to a kangaroo trying to get out of a river. Logistically, there is no reason that that scene and that kangaroo ever should have been there. It just didn't make sense.

And then people stopped and they thought about it for a minute. Holy crap. Kucha in Aboriginal language meant "kangaroo." And the two most beloved Kuchas left in the game were Rodger and Elisabeth. And, oh my God, that kangaroo was a baby, so it probably symbolized Elisabeth.

And that was when it resonated with a lot of people. Wow. So THAT is why that shot was included in the episode. This means that the Kuchas are going to fight and fight and fight, and finally, at the last minute possible, one of them (probably Elisabeth) is going to escape the danger and jump out of the floodwater and they are going to win the game!

Again, I know this sounds silly to somebody reading this fifteen years later. But in the summer of 2001 it made perfect sense. And I certainly wasn't the only one who believed that the kangaroo scene had been put in that episode for a reason. I was fully on the board with the Kucha Traitor/Kucha comeback spoiler the minute I saw that kangaroo in the river shot. Because, again, how on Earth could you have a season that ended with an Ogakor win after that inspirational speech at the end of that Mike episode? You couldn't. You just couldn't. The Kuchas couldn't lose. It didn't make sense.

So anyway, there you go. Two of the big "spoilers", which of course turned out not to be spoilers, that were running rampant through the second half of Australia. Everyone heard them. A good chunk of the audience actually believed them. And yes, that even includes me. At a certain point, I would have bet money that a Kucha was going to come back and win Australia. Yes, even after the Jeff vote. I mean, come on, it had to happen. All the clues were there. The producers were standing there handing them to us.

Now, why do I bring these Australia "spoilers" up in my book?

Well the reason I bring them up is because one of the comments I have heard throughout the years, particularly when it comes to Australia, is when a new school fan will ask me something like "How could you guys stand the second half of Australia? It was so boring. How can you possibly say that Australia was an amazing season and that the audience loved it? If it was me I would have been bored off my ass, it was so predictable."

As you can probably guess, the reason I bring up these fake spoilers is to point out that the second half of Australia was NOT predictable. Not if you were following it each week it wasn't. And certainly not if you were following the show on the internet. Because if you were an internet fan, and you heard all the "rumors", and you followed all the gossip, you would know that the ending of Australia was NOT considered to be a slam dunk at the time. There wasn't a single spoiler out there that Tina was going to win. Heck, there wasn't even a rumor out there that Tina was going to win. The only thing you heard on the message boards, day in and day out at the time, was that there was this rumor of a big Kucha comeback. And that some nasty interesting Survivor drama was about to go down. So of course we would all keep our eyes glued to the television each week just to see what it was.

And meanwhile Alicia went home. And then Jerri went home. And then Nick. And then Amber and Rodger and Elisabeth.

Oops. Well I guess so much for that big Kucha comeback. Never mind then.

Oh, and good job hiding it from us, producers.

This is the kind of stuff I am talking about when I say that you can't really understand the Australia phenomenon (and you especially can't understand the Borneo phenomenon) unless you were there. Unless you were there, in the trenches, following the gossip, reading the message boards, living and dying on every single fake spoiler or innuendo or rumor that you heard. If you weren't there for all of that, you will just think that Australia was boring. But it wasn't. Despite the fact that, in retrospect, it turned out to be boring, at the time it was anything but. At the time it was considered superior to Borneo. Because this was a time when the audience and the producers and the editors all still really cared.

And so there you have it. A summary of the two great spoilers in Australia. The Kucha comeback, and the Kucha traitor. Both of which, of course, turned out to be one hundred percent pure horse crap. Looking back on it now, it is amazing to think how naive we all were that we actually believed them.

Of course there was another HUGE spoiler that also came out around this time. And this one actually did turn out to be true. It was a picture of the jurors back in Ponderosa (or whatever passed for Ponderosa back in 2001.) It showed Jerri, and Nick, and Rodger, and Elisabeth. And it showed Amber. They were all hanging out in the jury lodge, and they appeared to be having a party. This picture showed up on the internet sometime around the Jerri boot, and it was clearly a leaked spoiler that showed who the jurors were going to be. But of course since most of the internet wanted a Kucha to win, since so many people on the internet were so heavily invested that the "Kucha comeback" spoiler simply had to be true, naturally most people kind of brushed off this "Australian Outback Jury Picture" as a fake. Naaaah, that picture can't be real. That picture is clearly photoshopped. No way could that be a real Survivor spoiler.

Of course I was one of the people who brushed it off as being photoshopped too, and look what I know. Turns out I was also an idiot.

So there you go. The history of spoilers in the second half of Australia, and how they fooled a good chunk of the audience. To this day I find it amazing that so many people believed them, and that so many people believed that a Kucha was actually going to come back and win the game. And I find it even more amazing that there wasn't a single "Tina is going to win Survivor!" spoiler out there, in any shape, form, or fragment, whatsoever. Seriously, NO ONE saw that Tina win coming. Not even me, and I was the world's biggest Tina fan. There wasn't even a hint of her winning anywhere in the clues available on the internet. And I find that just as impressive as the fact that there hadn't been any "Richard is going to win Survivor!" spoilers towards the end of Borneo either.

Seriously, how the producers managed to pull off hiding their winner for two consecutive seasons is just incredible. I don't think they have ever really gotten enough credit for that.

P.S. Okay, yes, I guess I might as well mention this little elephant in the room. There WAS one clue/theory/spoiler that Tina Wesson was going to win. It was called "The Dog That Didn't Bark", and it was posted after episode two by a guy named Tapewatcher. If you are interested in reading about a really fascinating piece of Survivor history, go Google that phrase or look it up at Survivor Sucks. This guy predicted that Tina was going to win specifically because she was the only player who didn't get a confessional in the premiere of Survivor: The Australian Outback.

I was familiar with 'The Dog That Didn't Bark" theory, of course, but don't believe any of the revisionist history floating around the internet these days that says that everyone read it and that everyone believed it. I remember hearing about The Dog That Didn't Bark when it first came out and I remember thinking it was a crock of shit. In fact a lot of people thought it was a crock of shit. So I don't consider it to be a true quote-unquote significant Survivor spoiler at all. Most people I knew didn't really take it seriously, and even then it was buried so deep in the Survivor Sucks message boards that most of the Survivor audience didn't even know about it. I mean, I think it is cool that "The Dog That Didn't Bark" turned out to be true in the end, because wow, whoever wrote it was likely some sort of an insider. But the truth is that it didn't really surface as being that big a deal until after the season was over.

P.P.S. Of course lost in the shuffle is the fact that our beloved hero, Nick Brown, was just voted out of the game. Saaaaaad panda. Oh but don't worry, I will have plenty to say about him in the next chapter. Yes, we have finally come to my big Nick interview.

37. The Interview

In the tenth episode of Survivor: The Australian Outback, Nick Brown of the Barramundi tribe was voted out of the game. And I am guessing that other than me, and perhaps Nick's family, and maybe some of his classmates at Harvard, nobody cared.

But with Nick out of the game, that meant it was time for my interview with him to finally take place. Finally, after months and months of anticipation and excitement and waiting and buildup, it was time for my introduction to the world as a famous Survivor writer. A week from now, finally, people would know who I was. I would no longer just be some random guy on the Television Without Pity message boards who went by the name of "Sandwich Artist."

I emailed Nick a couple of days after he was voted out. I asked if we were still on for the interview. He said, "Yeah, sure. No problem."

I was thrilled.

And unfortunately that is exactly when the rug was pulled out from under me.

My interview with Nick was set for two days away. I remember it like it was yesterday. I was collecting all the questions that readers had sent in through the Television Without Pity message boards, and that was when I received a strange email from a person I had never heard of before. I don't remember her name, but she was one of the site administrators at TWOP. She was one of the big shots.

"Hey, what's this I hear about an interview you are doing with a Survivor?" she wrote. "Can you give me a little more info about that?"

Sure, I said. And I explained how I was friends with Nick Brown through my brother. And how Nick had agreed to an interview. And how I was willing to offer it to Television Without Pity as a free exclusive. I said I had already cleared it with their moderator over at their Survivor board a couple of months ago and it was basically done.

"Well we're not really comfortable having you do a project like this for our website since we don't know you. We would really prefer if one of our staff writers did the interview instead. Would you be okay with that?"

Huh?

"This is a pretty high profile project," she explained. "It would look better for the site if one of our Survivor recappers did the actual interview. I hope you understand."

Well, needless to say, the string of expletives that came flooding into my head isn't really suitable for inclusion in a Survivor book. But I was pissed. In fact, it is now more than fourteen years later and I am STILL pissed. This was my very first time being screwed over by somebody in the internet writing world. And like they say about virginity, you never forget your first.

"Look," I replied back in an email. "I have been working very hard at this for over four months now. It has already been cleared by your admins. I have already even started gathering questions. Nick said he is okay with it, your readers are excited about it, there has already been a lot of publicity. Can't I just write it up and hand it over to you?"

"No," she finally said. "Either one of our writers does the interview, or it will not be posted at Television Without Pity. I'm sorry."

Well, crap.

To say I was a little bit pissed about this email would be an understatement. Are you kidding me? I worked this hard on this interview, for nothing? I spent nearly five months of my life putting this project together, gathering publicity, and setting up the whole thing with a Survivor. And now you are going to take it away from me? Just because you don't want me to take the focus away from one of the shitty writers on your shitty website? Are you kidding me?!?

I have dwelled over this issue, and why it played out the way that it did, for a long time now. I have thought about it for more than a decade and a half. And I have always wondered if that particular outcome could have actually been avoided. I mean, is there some other way I could have handled the Nick interview? Is there some other way I could have approached this with Television Without Pity and made the whole thing work out? And in the end I always believe that the answer is no. There is no way the people on that website were ever going to let me conduct that interview. At least not the way that I wanted to do it. They were only interested in it being THEIR project, written by one of THEIR writers, written in THEIR style. Also, I have to point out that since Television Without Pity was famous for being run by a bunch of snarky females, I am guessing they were probably none too happy about some random guy coming in off the street out of nowhere and trying to horn in on their turf.

So anyway, there is the backstory. The inside story of my infamous Nick Brown interview, and why it never happened. And why I have been talking crap about Television Without Pity and all the people who worked for that site for the past fifteen years. Seriously, don't ever read TWOP again. Even though it is shut down now, stay away from the archives. Only bad people who beat puppies and babies and vote for amendments against marriage for gay people hang out there. Remember, every time you read an old Television Without Pity article, you are breaking my heart.

As for Nick Brown, well I am sad to say that we never really spoke again after that. I mean, we didn't end on bad terms or anything. I just told him that the website had decided to cancel the interview, and I thanked him for offering to do it. I did let him know how bummed I was about it though. I really do think that would have been an awesome interview.

The last thing I heard about Nick was that he is living in Washington State now, and he is the lawyer for Governor Jay Inslee. I also heard he is very lazy.

As for me, well I learned a very valuable lesson through my dealings with Nick, and through my dealings with those assholes at Television Without Pity. I learned that if I ever wanted to become a Survivor writer, if I ever wanted to achieve any sort of internet fame or notoriety (however meager that notoriety might be), I wasn't going to be able to do it through somebody else's website. No, if I was ever going to become "a name" as a writer, it was going to have to be on my own terms, and through my own website. Because if there is one thing I have learned from my decade and a half of writing on the internet, it is that the internet doesn't like to share. If you have a really good idea and you want to get it out to the public, you are going to have to do it on your own. Otherwise somebody else will try to take a piece of it.

I actually stuck around the TWOP message boards for a couple more weeks after the interview debacle. Oh, I sulked about the way they tried to steal my project, of course. And I wasn't very happy about the way that things had gone down with the administrators. But it was still the best place to go on the internet at the time if you wanted to say snarky things about TV. In fact, I even wrote my very first Fallen Comrades Parody (which would later become my trademark) on the Television Without Pity Survivor message boards   Yep, you guessed it, my very first Fallen Comrades Parody was written during Australia, and it quickly became very popular. And of course, I love this part. Ironically (ha ha), because of my Fallen Comrades parody, I actually wound up with a fairly large fan base on the TWOP message boards. Gee, how nice. Looks like I actually got the readership I wanted after all. All it took was a feature that I wrote up specifically for the Television Without Pity website that everyone was talking about. How awesome. Wish I had thought of that for my Nick interview. God loves the concept of irony, I guess.

Unfortunately, if you try to find a copy of my Australia Fallen Comrades Parody on the internet now, you are going to be out of luck. I was kind of new to the concept of internet writing back then, and I wasn't smart enough to actually save a copy of it on my hard drive after I posted it. I just figured that once you posted something on the internet, it would stick around and be posted forever. So my first Fallen Comrades Parody hung around on the Television Without Pity message board for a couple of years, and then when they upgraded their website and they switched to a new server (around 2003 or so), it was swallowed up by the internets and it disappeared. Sadly, I haven't seen a copy of my Australia Fallen Comrades Parody in more than a decade. I don't think it exists anymore.

Oh, and as for the admin who wrote me and told me that TWOP was going to take over my interview? Whatever happened to her? Well I don't mean this in a bad way, but I hope she's dead.

38. Elisabeth Almost Died

Once Nick was out of the game, and once my interview with him was sabotaged by the bastards at Television Without Pity, my enthusiasm for Australia very easily could have just disappeared. I mean, 99 times out of 100, I probably would have just given up and not cared what happened the rest of the season. That's how deflated I was over what I felt had been done to me.

But luckily for me, and I guess luckily for anyone who has ever enjoyed my career as a Survivor writer, this wasn't 99 times out of 100. This was that other time. This was the special time.

Because this was the season with Tina, and she still had a very good chance to win.

Yes, we are now coming back to my fascination with Tina Wesson, who for years was my all-time favorite Survivor player. And yes, I know that will amaze the people who have only known me as a Chris fan and a Sandra fan for all these years. But yes, long before Sandra, and long before Chris, there was Tina. Tina was the original.

I really can't tell you what it was that I liked so much about Tina. I mean, Gretchen certainly wasn't my favorite player in Borneo. I am not just one of those people who always automatically likes a certain type of player. T-Bird wasn't my favorite player in Africa, and Kathy wasn't my favorite player in Marquesas. In fact Australia is probably the only season in 30+ seasons of Survivor where the older female player was my favorite.

But I don't know. There was just something about 95 pound little southern badass Tina that I thought was so cool.

Now keep in mind that I didn't actually think that Tina was going to win. Hell, I don't think that anyone thought she would win. If you had asked most people during the last couple episodes of Australia, I am guessing they would have assumed that Colby or Elisabeth was going to win. To most people, Tina was either "the nice one" or "the weird leathery one" or "that bitch who went through Kel's bag and will burn in hell for all of eternity." I guess that would depend on who you had asked.

In fact, I don't think most people at the time would have even considered Tina to be one of the major characters of the season. Even towards the end of the game, even when it was down to the final six, I know I was one of the only people out there who was publicly rooting for Tina to win on the message boards. And again, that wasn't because I thought she actually WOULD win. I was just saying that because she was cool and I liked her. Tina winning Survivor, as unlikely as it was, I figured was just some random Mario pipe dream.

Again, I need to emphasize once again that there were NO reliable spoilers out there about the end of Australia. There were none. There wasn't even a hint of one. No one out there knew that Tina was going to win. Hell, no one even knew that Colby and Tina were going to be the final two. I mean, you might have suspected that, if you followed the logic of the storyline, but just from spoilers alone the ending of Australia was a completely ironclad well-guarded secret. And I know how fascinating and bizarre that probably sounds to a person who didn't watch the show back in the early years. Yes, back then, the ending actually could be a complete surprise.

So Amber was voted out at the final six. She was blindsided. Whatever. Seriously, there may have never been a more useless, forgettable character in an early Survivor season than Amber in Australia. She was the original Kelly Purple. In fact, let's not say Amber was blindsided, let's just say she was blandsided. That is a much more fitting term to describe her Australia legacy.

> **Note:** In 2003 Amber was of course named as an "All-Star." After that, life never really made sense.

After Amber was voted out, good old Kentucky Joe was next. That's right, the old man took a bullet in order to save his surrogate daughter in the game, Elisabeth. I always loved that episode. In fact I have always loved Rodger Bingham as a Survivor character in general. He is one of those rare players in Survivor history who I have never heard a single person say a bad thing about. Seriously, go on to any message board on any Survivor website that has ever existed, and ask what people think about Rodger. I bet you won't find one person who can say anything bad about him. Well, other than maybe "Well I'm only fourteen and I never saw Australia. Who's Rodger?" He might be the only player in Survivor history who is universally respected by everyone.

> **Note:** I got to hang out with Rodger for about three hours once at a Survivor event in the winter of 2002. He is just as cool in person as

he was on the show. It will be fun to write up that event when we get there.

After we lost Kentucky Joe, we were down to the final four. And in a Survivor first (which would also be a Survivor last), the person who was voted out in fourth place didn't even make it to the finale. Yes, you got it. Survivor: The Australian Outback was the only season in Survivor history that lasted 42 days instead of 39. The producers were able to squeeze in that one extra episode that no other season has ever had. Elisabeth was voted out right before she would have made it to the finale.

Goodbye, Bessie. Onward and upward to Fox News, you sweet Colleen Haskell wannabe.

Oh, I should probably point out that one of the questions I get asked the most when it comes to Survivor is, "How come Australia was 42 days instead of 39?" I have to say, in nearly a decade and a half of following and writing about this show, that has got to be among the top ten questions that people ask me the most. Newer fans are always fascinated by why Australia had those extra three days that no other season has ever had.

Would you like to know the simple reason why Australia was 42 days instead of 39? Well it shouldn't take a rocket scientist to figure it out. Australia was 42 days because Survivor was such a big hit and because it was drawing such huge ratings. Since CBS was able to pull in millions and millions of dollars of advertising revenue for each episode, it was only natural that they would get greedy and they would want to fit in that one extra episode. This is also the same reason they started doing those stupid recap episodes in the middle of a season. Really, it just comes down to the network wanting to pull in more ad revenue.

By the way, I should also mention that even though the "Survivor is now 42 days long" decision was made primarily for financial reasons, money wasn't the reason they decided to drop it. No, the reason Africa went back to being 39 days was because some of the players in Australia almost died. People like Elisabeth and Colby and Tina were just so weak by the end of the season, they were so malnourished compared to the players at the end of Borneo, that the network was asking for trouble leaving them out there for those extra couple of days. In fact, Rodger Bingham once told me that Elisabeth came the closest to dying out of any player at any point of the first five seasons. And yes that even includes Mike. Rodger told me that Elisabeth's body was starting to shut down because of a lack of nutrients, and we only saw the tip

217

of the iceberg when we saw her hair falling out on TV. He told me she had to be given I.V.'s and she even had to be helicoptered out at one point because her body was just completely giving out on her. It was apparently way worse than what we ever saw on the show.

So anyway, if you are wondering why Survivor went back to being 39 days, and why Elisabeth never came back for All-Stars, well now you know. Those last few weeks in Australia were just absolutely brutal.

Oh, and the other reason why Survivor went back to being 39 days? Well because the Australia finale was just fricking boring. I mean, come on, how can you make a compelling two hour episode when there is only one person to vote off? You can't. The Australia finale (as much as I loved how it ended, and who won) is easily one of the worst episodes in Survivor history, and I am pretty sure that even the producers realized that. It was just three people sitting around and talking about the experience for two hours. And then a final Tribal Council where nobody was mad, and there were no angry jury speeches. You talk about a lack of drama at the end. I mean, you can bitch about Colby's decision to take Tina to the end all you want, and we will get to that decision in a minute, but at the very least that was a talking point. If Colby's... uh... questionable decision hadn't happened in that episode, you wouldn't even remember the Australia finale. It would be as forgettable as Amber's legacy was in Survivor prior to 2004. And that is saying something.

Believe me, the "42 days of Survivor" decision was a stupid idea, and there were many good reasons why it was quickly dropped. It would never be missed.

39. Colby's Choice

The finale of Survivor: The Australian Outback aired on TV on Thursday, May 3, 2001. And like I said, there really weren't any hints floating around about what to expect out of it. It was one of the those great moments in Survivor history that no matter who won-- Colby, Keith, or Tina-- it was going to be a surprise to everyone.

Obviously I was rooting for Tina to win. But I would guess that I was probably in the minority. Actually, no guessing about it, Tina fans were definitely in the minority. Colby was too darn popular and just way too likable. And, of course, he wasn't the bitch who went through Kel's bag. In order, I would estimate the general fan base at this point was something like 85% behind Colby, 14% behind Tina, and then probably Keith and his fiancée Katrin were the only two people rooting for Keith. Seriously, no one cared about Keith. No one cared enough about Keith to even hate him. Despite what the Australia editing would try to tell you, despite what Jerri would try to tell you, Keith has always been one of the more manufactured and ineffective "villains" the show has ever produced. I mean, come on, the guy proposed to his fiancée in one of the sweetest and most touching moments in Survivor history. No way could that guy be a TV villain.

It was very much a pro Colby fan base going into the finale. Remember that. This will become important in a minute.

> **Side Note:** Hey, remember the reward scene where Keith proposed to his fiancée? Remember the Outback Internet Cafe? Well don't forget that a future Survivor player actually showed up in that scene. Yes, that's right. It was Tina's daughter Katie, who would later show up as a contestant twenty five seasons later, on Survivor: Blood vs. Water! I don't really have anything interesting to say about the fact that Katie showed up on Survivor eleven years earlier. I just thought it was a fun little trivia fact that a lot of people don't know about.

Now, I don't remember a whole lot of specific details about the Australia finale. I don't know why. Maybe either because I have blocked them out over the years, or maybe there just wasn't anything in that episode that actually happened. Who knows? But what I do remember about that finale is this. I remember that my 12 month old daughter went to bed at 9:00 every night. And I remember that the Australia finale was waaaaaaaaay too big a deal for us to take 30 minutes out of the middle of it to go get a baby ready for bed. I mean, come on, this was before DVR's. You couldn't just pause live TV back then. You either watched a show live as it happened, or you were screwed.

Since there was no way we could ever watch three hours of uninterrupted TV at that point in our lives, what we did in the spring of 2001 was the only thing you could do in the spring of 2001. We taped the finale on our VCR. I set the timer on my VCR to start at 8:00, I set it to run for three hours (a two hour finale + a reunion show), and then we got the hell out of the house and away from the internet so that nobody could spoil it for us. I imagine I also took our phone off the hook so that my mom couldn't call me and spoil who the winner was.

At 8:00, I made sure that the VCR started to tape, and then we went out and we drove around Southern California for the next hour. Just to kill time. Just to think about anything else other than Survivor. We went to San Pedro. We headed up the coast to Hermosa Beach. We went out and we got some ice cream on the Redondo Beach Pier. It was a very nice evening.

And I swear to God, if I had heard anyone talk about who had just been voted out at the final three, I probably would have stabbed them.

At 9:00 we came back to the house and we got the baby ready for bed. She went down, and then for the next hour and a half my wife and I had to sit around and kill time and resist the temptation to turn on the TV. Or log into the internet. Or turn on the radio. For about 90 minutes of my life, I avoided all forms of communication whatsoever, and I learned a very good lesson about what it was like to be Amish. Trust me, being Amish is a pretty sad life.

Finally, at 11:00, once all the Survivor festivities were over (actually, 11:10, since I didn't want to be paranoid and actually catch the boot order at the end of the reunion show), we turned on the TV and I rewound the tape. And I said a prayer to whatever just and fair god there is in the universe that Survivor had managed to tape successfully. Had the finale not taped successfully, I honestly wouldn't have had a whole lot of options available to me. Remember, this was 2001. If your VCR didn't tape right, there wasn't a whole lot you could do about it. There wasn't any streaming video you could watch anywhere online. There wasn't a YouTube. The only thing you could really do was email a friend who you knew was a Survivor fan, and ask them if they had taped it and if you could borrow their tape. And then maybe 6-8 days later you would get the tape in the mail and you could finally watch it. Seriously, this was the ONLY option you had available to you if you missed an episode of Survivor back in 2001. And this is why the DVR is maybe the greatest invention ever. Because keep in mind, Survivor seasons were NOT released on DVD back then. Not in 2001 they weren't. At the time, CBS thought the idea of releasing a reality season on DVD (in its full form) would never sell and it would never make any money. So you either relied on homemade, probably illegal, tapes from other fans, or you were shit out of luck.

Well luckily for us, the Australia finale taped. Thank God for the Toshiba XX-7a model 42.

We got out our microwave popcorn and we sat down to watch it. And of course we were treated to one of the most boring and anticlimactic episodes in the history of Survivor. Seriously, don't ever watch the Australia finale. It is worse than listening to Russell Hantz. It is worse than listening to Amber being excited that she is at a buffet. There was at least one full hour in that finale where absolutely nothing happened. The final three players just sat around and they talked about what this experience had meant to them. Then they threw some stuff in a river. At one point I think Colby smiled and he revealed his brilliant white teeth.

And then, of course, the action happened. The one piece of action in the entire episode.

Colby won Fallen Comrades, which meant he won the final immunity.

Side Note: Okay, here is one of my biggest Survivor pet peeves. Please, let me finally set the record straight about this, because it is driving me crazy.

Fallen Comrades.is the final four immunity challenge (or final three immunity challenge in Australia) where the players have to answer trivia questions about their Fallen Opponents. Hence the name of the challenge: Fallen Comrades. Kelly Wiglesworth won the first one. Then Colby won the next one. Then Kim Johnson won the next one. And then, finally, Vecepia won. Fallen Comrades was a staple of the early Survivor seasons, although, for reasons we will talk about later, the producers have never done it again since Marquesas. The one that Vecepia won was the last one.

221

That challenge, that is Fallen Comrades. And that is the ONLY part of Survivor that is Fallen Comrades. The scene at the end of the finale where the last few players go for a walk and they share memories when they are standing at everyone's torch? That is called **Rites of Passage**. That is not Fallen Comrades. That has NEVER been Fallen Comrades. So please stop referring to that torch walk as Fallen Comrades, because it is hurting my ears. Thank you.

Once Colby won that final immunity challenge, I knew that the game was over for my ~~girlfriend~~ favorite player Tina. Because that was it, her game was done now. Colby was going to walk up to that podium, he was going to cast a vote for Tina, and the guy that nobody cared about and nobody loved (Keith) was going to make it to the final two. The very first goat in Survivor history was about to be crowned. And then, of course, Colby would win the final vote 7-0, which was exactly the ending that most of the world was probably hoping for. I mean, come on, Colby Donaldson had dominated this game (both physically and strategically) about as well as anyone ever had up to this point in Survivor. Or as well as anybody ever would. He was almost certainly a better Survivor player than Richard, despite what the revisionist history on the Survivor message boards will try to convince you. Going into that final three decision between Tina and Keith, Colby Donaldson was by far the biggest Survivor legend to have ever walked the Earth. And he was about to shatter any argument over who the all-time best player was going to be. In about twenty minutes, the debate question of "who is the all-time best Survivor player" would never need to be asked again. It didn't matter who won the next couple of seasons. The answer would always be Colby.

So Colby walked up to that voting urn in the final episode. He cast a vote for his best friend Tina.

The ending was now one hundred percent predictable.

As I was lying there on my bed, watching this happen, I remember congratulating Tina in my mind for putting up such a strong showing. I thought, wow, for a woman who is scared of pasty rice. For a woman who weighs 90 pounds. For a woman who single handedly cost her tribe immunity in episode two because she barfed up the cow tripe, that was a pretty good run. She came way closer to victory than she ever should have come, and I am going to miss her. And then I might have actually shed a little Mario tear.

222

And with that, I was resigned. Tina was going to lose Survivor. In my mind I quickly decided that after the show, I would write her a congratulatory fan letter.

And then?

Well in the words of a famous Survivor columnist, oh wowowowowowow.

Jeff Probst revealed Colby's vote to the audience at home, and it didn't say Tina. It said "Keith." And I am not exaggerating here, if I had been drinking a beverage at the time I would done the most majestically awesome spit take. I was so surprised that I would have wound up with Pepsi all over my bedsheet.

HOLY SHIT! COLBY JUST VOTED FOR KEITH?

THIS MEANS THAT TINA ACTUALLY HAS A CHANCE TO WIN!

I don't jump up and down very often in real life. And I especially don't jump and down very often in the pages of my Survivor book, because it is a completely stupid writing cliché and because nobody actually ever does that in real life. But I will be honest with you. I got out of bed, I stood on the floor, and I was so excited that I started jumping up and down. And I started pumping my fist. Because this was easily the biggest thing that had ever now happened in Survivor. Forget rats and snakes. Forget Mike falling in the fire. Forget Jerri being voted out. Colby had just single handedly sabotaged his game, and out of nowhere had given Tina a completely improbable chance to win. And THAT was the moment that I would now consider the best of the best. Again, forget rats and snakes. THIS was the Survivor moment that everyone would be talking about tomorrow.

I remember just staring there slack jawed as Keith was voted out of the game. Because my God, this wasn't supposed to happen on Survivor. Not like this it wasn't. Not when Colby was thiiiiis close to having an easy slam dunk 7-0 victory. He sabotaged all of that just to give his friend Tina a chance. He literally sabotaged every single argument out there that Survivor was a game that could only be played by selfish people, and that success in the game eventually turned you into a dick. And that people who did well on Survivor were horribly selfish assholes who only thought about money and personal glory and who had no interest in ethics or morality.

Colby dispelled all of those arguments in one vote. And the ramifications of his decision were enormous.

Colby's decision to spare Tina is a moment that people still talk about when it comes to Survivor. They still talk about it and they still debate it to this very day. And it has now been more than a decade. Colby's decision quickly grew into the most important and the biggest signature moment of Australia, and I believe it eventually became a bigger deal than even the Mike accident.

Now, why did Colby do it? Why did he spare Tina? What exactly was he trying to accomplish? Well understanding that, in my opinion, is the key to understanding the season. Because I know what you have heard. I know that the most common explanation for Colby's decision out there over the years has always been "Colby was an idiot." Or "Colby made a mistake." Or "Colby threw the game and lost on purpose." Or this one, this one always makes me laugh, "Colby was a bad player who didn't understand Survivor."

Well, here is the deal. Colby wasn't an idiot. And Colby wasn't confused about Survivor. And Colby didn't throw the game. And Colby didn't make a mistake.

Colby didn't make a mistake, he made a choice.

Personally, I thought what Colby did was one of the greatest things that has ever happened on Survivor. And that isn't just the ravings of a rabid Tina fan, that is the God's honest truth. I really did think what he did was awesome. And I still think that. And once you see my reasoning why, once you understand the big variables that were involved at the time, and what Colby's thought process probably would have been at that moment, I think you will agree with me that his decision to save Tina really wasn't as stupid as it seemed. At least, not at that moment it wasn't. In fact, in many ways, Colby's decision to be "the nice guy" at the end really wasn't even a mistake at all. In many ways, that was really the only way that Australia could have ended.

Don't worry, we will talk a lot more about this in the next chapter. Just keep in mind for now that Australia was supposed to end that way. The good guy was supposed to win. This was the exact ending that all sixteen players had been striving for all along.

Whether you agree with his choice or not (again, not a mistake, a choice), Colby's decision was one hundred percent determined by what had happened in Borneo.

P.S. One of the fun little trivia facts about Australia, and you will really notice this the next time you watch it, is that the editors NEVER spelled out, at any point during the season, that Tina and Colby were an ironclad final two pair. At no point, in any episode, for nearly three months, did the editors clue the audience in that Colby and Tina had a pact to the end and that they had pretty much always had a pact to the end. And this is why when people ask me nowadays "was the audience surprised when Colby took Tina to the end?" the answer is pretty obvious. Heck yeah we were surprised. NOBODY saw that coming. And the reason nobody saw that coming is because the editors had specifically hidden it from us.

After the season ended, all the interviews came out, and it was pretty obvious at that point that Colby and Tina had had that final two pact since about the tenth day of the game. Yet it was never shown in the episodes. And you know why it was never shown in the episodes? Well because Survivor was presented to the audience much differently back then than it is now. Back in the early days of the show, the name of the game from a production point of view was "hide the winner." The producers and the editors absolutely did not want anyone in the audience to know who the winner was going to be, and they especially didn't want you to know who the final two was going to be. So there was not a chance in hell that Colby and Tina's final two pact was ever going to be shown in the episodes. Nowadays, of course, Jeff Probst would have based his entire recap at the start of every episode around that final two deal, and how it was going to impact the rest of the season. But in season two? Nuh uh. That little piece of evidence wasn't shown, simply because Survivor wasn't interested in giving away its trump card at the time. The name of the game back in the early days was "keep the ending a surprise."

Also, this helps explain why so many people nowadays think that Colby was an idiot. He wasn't an idiot at all. That final two deal was there. He just honored it like he was supposed to do. Again, blame the editors if this is the very first time in your life you have ever heard that Colby and Tina always had a final two pact. Colby was a very smart guy, and he was just doing what he was supposed to be doing.

40. In Defense of the Colbster

Now, obviously, when I say that I was thrilled when Colby took Tina to the finals, the first thing you are probably going to think is "Well duh, of course you were thrilled. You were a Tina fan and Colby basically handed Tina a million dollar check. Of course you would have been in favor of that." But it goes a lot deeper than that. There was a far more important reason why I think it was great what Colby did. And it has absolutely nothing to do with Tina or the fact that I am the world's biggest Tina groupie.

Unfortunately, this is going to be one of those times where I use the cliché Mario phrase of "You just sort of had to be there." Because there is no way you can understand why Colby did what he did in its proper context unless you were there at the time and you were following Survivor at the time.

Like I said at the end of the last chapter, Colby's decision at the end of Australia was one hundred percent determined by what had happened in Borneo. Remember how I said that most of America hated the ending of Borneo? Remember when I talked about the outcry over Richard Hatch and the Tagi Alliance winning, and how the last few episodes of Borneo were seen as little more than "human beings devolving into their lowest possible form"? And "Well, the show started out good, but eventually they all turned evil and selfish and it devolved into a giant clusterfuck." Remember how so many fans said they would never watch a show like this again if it was possible for an asshole like Richard to win?

Well this was the thought process that was on EVERYBODY'S mind as the second season of Survivor came around. This was what the fans were talking about, this was what the media was talking about, and this is what the television critics were talking about. Heck, this was what preachers and psychology professors and priests and elementary school teachers and sociologists were all talking about. Why did Survivor turn ordinary people into selfish unethical assholes, and what did that say about us as a species? Why was it possible for a little bit of extra money (because really, that's all that a million dollars was, once you took all the taxes out) to turn normal rational human beings into emotionless self-gratifying sociopaths?

Again, I hate to keep harping on this, but this was what nearly EVERYBODY thought about Borneo at the time. They all viewed it as a fun little social experiment that had started off fine, but it had eventually devolved into something ugly and heartless and mean. And that as fun as the last few episodes had been to watch, most people felt that after you saw the

226

finale on TV you sort of had to take a shower afterwards. Because watching the way that Richard and Kelly and Sue had turned on one another (especially Sue turning on Kelly) had been like watching a suicide jump. It might have been interesting to see at the time, but after you watched it and you took pleasure out of it you kind of felt dirty about it.

Remember, this was Borneo's legacy. This was what EVERYONE was talking about. And you better believe that the applicants for season two knew full well what kind of a firestorm they were potentially walking into. They knew full well that the game they were signing up to play had the potential to turn ugly. And that they all had the potential to come off like grade-A assholes on national TV. They knew that, and they were probably all very affected by that. I mean, come on, Borneo had been such a big deal, and the ending had been so hated and so reviled, and so many people had watched it and were still talking about it as season two rolled around, that you would have had to have been an idiot to apply for the second season and not know what sort of a maelstrom you were walking into.

The players in season two were going to be scrutinized. They were going to be psychoanalyzed. They were going to be judged. And they were going to have their character called into question. A lot. By nearly everyone.

All sixteen of them knew that.

When you look at Colby's decision in this context, it makes perfect sense why he did what he did. Heck, you look at it this way, and there is almost no way he WOULDN'T have picked Tina. Because Colby knew full well that nobody in season two wanted to go down in TV history as the ~~Richard~~ asshole. They all knew that. They all saw what had happened to the Survivors the first time around, how they had all "turned evil." And nobody wanted season two to turn into the same sort of a debacle. The players who were cast in Australia wanted their version of Survivor to be more ethical, to be nicer, to just be more downright likable. And you can see it in just about every single decision and every single confessional they gave throughout the season. Seriously, go back and watch Australia, and watch it from this perspective the next time around. Read between the lines when you watch the episodes. Watch how the players interact. Watch what they do. And, more importantly, watch what they don't do. Keep in mind that nearly everything the players say or do throughout the season **is completely in response to how Borneo was received, and how the Australians just don't want to be come off as hated like the Tagis were.** That is the key to watching Australia and understanding it in its proper context. Count how many times during the season it is mentioned that "this time around, we want the good guys to win."

In any case, when you look at Australia this way, Colby's decision to spare Tina makes perfect sense. He had a chance to be selfish, and to take the easy win. He had a chance to stab his best friend in the back, and to betray the only person he ever had an alliance with in the game. He had a chance to choose victory over loyalty, and put the knife in the back of his outback mommy. And he didn't take it. And no, that wasn't Colby being "stupid" at all. So many people love to talk crap about Australia these days. They love to talk about how Colby's decision to save Tina was "the stupidest decision in Survivor history." And no, I'm sorry, but that's crap. If you are the type of person who is writing shit like that in your Survivor essay or on your Survivor webpage, please do me a favor and stop writing about Survivor altogether. Because you weren't there at the time, you have no business writing about something you don't understand, and I'm sorry, you have no idea what you are talking about.

Colby did not choose to lose to Tina. He was not stupid at all, he knew exactly what he was doing. He knew full well that season two was going to be "the season of the good guy"-- I mean, come on, how many times did the confessionals have to beat this into our heads?! He knew that whoever was "the most good good guy" at the end was going to be the one that everyone remembered. And that the hero was probably going to get the media endorsements, and the interviews, and the TV career, and the CBS insider jobs, and the Reebok commercials. In other words, Colby was playing a much bigger game than just winning the money. He wasn't just trying to win Survivor, he was trying to become the anti-Richard. He was trying to become the darling of the entire Survivor franchise.

And the fact that he still had a 50/50 chance of beating Tina even on top of that?

Well that part was just the icing on the cake.

If there is one thing I would like you to keep in mind when you think about Colby, it is this. He was an actor. He was a media personality. He had visions of being in Hollywood. And he had a chance to become the star and the face of the biggest damn TV franchise of the past 20 years. And he would have known it was something that the franchise needed, too, since most of the "names" in the first season had come off as such douchebags at the end. Colby had a golden opportunity to become the new and improved Colleen Haskell of Survivor. And it wouldn't even be that hard to do, since the original Colleen hadn't actually been significant enough to Borneo to ever really be considered "the star of the season" anyway. Nor had she ever really even <u>wanted</u> to be "the star." After her season ended, Colleen Haskell just wanted to say goodbye to reality TV forever and go home. As Australia rolled around, that meant that her former position as "the beloved icon of the Survivor franchise" was currently available.

To my dying day, I will always say that Colby Donaldson is the biggest hero in Survivor history. And he always will be. At his peak, the guy was revered. I mean, hell, my mom passed away in 2004, and even up to her final days she used to tell me how bothered she was that Colby didn't win that final vote over Tina in Australia. Here was my mom, in her final days battling cancer, and one of the things she thought about the most was "How could those jurors be so stupid? Colby was the best Survivor there ever was. How come those jurors didn't reward that?"

And why was Colby the best Survivor there ever was?

Easy.

He was the best Survivor ever because he made the smartest decision in Survivor history. He chose his friend Tina. And he demonstrated that Survivor actually could produce a good player who was also a good guy. Prior to May of 2001, most people would have said that was impossible.

Had Colby taken Keith to the finals, he would have won an easy 7-0 vote. It would have been a blowout. And if that had happened, I doubt that many people would still be talking about it these days. Australia's ending would be remembered as little more than "Well it was so predictable. The young guy won all the challenges and then he just steamrolled everyone. It was so boring." Also, every middle aged mom in America would have been disappointed because that nice young man Colby had turned on his outback mommy. Survivor never would have had its first big hero until the introduction of Ethan. And by then, it might have been too late. If Survivor had to wait three seasons to finally have "the most good good guy" make it to the end, it is possible that a good chunk of its audience might have already abandoned it, and they might have never come back. Because remember, it isn't just hardcore high school student and college student strategy gamers who watch Survivor. There is a good chunk of the world that watches Survivor who AREN'T hardcore strategy gamers. A lot of people watch the show just for the relationships and the personalities. And had Australia ended with a series of backstabbings and falling-outs and arguments just like Borneo did, it would have been a disaster for the franchise.

Side Note: By the way, I am well aware what the rebuttal is to my Colby argument, and I want to defend against it right now. So let's just get this right out into the open before it becomes a thing. Colby did NOT throw the game. Colby Donaldson did NOT lose Survivor on purpose.

Remember, there was a good chance that he could have beaten Tina in that final vote. He still had a very good chance. What happened is that Colby just decided somewhere along the way that winning or losing that way (against Tina) was a far more honorable accomplishment than running up the score with a slam dunk blowout against Keith. Because remember, just about every single player in that season had decreed that Keith was "undeserving" of being in the final two. And Australia was all about "deserving." The theme of that entire season, all season long, was that whoever won Australian Outback had to win the right way, with the right ethics, and against the right people. Remember, "deserving" is the key to EVERYTHING when you talk about Australian Outback. It really doesn't even fit the pattern of any other Survivor season. I mean, the goat that season (the player who never could have possibly won, aka Keith) was voted out at the final three. Name any other season where the goat was voted out at the final three. I bet you can't do it. And no, Jonny Fairplay wasn't the goat in Pearl Islands, Lill was.

And so there you go. My defense of Colby. And why what he did was incredible. And why he is so far from "the stupidest player in Survivor history" that I don't even think it is debatable. In fact, one could even argue that Colby could actually be considered the smartest player in Survivor history, simply because of the way that he outwitted the audience. Colby Donaldson took everything we thought we knew about Survivor, he took everything we thought we knew about greed, and about selfishness, and about "who was the most deserving", and about human behavior when money and fame and ego are around to influence it, and he turned it all on its head. He looked right into the camera, and he told the producers, "Look, I don't care how much money you dangle in front of me. I am still the Colbster and I am not going to backstab my friend." And he won America's heart in the process.

And the second season of Survivor was really the only season where something like that ever would have happened.

Remember, everything that happened in season two was a response to season one. That is just all there is to it. Everything in season one begat season two, just like everything in seasons one and two begat season three. There is just no way around that. And this is why when people tell me they have a friend who would like to start watching Survivor, and they ask me which season they should start them on, I always tell them the same thing. I always say to start with the beginning. Start with Borneo. Watch what happened in Borneo. And then watch how the players in Australia responded to that. And then watch how the players in Africa responded to THAT. In my mind there is really no other way a person should ever be introduced to Survivor. Jumping around, and watching seasons out of order, or even skipping seasons altogether, that is kinda just pointless. You are never going to get anything out of that. If you are introduced to Survivor that way, you will never get any historical context out of it.

In the end, all I hope you will take from this chapter is the idea that Colby Donaldson was not an idiot. Please stop saying that Colby was an idiot. He was not an idiot. In fact, I think he would have been an idiot if he HAD taken the easy money and he HAD come off like the asshole at the end of the season. Because that is what the behavior of a short sighted person would have looked like. That would have been a person who knew exactly what sort of a dilemma the Tagis had run into at the end of the game, and who chose the exact same path.

Well, Colby was not short sighted. And Colby didn't make a mistake, he made a choice. You can't make a mistake if you know what the consequences are going to be. He was simply playing a game that was much bigger than the game of Survivor, and he happened to win it. He won the hearts of the fans. He won the heart of my mom. Remember, winning Survivor (especially back in the early days) wasn't always just as simple as "winning Survivor." I mean, Richard Hatch won Survivor, but because people disliked him and they disliked what he stood for, after his season was over he didn't get jack squat. He barely got a single endorsement after the season. And no book publisher would touch him. Colby, on the other hand, wound up making a LOT more money than Richard ever did. He appeared in a few movies. He was in commercials. He was on a TV show. Hell, he even HOSTED his own TV show. And he didn't get those because he won Survivor. No, he got those because he did what was best for him at the time. He got those because he was The Colbster.

And now you know why I was so damn happy that Colby chose to take his

231

friend to the end over taking the money. Now you can finally understand what I am talking about when I say that. I was happy for the future of this franchise. I was happy about the fact that the audience actually had hope now, because they really didn't have that after Borneo. After Borneo everyone thought that the finalists would always turn out to be assholes.

Oh yeah. And I suppose I should mention that I was also very happy that my beloved favorite player Tina had just won Survivor.

I BELIEVE THAT CALLS FOR A REALLY BIG FIST PUMP!!!

41. Understanding Tina

Before I talk about Tina, there are a few misconceptions about Australia that I believe we need to clear up first.

The first thing I would like to talk about is this longstanding belief that "in the second season of Survivor, Tina won because she was nice." Or the ever-popular, "Tina winning made people forget about Richard, because Tina was so popular and Richard was so unpopular."

I hate to say this, because I am such a big fan of Tina, but bullshit. The nicest person didn't win Survivor the second time around. And Tina winning did nothing to make people forget about Richard. Indeed, if anything, there were just as many Survivor fans out there who hated Tina. This fifteen year misconception that Tina Wesson was a beloved fan favorite and that everyone loved her and that everyone loved her victory needs to stop right now. Tina was never the fan favorite in Australia. Ever. At any point. Never never never ever ever.

Furthermore, Tina did not win Survivor just because she was "nice." I mean, she probably is very nice in real life, I don't know. I have never personally met her. But that had nothing to do with why she won Survivor. The reason Tina won Survivor was because she was crafty. And because she was cagey. And because she had the right ties to all the right people at all the right times. And... I know how baffling this will sound to Russell Hantz and his nation of idiot disciples... she won because she had extremely good people skills and because the other players genuinely liked her and they genuinely respected her. After all, you can't win a game like this if the jurors don't want you to win. Right? I mean, duh. That is just Survivor 101.

Now as for the original question, was Tina "nice"? Wellllllllll, I'm not so sure I would really describe her that way. I certainly don't think she was nice the way that she blindsided Amber. And I certainly don't think it was nice what she did to poor Mad Dog. And I <u>really</u> don't think it was nice how she belittled and openly talked down to Jerri right out there in the open in front of everyone. I mean, go back and watch some of the Tina and Jerri interactions in Australia, and watch them from Jerri's perspective this time around. Most of the time Tina was just a stone cold bitch to her.   But it didn't really cost her in the end because most of the other players were annoyed by Jerri too, so no one really noticed. Tina was more or less just pandering to the jurors when she would openly defy Jerri in front of everyone. And, in as polite and as Southern a way as she possibly could, she would kindly ask Jerri to sit down and please shut the f up.

One thing that I think Tina was VERY good at, and this is something that I don't think she has ever gotten enough credit for over the years, was the way she was able to regulate the morality of the game. She flat out controlled the ethics of the other players around camp. She started doing it the minute she set foot in the Outback. And in the end I will always say that THIS was why Tina Wesson won Survivor. It had nothing to do with her being nice. Or her being strategic. Or the fact that she was the mom figure. Or the fact that she was cutthroat (although, oh boy, was she ever.)

No, in the end, I believe Tina won Survivor simply because she flat out mind-fucked everyone.

Remember how I said that everyone knew the players in the second season would have to be nicer than the first? Remember how I said that no one in the second season wanted to come off as being the Richard, or the Sue, or the asshole? Remember how they were all very cognizant of how they were going to come off on TV because of what had happened the first time?

Well guess who was the one talking about Christianity, and ethics, and "the right type of person needs to win this time" the most? That's right, it was our good little friend Miss Tina. Go back and watch Australia again, and watch how often Tina brings this subject up around the other players. Watch how often she stirs the pot of "Well we are all a little family here, and we want the good people left at the end." She is CONSTANTLY pushing that button with the other players. She knew EXACTLY what the mindset would be among the players going into season two, and if you pay attention and watch what she does, you can see that she completely milks it. All season long, all you hear in Australia is talk of "the good people." Or "the right people." And in my opinion, that is all Tina. She totally set it up so that a tiny little Christian woman with good people skills would actually be able to win Survivor this time.

And again, this is something that is so oblique, and so subtle, and is so hard to notice at first glance, that she has never really gotten enough credit for it. Honestly, I don't think anyone else could have ever pulled off the strategy that she did. Tina was the one person who could have formed a bond with (and given enough ethical guilt to) Colby, and actually make him feel bad about voting her out. If that duo had been made up of ANY other combination of players, in ANY other season, I don't think the Australia ending would have played out the way that it did. In fact, in many ways, I have always believed that Tina mind-fucked Colby as badly as Tom Westman

234

would later do to Ian in Palau. Except Tina didn't do it through intimidation, or bullying, or sheer force of her personality, like Tom would later do to Ian. No, Tina was much more subtle than that. She did it through ethics. She spent 41 days making sure Colby remembered that the audience would want to see "the right person" win Survivor this time around.

And that is exactly what happened.

Look, do I think that Tina is as Christian or as sweet or as goody goody as she tried to come off during the season? Hell no. Hell to the DurEEEtose no. I mean, I know she is Christian. And from everything I have ever heard about her in real life, she sounds like she is a very nice person. But do I think she was this innocent little sweet-as-pie daffodil that she tried to come off to the Ogakors? Not even close. I mean, Tina was not the audience favorite for a reason. In particular, from what I remember, she was NOT popular at all among most female viewers. My wife couldn't stand her. Most female fans I knew at the time thought she was fake, and that she was a huge hypocrite. And don't even get me started on how many females hated her just because she was tiny and cute and morally superior to everyone, and because she had a boob job.

In fact, most females I knew at the time wouldn't have described Tina as "the nice one" in the cast at all. Most of them at the time would have referred to her as "self-righteous." Or "holier than thou." Or "faker than Fakey McFakerson."

By the way, this is something that is kind of obscure, and you wouldn't really know about it unless you had been watching Australia as it aired, but do you know what kind of stories were floating around about Tina in the media at the time?

Well, okay, remember all those stories about Richard Hatch "abusing" his son that came out right around the time that he won Borneo? You know how they cost him a lot of goodwill among the fans? You know how all the bad press about Richard pretty much torpedoed any chance that he would ever become a celebrity at CBS?

Well there was a bad story floating around about Tina too. And it did not make her look good.

The story that came out about Tina was… well… do you remember the scene in the Outback Cafe, where Tina talked and flirted over the internet with her new husband, Dale? Well apparently Dale used to be married to

Tina's best friend. That is, until Tina allegedly stole him from her. And then when Tina got popular and she became a celebrity, the friend wrote an article and sent it to all the newspapers, in an attempt to expose her.

So here are all these news articles coming out in 2001 about our new beloved Survivor hero, Tina Wesson. And about what an amazing person she is. And about what a wonderful mom she is. And how close to God she is.

And meanwhile there was another story that was popping up all over the place, and it never really went away. This one was featured on Survivor News, and Survivor Fever, and all of the other big Survivor websites at the time. In fact, I am surprised that it never got as much national attention as the Richard child abuse story did. This story said something along the lines of "DON'T TRUST TINA! THAT BITCH IS RUTHLESS AND SHE STOLE MY HUSBAND! DON'T BELIEVE A WORD THAT COMES OUT OF HER MOUTH, TINA WESSON IS THE DEVIL!"

And well, I guess that was now <u>two</u> future Survivor winners that CBS was probably a little bit worried about. It wasn't until Ethan the next season that they would get their first winner who was completely controversy-free.

Please understand that I am not saying this just to try to make Tina look bad. Far from it, remember, she has always been one of my favorite players. In fact she is still maybe my all-time favorite player, even today. Even after the Sandra Diaz-Twine era. I am just saying it to point out that the "Tina only won Survivor because she was nice" argument doesn't really hold water. It didn't hold water in 2001, and it doesn't hold water today. Tina didn't win Survivor by default just because she was nice. She won Survivor because she is a shrewd and cunning little gamer who has the ability to mess with you.

Oh, and if you don't believe that "the right people need to win this time" didn't also include Tina reminding people that "Hey, I am one of the right people!" well I don't think you understand Tina. She was just as Machiavellian as Richard was. In fact it is possible that she was even MORE Machiavellian. If you don't believe she was cutthroat, just ask Amber. Or Jerri. Or Mitchell. Or Mad Dog.

No, Tina was just able to hide her Machiavellianism behind Christianity. And behind a sweet little accent and the guise of being a nice little mommy.

Remember, if there is one thing you need to keep in mind about Tina, it is this:

In this game (just like in many games), a girl with a sweet smile and a sweet little Southern accent can get away with <u>murder</u>.

42. How Tina Won

Okay, this is going to be my favorite chapter in the entire book. Here is a great rundown of how Tina Wesson won Survivor: The Australian Outback.

This is an essay that I have written many times before (and a lot of it forms the basis of what I have always called "The Badass Tina Theory"), but if you have never read it before I am sure you will find it interesting. Although, because Mark Burnett never put out an official book about the second season like he did with the first season, obviously some of these details I sort of have to speculate about. I am guessing this is pretty close to how it really went down though.

Okay, here we go.

Day one. Tina Wesson arrives in Australia. And right off the bat she knows that two things have to happen. There has to be a culture this time around that "okay, this time on Survivor, the good guys have to win." And it has to be known by everyone that she is one of those "good guys." So right off the bat she goes into Survivor with a unique strategy that no one player before or after her has ever been able to use. She literally USES THE FIRST SEASON AS A WEAPON AGAINST ALL OF THE OTHER PLAYERS. Oh, hey guys. Remember Tagi? Remember what jerks they were? Well let's not be like THAT. Oh, and did I mention I go to church and I am a mom and I work as a nurse? But hey, wasn't that Richard a creep? I mean, my goodness. Hey, do you guys want to pray to Jesus with me? Want to be my new little Outback Family?

Once the "good guys have to win this time around" mindset has been established, Tina goes around and she finds the goodest good guys she can align with. These are probably Amber, the sweetest and youngest girl on the tribe, and Colby, who is just like your mother's ultimate dream son. I am guessing (I can only speculate, of course, but if you know Tina you can guess who she probably aligned with) that Mitchell was probably in the mix somewhere too, because he was the heart of the tribe and because he was the nice guy who sang and who everyone loved. So I am guessing this was the heart of the Ogakor alliance at the start of the game. Tina, Amber, Colby, and Mitchell. The nice ones.

Now, obviously, Tina also makes friends with Mad Dog, simply because she is the only female on the tribe who is anywhere close to Mad Dog's age. So

Tina kinda sorta has to buddy up with her. Just in case. And then she does the same with Keith. Nobody else on the tribe is close to Keith in age either, so Tina more or less has to become one of his close friends out there. So she does. Now she has ties to just about everyone.

As the season goes along, it becomes apparent that Jerri is kind of becoming the Queen Bee of the Ogakors. Jerri is buddying up with Amber and Mitchell and Colby. And that is a problem. Not just because it isn't Tina who is becoming the Queen Bee of the Ogakors, but let's be honest, it is also because Tina just can't stand Jerri as a human being. Tina doesn't like Jerri, Jerri doesn't like Tina, the two of them will never get along. In fact, Tina would probably like nothing more than to wipe that smug little grin off of Jerri's face and knock her right off of her throne. So that is exactly what she does. Tina works her way into a final two alliance with Keith (the goat who nobody likes) and a final two alliance with Colby (the horse she can ride all the way to end and who will never turn on her), and this is where she begins her path of destruction against all the people who thought she had been their friend.

Mad Dog? Don't need you, baby. Buh bye.

Mitchell? Yeah, we're friends, I know. But take a hike.

Tina cuts two of her best friends off at the knees simply because she doesn't need them anymore. And because she wants to undercut Jerri. And from this point on, Jerri is now effectively neutered. She will never be in power again at any point in Australia. Oh, and the best part of it all? Tina votes off her friends prior to the merge so that none of them can hold it against her later in the jury. THAT is the sign of a savvy player. If you have to make the nasty cuts, you make sure you do them early on in the game so that nobody can ever get you back for them. That is how a truly ruthless player plays Survivor. You do the dirty work early.

Oh yeah, and Tina also more or less invents the idea of a "Survivor power shift" when she spearheads the Mitchell blindside in episode four. That was a very important moment in the evolution of Survivor, and it is one that has rarely ever gotten the credit that it historically deserves. Let's not forget that Tina Wesson was the person who was responsible for all of that.

Side Note: Okay, this is a fun one. You know how Tina was always harping on the fact that "the good guys need to make it to the end this time around"? Well if you stop and you think about it, you realize how full of crap she really was. Tina didn't want "the good guys" to get to the end. She wanted TINA to get to the end. If she really wanted "the good guys" to get to the end, don't you think she would have included her best friend Mad Dog as one of those good guys? Of course she would have. But no, she shamelessly cut her best friend's throat at the end of episode three just to fit in with the group. And she didn't spend even two nanoseconds afterwards feeling guilty about it or crying over it. And the only explanation you can come up with for that (especially in an early season, when you never voted out your friends) is that snipers don't cry.

Again, and I can't repeat this enough, Tina didn't "luck into a Survivor win" just because she was "nice." And she had no interest at all in "the good guys all getting to the end", unless that sentence got her further in the game. I mean, think about this. If Tina REALLY wanted the good people to make it to the end, don't you think she would have pushed for the power shift an episode earlier than she did, just so she could have saved her friend Mad Dog? She certainly had the votes to do it. Yet she sacrificed her best friend just because it was better for Tina. Think about it before you call Tina Wesson "the nice one."

Okay, back to how Tina won Australia.

So now we get to the merge. Tina wins the immunity challenge that night for the Ogakors (by stepping down and handing it to Keith, of course) and now we have reached a point where Badass Tina can never be stopped. With the Ogakors in the majority now she can simply waltz to the end. So, at this point now, she starts playing up the "good guys need to win this time" card around people like Rodger and Elisabeth. She starts playing that card HARD. She also starts talking about how amazing Mike was, and what an amazing leader he was. Oh, and she continues to take care of Colby and she starts playing mommy to him. Again, Tina is totally playing for the endgame at this point. She is totally using the perception of Borneo as "the mean, nasty season that turned bad at the end" as a weapon to use against her opponents in Australia. And not just because she wants to win that final jury vote. No, she also does it because she wants to be IN that final jury vote in the first place. She needs to be absolutely one hundred percent sure that Colby will take her to the end if he wins that final immunity challenge (because you know he will probably win it.) Remember, Tina's big fear at this point is that Colby will take Keith to the end simply because nobody likes

Keith. Tina doesn't want that. In fact, she needs to find some way to guilt Colby into NOT doing that. So she does it by constantly playing mommy to him. She does it by feeding into his need (and the need of the season in general) that Colby has to be the good guy. Again, she does whatever she can to basically mind-fuck the guy.

And, of course, you know what happens at the end. Tina cuts Jerri and Amber loose at the point that she simply doesn't need them anymore. Jerri just because ha ha lol Jerri, and Amber because well I'm sorry pumpkin, I mean you're a cute little girl and all, and you know I love you, but you really don't deserve to be here in this game with the grownups anymore. And I should point out, of course, that neither Jerri nor Amber sees it coming for a second. Tina just completely blindsides them. But hey, it's not that bad because Colby just blindsided them too. And guess which one Jerri has a relationship with and who she will blame for the backstab?

Rodger and Elisabeth are voted out next, and that is just fine with Tina because boy oh boy does she really need them to believe in her on that jury. After all, don't we really want to see a nice Christian mom win Survivor the second time around? And, hey, aren't I just the complete opposite of Richard? Have you two ever noticed that? Remember how we used to pray together and talk about our families all the time?

Then Colby wins the final immunity challenge (as everyone expected.) And at this point in the game Tina can do little but sit there and hold her breath and see if Colby really does believe that "the good guys need to win Survivor the second time around." Because this was the moment that she had been worrying about. And this had been her strategy all along. Make sure that everyone knows that the winner needs to be the opposite of Richard Hatch the second time around. Make sure they all know that. Always. The winner has to be the complete opposite of Richard. Remind everyone in Australia about this every single day.

And it is under this pressure, and under these forces, and with these variables involved, and at this point in Survivor history, that Colby makes the decision that it is more beneficial to him as a person, **AT THIS MOMENT**, that he be seen as the good guy at the end. And not just as the guy who backstabbed his outback mommy and who steamrolled his way to a Survivor win.

Now, of course, I can't sit here and tell you that Colby's decision was one hundred percent based on what Tina had been doing to him. That would be silly. But it would also be silly to think that Tina had nothing to do with it at all. Heck, she had been conditioning him to think that way since the minute

241

they set foot in Australia. This was the exact scenario at the end of the game that she had probably been HOPING for.

Oh, and if Colby hadn't won that final immunity challenge? Well that wasn't that big a deal to Tina. If Keith had won that final immunity challenge, he would have taken Tina to the end too. So she goes to that final jury vote either way.

And that, my friends, is how one of the most interesting players in the history of Survivor pulled off one of the all-time great Survivor wins.

43. My Mom and Gay Hairdressers

There is one Survivor question that I get all the time. People love to email me and ask, out of all the final Tribal Councils in the history of Survivor, which final matchup do you think was the most interesting? And really, this is a pretty easy question to answer. Whenever I get that particular question (and I really do get it a lot), I always tell the person, "Australia." Easy. The most interesting final Tribal Council was in Australia.

The reason I think the Australia final Tribal Council was so interesting is because it was one of the few times in the history of Survivor, indeed it was maybe even the <u>only</u> time, that you truly had the two best players of the season sitting up there facing one another in the jury vote. You had Colby and Tina, they were evenly matched in just about every strategic and social and diplomatic way possible, no one got dragged to the end as the other one's goat, the jury didn't hate either one of them on a personal level, etc. Really, it was one of the few times in Survivor history that either one of the finalists could have realistically won that vote. Colby and Tina were so good at Survivor, and they had both worked together nearly every single step of the way, and they both had the exact same friends and enemies once the decision was turned over to the jury, that honestly, in the end, it was really all just going to come down to a preference in game style.

At the end of the day, the jurors were simply going to have to decide. Did they prefer the physical dominant challenge-winning game style of Colby? Or did they prefer the subtle influencing social game style of Tina? No matter who won that vote, it was going to be close. It was guaranteed to be 4-3 in favor of one of them.

By the way, I say that this was the only time in Survivor history that two evenly matched dominators faced the jury at the end, but that sentence isn't quite one hundred percent accurate. If you wanted to, I think you could make a pretty good case that Yul and Ozzy in Cook Islands also fit this definition as well. They were both evenly matched in terms of dominating the game, and either one of them could have easily won that final jury vote. And either one of them would have been a satisfying winner. Just like in Australia, in Cook Islands the decision really just came down to game style preference. Do jurors prefer the subtle social diplomat game style of Yul, or do they prefer the physical dominant challenge god game style of Ozzy?

In the end, just like in Cook Islands, the Australia jury wound up preferring the social game. The Australia jury voted for Tina to win, just like the Cook Islands jury voted for Yul. Turns out that social beat physical in both cases.

And if you are interested in what the best way is to win Survivor, there is probably an important lesson to be learned from that...

Oh yeah, and I know that some people will claim that Tocantins had a similar showdown between the two best players at the end, when the season wound up with J.T. against Stephen. But come on, let's get real here. J.T. won that vote 7-0. That wasn't a showdown at all, that was a massacre. Let's try to be a little less liberal with our definition of "showdown" here.

> **Side Note:** I guess I have to add this part as well. Even with the Yul vs. Ozzy showdown at the end of Cook Islands, I still say that Tina vs. Colby was the ONLY real example of an evenly matched showdown between the two best players at the end of a season. Because let's not forget this important little fact. Yul vs. Ozzy only happened because Cook Islands was the first season with a final three, and none of the players had really been ready for a final three. If Cook Islands had been a final two, like Survivor is supposed to be, I can guarantee you that either Yul or Ozzy would have been voted out at the end right before that final jury vote. They would have become the next Jonny Fairplay. So let's not start throwing Cook Islands into the mix as being as big a deal as Australia was. Or that Cook Islands really means anything in the long run when it comes to Survivor. That showdown between Yul and Ozzy was great at the time, but it was also kind of a fluke. Also, the idea that "a final three" is the ideal way to end a season of Survivor is so ridiculous and so stupid on so many levels that it is not even funny. But we will talk more about that later, I guess.

Okay, back to Tina and Colby.

Now, obviously there was a reason that the Australia finale (and only the Australia finale) came down to two evenly matched dominators at the end. There was a reason that season was so much different than any other season that has ever happened, or ever will happen, on Survivor.

And if you have been paying attention to my last couple of chapters about Australia, it should be pretty obvious what that reason was.

The reason Australia was so much different than any other season, the reason it can't really be compared to any other season in Survivor history, as I keep repeating over and over and over, is because Australia had the weight of the

first season hanging over its head. Every. Single. Minute. Of the way.
 Every single thing that happened in Australia was in some way a response to
Borneo. Well okay, to be more accurate, every single thing that happened in
Australia was in some way a response to the audience's reaction to Borneo,
and how America hated the ending of it. So Colby's decision (again, a
decision, not a mistake) to face the other best player at the end, which again
would not have happened in any other season, can easily be explained when
you look at it in that context.

Simply put, there were different variables behind the scenes in Australia that
no other season ever really had to worry about.

And so this is how we wound up with that final two. The best male player
against the best female player. The dominator against the chess player. The
power duo. The perfect son against his mom. Two evenly matched players
who very easily could have both won that final vote. The reaction to Borneo.

And you know, at this point the question sort of has to be brought up. Did
Tina have an unfair advantage in that scenario?

Anyone who has read my Survivor writings in the past knows exactly where I
am about to go with this argument. I am about to go into the gender angle.
 Because you better believe that there were a lot of people in America who
were hoping that a woman would win Survivor the second time around.   In
fact, if you remember the reaction of feminists and college sociology
professors that I wrote about after the Borneo finale, you will know that
there were a lot of people out there who were legitimately asking this
question at the time: Could a woman ever win a Survivor jury vote? Was
that possible in a game based on strategy like this? This question seems silly
now of course, in 2015, but in 2001, since we had never actually seen it
before, it was still a very legitimate question in a lot of peoples' minds. Was
there a Survivor jury in existence that would ever vote for a woman to win
over a man?

And a lot of people in the media were claiming that no, such a thing
would never happen. A woman winning over a man in Survivor would be
next to impossible.

This is the type of stuff you have to keep in mind when you talk about
Australia. There was a LOT of stuff going on that season that wasn't going
on in any other season, and couldn't have gone on in any other season. A
good guy had to win Survivor the second time around. That was a given.
 The ending couldn't feature any backstabbing. The players in the game

245

all really wanted the people of America to root for them. None of the jurors at the end wanted to say anything embarrassing, or hateful and spiteful, or come off like a poor sport crybaby on national TV like Sue Hawk had done. Oh, and a lot of people out there in America would really like it if a woman won Survivor the second time around. You know, it would be really good for the franchise, and for the country in general, if the second time around, a man didn't win.

I'm not saying that Tina only won because she was a woman. I'm just saying that, because it was Australia, and because of when it happened, and because of what the opinion of the first season had been at the time, you sort of have to think about this.

Now, obviously you know which ending I was rooting for at the time. I was rooting for Tina. Not because I specifically wanted a woman to win (personally I always thought the whole "a woman can't win Survivor" argument was B.S.) No, I wanted Tina to win simply because I thought she was a badass. Of course I had nothing personally against Colby. Had Colby won Australia I would have been excited for him too. If I had been in that studio when they announced him as the winner over Tina, I would have stood up and I would have cheered for him along with the rest of the audience. Back then and even still today I have always thought that Colby Donaldson was awesome.

However, in May of 2001? I wanted Tina to kick his ass. I wanted her to kick his ass hard.

Of course you know what happened next. Four people voted for Tina, and three people voted for Colby. Jerri Manthey wound up being the swing vote. Tina Wesson won Survivor, and she proved beyond a shadow of a doubt that yes, a woman could actually win a Survivor jury vote over a man.

As a Survivor fan, I have never been happier.

> **Side Note:** Okay, here is some more Tina praise for you. Think about this for a second. Tina didn't just win a Survivor jury vote. She beat <u>Colby</u> in a Survivor jury vote. How many players in Survivor history do you think could have beaten Colby Donaldson in his prime in a Survivor jury vote? I bet you could count the number of players who could have done that on one hand.
>
> Again, before you call Tina a lucky winner, or an undeserving

246

winner, or even something ridiculous like a forgettable winner, just remember that. She didn't just win, she beat **Colby**. And she won because Jerri (who, remember, didn't even LIKE Tina) turned her attention from Colby to Tina at the very last second. And Jerri suddenly realized, "Holy crap, what kind of power did this woman have over you, Colby? What kind of voodoo was she putting on you out there?"

Again, Jerri couldn't stand Tina. Jerri has never been able to stand Tina. Yet Jerri still voted for her to win.

And Tina didn't just beat anyone, she beat Colby.

Never forget that.

I remember sitting there watching that final vote, and I remember it being one of the most tense TV moments I have ever experienced in my life. Because honestly, either Colby or Tina could have won that vote. It was that close. It more or less came down to the flip of a coin. And I remember nearly falling off my bed in shock and excitement when Jeff turned that final vote around and it said "Tina." I am totally not exaggerating here, that was easily one of the twenty most exciting moments of my life.

Oh, and there are two things I will always remember about that final vote.

The first thing I will always remember, of course, is Colby's reaction shot. I mean, that was cool. Tina wins, and Colby stands up and he starts pumping his fist like it was the greatest thing in the world. I know a lot of people like to make fun of that moment, I know a lot of people think that Colby was fake, or that he was just playing for the cameras, but I have always thought that was a genuine reaction of happiness from a very genuine person. I honestly think Colby was excited that his friend Tina had just won a million dollars. I have never read anything more into it than that. And wow was that a one hundred eighty degree turnaround from the blah reaction that accompanied the ending of Richard winning.

The second thing I will always remember about the Australia finale is what my mom said about it afterwards.

Now I don't talk about my mom very often. In fact, I bet a lot of people were surprised to see that I wrote she had passed away at all, this is something that I never talk about. Yes, I add a lot of personal details into my

Survivor essays, but writing about my mom dying of cancer? Well, no offense, but that is none of your beeswax.

In any case, my mom was a big Survivor fan. Well, she was a big fan of Colby, anyway. Like most of the moms in America at the time, she thought that Colby Donaldson was the absolute nicest young gentleman she had ever seen on TV. She thought he was the absolute epitome of what all young men in America should one day aspire to grow into. I mean, I know it is crude, but let me put it this way. If I was a girl, my mom would have been overjoyed if Colby Donaldson had hooked up with me. Heck, she loved Colby so much that she probably would have been thrilled if he'd had sex with me regardless, whether I was a female or not.

Needless to say, my mom was crushed when Colby lost that final vote in Australia. CRUSHED. She was just absolutely stunned. And she couldn't fathom how that possibly could have happened. Because like I said, she thought that Colby Donaldson was pretty much God's gift to the human race. She thought he was amazing.

Colby lost that jury vote in May of 2001, and my mom passed away in January of 2004. Which meant that for the next two and a half years, all I heard, week in and week out, even when she was sick, was some variant of "Mario, why did those girls vote for Tina? Why didn't they vote for Colby? I will never understand why Colby didn't win that game."

You see, this haunted my mom. It HAUNTED her. She would never be able to make peace with it. In fact, she would even arm herself with empirical proof just to back up her argument.

One day (this was many months down the road, I should add), my mom came to me and she pointed out, "You know Mario, the jurors with the most education all voted for Colby. The smart ones all knew that he should have won. I really think the producers need to reverse it."

And you know what, I looked it up. She was right. The three jurors with the most education DID all vote for Colby. He got his three votes from Nick (the law student), Rodger (the only juror with a master's degree), and Amber (who, as it was pointed out in the finale, had always made the Dean's List in college.) Colby got the votes from the three most educated ones.
Meanwhile, Tina got her four votes from Jerri, Alicia, Keith, and Elisabeth.

And my mom loved to point this out. She would point this out to anyone who would listen to her. "You know they only voted for her because they wanted a woman to win. The smart ones who had critical thinking skills and logic all voted for Colby."

And anyway, so there you go. The two things that I will always remember about the Australia finale. I will remember Colby's reaction to Tina winning, and how cool I thought it was. And I will remember how Colby's loss haunted my mom. And how she spent years trying to reconcile it in her head. In fact, even to this day, if my mom were looking down from above, I bet she would STILL be pissed that Colby didn't win. And like most of the females in America at the time, she would probably still think that Tina was fake.

Oh well. All I know is that I loved Australia. I have always loved Australia. It took everything that Borneo did, it took all the amazing things that Borneo pulled off the first time around, and it improved on them. In fact, I have always referred to Australia as Borneo on Red Bull. Or Borneo 2.0. It took what Burnett had managed to pull off the first time around, and it amped it all up to the next level. It was very exciting to dream about where the Survivor franchise was headed at this point.

And yes, I am probably only saying that because I was a big fan of Richard, and I was an even bigger fan of Tina. If I hadn't been so spoiled by my two favorite players winning the first two seasons, perhaps I never would have become a Survivor writer.

And yeah, there was definitely a flaw in Survivor at this point. Of course there was a flaw. There were still those damn boring unavoidable Pagongings. Those things were absolute momentum killers in the middle of a season, and they were going to have to be worked on. Hmm, maybe we could even start working on them next season, with the introduction of a twist...?

Seriously, if you could pick one point in Survivor history where you would have loved to have been a Survivor fan, the week after Tina's victory in Australia probably would have been the best spot to pick.

Because right here, right now, this was about as good as it ever got.

P.S. Okay I have to tell this story. I have been sitting on it for YEARS, but now after being patient for so long I finally get to share it with someone.

Remember how I said that there were no spoilers out there that Tina was going to win Survivor? Well it turns out that isn't quite true. About a week after she won Australia, I remember some guy showed up on the Survivor Sucks message board with a little announcement to make. He wouldn't give us his name, but he said he was a hairdresser in Hollywood. And he said it had been well-known for about two months that Tina was going to win Survivor. Except the only people who knew were the Hollywood hairdressers.

As the story goes, apparently one of the bigwigs at CBS liked to get his hair done. And whenever he was in the salon, he would start talking about Survivor. And oh, whoops, one day he accidentally told his hairdresser that Tina Wesson was going to win Australia.

Remember, this was back in 2001. Information like "so and so is going to win Survivor" just didn't fall out of the sky back then. This was an extremely big info leak.

Well apparently the CBS guy didn't realize he had spilled the beans. He never told his hairdresser not to share that info. So the hairdresser went to his hairdresser friends, and word got passed around. And pretty soon it became a big insider secret. Pretty soon every hairdresser in Hollywood knew that Tina Wesson was the next Survivor winner.

So anyway, jump forward about two months. Tina wins Survivor, and it spreads all over the news. The first female winner of Survivor, wow. And then this hairdresser guy logs on to Sucks and he is surprised that so many people were shocked that Tina had been the winner. He posts something like, "Really, you guys were surprised by that? If I had known it was such a big deal I would have told you two months ago. Every gay guy in Hollywood already knew that." Then he shared the story of how Tina's win was a lot less of a surprise than everyone thought it was.

I always loved that story. It was just one little moment that happened at Sucks in the summer of 2001, but I have never forgotten it. It also taught me a very valuable lesson about life.

If you ever want to know what is going on in the world, just ask a hairdresser.

44. The Australia Book

As Australian Outback ended, and as a legion of fans settled in for the long stretch afterwards known as the Survivor offseason, I sat there and I reflected on what Mark Burnett and company had managed to pull off. I mean, they had just produced the most fascinating psychological and sociological experiment in the history of television. Survivor was one of the most compelling dramatic soap operas I had ever seen on TV. And not only had they done it, they had now done it TWICE. Australia was even bigger and better than Borneo had been. It was mind blowing to think that Survivor was even bigger now than it had been a year ago. Your mind just raced, wondering, "Okay, now where are they going to go from here?"

Well okay, obviously, we knew where they were going to go from here. They were going to go to Africa. They had said so right at the end of the Australia reunion. And that was awesome. Survivor? Shyeah, awesome. Survivor in Africa? Shyeah, even better. Since Africa is one of those places that everyone and their mother is kind of fascinated by (yet most people will never have the balls to actually visit in person), to see Survivor go there was just a really big deal. In fact, in nearly thirty seasons of Survivor, I would say that Africa was the location that I was probably excited about the most going into the season. And yes that even includes the twelve consecutive seasons that they later phoned in in Samoa.

As I sat back and I basked in Tina's win in Australia, obviously the next step for any Survivor fan at this point was to wait for the book to come out. After all, Mark Burnett had written a book about the first season. And it had been just about the coolest possible thing imaginable. Once that first book came out, and it spilled all the insider dirt and all the true stories behind what had really happened in Borneo, it completely changed the way you followed the show if you were a Survivor fan. Because that first book was the key to everything. In fact, I still refer to Mark Burnett's book about Borneo as "The Survivor Bible." It is the one book about the show that every Survivor fan on the face of the Earth should be forced to read. And in my mind, now that we had finished the second season, the only step left to finish off the season, to give us the closure that we needed, was for Burnett to give away the insider dirt and publish his book about it.

So I sat there, and I waited. And I waited. And I waited.

And that book never came out.

251

Hmm, I remember thinking. What gives? No second book?

If there is no book, then how are we supposed to know what the "real" story of Australia was? How are we supposed to learn what the game was like behind the scenes, and what the people were like behind the scenes? Are you telling me that the only record we will ever have of Australia are the fourteen episodes that were shown on TV??

In all my years of being a Survivor fan, I have to say that this was one of the most crushing blows I have ever encountered. And that is saying something, considering how much CBS and SEG have crapped on their original fanbase and pissed us off throughout the years. I couldn't believe that there wasn't going to be some sort of an insider account of The Australian Outback. I mean, it was just unfathomable. Because here you had thirty million fans, who at this point in their Survivor fandom were so loyal and so rabid that they would have bought just about any stupid product that had anything to do with Survivor whatsoever, and you are telling me Burnett was too lazy to throw together some type of a cheapie insider guide for people to read during the offseason? Come on. Mark Burnett could have sold a pair of socks with the word "Survivor" on them at that point in history, and people would have shelled out twenty dollars for them. And you're telling me he is too damn lazy to even pay somebody to ghost write a book for him?

It pissed me off that there was no behind the scenes book about Australia. It still pisses me off to this day. Because what you wound up with then was one season that was incredibly well documented and incredibly well explained, right down to the last detail (Borneo), and then another season which no one really knows anything about, other than the edited episodes we saw on TV and what we later read in interviews. It just blew my mind that Burnett didn't want any type of record out there of what really went on in Australia.

I have always said that if I could go back in time to one point in Survivor history and I could change something, this is what I would change. This is the ONLY thing I would change. I would kidnap Mark Burnett with a BB pistol, Clark Griswold style, and I would lock him in a room. And I would not let him out until he wrote that second book about Australia. Or hell, I would force him to tell me what really happened so that I could write it. All I really cared about was that there was a second book. Because once there was no second book, I knew there would never be a third book. Or a fourth book. Once Burnett stopped writing insider accounts, I knew that the one lone book about Borneo would probably wind up being the only one of its kind. And I'm sorry, but I love the history of this show so much that that just pisses me off. At some point along the way, somebody should have been

252

concerned about documenting this stuff.

This isn't something I have mentioned to a lot of people before, but I actually wrote to CBS a couple of times about this subject. I wrote to them once in the summer of 2001, and I wrote to them again about a year later, in 2002. And all I did was ask them a simple question. I said, "Hey if Burnett isn't going to write a book about the seasons anymore, would you mind if a fan wrote one? I would love to be some sort of a ghost writer for him. I wouldn't even charge a lot of money to do it, I am just a big fan and I would like there to be an Australia book out there."

I sent this letter to CBS in the late summer of 2001. I never heard back from them. I didn't even get the courtesy of a denial letter.

Well okay, I figured at the time. That was probably to be expected. After all, who am I? I am just some nobody who watches the show and who thinks I can write a book about it. Why would CBS care who I am, or what I would like to do? After all, it's not like I have any sort of portfolio I can send to them. It's not like I am a professional writer or anything. If I was CBS, and if Joe Nobody wrote me out of the blue and asked if he could write a book about my franchise, I would probably ignore him too.

At the time I just sort of filed this away under "things that would be nice, but will probably never happen." But it never left the back of my mind. I obsessed about that Australia book for years. I racked my brain to figure out what it would take, and what I could do, to make something like that happen. Because that first book was way too amazing to wind up being the only one of its kind. I didn't want the awesomeness of Survivor to be cheapened and watered down just because the creator was too lazy to write a damn summary about it.

Now if you know my writing career, and you know where it later took me, what I am going to tell you next is probably going to surprise you. Because this isn't something that I have told a lot of people over the years. In fact, this is one of the best pieces of info I wanted to share when I sat down to write my Survivor book.

After fifteen years, I guess it is time to finally spill it.

My solution to how I was going to get that Australia book written (and how I was going to be the one to write it) was that I needed to put together some sort of a writing portfolio. I needed to give CBS some sort of proof that I knew how to write about a Survivor season. And that I knew how to make it

253

sound like I had been right out there in the Outback, even though I really hadn't been. Because obviously, if it was going to be a "Mark Burnett memoir", if it was going to be published by CBS, it had to sound like it was written by a guy who had actually been out there watching the action the whole time.

Well if you know my Survivor writing career, you will know how I did this. I started writing All Star stories. In 2002 I put together a project called "All Star Survivor: Hawaii." In theory this was just a fun little writing project where a few friends and I could collaborate to write an account of a fictional Survivor season. But in truth it was way more than that. In truth, this was my audition for CBS. Once Hawaii was published, once it was amazing and realistic and popular and it developed a readership, I was going to send it to CBS and point out to them "Hey look, I just wrote a Survivor season, and it sounds like I was actually out there. So how about you let me ghost write that book about Australia now?"

That's right. All along, any of the Survivor stories I ever wrote only existed for one reason. I only wrote them because they were my audition to be the writer of the Australia book.

Now obviously, I am jumping a little ahead on my timeline. Because at this point in my story I am still not even a Survivor writer yet. All I am at this point (summer 2001) is some guy who has written a funny Fallen Comrades parody about Australia. I only mention the connection to my later All Star stories because I wanted to point out that the Australia book (or rather, the lack of an Australia book) is something that stuck badly in my craw at the time, and it still sticks badly in my craw even today. This is something I have NEVER forgotten. There definitely should have been an insider book about Australia. And if Burnett was too lazy to do it then I should have done it. In fact it is now fourteen years later and I still want to do it. If CBS were to contact me today, and if they were to ask me to write a book about what really happened in Australia, I would start writing it tomorrow. And then I would ask if I could also do the one about Africa.

I will talk a lot more about my All Star Stories later down the road, I promise. I just wanted to throw this out there now to point out what a crock it was that we never got a book about Australia. Because I am telling you, people would have bought it. People would have LOVED it. The show was never bigger, the demand for Survivor products was never more ravenous, than it was during Australia. The idea that CBS didn't cash in and throw together something cheap to take advantage of their all-time biggest Survivor season has always just bothered me.

Oh, and you know how I said that I wasn't a Survivor writer yet? How at this point I was just some random guy on the Television Without Pity message boards who no one had heard of yet? Well, all that was about to change.

Because it was right after I wrote CBS that I met Murtz Jaffer.

45. The Birth of Survivor-Central

As I said before, I didn't really hang out at Survivor Sucks much back in the early days. I mean, I KNEW about Sucks, and I certainly read some of the stuff there. I have had an account there almost since day one (my original username at Sucks was SuperMario.) But I never really posted there very often. To be honest, I avoided Sucks in the early days because it tended to be a very negative place. People at Sucks had been particularly brutal in the early days in the things they had written about Richard and Jerri and Tina. And, well, since I happened to be a big Tina fan, I tried to stay away from that. Even back in the early days I saw that a lot of Survivor fans on the internet could be assholes.

But I was on Sucks one day, just minding my own business, and reading through some of the threads in the weeks after Australia, when something interesting caught my eye. It was a post I had never seen before, written by a poster I had never heard of before.

"Wanted: Writer needed to write recaps for Survivor: Africa. I will be starting a new Survivor website and I need somebody to write the episode recaps."

It was posted by some guy named "Murtz."

Well this was certainly interesting. A brand new Survivor website? Something that would be starting up in season three? Hmmm. I wonder if they would be interested in hiring me?

One thing that you have to keep in mind about this point in history is that there really weren't that many Survivor websites out there yet. I mean, yeah Survivor News was around. And I believe Survivor Fever might have been around that early. And of course there was Sucks. But if you wanted Survivor news or you wanted to read about Survivor back then, you really didn't have that many specific places you could go if you wanted to do it. Most people would just go to a generic television website and find the message board that was dedicated to Survivor (like at Television Without Pity, or on AOL.) The idea that there would one day be a vast network of websites that were all specifically dedicated to Survivor was still a couple of months off. So it was intriguing to hear that a new Survivor site was starting up and that they needed a recap writer.

Now I will flat out admit that I had never written a recap before. I mean, I had certainly READ a lot of recaps. For years I had been reading online recaps of my favorite shows like Road Rules and Real World (and of course every so often, about Survivor.) And of course I had been writing my own episode reviews of Saturday Night Live for a couple of years. But again, my SNL writeups weren't simply a recap of the facts, they were more of me giving my opinion about whether something was good or not. And that was an entirely different kind of writing. For a recap you simply had to go through the entire episode, from start to finish, and describe the action in a way so that someone who was reading at it home would feel like they had watched the episode. Writing recaps (for anyone who has never done it before) is not really satisfying at all if you are the one who is writing them. It is a massive, comprehensive, thankless, completely not-fun-at-all, bottom of the barrel undertaking that no writer in his right mind would ever, or should ever, want to do. It is the purgatory place where you always stick your rookie writer.

But hey, I did know one website that did recaps well. I knew Television Without Pity. They were widely known across the land as the TV website that wrote the most entertaining episode recaps.

And I also knew that it would be really easy to just steal their format.

You have to remember, because of the Nick interview (or should I say the failed Nick interview), I happened to have a grudge against Television Without Pity at this point. I was still furious with those bastards for the way they had strung me along, and for the way they had later sabotaged my interview. Even a couple of months later, I was still extremely pissed off about this. This was one of those things that I took extremely personally at the time, and I was not going to forget.

So when I saw that advertisement from Murtz looking for a recap writer, one thought immediately popped into my revenge-driven little brain. Holy crap, I thought. I can just copy the TWOP format and I can steal their act.

I know this was not the noblest way to start a writing career, I will freely admit that. But hey, it was what it was. This is how it began. The only way I became a Survivor writer was out of revenge. I wanted to take what Television Without Pity was doing, and was being praised for up and down the internet, and I wanted to do it better than them. In fact not only did I want to do it better than them, I wanted to do it EXACTLY like them. I wanted to make my recaps as obvious a ripoff of TWOP as I possibly could. If somebody from Television Without Pity ever ran across one of my recaps on this new Survivor website, I wanted them to be furious about it and I wanted them to email Murtz. And then I could tell them to f off because mine was better written, it was funnier, and it got more readers. Because as you will figure out very quickly when it comes to my writing, I can be very competitive.

Oh, and if I am pissed off about something, I can also be kind of a dick.

So this now became my new mission. I was going to become the best Television Without Pity recapper not actually on Television Without Pity. I was going to steal their bit. So I went back and I studied how their writers did it. How did they write such awesome recaps? In particular I studied a writer named Kim, who did their recaps for The Real World. She was one of the funniest people I had ever read on the internet, and she had an amazing effortless way of doing it. She made it look so easy. So I went back and I re-read all of her recaps from the last couple seasons of Real World, and I studied her style. I studied how often she used jokes, and how often she just stuck to the facts. I tried to soak it up like I was a sponge.

I also went over to the TWOP Survivor board and I studied the writer who did all of their Survivor recaps. I had never really read the Survivor recaps at Television Without Pity before (why did I have to read a recap? I watched this show so obsessively I already knew every little detail), but I paid attention to her style and the way that she wrote. And I have to say, it was nowhere near as impressive as Kim's recaps for The Real World were. I don't remember the name of the girl who did the Survivor recaps but they weren't very interesting at all. It was basically just a straight retelling of the episode, except every so often she would use a nickname for one of the players instead of their actual name. And this was so cutting edge that she would use it in an attempt to sound snarky. Oooh, she called Jeff Probst "Jiffy Pop." Oh, she called Elisabeth "Lizzie." She called Alicia "Muscles." That's pretty revolutionary stuff. I didn't know how anyone would be able to top it.

Anyway, screw Television Without Pity. I could do that exact same stuff, and I could do it funnier. And I was going to.

Once I had the style of recaps down, and I figured out how they worked and how they didn't, the next step for me was to write to this guy Murtz. So I wrote to him through Sucks and I told him I was interested in the recap job. And, of course, because I knew that 90% of an internet writer's job is to promote himself (more on this later), I made it sound like I had been writing recaps for years. "Oh yeah," I told Murtz. "I have been writing episode recaps of SNL and Real World and Road Rules for five years. I could do this stuff in my sleep. In fact, I used to even write recaps for Television Without

Pity." This wasn't even remotely true, of course, but I figured that if I made myself sound like I was a big deal and that my shit didn't stink that this Murtz guy would be impressed by me.

And, apparently, he was.

Just like that, I got the job. I now had my very first Survivor writing job. I was the recap guy for a new website that was going to be called Survivor-Central. Starting with season three, Survivor Africa, each and every week I would be the guy who summed up the episode in a recap in case you had missed it.

It certainly wasn't the dream job I had envisioned in the Survivor community. It certainly wasn't a glamorous job, it certainly wasn't a job that would get me noticed right away. And it certainly wasn't anywhere near the prestige I would have gotten as "that guy who did the interview with Nick." But hey, at least it was something. And everyone has to start at some point at the bottom, right?

I didn't know a whole lot about our new website at that time, other than it was going to be called Survivor-Central and that there were going to be four of us. There was going to be Murtz (our leader), there was going to be me (our recap writer), there was going to be a guy who did all of our graphic design (Steve Macks), and then there was some fourth guy who went by the name "Potato." I didn't know Potato at all, but apparently he was a really big deal in the spoiler community. In fact, not only was Potato a really big deal in the spoiler community, he was also going to get his very own column each week at Survivor-Central ("The Potato Perspective") where he could talk about the latest news and gossip in the world of Survivor spoilers.

Yes, between him and Murtz, their plan was that Survivor-Central was going to become the #1 website on the internet that was dedicated to Survivor spoilers.

And... anyway... well... barf.

Seriously, if you have been reading this book, if you know anything about me at all, you will know how much I hate Survivor spoilers. I mean, I HAAAAAATE them. I hate the idea of Survivor spoilers with every single bone in my body. To me the idea of ruining a TV show that millions of people love and look forward to each week to is the equivalent of just walking over to somebody's house and taking a dump on their rug. I think it is rude. And I hate it.

I couldn't believe it when I found out I was now one of the people associated with the world's new #1 Survivor spoiler site. And when I found out that the entire purpose of Survivor-Central was simply to glorify the idea of the Survivor spoiler community? I nearly threw up. I nearly emailed Murtz right there and then and told him I didn't want to be a part of this anymore. Because I didn't want my name associated with something that I hated so much.

However, I didn't do that. I didn't quit.

I <u>almost</u> quit. But I didn't.

I thought about quitting. But I didn't.

Because then I got hit with some news that made Survivor: Africa a lot more exciting for me.

46. You Have Got To Be Kidding Me

Before I get to the news that was so exciting for me about Survivor: Africa, let me go on a quick tangent first about spoilers.

I know that sounds random. But I promise, it will all tie together by the end of the chapter.

As I have said before (I know you are probably sick of hearing it already), I hate spoilers. I hate everything about spoilers. I hate that they exist, I hate that they are glorified, I hate that they are successful. Hell, I can't stand that there is even a Survivor spoiler community in the first place. It has always driven me crazy that not only do these people exist just to try to ruin the show for everyone else, they actually get celebrated and championed and held up as elite members of the Survivor fan community. And don't even get me started on that guy ChillOne who ruined Amazon for everyone and then went on to write a book about it. To me, I have always considered the spoiler community of the Survivor world to be the lowest of the low. That is the aspect of Survivor that I have always been the most ashamed of.

Well anyway, since I have always hated spoilers so much, one of the things I used to like to do during the offseason was I would try to mess with all the Survivor spoiler sites.

If you go back and you look at the potential cast list for Survivor: Africa, you will see my name on there. Yes, that's right. "Mario Lanza" was one of the rumored cast members for Survivor: Africa. Oddly enough "Mario Lanza" was also a rumored contestant on Survivor: Marquesas. And hey, he was also suspected of being one of the potential castmembers of Survivor: Thailand!

This was a little game I would play every offseason with the Survivor spoiler community. Once they went hunting for the names of the potential new castmembers (and they always did), I would do whatever I could to get my name onto that cast list. And I really didn't have any reason to do this, other than I just wanted to mess up everyone's spoiler accuracy. My only real goal was to make spoiler sites look as foolish as possible when they claimed that I was a Survivor contestant but I really wasn't.

Now, obviously, getting my name onto the suspected cast list was easy for Survivor: Africa. After all, I had never written anything under my real name at this point, so nobody out there knew who I was. All I had to do was log onto Sucks under one of my ghost accounts (good luck finding out what they are) and say something like, "Hey I have this friend named Mario who was at the Survivor auditions last month. He was supposed to be cast in Australia but they cut him at the last minute and told him to reapply for Africa. Anyway, he was gone for a month and he just came back and he has lost a lot of weight. I can send you guys pictures if you want." All you had to do was post something like that in the middle of spoiler hunting frenzy season on the message boards and pretty soon, like clockwork, "Mario Lanza" would show up as a potential Africa castmember. I used to do it all the time.

Again, this was easy to do for Africa since nobody had ever heard of me before. It got a little tougher the next season, with Marquesas. Because by then I was writing a weekly recap and a lot of people knew who I was. So I literally had to stay away from the internet for a month after the season ended to try and sell the illusion that maybe I had actually been cast this time. And then I finally got away with getting my name onto the "suspected cast list" one last time with Thailand. Although by that point I was far too well known. I knew that after Thailand I would never be able to pull off this little game again.

Why do I bring up this stupid little game I used to play with the spoiler sites?

Well the reason I bring it up is because it leads into the interesting part of my connection to Survivor: Africa.

Like I said, my name showed up on a lot of the early cast lists for Survivor: Africa. But so did a lot of other names. And if I ever saw one of these cast lists (I tried to avoid spoilers if at all possible, but sometimes they spilled over onto the legitimate message boards) I would generally scan them to see if there were any people that I recognized.

I knew it was a long shot that I would ever recognize anyone. But then again, hey, last time I had a connection to Nick. And what were the effing odds of that? So who knows, maybe I would have some random connection to an actual Survivor the third season as well.

> **Side note:** There was a great "oops" mistake that CBS made at some point during the summer of 2001. And a lot of people have never heard about this before, so if you weren't there watching the show at the time you will probably find this interesting.
>
> At some point during the summer of 2001, it was discovered that CBS had registered a bunch of new domain names on the internet. I

don't remember who discovered it, or how they discovered it, but about three months before Africa debuted, it was discovered that CBS had registered new domain names like bigtombuchanan.com. And teresatbirdcooper.com. And I think there was even a lilbitpowers.com or something like that. There were like six domains that CBS had registered overall, and lo and behold if those weren't going to become the major characters of Survivor: Africa. This was a major major MAJOR spoiler, and like I said it was one of the all-time greatest "oops" moments in Survivor history. CBS tried to jump the gun and register the domains that were going to be in demand a couple of months down the road, and somehow some Survivor fan got wind of it and he spilled it to all the message boards.

Now, since I avoided all spoilers like the plague, I never really paid attention to which names had been registered at the time. I knew there was a list floating around out there, and I heard a few of the names on the list. But I never really put two and two together that these were going to be the major characters of Survivor: Africa. I just assumed that CBS had registered all sixteen castmembers as domain names at some point, and that the spoiler community had only tracked down a couple of them. I assumed that the other ten names that hadn't been discovered yet would all be discovered at some point down the road.

In retrospect, I am certain I would have been furious if I had known just how accurate a spoiler those domain names really were. And this is the kind of crap from the spoiler community that CBS had to deal with back then. At the peak of Survivor's popularity, the spoiler community just had their noses into everything. CBS couldn't get away with anything on the internet, they would always get busted for it.

So anyway, yeah there were potential cast lists floating around for Survivor: Africa. And if I saw one, I would quickly scan it to see if I recognized anyone. Yeah, I knew it would be a longshot. But it's not like there was anything else that was going on at the time. It's not like the biggest terrorist attack in our nation's history was about eight weeks away or anything. This was back when all we had to do was obsess over stupid things like Survivor casts.

Well, one day I saw a list of potential new Africa cast members, and I quickly scanned down it. This was probably in July of 2001. And I saw a name on there that finally stood out to me. The name was Lex van den Berghe.

Van den Berghe? Well that sure was a distinct name. But it sounded familiar. I wondered where I had heard it before?

I scanned back in my brain and I tried to remember where I had heard the name van den Berghe before. And it took a while, but eventually I placed it. In college I had had a French teacher named Christian van den Berghe. And I distinctly remembered him telling us one day that "van den Berghe" was a Belgian name, and that the "van den" part meant he was descended from nobility. I don't know why I remembered that, but I did. Oh, and I also remembered him telling us that the "van den" part of his name was never supposed to be capitalized, only the "Berghe" was.

Wow, what are the odds of that, I thought. I am actually going to know two people named "van den Berghe" in my lifetime. I guess this really is a pretty small world.

I didn't really know much about "Lex van den Berghe" other than the fact that he had a cool name. And that I suddenly realized that I should have finished my French minor in college. In fact, now that I think about it, I think Dr. Christian van den Berghe was actually my advisor for a couple of months. I probably should have stayed in touch with the guy.

For now, I just filed away "Lex van den Berghe" in my head. I made a note to follow up on him later.

Then, a couple of weeks later, the official CBS bios came out.

And that was when my jaw nearly dropped to the floor.

Well first off, before I get to the fun part, let me tell you a little bit about where I went to college. Between 1992 and 1996, I attended Santa Clara University. It is a small Jesuit university in Northern California, and odds are that unless you are from California yourself, you have probably never heard of it before. It is a good school, and it has a good reputation, but since it is small and nondescript it doesn't get a whole lot of national media attention.

Oh yeah, and I can also count on two hands all the famous people I know who went to Santa Clara.

Well lo and behold, there were the CBS bios. And there was Lex's bio. And sure enough, right there on his bio was the school that he graduated from:

Santa Clara University.

It turned out that Lex had been at SCU exactly ten years before I had been there. And my French teacher, Christian van den Berghe, you know, my college advisor? Well it turned out that Lex van den Berghe was Christian van den Berghe's son.

And as the title of this chapter stated, well you have GOT to be kidding me.

You see, Santa Clara isn't all that big of a school. And we happen to have a particularly close alumni base. I mean, that is one of the benefits of going to a small school, you wind up knowing most of the people you went to school with. You often even know the alumni you <u>didn't</u> go to school with.

I knew full well that there was a Santa Clara alumni directory out there on the internet that had the contact information for each and every SCU grad going back to the 1900's. Including me. And including Lex. And I knew that it wouldn't be all that hard to get in touch with him. In fact, I was probably the only Survivor fan on the internet who knew exactly who Lex was, and because of our alumni directory, knew exactly what his email was and how I would be able to contact him.

All of a sudden, it was going to be two seasons in a row where I would have some type of a connection to one of the Survivor players.

Wow.

You have to keep this next part in mind. This was still very much a time when players were not supposed to have any contact with the fans whatsoever. This was years before Facebook, years before MySpace, years before podcasts and fan interviews and charity get togethers and Twitter. To have a connection to a Survivor two seasons in a row was practically unheard of back then. Heck, if I wanted to, with Lex, I could probably even start up my interview project again. Only this time, I could do it through MY website. And I could do it with a guy I went to college with. And this time, no one would be able to steal that interview from me.

From this point on, I knew that I was destined to one day become a Survivor writer. All the signs were there, fate was trying to tell me something. You didn't just get a random connection to a Survivor two seasons in a row, not back then you didn't. The odds against something like that happening back in the early days of the show were just astronomical.

The minute I saw that a fellow SCU grad was in the new Survivor cast, I didn't care that I was writing for a dumb spoiler site. I didn't care what Murtz expected from our new website, or what Potato expected it to be. All I wanted now was for the new season to start.

So that I could start my journey to becoming a Survivor writer.

P.S. Like I said, odds are that unless you are from Northern California, you have never heard of Santa Clara University before. Although there are some people who might have actually heard of it, especially if they are basketball fans. If you follow the NBA, I am sure you have heard of a little white point guard named Steve Nash. Well of course you have heard of him, he won the MVP Award in both 2005 and 2006. ESPN recently named him the ninth greatest point guard of all time. Anyway, Steve Nash is probably the world's most famous Santa Clara alumnus. He graduated from SCU in 1996, which hey is the exact same year that I graduated from SCU. In fact here is a little fun fact for you: In 1992 I was Steve Nash's English tutor.

47. Writing to Lex

The number one Survivor rule in the year 2001-- indeed the Golden Rule of Survivor Law if there ever was one-- was that if you were a fan, you were not supposed to contact a player who was currently on the show. If you were not an authorized representative of CBS, or of the mainstream media, or of the show itself, you were not supposed to have any contact with a Survivor in any way, shape, or form whatsoever.

The network was so worried about spoilers at the time that this rule had always been heavily enforced.

Now, I know how strange that rule must sound now, to newer fans of the show. I mean, here we are in 2015, and these days Survivors freely interact with fans all over Facebook. And of course there are some Survivors who will actually post spoilers right out there in the open on their Facebook page or on a Survivor message board. Oh, they might not be trying to post spoilers. They probably think they are just bantering with a bunch of random Survivor fans. But anyone who has been around this show long enough can identify something that shouldn't have been posted on a message board. And, believe me, there is a LOT of stuff floating around out there that in 2001 would have been deleted by the CBS spoiler police in about thirty seconds.

It's weird. This policing of Survivor/fan interaction has changed so much over the years. A decade ago it was almost completely forbidden. Nowadays nobody at CBS seems to give a crap anymore.

Now obviously, because this "fans are not allowed to contact Survivors!" policy was so stringent and was so heavily enforced in 2001, as a rebel I knew that I wanted to make it my mission to get in contact with Lex. After all, I wasn't just some random anonymous fan anymore. No way. Now that I was writing for Survivor-Central, I was a BIG SHOT SURVIVOR WRITER. Who was CBS to tell me what I could do and what I couldn't do? In a couple of months I figured I would have millions of readers and I could just do whatever I wanted at that point.

Okay, I'm kidding. I didn't contact Lex because I thought I was a big deal. The only reason I contacted Lex was because we both went to Santa Clara University, and because it was such a small world. And because I thought he would find it amusing that there was a Survivor fan out there who had actually had his dad as a French advisor.

Now, you would think that after my disastrous experience with Nick in Australia that I would have been a little more gun shy about contacting a Survivor again. You would think I would have learned a lesson from that experience and I would have been a little more cautious the second time around. But then again, I am guessing you probably assume that I am smart.

Well here's the deal. I am not smart. I didn't learn a thing from the Nick experience. The minute I saw that Lex and I went to the same school, I didn't care if it was against the rules. I was going to contact him. Oh and of course I was going to tell him all about our new Survivor-Central website so that maybe he would read it. And then maybe he could get all of the Africa cast to read it. I mean, you can say I wasn't very smart but at least you can't say I'm not Machiavellian. At a certain level we needed to find some way to build ourselves a readership.

As I predicted, Lex was easy to track down in the SCU alumni directory. Like I said before, we have a very close and a very small alumni base. I found his personal contact information in about five minutes.

Once I had Lex's contact info, I decided that I needed to learn a little more about the man before I attempted to contact him. So I took a trip over to the Santa Clara campus to dig up a little more info. The reason I went to the campus is because I knew that there was a corner deep down in the basement of the library where they had a copy of all of the old SCU yearbooks. I don't remember how I knew about that corner, but do I remember stumbling onto that yearbook section one day back when I had been a student myself, about ten years earlier. I had been exploring the bowels of the library one day, around 1993 or so, and I remember stumbling onto the yearbook section and thinking, "Hey neat, I can look up anyone who has ever been a student here going back to 1906."

Since I knew that all those old yearbooks were still stored down there in the corner, I took a trip to the SCU campus, I went to the library, and I found Lex's old college yearbook. And I decided to learn a little about the guy before I wrote to him.

Now obviously this is something that only an SCU alum would know, but did you know that Lex was a radio DJ in college? And that in college he wasn't known as "Lex", he still went by his full name, Alexis? In fact, in the 1985 SCU yearbook there was an entire article written about him because he was such a unique character around campus.

This really doesn't have anything to do with Survivor, but I always thought it was funny. There was an entire half page article in the 1985 SCU yearbook about Alexis van den Berghe '85 because no one had ever heard of a straight guy who walked around a conservative Jesuit college campus wearing earrings. In 1985 this was the equivalent of a guy who went to class every day wearing a Darth Vader mask. A guy with earrings was so out of character at a place like Santa Clara in the mid 80's that Lex actually got an entire article in the yearbook dedicated to him.

Oh, and then at the end of the article, Lex asked that any woman who wanted to donate her old earrings, to please just send them to him where he worked at the radio station.

I remember seeing that article in the yearbook for the first time, I remember seeing the pictures of 22 year old counterculture earring-wearing Alexis, and I just thought it was hilarious. So here was this guy who wanted nothing to do with the status quo, who wanted nothing more than to shake up the system and just do whatever he wanted to do in the world, and he was going to be one of the stars of the next Survivor season. Only he wasn't 22 anymore, now he was 37, and he had added a ton of tattoos and he had also had a lot more earrings. Oh yeah, and he also had a very conservative job now working as a software manager in Silicon Valley. Even before I met Lex (even before any of us met him), I knew that he was going to be an interesting one.

The next thing I did was I made Xerox copies of all of Lex's old yearbook pictures, and of course I also made a copy of the earring article. And I decided that I would send them to him. After all, I wanted to be able to prove that I was actually a SCU alumnus. I wasn't just making this up, I really did go to school there. Also it was kind of important that I established that I wasn't just some everyday random internet stalker.

With all this information and all this background in mind, I sat down and I finally wrote a letter to Lex. Now, obviously, I had never met him in person before (again, he is ten years older than me). But since I had read so much about him and I knew his family a little bit, I figured I finally had enough info to write to him and say hi. So I sat down one day at home and I wrote him a nice little handwritten letter. I introduced myself, and I said I was a Santa Clara grad. And that his dad had been my French teacher, etc. I also shared some stories of all the Santa Clara basketball games I had been to over the years, and how I had almost been stabbed a couple of times when I heckled the opposing players too much and the other team's fans got upset with me. I figured, well if Lex knows that I am a bit of a wild card, he will probably appreciate it since he is probably a bit of a wild card too. I figured he would be able to relate to that.

> **Side note:** I'm not sure if you will be surprised by this or not, but I used to be a merciless heckler at sporting events. I mean, when I was in high school and college I was just vicious. To the point that my girlfriend refused to sit next to me at basketball games because she was afraid we would get jumped by somebody in the parking lot after the game. In fact, to this day, I still say that one of the proudest accomplishments of my life was the time that I got our student section banned from attending wrestling matches for an entire month in high school. That was all because of me. Ask me how I did it sometime, it was spectacular.

So anyway, that is the kind of stuff I told Lex when I first wrote him. I told him a few of my greatest heckling adventures, and I how I almost got stabbed once in the parking lot at St. Mary's College. I told him how I got our student section banned from the wrestling matches in high school. I figured, well, if nothing else an iconoclast like Lex will probably get a kick out of that. And then I settled down at the end of the letter and I told him about Survivor-Central. And how we were going to be the newest Survivor website. And how I was a writer there. And if he wasn't too busy during the day, if... you know... maybe he could check our site out.

What I DIDN'T do was ask Lex for an interview or an autograph or for any information about the new season. Because I knew that he couldn't give them to me anyway. At least, not at that point he couldn't. I didn't want the guy to get into trouble. I just wanted him to know that there was at least one SCU grad out there who was going to be rooting for him. And that if I wrote any commentary about him during the season I promised I would only write nice things. After all, I might have been a merciless heckler when I had been younger, but that had been nearly a decade ago. By 2001 I was a lot older and I was a lot wiser, and I had eventually calmed down. I even had kids of my own now. And I knew that the Survivor internet fanbase could often be a nasty place, where people would often write the most horrible things. I promised Lex ahead of time that I wanted be the one and only Survivor writer out there who would only say nice things about the castmembers.

I sent my letter to Lex in July of 2001. And I didn't expect to hear back from him. At least, not until after the season was over I didn't. But he actually did write back to me. Oh, he couldn't say anything about the season, of course, but he told me he had once gotten into a lot of similar trouble as a heckler too, and that he loved all my SCU basketball stories. Then he signed off by thanking me for the letter, and he told me we could talk more in depth about Survivor after the season was over. And he promised that he would read all of my episode recaps.

And with that, I now officially had my very first Survivor friend.

Lex and I would stay in touch with one another for years.

48. And Then 9/11

The year leading up to Survivor: Africa was completely saturated with
televised reality shows. I mean, it was just crammed with them. 2001 was,
and it always will be, the year that reality shows came in and they completely
took over television.

Let's look at the evidence here. Aside from Survivor: The Australian
Outback and Survivor: Africa, you also had The Amazing Race. And then
there was also The Mole. And Mole 2. And then there was Big Brother.
And Big Brother 2. And Chains of Love. And Boot Camp. And an
Amazing Race ripoff called Lost. And Making The Band. And Temptation
Island. And Fear Factor. And Murder in Small Town X. The list goes on
and on. There were even plans for Donald Trump to do his own TV show
called The Apprentice. 2001 was the year that reality came in and it
completely took over everything. And like I already mentioned in an earlier
chapter, if you were an actor or a writer in Hollywood at this time (or, more
often than not, if you were a TV critic) you just absolutely hated this
development. Because remember, what "a reality show" is really code for is
"a show where they don't have to pay for any writers or actors." In fact,
when it comes to reality TV, almost nobody but the network ever gets paid.
Which in the world of unions and actors in Hollywood is a very big no-no.
Seriously, there have been wars that have started up over smaller issues than
this.

Yes, 2001 was the year that the war between "reality TV fans" and "reality TV
haters" really sort of developed into its own little thing.

On one side of the coin you had people who LOVED reality TV. You
had people who loved this genre right down to the bottom of their hearts,
and who were completely addicted to it and to all of the shows in it. And
then on the other side of the coin you had the writers and the actors and the
TV union people in Hollywood who just HATED it. They hated reality TV
so much, in fact, that they were getting ready to file injunctions against CBS
and ABC and sue to stop reality shows from being made that were taking
jobs away from people in Hollywood.

And then, of course, there were the media critics on the side who did nothing
but talk smack every week about reality TV and how it was destroying
America.

All in all, 2001 was a really awkward time to be a reality TV fan, because there
was a very visible line being drawn in the sand. Either you were with reality

TV or you were against reality TV. That was it. America was pulling a Russell. You were either with the networks and the viewers who loved it, or you were with the unions and the actors who hated it. There really was no middle ground when it came to watching TV around that time. You simply had to be on one side or the other.

And then, of course, on September 11, 2001... things suddenly got worse.

Now obviously you know what happened on 9/11. Islamic terrorists hijacked four commercial flights on the east coast of the United States, and they intentionally crashed them into American landmarks. Thousands of people died. Millions more were traumatized for life, because they watched it all happen live on TV. The landscape of New York was changed forever because of the loss of the Twin Towers. The airline industry and the economy were devastated for years. All in all, it was pretty much the single worst day in American history. The tragedy of 9/11 (rightfully so) was all that anybody thought about or talked about or was going to care about for the next year and a half.

And of course Survivor: Africa was scheduled to debut the very next week.

This is something I have written about many times before in my essays, and I have talked about so many times before on Survivor podcasts. And I know that if you know my writing and you are familiar with my backstory you are probably sick of hearing it. But there is no way you can talk about Survivor history without talking about 9/11. You just can't do it. 9/11 is intertwined with Survivor history as much as Friends is. It was a pivotal moment on the Survivor timeline that pretty much affected everything.

Now clearly I am not going to sit here and complain that 9/11 sucked because it ruined Survivor. That would be tacky, it would be stupid, and it would be ridiculous. It would also be pretty disrespectful to the thousands of people who died and to the hundreds of thousands of families that were affected by that tragedy. So no, I am not going to sit here and claim that 9/11 was bad because it was a bad day for Survivor.

However.

Like I said before, keep in mind that Survivor: Africa was scheduled to air the following week. I don't remember how close it specifically was to 9/11, but I remember it was really close. I mean, it could have been scheduled to air as early as two days later (9/11 was a Tuesday, Survivor: Africa ran on Thursdays, so the original air date could have been Thursday, September

273

13th.) All I know for sure is that the minute 9/11 happened, the minute it was evident that this was all that America was going to talk about for a while, that this was all that anyone in America was going to <u>care</u> about for a while, CBS took their new fall schedule and they wisely pushed it back. Survivor: Africa didn't debut until nearly a month later, on October 11th.

And by then? Man, the momentum was over.

A month after 9/11, most of the big names in the media were already calling for an end to all the frivolous unimportant crap in America. A month after 9/11, it was already being beaten into our heads over and over and over that as Americans we were at war now. And that we lived in a new world. And that we all had to come together now as a country in support of what had happened on 9/11. Oh yeah, and those new "reality TV shows" that were supposed to debut in a couple of weeks? Well those shows might as well now be called "Here is the crap we used to care about, back in the olden days. Back when our loved ones weren't being crashed into buildings."

Needless to say, let's just say there wasn't a big demand for reality TV in America at that particular point of time.

Now, obviously, Survivor wasn't the only show that took a huge hit because of 9/11. The TV show Lost (not the J.J. Abrams one, but the reality show one) debuted on September 4th. Episode two was scheduled to air on 9/11. You talk about the world's worst timing. The Amazing Race debuted six days before 9/11, on September 5th. And then my personal favorite show, Mole 2: The Next Betrayal, well that was the first reality show to actually try to debut <u>after</u> 9/11. It premiered on ABC on September 21, 2001. And, well, yeah, big surprise. Three weeks later, after drawing about a hundred and fifty viewers total, it was mercifully canceled. ABC wisely pulled it off the air and decided to bring it back and try again the following summer.

Side note: Mole 2 was the show that suffered the most because of 9/11, but if you want the eeriest connection between reality TV and 9/11, go to Wikipedia and look up a show called Murder in Small Town X.

Murder in Small Town X was an innovative and really neat little detective show that aired throughout the summer of 2001. Basically what happened is that the producers rented out an entire little fishing village in the state of Maine and they staged a murder. They faked

274

the death of a family. And then they hired ten ordinary people to come into town and try to solve the murder. Only instead of this being a real town with a real fishing port and real people, all the "villagers" in the town were actors who could hopefully give clues to help the players solve the murder. It was a really high concept, innovative, and interesting idea. To this day I have never seen another show quite like it (although Whodunnit? in 2013 came pretty close.)

Murder in Small Town X never drew great ratings. Despite its awesome premise it was probably a little too complicated for most people. It flatlined in the ratings all summer, and I am sure it barely avoided cancellation a couple of times along the way. But it finally crowned its winner on September 4th, a week before 9/11. A New York City firefighter named Angel Juarbe solved the murder, he won the show, and he won the grand prize of $250,000. And I still remember that finale like it was yesterday. I remember seeing Angel win that night, I remember how happy he seemed that he had won, and I remember thinking "Wow I bet that Angel Juarbe is a really nice guy in real life."

Remember, this was a time when nice guys usually didn't win reality shows. Ethan hadn't won Survivor yet, so Survivor had not yet had a 100% popular winner. A good guy like Angel winning a competitive reality show was actually a pretty big deal.

So anyway, Angel won Murder in Small Town X on September 4th, 2001. And then a week later he was dead. He died in the collapse of the World Trade Center exactly seven days later, on September 11th.

See, I told you that was eerie.

Like I said, Mole 2 was the show that obviously took the biggest hit in the ratings because of 9/11. The minute that 9/11 took place, the minute that the analysts and the hand wringers came out on TV to decry everything that was wrong with America and how everything in our culture was going to have to change and get more serious RIGHT NOW, entertainment was obviously one of the first things that the critics all decided to focus their attack on. And if you want to know what the biggest fish was at the top of that particular pond at that particular moment, well that's easy. The biggest thing in entertainment in the year 2001 was reality TV. Like I said at the start of this chapter, in 2001 television was just completely saturated with brand new competition reality shows.

And, well, you can probably guess what happened next.

I swear, it wasn't even a week after 9/11 before the commentaries came out in magazines and in newspapers. They stated that we were focusing on way too much mundane unimportant crap in our lives in America, and that that kind of behavior needed to stop NOW. After 9/11, it was claimed (by Time Magazine!) that there would be no more irony in America. There would be no more frivolity. It was predicted that we would never laugh the same way that we had before. It was stated that we would never be the same type of society that we had been before. We were going to have to change our lives and get rid of all that and start focusing on the things that were important now. Such as the fact that we were at war now and we probably would be at war for the next twenty years. Oh, and also the fact that our enemies were probably already here and that they could attack us anytime they wanted. And that they probably would.

Simply put, if you thought that TV and movies were important after 9/11, according to the media you were now officially an asshole.

This was the mood in the country leading up the premiere of Mole 2 (and of course the premiere of Survivor: Africa) in September of 2001. There was almost NO hype about either one of them. In fact not only was there no hype, it seemed to me like the networks were almost embarrassed by the fact that they even existed in the first place. If there were any articles or previews about Survivor: Africa at all, the general tone behind them was usually something along the lines of "Well we taped this a couple of weeks ago, before 9/11. If it doesn't offend you too much, we would appreciate it if you watched it."

Oh, and remember how I said that television critics and actors and unions all hated reality TV prior to 9/11? Well after 9/11 they REALLY hated it. After 9/11 the entertainment critics and the Hollywood unions jumped onto the "we need to stop caring about frivolous crap in America!!!" bandwagon right along with the rest of the media full force. And reality TV quickly became numero uno on just about everyone's hit list. It was just the perfect storm of the media hating reality TV, the critics hating reality TV, people in Hollywood already hating reality TV, and just a complete oversaturation of reality TV shows at the time in general. Even if 9/11 hadn't happened, people were already starting to feel swamped by how many new shows there were in the genre and how much time it was taking to follow them all. So it is entirely possible that America would have eventually turned on reality TV even if 9/11 hadn't happened.

However, that argument is kind of pointless in the end because 9/11 DID happen. It happened, and then everyone jumped on the "anti-reality" bandwagon with the people who already hated it before. Which meant that after 9/11, if you still watched reality TV and you admitted that you liked it... people thought you were a dick.

And of course, as the highest profile show (not to mention the most successful show) in the genre, if you still watched Survivor after 9/11, that meant you were an enormous dick.

An enormous dick who hated America and who didn't care about Manhattan, and who mocked the suffering of the 9/11 victims.

I know that sentence seems ridiculous to write now but trust me. It's true. It was a weird time. If you were there, if you lived through this and you saw everyone in the media completely turn on reality shows over the course of about two weeks, you will know exactly what I am talking about. You will understand. This was the time that NOBODY in their right mind would admit that they were going to watch Survivor anymore. Heck, I wouldn't have even admitted it to my mom. And I knew she was a Survivor fan too!

> **Side note:** I actually got an email about this subject just the other day. One of my readers wrote me and said "You know, Mario, I never believed you when you said that people in the media all bashed Survivor after 9/11. I thought you were exaggerating. But then I pulled up the first Daily Show that Jon Stewart taped right after 9/11 and sure enough, there it was. A few minutes in, he starts trashing Survivor."

There is one question that people ask me all the time. They say "Hey Mario, how come Survivor was once a cool show to be a fan of? How come in the summer of 2000 and 2001 everyone watched it? And how come when I mention to people that I watch it now, they look at me like I am a huge dork? When did that change?"

Well the answer to that is easy. It happened on 9/11.

Survivor was once a very mainstream show that just about everyone in

America watched. You could go up to pretty much any random stranger in the country in 2000 and 2001, and you could ask them what they thought of Rudy Boesch and Jerri Manthey. And about 75% of the time they would know exactly who you were talking about. In fact you probably wouldn't even have to mention their last names. You could just walk up to a stranger in 2000 and say "Hey do you think Richard deserves to win?" and you would probably get a very animated response. And since it involved Richard it would probably involve a couple of curse words. And you could say the same thing about Jerri the following year in 2001. In fact, I have heard stories about how teachers would make their students watch Survivor just so they could talk about the latest episode in sociology or psychology class.

That was all prior to 9/11.

After 9/11? Well if you watched Survivor after 9/11 it was more like watching porn. It was like watching dirty, dirty porn. After 9/11 you generally had to watch it alone, in the dark. And in shame. And if you wanted to talk about it afterwards you had to go to a very special message board. And yes, like porn, most of the people you discussed Survivor with were going to be creepy and awkward.

So there you have it. The impact of 9/11 on Survivor (actually on reality TV in general) and why Survivor: Africa had absolutely no chance whatsoever to ever be a hit. It was doomed before it started, there was no way the biggest show in the most hated genre on TV at the angriest time in American history was ever going to be loved or accepted. Not under those circumstances, not at that point in history, and certainly not with that kind of baggage behind it. In fact, you will think I am kidding, but I am quite surprised that CBS even decided to air it at all. I bet the only reason they DID air it was because of the prevailing belief among some that "well we have to bring back some sense of normalcy to the country eventually, or else the terrorists have won." So I am guessing that CBS aired it simply because they had nothing else to air in its place. Because believe me, Survivor coming back for a third season (hey look, Americans faking suffering just to win money!) was just NOT what most of America wanted to see in the weeks following 9/11. In fact, I would be surprised if Mark Burnett and CBS didn't receive a truckload of hate mail.

In the end, did America recover after 9/11? Of course it did. Three years after 9/11 there was just as much frivolous stupid pointless crap in the country as there has always been. In fact, I have always thought we sprung back to normal pretty quickly, all things considered. I mean, remember, prior to 9/11 nobody had ever heard of the Kardashians. There was no Honey

Boo Boo. There was no such thing as gluten free dog treats or a selfie stick. We actually have more stupid pointless crap in the country NOW than we have ever had before, which is pretty incredible.

But did Survivor recover after 9/11?

Well if you look at the ratings, you would have to say yes. I mean, the show still exists today, even 27 seasons later. That is pretty impressive on its own. Most TV shows in history haven't lasted for 30 seasons. And that is especially true for TV shows that were once marked for death, and were once called "the downfall of America" way back in their third season. So yes, as a franchise, it is amazing that Survivor recovered as well as it did.

But did the coolness factor of Survivor ever recover? Did it ever go back to being a TV show that you could talk about with your friends? Or that teachers would routinely show and would talk about in class?

Um, I think you know the answer to that one.

Survivor fans went and they hid in their own little personal foxholes after 9/11. And for the most part they have never returned. 9/11 was the day it went from being a mainstream cool hip show to a show that is only followed by dorks. And believe me, I am not slamming you if you are a Survivor fan. Trust me, I am a huge dork too. I have nothing but respect for my people. But we would be fools if we thought of our Survivor fandom as anything but an embarrassing little niche hobby at this point. That was the truth of our situation in October of 2001, and it remains the truth of our situation very much today. If we like Survivor, and if there wasn't an internet or such a thing as internet message boards where we could interact with other Survivor dorks, we would have very few people in our lives who we would be able to discuss it with.

More than anything, it is the internet that has kept Survivor alive over the years. It is the internet that allows Survivor dorks to crawl out of their hidden dark corners where they watch the show alone and in shame, and find and interact with other Survivor dorks every Wednesday. The mainstream media might still laugh at Survivor, but the internet has always been the great equalizer in this game.

Had there been no internet, I am pretty sure that Survivor would have died in 2001 just like so many other TV shows. It would have been another 9/11 casualty. In fact the media would have LOVED if it had been another casualty. It very easily could have turned into The Mole.

However, it didn't die. Its coolness may have died, but the show itself didn't die.

Which was awesome. Because the next installment, Survivor: Africa, gets my vote as one of the all-time most underrated Survivor seasons.

P.S. Mole 2: The Next Betrayal, we will never forget. Team Meadow Muffin 4 Lyfe.

49. Diane Is Nothing Like Your Mother

Survivor: Africa debuted on CBS on October 11, 2001. And as you can imagine, it was a very odd and muted experience. Thanks to 9/11, and thanks to all the aftermath of 9/11, this was a far different experience than the premieres of Borneo or Australia. There was no fanfare involved. There was no excitement. It was honestly one of the weirdest TV experiences I have ever been a part of in my life. Africa just sort of showed up at 8:00 and it hung around for a while, and then after it was over you went on the internet and nobody was talking about it. It might as well have just been a PBS documentary about Africa.

Huh. Interesting.

It's funny, when I think back about the Africa premiere. It really wasn't one of the more amazing or interesting episodes in Survivor history, yet because of the circumstances and because of what was going on in the world at the time I remember pretty much every single little detail about it. Right down to how blue Ethan's shirt was, and the fact that Lex's first confessional was about how you didn't want to drink the water in the watering hole because otherwise "you will be puking and crapping your guts out."

> **Side note:** By the way, remember how Lex lost Africa? Remember why he fell during the final immunity challenge? It was because he had been drinking tainted water the day before, and because he spent the night before the big challenge... you guessed it... puking and crapping his guts out. You talk about one of the all-time best ironic character arcs.

So Africa premiered and I watched it like millions of other (now closeted and hiding in shame) Survivor fans. And of course I loved it. Seriously, there really wasn't a bad episode the first three seasons of Survivor. Well, okay, maybe the Australia finale was kind of boring. But even by lofty Survivor standards the premiere episode of Africa was still pretty darn good. In particular, if you go back and watch it again, pay attention to the immunity challenge where they had to push the fire cart through all the obstacles. Watch how exciting that challenge is. And pay attention to the music, and how over the top and epic it is. And watch how well the editors timed the music to sync up with everything that happened in the challenge. It is amazing. To this day, I consider that fire cart immunity challenge in the Africa premiere to be one of the all-time best moments in Survivor editing.

Now obviously, like I said before, the excitement and buzz around Africa was much smaller than it had ever been for the previous seasons. And I mean, it was like a whole different show now, it wasn't even in the same universe. If there was any excitement about Africa at all, people on the internet tried their best to keep it on the downlow.

However, I can't necessarily say that I wasn't fully invested in Survivor: Africa.

I mean, yeah, 9/11 was a big deal and all. And I'm sure 9/11 sucked for a lot of people in America and all. But 9/11 and the healing after 9/11 be damned. This was a month later, and there was important Survivor business to attend to!

As you can probably guess, the reason I was so invested in Africa was the same reason I had been so invested in Australia. I was invested because I actually knew one of the players. In fact, not only did I know one of the players (Lex), but we had already corresponded with one another through the mail. So I was about to strap myself onto the exact same stress-filled rollercoaster following Lex as I had been on last season while following Nick. His success in the game would be very much tied to my own enjoyment of the season. If he did well, it would be like I did well.

I know I have said this before, but it bears repeating again. This is a VERY stressful way to watch Survivor. I do not recommend it. Watching the show when you actually know one of the players will really mess with your blood pressure.

Of course, in episode one of Africa, there was talk that Lex was too bossy and that he was starting to annoy people. Oh great. Here we go again. The guy I know is going to be discussed as a boot option in the very first episode. Because remember, that had happened to Nick too. Right off the bat, I was already regretting the fact that I knew one of the players again.

However, luckily for me, Lex rallied. Even though the players complained about him at the start of the episode, about midway through the episode it didn't matter anymore because of Clarence and the cherries. And then because of Clarence and the beans. And then just because of Clarence in general. And then because Tom did that hilarious thing where he was racist. Oh and then also because Diane died about midway through the first immunity challenge.

I don't mean to cheer when somebody else fails but YES SCREW YOU CLARENCE AND DIANE! THANK YOU FOR KEEPING THE VOTE AWAY FROM OUR HERO LEX!

I am just kidding, of course. I happen to be a big fan of both Clarence and Diane. In particular, Clarence. I always thought he got a raw deal in the way the Borans effectively neutered him in the first episode. He just never really had a chance to win after that first incident with the cherries. In fact, when you get right down to it, he never really even had a chance to go far. The Borans just wouldn't let him. After the cherries incident in episode one (and other similar incidents that we probably never saw on camera), the Borans were only going to let him linger and hang around up until the point where they didn't need his strength anymore. And I thought it was a shame because he was such a funny guy and because he was such a good Survivor character. Oh well. Don't worry though, we'll talk more about Clarence (aka Clanence) a little later.

Oh yeah, and Diane Ogden and I would become email friends much later down the road. So I have nothing bad to say about her either. But more on her later too.

So anyway, Samburu won that first immunity challenge, and just remember that when people say that Samburu was a horrible tribe and that they were the biggest disaster of a Survivor tribe ever. They were actually a very good tribe when it came to winning challenges. In fact they actually dominated the Borans pretty well up to the twist. Never forget that. Don't let history rewrite the Samburus and turn them into the Ulongs. They were the opposite of the Ulongs.

Aside from the awesome music in that first immunity challenge (seriously, I can't say enough about that, go watch that editing again, it is spectacular), the thing that I remember the most about that first episode is Ethan. And the many many many times he tripped over something and flopped face first into the dirt. Again, if you don't remember that, go back and watch that first immunity challenge again, and count how many times gravity decides Ethan is not a part of the system and it Throws Him To The Ground (tm). I swear, at a certain point he starts flopping around more often than a soccer player. Which, considering that Ethan actually is a soccer player, is mighty impressive.

So that was the premiere of Survivor: Africa. The Samburus won immunity.

283

Ethan flopped around like a rag doll. Lex gave us a prophetic quote about how he would one day wind up with the Hershey Squirts. And then Diane died. Oh and then Clarence and the corpse of Diane (who is nothing like Clarence's mother) got in a really nasty fight over a can of beans. All in all, it was probably the strongest premiere out of the first three Survivor seasons.

And of course, since this was a month after 9/11, no one cared.

Right off the bat we had the makings of a new and fantastic new Survivor season, and the audience just wasn't there. Oh, the ratings might have been there. History will show that people did turn out to watch Survivor: Africa, just like they turned out to watch all of the early Survivor seasons. Go look it up on Wikipedia, you will see that people did watch it. But in terms of buzz? None. There was almost no buzz and no excitement about the premiere of Survivor: Africa whatsoever. We might as well have just watched an episode of the evening news.

If you were a Survivor junkie like me, this was very depressing.

By the way, I suppose I better bring this up since people who are reading this book will probably want to ask about it. I bet a lot of you are wondering what really happened with Clarence and Diane, and what the real situation was behind that can of beans. Because the question has sort of lingered in the air now for a decade and a half. Which one of the two of them was actually lying about opening those beans?

Well unfortunately, I don't really have an answer for you. I wish I had an answer, but I don't. All I know is that Clarence has been very consistent with his story throughout the years ("Diane asked for beans so I opened a can") and Diane has also been very consistent with her story throughout the years ("I never asked for beans, Clarence opened them because he was hungry.") So where does the truth lie? Who knows. I imagine it is probably somewhere in the middle. This is one of those moments in Survivor history that was kind of pivotal in the way a season would play out, but thanks to a lack of evidence (and of course thanks to two consistent but completely different versions of the story) I am guessing we will never know. In other words, I suppose it is up to you to decide. Who do you think was telling the truth? Do you think it was Clarence or Diane?

If you want my opinion... well... I am sure that Diane is going to get mad if she ever reads this, but I have always suspected that she was the one who was lying. What I think happened was that Clarence was already in hot water because of the cherries incident. And I think Diane knew that she could get him in even more hot water right before the vote if there was a second incident. So I think it was a ploy to kind of distract from the fact that she lost the challenge for Boran and that she was such an obvious first boot.

Not that I would hold it against her, of course. I mean, come on. Survivor is a nasty game. You do what you gotta do to survive.

Again though, none of this is actually fact. It is only me trying to speculate. The only thing I can base my opinion on is the fact that Clarence was so pissed off and he was so wounded when he went up and he cast his vote for Diane. Just from that angry voting comment alone ("You are NOTHING like my mother!"), I suspect that he had kinda been framed.

Oh yeah, and also every time my wife watches that first episode of Africa, she always says the exact same thing: "That Diane, I just don't trust her."

> **Side Note #1:** Now obviously there is no reason we still need to speculate about this sort of thing. Mark Burnett clearly answered the question of whether Clarence or Diane was lying when he wrote his tell-all book about Africa. Wait. What's that you say? Mark Burnett didn't write a tell-all book about Africa? Wow. Well I guess we can see a pattern starting to develop here. Thank you for making us all speculate about the important moments in Survivor history, Burnett.

> **Side Note #2**: By the way, just to stir up the pot a little, I asked Diane about the beans incident one more time right before I published this book. And her answer? She said that Clarence was lying and that he has since fessed up to her that he had been lying. Diane claims this isn't even a controversy anymore, Clarence has now admitted his guilt.

So anyway, that was that. Survivor: Africa premiered, our beloved fan favorite Lex survived, Clarence got accused of being a bean thief, and Diane Ogden went home. Oh, and Frank said something bizarre about crawling out of his mother's womb. All in all it was probably the single most successful premiere in three seasons of Survivor. Well okay, except for the complete lack of buzz and the complete lack of an audience. But oh well. Whatever. All you could hope for at this point was that fan favorite ~~Ethan~~ Lex would find some way to win them all back along the way.

285

However, the premiere of Survivor: Africa was NOT the only important thing that took place in the world of Survivor that night.

Nope. You are forgetting about one thing.

The minute that clock struck 9:01, that meant it was time for me to sit down at my computer and start writing my very first Survivor episode recap.

50. Writers Are Needy

Before I get into what it is like to be an internet writer, I feel that it would be appropriate to first tell you a little something about writing in general. Or, I guess to be more specific, I would like to tell you a little something about what writers are like.

I know this isn't going to be very pretty but here we go. To make a long story short, writers are needy. They only do what they do because they need your approval. I know that will sound like a stereotype but from my experience it has always been true. People who write for a living, people who make a living putting their thoughts down onto paper, and begging you to read and comment on them, are perhaps the saddest, neediest, most lacking in self-esteem creatures that have ever walked the Earth. Yes they are probably even sadder than professional reality TV contestants.

And I know what you're thinking. You are probably reading this and you're thinking, uh Mario, aren't you a writer too? Aren't you basically just slamming yourself?

You're damn right I am slamming myself. Remember, I am a writer too. That means (like all writers) I am needy and I lack self-esteem. So of course I am slamming myself. After all, the only way one can become a great writer is to point out how writers lack the ability to ever become great. And also, Inception.

Now of course I am exaggerating a little. Writers aren't terrible people. Well okay, Hitler was a terrible person, but I am guessing more people think of him as a dictator rather than as an author. So he probably doesn't count. But there is definitely some truth in what I said above. Writers only become writers because they seek approval.   In fact, not only do writers seek approval, if you write for long enough this need for approval more or less turns into a drug. The more prolific you are as a writer, the more successful you are as a writer, the more readers you amass along the way, the more addicted you become to success and readership and approval and fame.   And this all has an enormous effect on a person who is generally needy and who seeks attention in the first place.

I don't know if there is any actual scientific evidence to back up this theory of "writing = drugs", we might have to call in Yau-Man to clarify this for us.   But I am guessing that after a while, this "writer's high" actually starts to affect your dopamine levels and it starts to alter your brain. Like I said, if you write for long enough (and you are successful enough), I am guessing you actually do start to become physically addicted to it.

Why am I bringing all this up in my Survivor book? Well that's easy. Because the minute I posted my first Survivor recap (Survivor: Africa - episode 1), I realized very quickly why so many people consider writing to be a drug. The minute I wrote up my recap and I hit "publish", the minute I realized I had just posted something on the internet that hundreds of thousands of people were possibly going to read, I received a rush of adrenaline so intense and so powerful that you might as well have just injected me with heroin. I experienced such a rush of power in that one moment that I actually had to sit down and rest for a while because my legs were shaking.

Yes, if you ask me what the one moment was where I officially became "a Survivor writer", it was right there. And no, not because I had just published my first Survivor piece. No, I became a Survivor writer because it was a drug and because I was now addicted to it. Once I got that first hit there was no way I was going to stop until I got that second hit.

> **Side note:** By the way, before you think I am some junkie or something, I should point out that I have never even tried alcohol in my life. I have never even had a sip of coffee. I am as close to Mormon as you can be without wearing the magical underwear. So the idea of me receiving these huge dopamine hits of stimulant is not something I had ever experienced before. In fact, in a lot of ways, it probably would have been easier if I <u>had</u> been some sort of a habitual drug user. Since writing was the first drug I ever experienced in my life, it probably had a stronger effect on me than it would have had for most people.

So yeah, I wrote my first recap for Survivor-Central, and I posted it on the web. And then like all writers do (no one else will admit to this, but I will) I sat there and I played A.D.D. Feedback Hunter for the next four hours. I just sat there and I hit refresh on the website over and over and over, just so I could see my name and my recap in print. And I also went to EVERY SINGLE PLACE ON THE INTERNET THAT DISCUSSED SURVIVOR and I looked around to see if people were talking about it yet. Oh my God, my recap has been up for 20 minutes already. Why aren't people talking about it on Sucks? Why isn't it being discussed on Survivor News? How come I checked my AOL account and I haven't gotten any emails about it yet?

Oh no, what's wrong?

Does my recap suck?

Did I accidentally write something offensive??

Was I wrong about some of the facts????

OH MY GOD, WHAT'S WRONG WITH MY RECAP?! WHY AREN'T PEOPLE TALKING ABOUT IT YET?!?!?!??

See, I told you that writers are needy. This is how it works. Especially when you are talking about a newbie writer like I was. They will post their thoughts, and then the only thing they will do for the next 24 hours is obsess over the internet to see if people are talking about it yet. And if the first feedback that comes in is negative... well I'm sure I don't have to tell you this... but if the first feedback that comes back is negative then may God have mercy on your soul. You are probably going to be devastated for the next two weeks.

Now here is the funny thing. I go back and I look at my first Africa recap now, and it was just terrible. It was a complete and utter piece of crap, especially compared to the writing style I would develop later on. But man, at the time, I just thought I was a god. And I'm not saying that because I have an actual god complex or anything, I am saying that because all writers feel that way. When you post something for public consumption, and you sit back and wait for the praise and the adulation to come rolling in, you literally do feel like a god. Any writer will tell you this. Posting something and waiting for feedback about it is the most powerful and amazing (and yes, somewhat scary) feeling in the world.

But yeah, I look at my episode one recap now and it was a complete piece of crap. I mean, the very first sentence I ever wrote contained a joke about Hakeem Olajuwon. That's right, I led off a Survivor recap with an obscure homage to a retired NBA basketball player. That sure is writing for your audience. Trust me on this one, the vast majority of the online Survivor fanbase is made up of middle aged females and younger gay males. I am guessing that references to retired 1990's basketball stars is not what most people are looking for when they read a Survivor recap.

So anyway, I posted my recap (complete with 100% more Hakeem Olajuwon jokes!) and I sat there and I waited for the feedback. I sat back and I waited to see how my words were going to inspire the world, and how my rapier wit and keen observational skills were going to bring all the other Survivor sites on the internet (especially Television Without Pity) down to their knees.

Um yeah, that didn't happen.

To tell you the truth, I'm not sure I got <u>any</u> feedback about my first Africa recap. And the reason I didn't get any feedback was because... okay here we go. I am about to drop a pearl on you, so be sure to write this down. The reason I didn't get any feedback from my readers was because <u>nobody on the internet reads episode recaps!</u>

Seriously, have you ever gone onto a Survivor website and read a recap of an episode? Of course you haven't. People who are truly addicted to Survivor (which is like 90% of all online Survivor fans) are so obsessed with this show that they don't have any reason to read recaps. They don't have to read the recaps because <u>they already watched the show and they already know what happened!</u> In fact, by the time your recap is posted, most Survivor fans have already watch the episode a second time or maybe even a third time. Some of the true diehards have already written fifty posts on the message boards about it.

From my experience (and trust me, I have lived through this) recaps don't accomplish crap. Nobody cares about them. They are the absolute lowest rung on the ladder if you write about a television show. In fact, let's put it this way, if you ran a website about a TV show, and if your ten year old brother said he wanted to write for your site and help you out, you would stick him on recaps. Because that is the job that nobody wants to do. That is the place on any website ever, about any TV show ever, where you put the new guy. To steal a line from Austin Powers, being a recap writer is the Diet Coke of evil. It is only quasi-evil.

Now I'm not saying that websites about <u>other</u> shows don't get some recap readers. I mean, if people didn't read recaps about other television shows, there would have been no reason for a website like Television Without Pity to have even existed. TWOP wrote recaps. And one out ten of them were actually even pretty good. So yes there are some TV shows out there where recap writers are actually needed every once in a while. Just like there are some people out there who still actually read Television Without Pity. And who actually thought it was a good site.

But recaps about Survivor, well that is a whole different thing.

290

From my experience, if there is one word you can use to describe a Survivor episode recap, it is "unnecessary." Nobody is going to read it. Hell, 90% of the time nobody is even going to notice it. It is just going to sit there unnoticed at the bottom of a website. If you are a Survivor recap writer, your prime audience is going to be little more than amnesia victims, people who were in a coma, people who are on a cruise ship and who missed the episode, and people who were home but were too stupid to figure out how to program their DVR. That's it. Anyone who is actually interested in the show would have already made the time to sit down and watch it. Probably twice.

So this was my first experience as a "famous" Survivor writer. I wrote up my recap of episode one of Africa, and I posted it at Survivor-Central.com. And I sat back as the rush of godlike power came flowing into my veins. I took my first hit of the drug called writing, and now I was officially an approval addict.

And then I didn't get a single piece of reader feedback. From anyone. Anywhere. Frankly I'm not even sure that Murtz noticed I had posted it.

Well hey. Well wasn't that just a huge enormous waste of time.

My first recap didn't get noticed. My second recap didn't get noticed. My third recap didn't get noticed either. And by the third week, I realized that something was wrong. There was just no way you could write about Survivor unless you were also offering some sort of commentary on it. After all, that was what Potato was doing in his weekly Survivor-Central column. He was writing about the state of spoiling in the Survivor world. He was offering insight. He was offering opinions. And he was getting a fair amount of readership because he was doing this.

Meanwhile all I was doing was sitting here regurgitating the details of the episode. Yes, I was adding jokes to the commentary, sure, but jokes buy you nothing if there is no substance behind them. If you are just spitting out jokes without offering insight you might as well be Dane Cook. You are nothing but fluff.

It took me a while to figure out how to start adding commentary to my recaps, and how to get people to read them, but I did get there. Eventually. But now I am jumping too far ahead in the story. Because that development didn't happen until episode seven. And we still have episodes two through six of Africa to talk about.

51. Lindsey Richter's Only Fan

For more than a decade, whenever people talk about Survivor: Africa, they will generally always say something along the lines of "Wow, that Samburu tribe was a huge disaster." Or "I think the Samburus were the single worst tribe in Survivor history." For years, this Samburu-bashing has been the prevailing opinion when it comes to Survivor: Africa.

Well, let me say right now that this opinion is completely wrong.

The Samburus were one hell of a kickass Survivor tribe.

If you go back and you rewatch Africa now, watch how dominant Samburu was. Pay attention to how good they were. Take note of how they dominated the early episodes, and how Boran (because of weak links Diane, Kim Johnson, and sick Jessie) had almost no chance to compete with them. Yes, this is an aspect of Survivor history that has been completely forgotten over the years, but for the first couple episodes of Africa, the Samburus nearly blew the Borans right out of the water. It wasn't even close. In fact, it was only by the grace of God that Boran went into the twist with six members left at the start of episode five. If you ask me, the Borans were a much weaker tribe that season and they got very lucky.

Now, I'm not saying that Samburu's bad reputation over the years has been completely undeserved. That tribe really <u>was</u> a disaster when it came to getting along and thinking ahead and planning out their strategy as a team. I really don't think that was all editing, I am guessing that half of that tribe really wasn't talking to the other half of the tribe at the time of the twist. So no, I do not think that all criticism of Samburu as a tribe is completely unwarranted. But I do think they have gotten a lot more crap over the years than they have probably deserved. And it is time that somebody out there finally stuck up for them.

For starters, why don't we delve into some of the awesome characters on the Samburu tribe. Who, let's be honest here, were light years better than most of the characters on Boran. And yes, I know that is a dagger to the heart to the fans of Big Tom and Jessie and... especially... Kelly. I apologize. Although I'm sure that won't be the last snide remark I make in this book about the legion of "Kelly Goldsmith was the greatest Survivor character ever!!!" devotees out there who I have never really understood. So, uh, yeah. Get ready for that.

If you ask me, nearly ALL the big characters in Survivor: Africa were on Samburu. Those guys were the meat of the season. From Silas to Lindsey. From Brandon to Frank. From T-Bird to Linda Motherfucking Africa. If you ask me, THAT is Survivor: Africa. Those are the characters I look forward to when I go back and I rewatch the season. Those guys are where most of the entertainment happens.

Now, am I saying that you have to like all of the players on Samburu? Am I saying that you had to be rooting for them all to get far? Of course not. Hell, if you think most of America was rooting for Silas and Lindsey at the time the season was airing, you're nuts. I know this will be almost unfathomable to a person who wasn't watching Survivor in 2001, but it is possible that Lindsey Richter in Africa might have been the single most hated female in the history of Survivor. And yes, that is even including Jerri the season before.

If there is ONE Survivor who can say they might have been hated by the audience even more than Jerri was, that person would be Lindsey.

> **Side note:** Okay, here is a funny story for you. I actually had a chance to meet Lindsey Richter at a charity event in 2002. It was the night before the Thailand finale, and since this was a year after Africa had aired, most Survivor fans had already forgotten about her. Luckily for people like Lindsey and Jerri, Survivor fans tend to have always had a very short memory.
>
> I remember seeing Lindsey at the charity event all night, just sitting there eating her dinner, and I don't think a single person actually came over to talk to her at her table the entire night. It was the saddest thing. It was almost as sad as watching Keith Famie standing there alone at the bar, and no one talked to him either. Poor Keith and Lindsey. They really never caught on with the Survivor audience like they were probably expecting.
>
> Okay, so here is the funny part. T-Bird (Teresa Cooper) was one of the hosts at the event that night, and she and I were pretty good email friends. And for some reason T-Bird thought I was a big fan of Lindsey's. I have no idea why she thought that, during Africa I had been annoyed by Lindsey pretty much as much as everyone else was. At no point ever would I have claimed I was actually a "fan" of hers. But hey, T-Bird thought I was a big Lindsey fan, and that was

293

good enough for her. She was bound and determined that she was going to introduce me to Lindsey that night.

So anyway, here comes T-Bird over to my table. And she takes me by the arm (T-Bird is not shy). And she marches me over to meet Lindsey. And she introduces me to her as "The #1 Lindsey Richter fan on the internet."

And, oh, you should have seen Lindsey's face just light up.

Lindsey was SO excited that she had a fan. Any fan. I don't think she had ever actually had one before. She had just been brutalized for a year on the internet, with people on every Survivor website calling her a bitch, and calling her fake, and saying she was annoying and that they wished she would die. And calling her things like "a dumb twat" and "a spoiled brat." You could just see it in her eyes when I was introduced to her. She was SO excited that there was one Survivor fan out there who was actually a fan of hers.

T-Bird introduced me to her, and Lindsey got this huge smile on her face. And then, of course, because she is Lindsey, she started talking a mile a minute. She wanted to know all about me. She wanted to know all about my website. She wanted everyone around her to know that "MY ONLY FAN IS HERE! I FINALLY HAVE A FAN!" She gave me a big hug. Then she tipped me off that when they were playing the game, Frank was actually even more annoying out there than she was. The whole conversation was actually quite cute.

And then we got to the best part.

At some point during the conversation I actually got a word in, and I mentioned that aside from Survivor, I was also a fan of The Amazing Race. And Lindsey's eyes got really wide. Because, you know, it turned out that she was a fan of The Amazing Race too. In fact, we had both just watched the finale of Amazing Race 3, which had aired on TV about 24 hours ago. It had been won by a particularly annoying young woman who never shut up named Flo.

The minute I mentioned The Amazing Race 3 finale, Lindsey suddenly got even more animated.

"DID YOU SEE THAT FLO CHICK!" she practically shouted with

delight. "DID YOU HEAR HER WHINING? OH MY GOD! SHE WAS EVEN MORE ANNOYING THAN I WAS!"

At this point I agreed. Yes, I would say that Flo was just about the single most annoying person I had ever seen on reality TV. Just like Lindsey the year before, the audience absolutely could not stand her.

"Do you know what this means??" Lindsey concluded with delight. "I'm not the most hated person in reality TV anymore! Flo beat me! Flo was even worse than I was!! I'M NOT THE ONE THAT EVERYONE HATES ANYMORE!"

She was so excited by this development that I had to admit, okay now I was a Lindsey fan. She won me over. I told her it was nice meeting her and I promised her that one day I would write a Survivor All-Star story and I would use her as a character. And I would turn her into a fan favorite. She seemed excited by that news too. That was clearly something she had never experienced, nobody on the internet had ever written anything nice about her before. So we said our goodbyes and I got a picture with her and that was the last time I ever talked to her.

Sadly, I never did get to use Lindsey Richter in any of my All-Star stories. I really did intend to turn her into a fan favorite if I could, but for whatever reason, it never quite happened. Oh well. But we will talk more about my All-Star stories later down the road. As you can guess, I have a lot to say about those.

Oh yeah, and Jerri Manthey was at that event too, but I never talked to her. Quite frankly, I stayed away from Jerri because at the time I was scared to death of her. In fact, I have never had a single interaction with Jerri over the years. I mean, meeting Lindsey in person was one thing, but meeting JERRI, well that was another. Hmm, maybe Lindsey really <u>wasn't</u> an equal to Jerri when it came to the Survivor villainess department. Maybe I need to rethink this hierarchy a little bit.

Lindsey is another one of those Survivor players that I tend to get asked about a lot. People love to email me and ask about Lindsey Richter and where she ranks as a villain in Survivor history. Because a lot of newbie fans will watch Africa now for the first time, fourteen years after it aired, and they will hear that Lindsey used to be hated, and they can't understand why that would have been the case. It just doesn't match up with the season that they just watched on the internet. So people will often email me and ask "Why?" It just seems incomprehensible to a lot of first time Survivor fans that a character who was that minor and who was that insignificant to the season could have somehow been hated by the audience that badly.

And what is my answer when people ask me about this?

Well, to be honest, I can't really explain to you why Lindsey was so hated. I mean, she just _was_. People found her annoying. People found her whiny. People found her self-important. The audience just didn't like her. She was absolutely trashed on every single Survivor message board that I ever paid attention to at the time.

But why didn't the audience like her?

Who knows.

I know this theory will make some people upset, but I am guessing there was probably a fair amount of sexism in there. In other words, male characters are allowed to come off as cocky and self-centered on Survivor (Hello Richard! Hello Silas!) but if a female tries it? If a female gains power on Survivor and she suddenly gets all cocky and she starts demanding things? Well God help her. I think what happened to Lindsey was exactly what happened to Jerri. I think that the TV audience just could not handle a young female who was in power and who started to throw a little arrogance around. Lindsey gained a little power on her tribe, she started to act cocky and whiny and make demands around the older Samburus, and the audience just absolutely BLASTED her for it.

This is something I am going to talk about more as this book goes along, but I have always found it sad how the Survivor audience has never really been able to handle a good female villain. I mean, you look at Lindsey now and she really wasn't that bad. You look at Jerri now and she really wasn't that bad. Yet the audience treated both of them like they were out there drowning their babies in bathtubs. The audience just absolutely crucified them. And it is ridiculous to think how little venom Silas or John Carroll in Marquesas got for doing what was basically the exact same thing.

I don't know. The Survivor audience has always seemed very strange to me, and this is one of the things about it that has always stood out to me as being particularly strange. Survivor fans simply can NOT handle a good female villain. It happened with Jerri. It happened with Tina (to an extent.) It happened with Lindsey. And it definitely happened down the road with Heidi in Amazon and to a lesser extent even with Ami in Vanuatu. The venom directed at female villains over the years has just been completely disproportionate to the venom that the males get.

I mean, even if Richard Hatch was hated, he still had fans. Even Boston Rob in All Stars had fans. Even Brian Heidik had fans. I mean, fricking Russell Hantz would later win Fan Favorite. Twice! How does that douchebag win Fan Favorite twice?? And meanwhile here are Jerri and Lindsey, who really didn't do anything all that bad, yet who were practically run out of the Survivor community and who weren't even talked to at charity events because the audience hated them so much. I don't know. This entire aspect of the Survivor fan base has always been embarrassing to me. Why do we always hate the women so much?

In any case, I met Lindsey Richter in person in 2002 and she was a very nice girl. And she was well aware of her reputation in the Survivor world. And it bothered her. And I really wish I could have used her in one of my later All-Star stories. I don't have many regrets when it comes to my career as a Survivor writer, but this is one of those things that has always bothered me. I really should have done more to get people to appreciate Lindsey more.

Oh well. In the end, Flo from The Amazing Race came along a year later, and she was way worse than Lindsey, and we both got a good laugh over it. And then the baton was passed from one great reality TV villainess to the next. And Lindsey was very happy about it.

I have no idea what Lindsey Richter is up to these days. I don't know if she even still watches Survivor. I am kind of hoping she stumbles onto this book one day and she actually reads this chapter and she remembers this. Who knows. Weirder things have happened, I guess.

Oh, and now that we have properly chronicled Lindsey's place in the history of Survivor, that means it is time to talk about her male equivalent.

Yes, the time is here.

It is finally time to talk about Silas.

P.S. No, I never did find out why T-Bird thought I was a big Lindsey Richter fan. My guess is that she knew I was a big Tina Wesson fan (this was no secret, I used to mention it every single week in my column) and I think she somehow got one blonde Survivor confused with another. And that is how Lindsey finally met her "number one fan."

By the way, I changed my mind. Now I am hoping that Lindsey doesn't ever read this.

52. Chip

Ah yes, Silas. Or, as some people know him, Chip. One of my all-time favorite Survivor characters. And sadly, one of the players that has never really gotten the credit he deserves for how important he really was to Survivor history.

Let me take you back to the fall of 2001.

As the first few episodes of Survivor: Africa played out on TV, it became clear to just about everyone who was watching that the Samburus were going to be the power tribe of the season. I mean, go back and watch Africa again, see for yourself what I am talking about. The Samburus were just dominant those first couple of episodes. They just steamrolled all over the hapless older Borans.

And, of course, since the Samburus were going to be the dominant tribe, the game back in the early days of Survivor was to try to pick out which member of the dominant tribe was going to wind up being the winner. I mean, that was really the only way you could watch Survivor back in the early days. Since the smartest member of the dominant alliance on the dominant tribe always won the game (based on what had happened in Borneo and Australia), it was pretty easy to pick out who the likely winner was going to be in the first couple of episodes. By the time the show made it to the merge, it was usually pretty easy to tell that the winner was going to come from a pool of maybe two or three people.

Again, this sounds like a very boring way to watch Survivor now, when there are twists every two or three episodes and players are constantly switching alliances and flushing out idols and splitting their votes. But back in 2001 there were no twists and nobody ever switched alliances. At least, not that we ever saw on television. Once the power alliance took over the game, man they just took over the game. And this was not considered boring TV at all at the time, this was just what Survivor _was_. It was a game of which alliance was going to become the power alliance. And then what was going to happen at the end when the power alliance had to turn on itself.

So keep that in mind. Survivor was incredibly different back then because the dominant alliance ALWAYS won the game. And after two seasons of seeing it happen, anyone who followed the show obviously expected it to happen again in Africa. I mean, again, that was just what Survivor WAS. There was no reason to ever expect it to be anything different.

And, well, in the third episode of Survivor: Africa, the dominant alliance of the season finally revealed itself.

Anyone who was watching the show back then will remember the third episode of Africa. The Carl vote. It was a really big deal. In fact, in many ways it was just as big a deal as the Gretchen vote had been back in Borneo. Or the Mitchell vote had been in Australia. Honestly, if you had taken a poll around the time of All Stars, and you had asked a hundred diehard Survivor fans what the ten most memorable Tribal Councils had been in Survivor history, there is no doubt in my mind that the Carl vote would have been mentioned by just about everyone. And I find it kind of sad that now, fourteen years later, the early seasons have been so completely forgotten that 90% of Survivor fans in 2015 don't even remember this episode and they have no idea who Carl was.

But I digress.

Yes, episode three of Africa was THE big episode at the time. It was the big showdown between the two warring factions of Samburu. The Elders versus the Youngsters. The battle. The vote to determine which alliance in Samburu was going to dominate the rest of the game.

And yes, I know that isn't how the season eventually played out. I know that a member of Boran ended up winning the game, not a Samburu. But at the time, you have to understand that simply wasn't the case. Anyone who knew how Survivor worked back then knew that the winner of this showdown was going to become the dominant four member alliance. They were going to become the Africa equivalent of the Tagi Four. Or the Ogakor Three. Again, no one questioned it at the time, this was just how Survivor had played out every single time we had ever seen it before. Everyone knew that the first Samburu Tribal Council was going to be the important one.

So here comes Africa episode three.

And here is the interesting part.

Up to this point in the season, the editing of the episodes had been very skewed in favor of the older members of Samburu. Almost every single scene we saw the first three episodes of Africa had some mention of how noble and hardworking and wise the older members of Samburu were. And how lazy and spoiled and worthless the younger members of Samburu were. Right down the line, this is practically all we were ever told when it came to Samburu.

Now, of course, nobody watching the show in 2001 was any sort of an expert in Survivor editing back then. Most people who watched the show in 2001 didn't even realize that there <u>was</u> such a thing as "editing." Most people who watched the show back in the early days took most of what they saw on Survivor at face value. They thought that the older Samburus were all just awesome wise older people. And they thought that the younger Samburus (aka "The Mallrats", as they were nicknamed on the message boards) were all just awful lazy terrible people.

> **Side Note:** Seriously, I can't overstate this enough. If you had gone up to any random Survivor fan in the fall of 2001 and said, "By the way, the Mallrats are only being edited that way because it makes the storyline better", he probably would have looked at you like you were speaking Swahili.

So this was the scenario leading up to that important episode three Tribal Council vote. The older Samburus were old and likable and wise. The younger Samburus (particularly Lindsey and Brandon) were lazy little shits. And then of course there was the guy in the middle, Silas, who the elders thought was on their side but who really wasn't.

And Silas was about to become possibly the most irritating little dickhead up to that point in Survivor history.

We get to episode three. The Elders have it in the bag. They have the numbers. They have the votes. And then Silas announces to us that he doesn't consider himself a free agent anymore, he has decided that he is going to team up with the Mallrats.

Hmmm, that's interesting, most people in the audience would have thought. So you have decided not to be a part of the dominant five person alliance that is going to control the rest of the game. Instead, you would rather team up with the lazy little annoying children who are about to be picked off one by one. Well good luck with that I guess, Silas. It was an honor and a pleasure getting to know you.

I mean, even if none of us in the audience were really "students of Survivor editing" yet, it was pretty clear that none of the Mallrats were ever going to win the game. They were just getting completely crapped on in the edit every week. And the idea that somebody like Brandon or Silas, or god forbid Lindsey, would rank up there with Tina Wesson and Richard Hatch at the end of the season as a Survivor winner? Well if you had mentioned that to any Survivor fan about midway through the third episode they would have laughed in your face.

And that is what made the end of Africa episode three so completely shocking to everyone.

So here comes the big showdown. The Elders against the Mallrats. T-Bird and her heroic band of noble warriors against Silas and his douchebag patrol. I can guarantee you that NOBODY in the audience thought that the Mallrats were going to win that particular showdown.

And then?

To quote the great Kathy Vavrick-O'Brien, "Holy Mother McCready!"

The vote is a tie. They go to a tiebreaker. And then, in easily one of the ten most shocking moments in the history of Survivor, Lindsey Effing Richter, the A.D.D. Queen, beats Doctor Carl Bilancione in a question about medical knowledge.

Wait, what?

What the hell just happened?

The Mallrats WON?

One of those little pukes is actually going to be a Survivor champion now??

I can honestly say that this was one of those rare moments in Survivor history that jaws actually dropped to the floor. Because the editors had completely set that showdown up to go the other way. And those bastards got all of us.

At the end of episode three, as the smoke cleared after the Carl vote, it was clear to everyone who was watching the show that Africa was going to be a different type of season than we had ever seen before. Because all of a sudden, the people we thought were going to dominate the game were not the ones who were actually going to dominate the game. And that had never happened before. I mean, yeah, Ogakor kind of came back and won because of the Skupin injury, but Tina and Colby were both major characters well

302

before the merge. So their rise to power, while lucky, wasn't really much of a surprise.

But the Mallrats becoming the major alliance in Survivor: Africa? THESE four people were going to be the stars of the season? With the edit (whether deserved or not) that THEY had been getting?

To quote Wayne Campbell from Wayne's World, shyeah right!

There have been very few moments in Survivor history that honestly caught me off guard and knocked me for a loop. But this was one of them. This one just completely blindsided me. And I loved it. I loved that I thought I had known everything there was to know about this show. I loved that I thought I could predict how Survivor was going to play out each and every time, just because of the way it had always played out before. But I hadn't predicted this. I hadn't seen this Mallrats dominance coming for a second. The editors had just completely blasted me with this one.

As episode three ended, and we saw Silas and Brandon sitting there with those smug little grins on their faces, as we saw Lindsey sitting there in complete shock that she had managed to survive that tiebreaker and take over the game, it became clear to everyone who was watching the show that one of these four people was probably going to win Survivor now. A young person. A lazy, smug, annoying, young person. And this was incomprehensible. Remember, through the first two seasons of the show, we had never had a Survivor winner who was under the age of 39 before.

And at this point this is where the outrage kicked in. Because as a fan it was like, come on. Seriously? Silas as a winner? Brandon as a winner? Lindsey as a winner?? We are going to have a lazy winner??

Silas or Lindsey as a Survivor champion? That just wasn't how Survivor was supposed to work!

Now, this isn't something that I like to talk about all that much anymore (for obvious reasons), but I used to have a theory about Survivor that I always referred to as "Mario's Theory." This was a very simple theory, and starting with Africa I used to reference it all the time in my Survivor writings. Mario's Theory simply stated that **"No one under the age of 30 will ever win Survivor."**

Mario's Theory was something I used to believe in with all of my heart. And the reason I believed in it was because of what I had seen in the world and because of what I knew about life. And because of what I had seen happen last season on Survivor with Colby. The reason I believed in Mario's Theory, the reason I hyped it so often in my writings at the time, was because I just didn't think it was possible for a young person to be wily enough or cutthroat enough to ever be able to win a game that relied on social politics like this.

Well, after episode three of Africa, now that I saw what was going to happen, you better believe that my stomach dropped.

Thanks to the rise of the Mallrats, I knew that Mario's Theory was about to be put to the test.

Because at the end of episode three, there was Silas. A.k.a. Chip. With that smug little grin on his face. And that knowing little wink to the audience. He knew that he had it. He knew that he was the smartest and the most dominant member of the Mallrats. He knew that nobody was going to be able to stop him now. He knew that he was now the 2001 equivalent of Richard Hatch.

In fact, if you remember, it was at that point that Silas even dropped a Richard Hatch QUOTE on us. I forget if it was in episode three or episode four, but in one confessional around this point in the season Silas becomes so confident that he is going to win that he literally drops a Richard Hatch callback quote on us. In one of his confessionals, he states that "they might as well make out the million dollar check to me right now, because I am the winner."

Oh crap.

Remember, the editors had already done that to us once before, in episode one of Borneo. They did that to foreshadow a Hatch win. The precedent had been set. Anyone who was a fan of Survivor at the time would have recognized the significance of that Silas quote.

And that meant that the signs were all there now.

Barring some miracle, or some inexplicably awesome collapse of the Mallrats, this guy-- this douchenozzle-- was going to be our next big Survivor winner. He was going to join Richard Hatch and Tina Wesson in the pantheon as the three all-time Survivor greats. After all, why wouldn't he win? He was now the smartest person in the dominant alliance on the dominant tribe. At this point in Survivor history there was simply nothing to stop him. Some bartender whose nickname was Chip was now going to become a Survivor legend.

Oh great.

Well wasn't this just a wonderful development.

53. Mallrats, Jessie, and Boners

I can't tell you what an honor it was to have Africa as the very first Survivor season I ever wrote about. Because even though no one was reading my recaps (yet), and even though the country hadn't fully come back to embrace the show after 9/11 (yet), you could tell after only three episodes that Africa was going to turn out to be a memorable season. Oh, it might turn out to be a complete trainwreck of a season, and it sure looked that way now that Silas or Lindsey were probably going to win the game. But hey, nobody ever said that watching a trainwreck happen wasn't memorable. A trainwreck might be horrible, sure, and people might die in it, true. But it is also one of those things you are going to tell all your friends about.

And the Silas and Lindsey power grab definitely had the fan base talking again. After episode three, the internet was buzzing the loudest it had buzzed about Survivor in a long time. People were ANGRY about what was happening on this show. People were ANGRY at the Mallrats. And it was kind of nice to see that for a change.

Remember, this was still only about a month and a half after 9/11. Most people in America still hadn't come back to care about network TV. It was nice (at least from a normalcy perspective) to see that America was starting to get invested in what was happening on television again.

So anyway, episode three passes and Silas takes over the game. Then he drops that quote on us that he is the winner of Africa and that they might as well write him a million dollar check right now. He steals the famous Richard Hatch line. Then in episode four he does that douchy thing where he takes a knee and he tells all the elders to gather around him. And his sidekick Lindsey starts yelling at all the older people that they better shut up and they better not f with her.

Then, at the end of episode four, right before Tribal Council, Silas tells the elders to stack all their votes onto Lindsey, simply so that the Mallrats will be better off down the road in the case of a future tie. And the Elders say "no way, f.u. Silas" and they all just cast their votes for him instead. One of the most awesome moments of the first three seasons, by the way.

Oh, and Silas just sits there and he has to watch his name come up over and over again at Tribal Council. He just sits there and has to watch this with a very angry little Tom Cruise grin on his face.

I mean, my goodness, this was great drama. I had never seen anything like it

306

before on Survivor. And the audience was just eating it up. The internet audience HATED the Mallrats. Especially after episode four, they just HATED Silas. They just hated Lindsey. Anywhere you looked on the internet, you would hear that this was an alliance that was just BEGGING for a downfall.

And I have to again point out that little subplot at the end of episode four where Silas tells the Elders how to vote, and they give him a big middle finger and they all just vote for him instead. That is easily one of the ten most underrated moments in the history of Survivor. Nobody <u>ever</u> talks about it. Yet I rewatch that episode and it just kills me every time. That is one of those magical little Survivor scenes that immediately jumps out at me when I think of Africa, and what a great season it was.

Oh and then of course Silas follows it up by saying something like, "There's not an event in this game that could possibly concern me in the future." Which of course he says one episode before the most famous twist in Survivor history. And the downfall of Silas. I mean, if that isn't good TV, if that isn't an amazing transition from setup to punchline, I don't know what is. It is ridiculous how good the first couple seasons of Survivor were.

And yes, that even includes Linda and her endless ridiculous monologues about Mother Africa.

By the way, there are a few things I would like to point out about this season before we move on to the twist. Or THE TWIST, as it should always be called, since it was such a big deal. And because it was so important to the development of Survivor as a TV franchise.

The first thing I would like to point out about the first couple of episodes is Jessie Camacho. Do you remember Jessie? On Boran? Of course you don't. She was the hot young Latina deputy sheriff who got dehydrated because she refused to drink the water, and she was voted out of the game at the end of episode two. And who made no impact on the season whatsoever. Well, other than the fact that she insinuated she would let Big Tom have sex with her during her final words. I have never really understood what was happening there in Jessie's final words, but whatever. Who knows what was going on between the two of them. I mean, Big Tom might be a simple goat farmer but maybe he is like Gene Simmons and he also has an eight inch tongue. We will probably never know.

Anyway, what I wanted to say about Jessie is, did you know that she has the all-time highest approval rating of any player in Survivor history? Yep, that's right. Back in the day CBS.com used to have a popularity poll that they would hold after every episode, and they would track who the fan favorites were and which players the audience thought should be getting all the airtime. And, sure enough, Jessie (because she was hot) had something like a 100% approval rating after episode one, and a 95% approval rating after episode two. And then she was voted out at the end of episode two so it never had a chance to drop any lower than that.

Which meant she retired from Survivor with an average fan approval rating of something like 97 percent.

So there you go. There is your obscure little Survivor trivia fact for the day. If anyone ever asks you who the most popular and beloved contestant was in Survivor history, you can say it was Jessie. And you will be right. Even though, technically, most Survivor fans don't even remember who she was anymore. The world is an interesting place.

Oh yeah, and this also backs up another old theory of mine. If you ever have a hot girl (aka Jessie) in a popularity poll, straight guys will always vote for her simply because they think she will find out, she will be impressed, and then she will sleep with them. Or, if gay guys are voting, they will vote for her because she is fierce. Because of this, it is amazing that we have never had a hot young female president yet.

Side Note: Oh yeah, I have a funny story about Jessie that you will enjoy.

I actually used Jessie Camacho as a character in the third All-Star story I ever wrote, All Star Survivor: Greece (in the year 2003).

Now, Jessie was never really a big enough character to feature in an All-Star story. It's not like she ever said more than about four things during her entire Survivor run in Africa. But since this was a "Second Chances" story, I figured I could get away with casting her even if she was forgettable. I also remember thinking, well if nothing else she's still got that 97% fan approval rating, right? At the very least I should be able to do SOMETHING interesting with her.

However, the problem was that when I sat down to actually write the story, I realized very quickly that I had absolutely no idea how to portray Jessie as a Survivor character. I mean, what do you know

about Jessie from Survivor? Quick, tell me three things about her.
 And no, "she gets dried out very easily and she has gross lips"
doesn't count, so not so fast.

I drew a complete blank when it came to actually writing Jessie, so I
turned to my friend Murtz Jaffer (our Survivor-Central webmaster)
and I asked him for some ideas. Okay Murtz, so how would YOU
write Jessie?

Murtz's answer was the same answer he would always give about any
young female contestant. He said I should make her super sexy and
I should have her flirt with and mess with all of the guys. Any time I
had a young female character in one of my stories, Murtz would
always beg me to turn them into what would later become Parvati
(or, more specifically, Jeff Probst's version of Parvati.)

Well, normally, I would scoff at this type of a Survivor character in
one of my stories, but in Jessie's case it wasn't actually a half bad
idea. I mean, she was hot. There was no denying that. At the time
she was considered to be easily the hottest female in Survivor history
(sorry Sue). And she was young. And I had to imagine that if she
ever had a second chance to play Survivor, she would probably know
the second time around that she was super popular with the audience
and that she was super popular with all of the guys. So I thought
about it and I figured, why not? Okay, the second time around let's
turn Jessie into a professional reality star super vixen. Let's play
around with that 97% approval rating and see if I can get my
readership to go with it.

So I started writing my Greece story, and I immediately turned Jessie
into a little vixen. I had her flirting with Ryan Aiken. I had her
totally manipulating Dirk. I had her walking and prancing around
camp in a tiny little bikini. I had the older women on the tribe all
hate her guts. It was a lot of fun.

And sure enough (the Survivor audience is nothing but predictable),
here came the hate mail.

"Um, Jessie is a deputy sheriff and a highly respected police officer in
real life," one guy wrote to me. "Don't you think it is irresponsible
to portray her like that?"

"Who is this Jessie chick you are using in your story?" some other guy wrote. "That isn't the Jessie that we saw in Africa. I thought your characters were supposed to be realistic!"

And then of course there was this one. "I don't know who the Jessie is in your story but this character is awesome. The real Jessie sucks!"

Meanwhile here was Murtz off to the side absolutely loving my new sexier Jessie, and begging me to make her more and more over the top in every episode. I think he wanted me at one point to show her actually sleeping with a guy and then voting him out. Murtz was always a big fan of trying to push my characters to be completely over the top. I can't even imagine how much joy he must have received when we finally got a Black Widow Brigade in Micronesia. He had been dying to watch that character on Survivor for YEARS.

In the end, I wasn't 100% proud of the Jessie Camacho in my story. I mean, she was a fun character to write, sure, but I did think I had been a little irresponsible in the way that I made her so flirty. I was actually stung a little bit by that first email that pointed out that she was a sheriff in real life and that I probably shouldn't be doing that. So yeah, even though I had fun with her, and even though by definition a Second Chances story means you have a lot of leeway to do whatever you want with characters you barely knew from TV, I wasn't entirely comfortable with how over the top and sexy I portrayed her in my story. In fact, over the next couple of years, I tended not to talk about Jessie whenever people asked me about my Greece story. I just sort of hoped that people would forget she had ever been a character in one of my All Star stories.

Once my Greece story was done, I figured that would be the end of it. I figured I would never have to think about her again. I figured that Jessie Camacho would just fade away back into the real world into law enforcement, and people would forget that she had once been a minor character on a reality TV show.

And then, of course, this story wound up having a hilarious conclusion.

A couple of years later, Jessie Camacho randomly popped up again on reality TV. I didn't realize it at the time, because I don't speak Spanish (and because I don't give a crap about Big Brother), but she randomly showed up as a contestant on the Spanish language version of Big Brother. And the second time around she was EXACTLY

LIKE I PORTRAYED HER IN MY GREECE STORY! She was sexy. She was cartoony. She was over the top. She manipulated the guys. She flirted with the cameras. Somebody told me a couple of months ago that, to this day, she is still considered the all-time greatest character in the history of Spanish Big Brother.

Now, I thought that my association with Jessie as a character was over after my story was over. But nope. Because here came the emails again. Now that Jessie was a huge reality TV celebrity, people were discovering her in my Greece story and they absolutely loved it. You should have seen all the emails I got from Big Brother fans who just randomly ran across my Survivor story on the internet one day, and they loved that I had portrayed Jessie "so accurately." They said it was amazing that I predicted what she was like in real life before she ever wound up on Big Brother.

And I am sitting here thinking, that wasn't me portraying her accurately. That was me making her sexy in my story because Murtz thought it would be awesome. The only reason Jessie the Greece character existed at all was because she gave my webmaster a boner.

To this day, I cannot believe that Jessie story ended the way that it did. And that she became an international sensation by vamping it up on Big Brother. And that I accidentally predicted that. And that Jessie Camacho is a giant celebrity now.

I tell you, the reality TV universe is weird.

54. Silas Screws... and Gets Screwed

The first twist in Survivor history (The Africa Twist) was such a big deal at the time that it is almost impossible to come up with any sort of a modern comparison. I mean, that episode wasn't just a big Survivor moment, that was flat out a big TV moment. Africa episode five was one of those rare "holy shit!" episodes that I wrote about back in my Michael Skupin chapter. Which is pretty amazing, considering that Africa episode 3 was also a "holy shit!" episode. Africa and Australia have so many amazing pre-merge episodes that it is almost unfair to expect any seasons following them to have to live up to that.

Of course, I would argue that Marquesas did exactly what Africa and Australia did, and it did it even BETTER. But we will get up to that when we get to it.

So anyway, here we are at The Twist. Episode five. The first twist in Survivor history. The one that changed everything. It changed everything you knew about the show, it changed everything you knew about the game, it completely changed the way that the players approached the game, it was responsible for everything.

And of course what the very first twist in Survivor history really needed was the very first victim.

And hey, well look at that. Luckily, we just so happen to have the perfect guy for you. And he is already standing right here.

We have Silas.

Lord Douchy McDouchington.

Yes, Silas (Chip) Gaither was about to take his step into Survivor immortality. And I will always remember where I was when it happened, and what a big deal it was.

> **Side Note:** By the way, a lot of people have never understood the whole Silas/Chip dichotomy, and what the deal was with the Samburu elders casting votes for "Chip" and why it pissed him off so much. Here is the backstory behind that.

312

In real life, Silas Gaither goes by the name Chip. That is apparently what everyone knows him as. The reason people call him Chip (or at least called him Chip at the time) was because he was a boxer. And because his father was also a boxer. And since Silas reminded so many people of his old man, the word around the world of boxing at the time was that he was "a chip off the old block." Hence his boxing nickname, Chip.

So here comes Chip Gaither, and he decides to apply for Survivor. And CBS casts him as Chip. And then after all the casting process and everything has been finalized, he decides that he wants to go by his real name instead. On Survivor he wants to be known as Silas. So he has them change his name in the cast list to Silas Gaither.

Here comes Silas out to Africa, and he starts playing the game, and he tells everyone on Samburu that his name is Chip. He says everyone back home calls him Chip. Oh, but his real name is actually Silas. He tells the Samburus that they can call him whatever they want during the game, but in interviews and during the episodes they are supposed to refer to him as Silas.

I don't remember where I saw this next clip, it might have been a secret scene on CBS.com at the time, or it might have been in one of the postgame interviews, I don't really remember. But there is a clip somewhere where Linda Spencer is complaining about Silas. She is complaining because none of the older players can stand him. And the thing they particularly can't stand about him is the fact that THEY DON'T EVEN KNOW WHAT HIS FUCKING NAME IS. She complains that half of the time he goes by Chip, and the other half of the time he goes by Silas. She complains that no one on the tribe has any idea what is going on in his head or who he is, and she thinks that HE doesn't even know what he is going on in his head or who he is. And believe me, when Linda "Mother Africa" Spencer is calling you crazy, that's saying something.

So anyway, there is your backstory. When the elders wanted to piss off Silas at the end of episode four by casting votes for him, that's how they did it. They cast votes for "Chip." And for "Silas." And for "Silas a.k.a. Chip." And you can even hear Silas bitch about it at the start of the next episode in a confessional. "They did it with an a.k.a.!" he complains at the start of episode five. There was clearly no love lost between Silas and the older members of Samburu.

313

Oh and yes, I have also heard that Survivor was the only time in his life that Chip Gaither has ever really gone by "Silas."

Okay, so here we go. The first Twist. The fall of Silas. All the hints were there. All the foreshadowing was there. Heck, if you go back and you rewatch Africa, pay attention to how many times the editors decided to show a shot of a dust devil swirling its way through the Samburu and Boran camp scenes. Dust devil = small tornado = twister. Get it? As usual, the editors were having a lot of fun with it.

Oh and I should also point out that the main sponsor of Survivor: Africa was a soft drink called **Pepsi Twist**. Pepsi Twist has never sponsored any other Survivor season. In fact, I am pretty sure that Pepsi Twist doesn't even exist anymore. In any case, Pepsi Twist was the sponsor for the very first Survivor twist season, and I am quite certain that wasn't a coincidence.

Again, go back and rewatch Africa some time, and look for all of the twist foreshadowing. See for yourself. There are a ton of little jokes in the episodes. There is a ton of little "Silas is about to take a huge fall" foreshadowing.

Now here is a question that I get asked a lot. A lot of people write to me and they ask me, "What did the Survivor audience think of the Africa twist at the time? Did they know it was coming?"

The simple answer to that is no. No one knew it was coming. I mean, a lot of people <u>suspected</u> that something like that might happen. There had been hints in the episodes that Silas was getting cocky and that he was headed for a fall all season. And of course the preview at the end of episode four hinted that SOMETHING AMAZING IS GOING TO HAPPEN AT THE START OF NEXT EPISODE! But no one knew exactly what that amazing thing was going to be at the time. Sure, some viewers predicted that there would be some sort of a tribe switchup, but anyone who says they knew for sure these days is lying to you. No one knew for sure. Yes, there were spoilers back then, but the spoilers were in no way as accurate or as definite as the types of spoilers that get dumped onto the internet now. Back in 2001, even the hardcore spoiler community tuned in with baited breath to see what THIS AMAZING THING THAT IS GOING TO HAPPEN IN EPISODE FIVE was going to be.

Now, this is a story that I have told before, but I always like telling it so I will share it again.

I did not watch the Africa Twist at home in my living room. Nope. By some weird coincidence, this was one of the rare episodes of the first eight seasons of Survivor that I did not get to watch at home. That week (the second week of November, 2001) happened to be the week that my family was on vacation in Las Vegas.

I love telling this story because this is one of those TV moments of my life that I will always remember because it was so surreal.

Survivor: Africa episode five (The Twist) aired on Thursday, November 8, 2001. Just about two months after 9/11. It aired at 8:00 PM. Which, by some strange coincidence, was the exact same moment that my wife and I happened to be walking through the mall underneath the MGM Grand Casino in Las Vegas.

Now, I'm not sure if you have ever been in the MGM Grand Mall in Las Vegas, but back in 2001 it was a big bright hallway that was lined with TVs on either side. There were just TVs and other media displays lined up as far as the eye could see. Which makes sense, since I am pretty sure that MGM owns (or at the very least was affiliated with) CBS. And sure enough, since this was 8:00 on the night of THE GREAT BIG SURVIVOR EVENT, all the TVs down that corridor that night had been tuned to Survivor.

Yes, I know this visual is almost unfathomable to a modern Survivor audience, who pretty much watch Survivor these days in shame and in secrecy with nobody else around, but this episode and this event (Africa episode five) had been hyped up so much that week that pretty much every single TV in the MGM Grand Casino had been tuned to Survivor that night. Everywhere you looked, people were stopping what they were doing (talking, shopping, gambling, eating) to turn around and watch what this big Survivor event was that everyone was talking about.

Even though I had programmed my VCR to tape the episode back home, I couldn't believe the coincidence that we had stumbled into that night. We happened to walk through that mall with those TVs on those walls at this exact moment. It was like it was fate. I mean, it was literally like 8:07 PM. I walked down that TV corridor the exact minute that Silas and Lex and Big Tom, etc., arrived for the twist. So I stood there, with about 200 strangers around me, and we all watched the first major twist in Survivor history. On the walls of the MGM Grand Mall in Las Vegas. It was one of those strange little life moments that I will never forget.

Now of course, you know what happened next. Silas got screwed by the twist (ooh! aah!), the Borans threw a challenge just to be able to get rid of him (yay! cheer!) and we got one of my favorite scenes in Survivor history where Silas wants to talk strategy with Ethan, and Ethan just gets annoyed and he sighs at the camera and he rolls his eyes. Seriously, that is a hilarious scene, go watch it again. My wife claims that is one of her top ten all-time funniest Survivor moments. Everyone knows that Silas is dead meat, but Silas himself hasn't figured it out yet. So Silas is wheeling and dealing and trying to save his ass. And Ethan just rolls his eyes at the camera any time Silas tries to put together some sort of a strategy discussion.

Side Note: You know, people claim that Ethan is dull and boring and that he is unmemorable as a TV character. And those people have always been wrong. Ethan sure isn't boring and dull and unmemorable during the Silas episode. In fact, the second half of the Twist episode has pretty much always just been the Ethan show. And let us not forget that Ethan Zohn was pretty much the first player in Survivor history to go through with the idea of throwing an immunity challenge just to get rid of someone. He was nowhere near as passive or boring or forgettable as you probably think he was.

And with that, with the thrown challenge on top of the twist, Silas Gaither was voted out of the game. The Fall of Silas was officially complete. It was the death of Chip. He went from the top of the peak to the bottom of the trash in less than an episode.

This was a big deal.

Remember, up to this point in Survivor history, there had never been a storyline even remotely like this before. No one had ever had a fall like that before. And yes, I need to point out again that Africa episode five was likely the first time in Survivor history that a tribe actually threw an immunity challenge just to get rid of someone.

Again, Ethan is forgettable? Ethan has no legacy in Survivor history? Ethan

316

is just a weak little sheep? Think again.

Ethan was the mercenary who threw the very first immunity challenge just to get rid of Silas.

-----Great Moments in Survivor History (re-enacted)!-----

[Silas arrives at Boran.]
Silas: Oh hey guys! My name is Silas but you can call me Chip.
 Let's take this game to the end!
[Ethan walks over to smile and shake his hand.]
Ethan: Oh hey Chip, nice to meet you. My name's Ethan. Don't unpack.
Silas:
Silas:
Silas:
Silas: Wait, what?

So anyway, I guess the question at this point in the book is this: What is the legacy of Silas Gaither?

How should we remember this guy in Survivor history?

Should he be remembered as a douchebag who got cocky and who was responsible for his own downfall? Is he a bad player who had an easy chance to win, but threw it all away because he got so full of himself? Or was he a legitimately good player who easily could have won, but who got screwed by a twist that he absolutely could not have seen coming because something like that had never happened on Survivor before.

How should we remember the Chipster in the history books?

I don't really know. I guess it is up to you to decide. You tell me what you think Silas's legacy should be.

All I will say about Silas Gaither at the end of the day is this.

He got killed by that twist. That twist came out of nowhere and it just hit him HARD. Like I said before, prior to Silas, nobody in Survivor history had ever gone from complete power to being a unanimous vote off in the span of

317

one episode. That was all him. Silas was the Jackie Robinson of downfalls. But at the same time, you have to have a little sympathy for the fact that there was absolutely no way he ever could have seen something like that coming. I mean, that tribe swap in episode five just came completely out of nowhere. There had been no precedent for something like in any episode of any season of Survivor before. Silas walked right into the trap that the producers had set for him, there was no way he EVER could have seen it coming, or planned for it, and he just got completely blindsided by it.

And this is why I have always had a bit of a soft spot for the guy.

It is now fourteen years later, more than a decade has passed since that very first twist screwed the very first Survivor victim, and I have NEVER heard Silas complain about it. Ever. He has never complained in an interview, he has never complained to any of the producers, he has never complained to any of the fans. Heck, I know dozens of people who have met Silas in person in real life, and he has <u>never</u> had a single bad thing to say about his Survivor experience. Ever. To anyone!

And you know, after watching Stacey Stillman sue CBS, after hearing Russell Hantz harp on that the game is flawed and that he always gets screwed by bitter juries, after seeing Coach Wade and Mike Skupin and Parvati Shallow (among others) complain that they got screwed at the end and that they should have won and that the game doesn't work, it is refreshing to know that Silas Gaither (of all people) is the one person who COULD have complained and bitched and threw a fit about Survivor but who DIDN'T.

I mean, Silas got screwed worse than anyone. There is no getting around that. The producers just totally blindsided him. If he had hired a lawyer the very next day and had taken CBS to court and had claimed he was robbed, I believe the fan base probably would have been fairly sympathetic towards him. I think most people would have heard about his lawsuit and they would have thought to themselves, "You know, the guy is a smug bastard but he makes a good point. That twist was really unfair."

Yet Silas DIDN'T. Again, he is the ONE guy in Survivor history who has a very valid case that the producers probably screwed him out of a lot of money, yet he has never even hinted at it. He has never even implied it. All Silas ever said in interviews after the game was over was, "Survivor is amazing. I want to thank Mark Burnett and CBS for casting me and for giving me a chance to play."

I mean, say what you want about the guy. I know I sure have taken a lot of cheap shots directed at him throughout the years, but Silas Gaither is a class act. And I am glad I finally get to say that about him in my Survivor book. I think it is ridiculous that his storyline (and the fact that he was such a good sport about it afterwards) has been so completely forgotten and overlooked when it comes to what an important part of Survivor history he was.

Silas is one of those alums that I have never been lucky enough to have a chance to meet. But I always wished that I could, just so I could say thank you and I could walk over and I could shake his hand.

Like him or not, in many ways, Silas "Chip" Gaither was really the biggest character when it came to Survivor: Africa.

He really should have received more consideration when it came to All Stars.

P.S. Okay, there is no way I can write a chapter about Silas without mentioning "Silas Screws." If you have never heard of it before, you are in for a treat. For most people (sadly), this is Silas Gaither's only big remaining Survivor legacy.

"Silas Screws" is one of the most popular features over at Survivor Sucks. And it has been a beloved running joke for nearly a decade and a half. It is also one of the funniest damn things I have ever seen in my life.

See, what happened was that at some point after Africa, Silas Gaither appeared at a charity event. And he wasn't wearing a shirt. And at one point he did a dance where he threw his head back and he thrust his hips forward. And of course, naturally, somebody at Survivor Sucks found the screen capture of this moment on the internet and they posted it over at Sucks. Because... well... because that's how Sucks do. They find embarrassing pictures of people and they make jokes out of them.

Note: Since I don't actually own the famous "Silas Screws" picture, here is me trying to recreate it in Paint. I'm sorry, legally, this is the best I can do. Just imagine Silas leaning back with no shirt on and joyfully thrusting his hips up into something. Oh, and he seems very happy about it.

In any case, if you know anything about Survivor Sucks (which is a comedy site more than anything), you will know that what happened next was that people started posting pictures of other people next to Silas. So that it looked like he was screwing them. Again, since I technically can't use any CBS photos in this book, you will just have to use your imagination. Just imagine a picture of Eliza wide-eyed in surprise next to Silas. Or a picture of Coach bending over and looking like he is in pain. When the two pictures are posted side by side it totally looks like Silas is gleefully boning them.

And that is how the legend of "Silas Screws" was born. Funniest damn thing I have ever seen when it comes to the Survivor fan community.

By the way, it is now fourteen years later, and Silas Screws is STILL going strong. On Survivor Sucks there are currently at least 200+ pages of people trying to come up with the funniest picture of something/someone being backdoored by Silas. Without question, this is my favorite thing that has ever come out of the online Survivor world. I will never find Silas Screws not funny.

Oh, and if Silas himself ever learned about this particular legacy? Well I am sure he would be quite proud of it. Strength and honor, baby.

P.P.S. I am not kidding. Google "Silas Screws" some time. Find the best ones. Then sit there and try not to laugh. I dare you.

55. The Reaction to the Twist

One question that I have heard a lot from Survivor fans over the years is, "What was the audience reaction to the Africa twist? Did they love it or did they hate it at the time?"

Well, before I answer that question, what I would like to do first is delve into the bigger question that actually comes before it. As in, why was that twist even there in the first place? Why did the producers suddenly need a twist in the third season of Survivor when they had never used one before?

To me, it is fairly obvious why the producers introduced a twist into Survivor. I believe it was all about manipulation. I think the producers wanted a way that they could manipulate the outcome of the game and change it if it was headed in a direction that they didn't like. And I think it took them three seasons to come up with a way that they could do it and not get in trouble for it.

I mean, think about it. Remember the Stacey Stillman fiasco in Borneo? Remember how much trouble the producers got in for trying to manipulate the way that the first season was playing out? Remember all the bad publicity that came down on them? And yes I know a lot of people will still argue that the Stacey stuff was "a rumor" and that there was no way to prove that it happened at all. But honestly, at this point, after all the evidence that came out afterwards (seriously, just google the Stacey Stillman lawsuit on the internet, the depositions are all public), I don't think there is any way you can say that Borneo played out 100% completely untainted with a straight face. In fact, the more I have heard about Borneo over the years, what surprises me the most about that first season is the fact that the producers only got nailed for ONE such incident.

So anyway, the producers tried to push the game in a certain direction in Borneo, and they got busted for it. They got busted hard. And the publicity that came out about it afterwards (and the accompanying lawsuit) very nearly could have ended the franchise. That was a really dark chapter in the history of Survivor. In fact, I would guess that was probably the closest the show has ever come to just flat out being canceled.

Then season two came along.

You know that the producers were dying to stick their hands into the game again. You know they were just DYING to do it again. I mean, come on, that would just be basic human nature. If you have a TV show that is worth this much money and is pulling in this much advertising revenue, of COURSE you want to have some control in the way it plays out. That is just common sense. Honestly, if you didn't want a single bit of control in the way your game played out, you really wouldn't be a very good TV producer.

The producers would have wanted some way to influence the way that Australia played out, but they didn't do anything. In fourteen years of writing about this show, I have never heard a single rumor that Australia was manipulated or fudged or influenced in any way whatsoever. It is like the polar opposite of Borneo. In fact, if you ask me, Australia is probably the only season in fifteen years of Survivor that I think the producers left completely alone. I think that is the one season in Survivor history that the producers had to stay away from and keep their grubby little hands off, simply because everyone in the media and the fanbase was watching them and they didn't want to get busted again.

Now, I have no way to prove that this next part is true, it is just a theory of mine. But I have to imagine that the producers were probably DYING to manipulate Australia a little. I mean, look at that Skupin episode. Look at the edit that Colby got all season. The producers were just dying to have a noble heroic winner after the disaster of Richard Hatch winning. What the producers would have wanted (at the time) was for one of the Kuchas to come back and win the game in honor of their leader, Mike. Or they would have wanted the Colbster to win. Right there, one of those two scenarios (Colby or either Elisabeth/Rodger winning), that would have fixed everything that people perceived had been wrong with the end of Borneo.

But it didn't happen. Neither of those scenarios happened.

I think the producers held back on Australia. I think they let it play out exactly how it would have naturally played out, and in my opinion it is probably the only time in Survivor history where they let a season do that. And I don't think they were all that happy with what happened in the end. Because as much as I love Tina, she was never all that beloved by the general audience. And I have never thought she was all that beloved by the producers or the network either. After all, this might seem like an insignificant fact to some, but I don't think it was: Tina was never even supposed to be in that cast in the first place. She was only one of the alternates. The only reason she was an Ogakor member at all was because some other woman dropped out at the last minute.

So Australia ended, and my guess is that the producers got together and they had a little powwow. I think they sat down and they brainstormed how they were going to handle the third season. Because even though Survivor was an amazing smash hit, and even though the audience was currently enamored with it, there were still a couple of flaws in the format that they wanted to smooth out.

Flaw number one? Well, that's easy. Pagongings are boring. We have powered our way through two of them now, and as producers they drive us nuts. And if they drive us nuts, they sure as hell probably drive the audience nuts. So we need to find some way to "encourage" those season-killing Pagongings not to happen anymore.

Flaw number two? We need to have some control over the way that the story plays out. If a season starts heading down a direction that we aren't comfortable with, we need to have some way as producers to right it and steer it the other way. And we need to do it in a way that no one can ever nail us for it.

Flaw number three? The audience hated Richard. The audience was mostly indifferent to Tina. We need to find a way to produce a likable winner one of these days. If we wind up with an unpopular (or meh) winner three seasons in a row, there is the potential that the audience might simply revolt on us.

And this is how I have always believed the Africa twist came about.

The minute Silas and Lindsey grabbed control of Samburu, the minute it became clear that one of the Mallrats was probably going to win the game, I think the emergency super secret backup plan quickly went into effect. My guess is that "Operation Stop The Mallrats" (or whatever they called it) was quickly approved. And I think the producers had done enough research and they had worked it out carefully enough ahead of time that they knew they could never get busted for it.

"Oh, the twist? Well we planned to do that back in Australia but it didn't work out. Basically we do that to keep the players on their toes and to make the endgame less predictable. And it was carefully planned out ahead of time to always happen in episode five."

Yeah okay, sure.

Check out how impossible it is to prove that the producers are lying about that. That is a carefully crafted explanation without any loopholes or possible rebuttals whatsoever; there is simply no way to call B.S. on it because it is intelligent and it makes logical sense.

Yet it also makes logical sense to point out that the minute that Silas and Lindsey and Brandon took over the game, we immediately got the first twist. Just like that. Silas is king. Silas is ready for his check. Annnnnnnd now Silas is gone.

And the audience cheers.

Now, again, I don't have any proof of any of this. I have never heard anything that proves one way or another that the producers tweaked Africa simply so that Silas and the Mallrats wouldn't win. But if you follow everything that had happened in Survivor history up to that point (remember, think of Survivor as an overall timeline, don't think of it as a bunch of different seasons), it all makes perfect sense. Do you think that twist would have happened if Ethan and Big Tom had risen to power in episode three? Do you think that twist would have happened if it looked like T-Bird was going to win the game? Fat chance. I'm sorry, but that just isn't how TV works.

Again, this is all that I'm saying. I'm not saying that Africa was fixed. I'm not saying that Ethan didn't deserve his win, or that the Borans weren't responsible for their amazing comeback. The Borans worked their asses off that game, and Ethan to this day is one of the all-time great Survivor winners.

What I AM saying is that Silas or Lindsey winning Survivor would have been a disaster. It would have been a public relations disaster of epic proportions. It would have made the fan fallout after Richard won look like a joke. Oh my goodness, I mean, I can't even put into words how hard the fanbase would have revolted if Silas Gaither would had won the third season. Or my God, if Lindsey had won? Lindsey, who might have been even more hated than Jerri? Or if weaselly little Brandon had won??

There is a really famous rant out there by comedian Chris Rock, where he talks about if O.J. Simpson really killed his wife Nicole. Rock lists all the terrible things that Nicole did to O.J. in the years leading up to her murder. She took his money. She slept with his friends. She drove around in his car. She got control of his house. She had sex with guys on his bed. And then at the end of the rant, Rock says "Now I'm not saying he should have killed her. But I understand."

This is the tactic I have always taken when it comes to discussing the Africa twist. Or when it comes to the question of whether Survivor has ever been manipulated or not in general.

Should the producers have stepped in and made it so that a Mallrat wouldn't win the game? Should they have thrown in a twist right there to save the heroic T-Bird and Frank right before they were voted out? Should they have tweaked the structure of the game to ensure that the Samburus were going to splinter and fall apart, and that a Boran was probably going to take control of the game?

No, they probably shouldn't have.

But if they did, then I understand.

P.S. Oh yes, and to answer the second question, "What was the audience reaction to the Africa twist?" Well the answer to that one is easy. The audience absolutely loved it, because lol Silas.

56. Did The Twist Actually Change Anything?

In the last chapter I talked about how Silas and the Mallrats would have easily waltzed to the end of the game, and how Silas would have probably walked away with a million dollar check if there had never been a twist.

I know a lot of Survivor fans will probably disagree with me on that particular opinion, so why don't we take a moment to delve into this a little bit?

For starters, yes. The perception at the time was that Silas had an easy million dollars taken away from him because of producer interference. Oh, I'm sorry. I mean because of "a twist." Remember, it's only "producer interference" if it happens to a player you <u>don't</u> like. Because it happened to Silas, most people were fine with it because it was "a twist."

But yes, this was definitely the prevailing opinion among the internet fan base at the time. Silas got screwed. After all, through two seasons of Survivor, what other knowledge did we have available to us other than the precedent that had been set by the first and second seasons? When you had a dominant tribe that had the numbers going into the merge, one of the members of that tribe was going to win the game. I mean, this opinion really wasn't all that negotiable at the time. That was just how Survivor worked. You would have been a fool at the time to argue anything other than "Well that Samburu tribe looks strong. If they go into the merge with numbers, one of them is probably going to win the game." And again, since Silas and Lindsey were clearly the two players at the forefront of that tribe, the winner was likely going to be one of them.

Much as Survivor history would have hated it, that was definitely the perception at the time. And it was widespread. That was what everyone believed.

Now, looking back at things in retrospect, was this reasoning one hundred percent correct?

Many people (including me at times) have argued over the years that there was NO WAY that a Mallrat was ever going to win that game. Because the minute that merge hit, the minute T-Bird or Frank made that merge and saw that there were people other than Silas and Lindsey who they could potentially team up with, well then it pretty much would have been game over for the Mallrats. All T-Bird or Frank would have had to do was switch

327

sides, team up with the much nicer and easier to work with Boran Tribe, and take out the Mallrats. In fact if Africa had been season eighteen instead of season three, that is <u>exactly</u> what would have happened. In later seasons, players will routinely bail out on their alliance and team up with new people on the other tribe to form a new bloc. Once you get to about season six (thank you Rob Cesternino), Survivor players start jumping from tribe to tribe and doing stuff like that all the time.

But again, and here is the tricky part, in season three the players just didn't do that yet. Remember, NO one had jumped ship from a dominant tribe to the other tribe at this point in Survivor history. NOBODY.

And so here is where we come to the big question. The million dollar question, if you will.

If there had been no twist in Africa, if Silas and Lindsey had led the Mallrats into a merge with the way that Samburu had been structured at the time, would they really have won? Is the perception accurate that Silas had a very good chance to win the game, and The Twist was the only thing that screwed him over and took away his million dollar check?

Well first off, there is no way to know the answer to this for sure. I mean, I've read interviews with Ethan and Lex. I've seen comments from Frank and T-Bird and Silas. I've even had a personal conversation about this question with Lindsey. Heck, I even had a phone conversation with T-Bird about this very subject just a couple of weeks ago. And you know what? <u>Everyone</u> who has ever talked about this topic has said something different. Naturally, the players who were on the opposite side of Silas (the Borans) say that they would have taken over the game even without the twist. And Silas? Well Silas is too much of a diplomat to ever say that he got screwed. But if he was ever pressed in an interview, he would always say that he had a decent relationship with T-Bird and Frank, and that the two of them probably would have stayed on board with him after the merge.

And, of course, you know how Survivor works. Remember, this is an important mantra that I think all fans need to memorize, <u>Survivor isn't a game with one storyline, it is a game with SIXTEEN storylines</u>. And it is only possible for people to see the game one way. They are only able to view it from their own individual biased perspective. In other words, the Borans say one thing, the Samburus say another, and I hate to say it, but it is entirely possible that both sides might actually be telling the truth.

Remember these next two paragraphs, because they are important ones. This is something that will never change throughout fifteen-plus years of Survivor history. Get ready for the Golden Rule of Reading Survivor Interviews, because here we go:

> **The Golden Rule:** Ask any player in Survivor history what they would have done in a theoretical situation, and the answer will always be the same. It will never change because Survivor is a predictable game, and because human beings are predictable creatures.
>
> Survivor players can only see a game like this from one perspective. They can only see it from their own. Which, according to basic psychology, is generally an inaccurate perspective anyway. In other words, ask any player in Survivor history what they would have done in a theoretical situation and they will always say the same thing. Of COURSE I would have made the right move. Of COURSE I would have maximized my chances to win. Of COURSE I would have seen the danger and I would have avoided it. Of course, of course, of course, of course, of course.

This is an aspect of Survivor that is very difficult for the average fan to understand, and it wasn't until a few years after Africa that I really sort of "got it" myself. It is really hard to grasp the concept of "Sixteen storylines, yet none of them are necessarily accurate" when you sit down and you read retroactive Survivor interviews. Yet fans do it. They will read an interview by Lex, and they will read, "Oh yeah, of course we would have swayed T-Bird over to Boran. We knew she was a free agent and we had her." And they will treat that as gospel. Yet it is not gospel. That is just Lex's opinion. Just like it is Ethan's opinion that he would have won even without a twist. Just like it is Silas's opinion that he had the game in the bag.

Those are all opinions, and none of them are necessarily wrong. Just like none of them are necessarily right. But they are all 100% completely accurate and correct from the point of view of that particular player. From THEIR vantage point, that is EXACTLY how the game was going to play out. They can see it crystal clear in their mind. That is how the game would have played out if there had never been a twist.

But again, what players do NOT see, what they couldn't POSSIBLY see, is that there are fifteen other storylines in the game other than theirs. And a lot of times there are variables and situations and circumstances that they couldn't ever possibly predict. I mean, maybe T-Bird and Frank would have stuck with the Samburus after the merge. Maybe they wouldn't have. Maybe they wouldn't have even been there at the merge. Maybe relationships would have changed in those last six days leading up to the merge. Maybe Lindsey would have said something on day 17 that freaked out Silas. Maybe he would have made a super secret counteralliance with T-Bird just in case he needed it. Maybe Kim Powers would have subtly taken control of the Mallrats. There is just no way to know.

What I guess I am saying here is that there is NO way to know what would have happened if there hadn't been a twist. Oh, the players might <u>tell</u> you what would have happened if you ask them in an interview, months or years or even decades after it happened. But they couldn't possibly know. And they couldn't possibly have known at the time either. Any opinion they have (or had) will always be skewed by the way THEY saw the game, and the facts that THEY saw, and the variables that THEY controlled. And the image in the Survivor fan base that THEY want to give off.

Always remember that when you read a Survivor interview. Because players aren't lying. From their point of view, hell yeah, what they are telling you is the God's honest truth. When somebody asks Lex if a Boran would have won even without the twist, he honestly believes that yes, that would have happened. Just like Lindsey more than likely believes otherwise. They aren't lying, they are just telling you what the reality was.

Except... reality isn't always reality. Especially when it comes to a game made up of sixteen different storylines. If you know what I'm saying.

So what is the point of bringing all this up? Well my point is that we couldn't possibly know what would have happened in Africa if there hadn't been a twist. I mean, I could give you my opinion. I could give you what I <u>think</u> would have happened based on the facts. In fact I believe I will do that right now.

Here are the facts:

* Kim Johnson was a HUGE challenge liability. She was by far the worst challenge competitor in the entire game, and she almost single handedly cost Boran several challenges early on in the season. And she was still there hanging around on Boran in episode five.

* Had there not been a twist, I believe that Kim would have cost the Borans at least one more challenge. I mean, she was so bad at challenges that just

sort of makes logical sense. So right there, without a twist, I think the best that Boran could do is probably go into that merge 5-5. And remember, that is a BEST case scenario. There is almost no way that Boran goes into a merge up 6-4. And if they lose one of the two final immunity challenges (which they probably will), and they have to vote out Kim Johnson (which they probably will), well that sort of changes the dynamics of the tribe significantly. Because remember, Kim was tight with both Lex and Ethan. So right there, they vote her out, and they just lost one of their big allies.

* Without a twist, there is no way to know if Kim Johnson would have gone home pre-merge or not. So therefore the only fact I can give at this point is that had there not been a twist, Silas would have definitely still been there on Samburu at the start of episode five. And Silas was a challenge beast. And Kim would have definitely still been there on Boran in episode five. And Kim was pretty much the opposite of a challenge beast. And nobody would have been trying to throw a challenge in this storyline because both tribes would have still been trying to win.

Could the Borans have made it to the merge even in numbers if there hadn't been a twist? It's possible.

Would T-Bird and/or Frank have flipped over to Boran the minute they hit that merge? It's possible. But remember, Clarence was on the outs with the Borans just like T-Bird and Frank were on the outs with the Mallrats. And Clarence was just as likely to switch tribes as they were once they got to the merge. A flip could have happened on either side, we will never know. But it would be foolish not to point out the parallels there.

In the end, there is one lesson I learned in my college psychology classes that I have always held near and dear to my heart. And I always come back to this lesson when I am trying to predict what a human being will or will not do in a particular situation.

The number one lesson when it comes to predicting human behavior is this.

Any behavioral psychologist will tell you this:

The best predictor of future behavior is past behavior.

And so there you go. If you want to guess what would have happened in

Africa if there had never been a twist, there is the golden rule of psychology that you probably need to go by. **The best predictor of future behavior is past behavior.**

Here's the deal. The tribe that went into the merge with numbers and a dominant alliance had ALWAYS won Survivor prior to Africa. Remember, this was 2001. Nobody had ever willingly jumped out of a position of dominance in this game before. Never. Hadn't happened before, wasn't going to happen now. At least, not without some assistance or a little bit of a nudge from the producers (aka a twist). So I am guessing that had Teresa and/or Frank made it to the merge as a part of the dominant Samburu Tribe, I am guessing that is exactly where they would have stayed. They would have stayed with the group that was winning. Just like you always did.

In particular, I believe that T-Bird probably would have stayed with the Samburus.

Now, I know what you're thinking. If you know Africa at all, you are probably sitting there reading this and thinking, "But wait, T-Bird was the best player on Samburu. She would have been smart enough to know that if she stayed on Samburu, she would have wound up in fifth place at best. She would have jumped over to the Borans in a heartbeat."

I disagree with that. And I will tell you why.

Yes, I agree that T-Bird was probably the savviest player on Samburu. No disagreement there. But what that means to me is that she would have been smart enough to go with the strategy that she knew worked! I mean, remember, riding a dominant alliance to the end was the only way that Survivor was played back then. People didn't just switch alliances or switch tribes at the drop of the hat. That kind of strategy wouldn't become a thing on Survivor until a few seasons later, in particular (like I said before) with Rob Cesternino in Amazon.

I am pretty sure T-Bird realized she was fifth place at best on Samburu. And I think she knew that Silas or Lindsey were probably going to win the game. And I also think she knew that YOU DON'T SWITCH ALLIANCES AND JUMP OUT OF A MAJORITY AFTER THE MERGE BECAUSE MILLION DOLLAR WINNERS ON SURVIVOR DON'T DO THAT!

Remember, past behavior predicts future behavior. A successful player on Survivor had never done that before. I think T-Bird was smart enough and would have been savvy enough not to be the first.

Now when it comes to Frank, all bets are off. Because Frank, well he always came off a little bit crazy. And a little bit impulsive. So I could easily see him switching sides and teaming up with the Borans. Not necessarily because it was the smart move, but just because he wanted to say ha ha f.u. Silas and f.u. Mallrats. And this is why I think pulling T-Bird back into Samburu would have been the Mallrats' next move if there hadn't been a twist. Because they weren't idiots. They knew darn well that if they kept T-Bird in the mix they could probably keep Frank. I have always believed that T-Bird was the single most important variable there. She was the mother figure and they would have wanted to keep her.

In the end, if you ask me what I think would have happened in Africa if there had never been a twist, this is what I would say.

I think that T-Bird would have stayed with the Samburus, simply because she knew a good thing when she saw it. And "a good thing" in Survivor's early days simply meant "you had the numbers." I think she would have stuck with the Samburus, and I think she would have tried to make a strong bond with the less dominant member of the Mallrats (Brandon and Kim). And I think she would have said a prayer in her head each and every night that the Mallrats were going to fracture down the road. Because if they fractured, if they suddenly turned against each other after the merge, well guess who might sneak right in to that final two? It really isn't all that improbable that we could have had two sweet southern female flight attendants win Survivor in a row.

Now, of course, none of this is fact. This is just my opinion. I don't know anything more than anyone else knows, I am simply basing this on the facts of what Survivor was like at the time, what the dynamics of the game were at the time, and how human behavior works. And also what we know about Survivor: Africa. Had there not been a twist, I think the most dangerous player in the game (T-Bird) would have ridden that Samburu dominance as far as she could go. I think the Samburus would have taken over the second half of the game. And whether Silas, T-Bird, or Lindsey wins would have mostly been determined by when and how and whether or not the fracture occurred.

To me, that sounds logical. That was how Survivor was played back then. That whole scenario passes the sniff test.

In other words, yes, I am sorry Ethan and Lex, I think it has to be said.

I think the twist really did make a difference in how Survivor: Africa played out.

P.S. Okay here is some juicy Survivor gossip for you. I have no idea if this is actually true or not, but I have heard it repeated several times over the years, by several different people, and I thought you would get a kick out of it. Because it is no coincidence that I just compared Teresa Cooper to Tina Wesson. There is a reason I said we very easily could have had two sweet southern female flight attendant winners in a row.

The rumor I have heard over the years (again, from several different sources) was that T-Bird was originally supposed to be a member of the Boran Tribe. That was the plan. When the producers laid out the tribes and they planned out the season, she was supposed to be on Boran and Diane Ogden (the postal carrier) was supposed to be on Samburu. But at the very last minute, I heard that the producers saw the problem with this so they flip-flopped T-Bird and Diane and they made them switch tribes.

And what was the problem the producers saw?

Well again, this is just gossip, but I have heard it so many times over the years that I should at least spill what I have heard.

The story I heard is that the producers expected that the Samburus were going to be a mess. That Frank/Brandon personality clash was going to be a problem just from looking at their biography pages, and it was expected that there was going to be an ugly old/young split in the Samburu tribe the minute they set foot in that boma. So, right off the bat, the producers expected that Boran was going to be the more successful of the two tribes in Africa.

And if you look at Boran, who is the strongest looking player on paper? Who is the smartest, and the savviest, and the most people-friendly strategist of the bunch? Well if you look at all the bios on paper, that person is probably T-Bird.

And if you look at T-Bird's bio, well look at that. She's a flight attendant. Just like Tina Wesson used to be. And she's from the south. Just like Tina

Wesson is. And she is sweet and she has a distinct accent. Again, just like our last winner. Oh, and both of them happen to be moms with two kids.

The rumor I have heard over the years is that Teresa was SO similar to Tina that the producers didn't want two similar winners in a row. They wanted the winner demographic to be a little more diverse than that. So they took the best player off of the best tribe, and they dumped her over onto the "other" tribe. You know, just as sort of a handicap. And then T-Bird got the last laugh anyway when she very nearly won.

Again, I have no idea if any of this is true. And I certainly can't tell you all the people I have heard it from because I don't like to name names. But I have heard it, a lot. It has been a well-known piece of Survivor gossip for years.

And these are the kinds of stories you hear when you become a Survivor columnist. :)

P.P.S. By the way, I actually ran this chapter by T-Bird right before I published it. Out of all the chapters in the book, this is the only one that I wanted to run by a Survivor before I committed it to my book. And no, not because I necessarily think that her opinion (or any Survivor's opinion) is gospel. No, I simply didn't want somebody to show this chapter to T-Bird six months down the road and for her to find me and tell me that I was 100% full of crap.

So anyway, I ran this chapter by T-Bird a couple of weeks ago, and here is what she had to say about it. She didn't disagree with me that there was a chance she might have stayed with the Samburus, at least at the beginning. Because as she pointed out, yeah working with Silas and Lindsey would have been a disaster, but at the same time it's not like she ever could have broken into the Lex/Ethan/Tom triumvirate either. Those three were completely unbreakable and nobody was ever going to get in to wedge them apart. Either way, no matter which side she went with, after the merge she would have been in a difficult scenario.

However, and this is the interesting part, the one thing that T-Bird wanted to point out to me was that if there had never been a twist, it was unlikely that she ever would have made it to the merge in the first place. Because she was going to be the next person voted out of Samburu. She said that the Mallrats (or "the kids" as she calls them) pulled her aside after the Linda vote, and they told her that she was going to be voted out before Frank. Simply because she was a way better player than Frank was, and they knew damn well that she could cause more trouble than he could after the merge. So they preferred to keep Frank around over her, simply because Frank was a social spaz and he would never be able to work with anyone. And T-Bird wasn't.

And so there you go. Before we get too far into the question of "what would have happened if there had never been a twist in Africa?" it is important as fans that we know all of the variables. And that is a really big variable. If Samburu had lost another challenge after the Linda vote, T-Bird was probably dead meat.

But still, I will always believe that they never would have lost another challenge. And that T-Bird would have made it to the merge. And at that point, well then all bets are off. But who knows. As I said at the start of the chapter, all we can really do at this point is speculate.

57. Dr. Sean Saves The Day

So here we were, midway through the third season of Survivor, Survivor: Africa. I was writing recaps for a brand new Survivor website called Survivor-Central. And it was a magical time for me because I must have now put together an audience of about three readers. Oh, such an amazing accomplishment. Oh, such glorious times. Over the past five weeks of my life I had gone from zero readers all the way up to three readers. These were such heady times to be a well-known Survivor writer on the internet.

By the way, there were two events around this time period that made a big difference in how I eventually went from being "Some guy who writes the recaps" to becoming "Mario Lanza, Survivor Writer!" And I thought I would write about them now because, even though they might seem like they are laughably small to you, they were both a really big deal at the time and they both made an enormous impact. And since you are here for the Survivor history, you will hopefully find them interesting.

The first person who made a big difference in my Survivor writing career was Dr. Sean Kenniff.

Yes, Dr. Sean Kenniff from Borneo. Dr. Doofus. The alphabet guy.

I have never actually talked to Dr. Sean before. The two of us have never had any sort of interaction whatsoever over the years. There have been no emails, no texts, no face to face meetings, no interviews, no Facebook pokes, nothing. Like I said in my Borneo chapters, it was almost impossible for a fan to have any sort of interaction with one of the Borneo castaways back in the early days. So Dr. Sean and I never interacted at any point back when I was a Survivor writer, and we still have never had any type of interaction whatsoever up to this day.

However, Murtz Jaffer (my boss at Survivor-Central) did have some sort of an in with Dr. Sean. I have no idea how he made that contact, especially at that point in Survivor history, but he did. Somehow Murtz had an inside connection to Dr. Sean. And a couple of episodes into Survivor: Africa, all of a sudden Dr. Sean Kenniff joined the Survivor-Central writing team as one of our columnists.

And let me tell you, (this is not me being sarcastic) our readership just SKYROCKETED.

There is no way I can emphasize to you what a big deal this was at the time. An actual Survivor alum is now writing for a Survivor website? Holy crap. That was just effing unbelievable. NO Survivor website had a Survivor writing for them at that time. Nobody. In fact, I'm not even sure the players were allowed to do that in their contracts. Back in the early days of the show, Survivors were contractually obliged to be seen on the show, they were expected to be available to do CBS/SEG approved projects after the show, and that was pretty much it. They were NOT supposed to be interacting with fans on the internet or be talking about the show unless it was in an approved CBS/SEG format. This "don't talk about the show unless we say you can talk about it" rule was the absolute golden rule among alumni, it was enforced by the all-seeing CBS overlords on the internet twenty four hours a day on every single website, and this was well-known and it was understood by pretty much everyone.

And then Murtz somehow gets Dr. Sean to be a part of our writing team.

I still have no idea how Murtz managed to do that. In fact, to this day, I have never asked him, and I really don't even <u>want</u> to know. I have no idea what part of his soul he had to sell to the devil to get a Survivor to come write for our Survivor site.

But here came Dr. Sean, with a column every week that was called "Ask Dr. Sean." Fans could write in with questions, and The Alphabet Strategy Guy would answer them. Your question could be about the show, it could be about neurology, it could be about the alphabet, it could be about Superpole. It could be about autoerotic asphyxiation. It could be about anything. And like I said, the minute that column showed up at Survivor-Central, our readership just <u>skyrocketed</u>. Within the span of about two weeks, we went from being "one of the nameless Survivor websites that sprung up after Australia" to "ONE OF THE MUST-READ SURVIVOR SITES!" Just like that, and all because of Dr. Sean, we quickly became one of the two or three biggest Survivor websites on the internet.

> **Side note:** By the way, lest you think I am exaggerating about this, this is something that Murtz used to tease me about all the time. He used to tease me about the fact that I could write a 10,000 word essay on how Survivor works, how the jury works, and why players who think they are playing a good game on Survivor really aren't. And then Dr. Sean could write twelve words on why Lemony-Fresh Tide smells nice. And his column would wind up getting 420,000

more hits than mine would. Murtz loved to point that out and tease me about it. Naturally, because of this, Dr. Sean's column quickly took the place of Television Without Pity and became my new Lex Luthor.

All joking aside, Dr. Sean really did "make" Survivor-Central. He really did turn it into the behemoth that it would later become. Murtz has said this to me on many occasions, and I feel it is important to document it here in my Survivor book as well. Because of Dr. Sean Kenniff, because of his decision to write a column for a no-name Survivor website, Murtz Jaffer soon became the biggest Survivor superfan and the biggest reality TV expert of them all, and I soon became the most widely read Survivor writer on the entire internet. Again, it all goes back to him. It all goes back to the guy who invented the Alphabet Strategy.

And to think, the only reason he chose to write for our website is because, alphabetically, we came before Survivor Fanatics and Survivor Fire.

I know, I keed, I keed. In any case, thank you Dr. Sean. Thank you for everything. I sure hope that your Etre the Cow book worked out for you.

So that was the first thing that made a really big difference in my writing career. Dr. Sean. It all started because Murtz got him to write for our website. And again, I don't know how that happened, and it is really better not to ask how it happened. It is really better not to know what kind of a monetary payment was involved in those negotiations.

The SECOND thing that made a big difference in my writing career, however, well that was all me. Although just like the Dr. Sean thing, it will seem minor to you unless you put it into perspective. Because this was a really big step in the way that websites presented Survivor to their readership back in the early days.

Remember how I said that I was the recap writer for Survivor-Central? And that nobody read my recaps. And that nobody on the internet EVER reads Survivor recaps? Remember how I said it was a loser job?

Well like I said in an earlier chapter, there was a guy at our website named "Potato" who wrote a weekly column he called "The Potato Perspective." Every week he provided commentary on what the current state of spoiling was in the Survivor world. This was his chance to put his thoughts out there each week about which spoilers floating around about Survivor were important, and which players had clues about them that pointed out they were probably going to go far. He would also add his prediction each week on who he thought was going to be the next boot. Basically, what Potato was doing was he was writing was an opinion piece. It might have been the very first internet Survivor opinion piece.

And, well, you know, I kind of wanted to write an opinion piece too.

So this is what I did.

At the end of my second recap (Africa, Episode 2), I decided I would add a little opinion piece at the bottom. You know, at the very end of my recap. It wasn't anything major, it was just a quickie little summary of what I thought was going on in the game, and which players I thought were playing particularly well. And why the episode we just saw played out the way that it did.

Again, this sounds minor, it sounds like it was no big deal. I was basically just doing the exact same thing that Potato was doing. Only instead of writing it from a spoiler perspective, like he was doing, I was writing it from a game perspective. I was writing it from a psychology perspective. I was spelling it out as "Hey if you are ever a player on Survivor, this is how you would want to play. Because these are the players that are playing well and they are going to go far."

I had no idea that these were the kinds of essays that would one day become my legacy. I had no idea that this was the kind of stuff that the fan base really wanted to read when they scoured the internet for stuff about Survivor. I also had no idea that NOBODY ELSE ON THE INTERNET WAS DOING THIS AT THE TIME and that I was probably the first.

All I knew at the time was that I added my first little opinion piece at the end of my Africa episode two recap. Just a tiny little seven paragraph opinion piece.

And just like that, between that and the draw of sharing a website with Dr. Sean, I would start to get a readership.

P.S. And here you go. The very first opinion piece I ever wrote about Survivor. These are the actual comments I tacked on at the bottom of my

Africa episode two recap:

MARIO'S COMMENTS:

A big chunk of the middle of this episode dealt with paranoia and the double crossings by Silas, and it was pretty boring. But other than that, this was another strong episode. The Samburus look like they are in deep trouble. Even with an 8-6 lead, they are crumbling faster than the Taliban defenses.

Ever since the spoiled brats of Pagong voted out B.B., I have wanted to see the elders in a tribe go medieval on the younger members of a tribe, and it looks like it may finally happen in Samburu. Lindsey and Brandon will be the first to go, and I don't think anyone in the audience will miss them very much. I thought Brandon was going to be entertaining like Jeff Varner, but he hasn't done anything yet to be even remotely likable. I am liking Frank and Carl more and more though. Although Frank may be in some peril, I hope he sticks around just for the humor alone.

Teresa looks to be a very strong player. She is likely past the most dangerous part of the game for her (as the oldest female in the tribe), so if she makes the merge she could become an easy candidate to make the Top 5. Plus she seems so nice. Linda is tough as well, although she seems a little shady to me. And Silas, of course, is the big wildcard. He could go any way, he could do anything, no one has any idea.

Over on Boran, the duo of Lex and Ethan are still my favorites to win, although I am liking Kelly more and more each episode. She's not your stereotypical "cute girl just getting by because she is non threatening." She actually has some fight in her, and I like her more than any of the other young players in the game by far. Clarence is okay, but he seems awfully eager to blame others for things just to get the attention off of him.

I wasn't the least bit sorry to see Jessie go home this week. If you are dying of dehydration and you willingly refuse to drink water, you have no business playing this game anymore. I'm sure the CBS executives are crapping their pants about it though. "We had a beautiful Latina who was a cop AND a model and she is out in two

341

episodes??" I'm sure they expected more out of her. I probably shouldn't have joked earlier that she should be able to outrun Tom. If she was legitimately sick, I'm sure that must have been a factor. But still, as Rick Springfield once sang, "I wish I hadn't seen Jessie hurl!"

My picks to go home next week? For Samburu, Lindsey. Whether it is the dehydration thing or the vote itself, she is dead meat in the next episode or two. It is just common sense. She is the most visible member of the weaker alliance. For Boran, it will probably be Kim Johnson. That just seems like a common sense pick too. I am big on common sense picks. Lindsey and Kim Johnson seem like pretty obvious boots in my mind.

Until next week, remember to mix in some milk with your blood!

58. Some Random Anecdotes

Before we get to the merge in Africa, I think this would be a good time to share a couple of personal Survivor anecdotes with you. These will give you a good idea of what it was like to be a Survivor fan back in November of 2001.

For starters, let's talk about All Stars.

Yes, even though we were only in the third season of Survivor, even though only 48 people in Survivor history had ever been cast on the show up to this point, there was already a buzz among the internet crowd as to what a Survivor All-Star season would be like if they ever decided to do one. Specifically, what would happen if Richard Hatch went up against Tina Wesson? If the two winners from seasons one and two went head to head against one another, which one would truly turn out to be the better Survivor player?

There wasn't a strong buzz about any sort of an All Star season yet. It certainly wasn't as strong as it would be later, after season four, or after season five. But it was definitely there. It was right there, lurking under all the discussion on the internet about whether the Mallrats got screwed by the twist, or if Ethan was too nice to win a game like Survivor. Or what the hell was up with Kim Johnson wearing that thong.

Fans were openly starting to wonder if Tina was a better player than Richard. Or if Richard was a better player than Tina.

They were starting to wonder what would happen if Mike Skupin ever got a chance to play again, and what that would be like.

They were already starting to discuss... if there WAS a Survivor All Stars... who the representatives from Africa would be.

There isn't much to say about All Stars yet. And I stress "yet." But there will be soon. For now, just file away the fact that fans were already starting to wonder what would happen if Tina played against Richard. They were already starting to wonder what Sue and Kelly's relationship would be like if they actually went out and they played Survivor against one another again. Because, man, oh my God. Remember the rats and snakes speech?? Wouldn't the two of them playing against each other after the rats and snakes speech be dramatic as hell?

No one was thinking there would actually <u>be</u> a Survivor All Stars yet. For now this was all just theoretical. In fact, I remember that whenever I would talk about this subject on a message board around this time, I would always say the exact same thing. My suggestion was always something along the lines of "After season four, they should take the final four from each of the first four seasons. And then just split up all the alliances. Split Colby and Tina apart, split Richard and Rudy. Split Kelly and Sue. Voila. A sixteen person cast with a ton of big names and a ton of inherent drama." I mean, who wouldn't want to watch a TV show like that?

By the way, I just mentioned the existence of a theoretical "Survivor season four." Which, of course, as Africa was airing, most people didn't know a thing about. Around this point in late 2001, most fans (including me) didn't realize that there was actually a <u>ton</u> of drama going on behind the scenes about "Survivor season four" and "if there actually would be a Survivor season four because of what is going on in the world."

Now, this is a pretty well-known bit of trivia by this point, so forgive me if you have already heard about it before. But there are a lot of newer fans out there who might not know about it yet. So here we go. Here is the big drama that was going on around Survivor Season Four behind the scenes at this point in the franchise:

Survivor 4 wasn't supposed to be set in the Marquesas Islands. Nope. The <u>original</u> plan was that it was supposed to be set in the country of Jordan.

Now think about that for a minute. Survivor Four. Survivor: Jordan (or Survivor: Arabia, as they planned to call it.) A season of Survivor set out in the middle of the desert. A season of Survivor set somewhere in the Middle East.

Sounds like an interesting season, doesn't it?

Doesn't that sound like a season that would be fascinating and unique?

Well not after 9/11 it didn't. I mean, remember, we are talking about a timeline here that is about 45 days after Islamic fundamentalists just crashed planes into lower Manhattan. For all intents and purposes, The United States was now at war with half of the Middle East.

You think the producers were going to dump sixteen Americans and a camera crew out into the middle of the Jordan desert? Where they would be

344

sitting ducks and totally defenseless against any sort of an ambush? You think the companies that insure CBS and CBS talent were going to allow that?

So anyway, yeah. Survivor Four in Jordan was canceled. And I mean QUICKLY. There was no way in hell that location was ever going to happen. And it is too bad, too, because they apparently had a logo created and they had the location all mapped out and everything. Had the timeline of Survivor worked out a little bit differently, I have no doubt that Arabia would have turned out to be a kickass Survivor season. I think that would have been one of those seasons that everyone in the fan base would still be talking about even today.

I mean, come on. Rob Mariano would have started his legacy in Survivor: Arabia. He could have been Madaba Rob. Vecepia Towery would have praised Jesus approximately eleventy billion times while standing in the middle of Islamic Holy Ground. Tell me that isn't a scenario that would have drawn some ratings. Peter Harkey would have been upset that his holes were all being plugged up with sand.

We will talk more about Marquesas when we get there (trust me, we will talk about it a LOT, it is my second favorite season), but let's just say for now that the producers completely threw that season and that location together at the very last minute. And it is AMAZING that Marquesas turned out as good as it did. I mean, that was Survivor: Arabia up until about three weeks before they started filming it. They just picked a backup location at the very last minute and they threw together a Tribal Council set and a "Back to the Beach" theme and a couple of challenges. And it turned out to be great.

In other words, Survivor the franchise got really REALLY lucky right there.

Again, we will get more into Marquesas later, so just file this info away for now. Also file away the fact that I have always believed that Survivor: Arabia would have been a terrible, terrible idea. And that the producers got lucky that they switched to a milder location. Because I have always believed from the bottom of my heart that had the seasons continued to get harder physically, and more demanding location-wise, as they were doing with Borneo through Africa, I have no doubt that by season four or five the conditions would have been so bad that one of the players might have actually died. I mean, not too many fans realize this, but we came awfully close to a player dying in both Australia and Africa. In particular, Africa. That location and that setting and that watering hole situation in season three was just brutal. I have no doubt in my mind that had Survivor

345

continued on the course it was headed, where every location got more and more brutal and the players got less food and less water every season, I can almost guarantee you that by season five we probably would have had our first Survivor casualty.

And that is why I have always said that the producers got really lucky that they were forced to move Survivor away from the desert.

I know this is weird to say. But in the greatest irony of them all, it is possible that the events of 9/11 might have actually saved a life.

Okay that story was kind of a downer. And I don't like ending my chapters on a downer. I am like George Costanza, I want to leave you laughing. So let me end this chapter on a funny anecdote.

Do you know what an ORG is? Chances are, if you have spent any time at all in the Survivor online community over the years, you have probably heard of an ORG before. An ORG stands for an Online Roleplaying Game.

ORG's (or the precursor, just RG's) have been around for years. And they have been associated with all sorts of themes and movies and TV shows throughout the years. Pick any aspect of popular culture that has had a fan base over the past twenty or thirty years, and chances are at some point there has probably been a roleplaying game based around it. I mean, dang, it's possible that back in the early 70's, people were playing dice based roleplaying games based around The Partridge Family.

> **Side Note:** Danny Partridge rolled a 2d20. Danny Partridge gets initiative! Danny Partridge takes out Greg Brady by pulling a Fairplay and tossing him face first over his shoulder!

Well, as you can imagine, Survivor and ORGs have always pretty much gone hand in hand. From the minute that Borneo ended, I can guarantee you that people on the internet were playing online Survivor simulations. And I can say that because I happened to be a player in one of the early ones.

Yes, this is a dirty little secret that I can let out now. I have held it in for years, this is actually the first time I have ever told it before. Even my own wife has never heard this particular anecdote before.

At some point in 2001, an advertisement showed up on the AOL message boards for "A new online Survivor game!" It was promised that sixteen people were going to get together on the internet, and they were going to play Survivor against each other and it was going to be just like the actual TV show.

And, well, come on. The internet is awesome. Survivor is awesome. I love Survivor. Online games are awesome. How could this not turn out to be a lot of fun?

So I signed up for the game.

It was advertised as "the first great Survivor roleplaying game!"

It was advertised as "the closest thing you will ever get to being on the actual show!"

And here is what happened.

Sixteen people applied for the game, and we were given a character to play. You got to be any one of the thirty two contestants from the first two seasons. I was randomly assigned to be Dirk.

Dirk? Um, okay.

Yay, okay now I guess I am Dirk.

So I got online. I exchanged emails with my seven tribesmates. We all said hi. That was about all we ever got a chance to say to one another.

Then the host emailed us and said "Okay now you have to vote somebody out. You have an hour to do so."

Wait, what?

Sixty minutes later I got another email from the host. He told me I had been voted out of the game. He said that not enough people had cast votes by the deadline, so as host he got to decide who was voted out. And he chose me because he watched Borneo and he didn't like Dirk.

And then, to make matters worse, instead of hearing the famous parting words, "The tribe has spoken," I was forced to hear my host's dread catchphrase instead. The very last thing Dirk heard as his online Survivor torch was snuffed was "Sorry dude."

So anyway, that. That was my introduction to the world of online roleplaying games. That was my introduction to the world of Survivor played online. A world that I would spend a significant amount of time in much later on.

Yes, I popped my Survivor ORG cherry as Dirk Been. I was Dirk in one of the very first Survivor ORGs. And I was voted out first. I was voted out randomly.

And then the fucker didn't even have the courtesy to tell me "The tribe has spoken." Instead, all I got was a "Sorry dude."

Let's just say that the authenticity of Survivor roleplaying games would eventually get a lot better than that.

59. Ethan

A lot of people don't realize this about me, but I am actually not a writer in real life. In real life I am actually a computer programmer. I only write on the side when I am bored and I am looking for something to do.

And it was one day at my programming job when I had one of my all-time favorite Survivor experiences.

It was the fall of 2001, and I was working in the I.T. department at Cedars-Sinai Medical Center in Beverly Hills. And one day I was walking around the main business office at Cedars, on my way to a meeting, when I spotted something on the wall that caught my eye.

It was Ethan Zohn.

One of the workers in the business office had taped a picture of Ethan to her door.

Well, when I saw this, I immediately peeked my head around the corner because I wanted to say hi to her. Because remember, Survivor might not have been nearly as cool as it had been a year ago (prior to 9/11), but there were still a lot of fans of the show out there. And it was always fun to run into a new co-worker who was also a Survivor fan, because you immediately had something in common that you would be able to talk about. In other words, a picture of Ethan on your door was basically an invitation for anyone else who worked in that building who was a Survivor fan to come over and talk to you. Whoever had posted that picture on the door had known that.

So I peeked my head around the corner of her door and I introduced myself. I said my name was Mario Lanza and that I was a big Survivor fan. I said that I wrote a weekly column for a website called Survivor-Central. And I mentioned that my wife was completely in love with Ethan this season and it was cool to meet another fellow Ethan fan out there.

"Your wife is in love with Ethan?" my co-worker said. "I am too! I hope he wins!"

It turns out that this lady's name was Susan Jordan. We sat there and we started talking about the show, and about Ethan. And about Borneo and Australia and Africa. And, well, to make a long story short, it is fourteen years later now and we are still friends. Even though we haven't worked with each other in more than a decade, even though I don't think she even watches Survivor anymore, Susan and I are still friends and we still talk to each other on Facebook to this day. And all because she had a little Ethan face on her wall back in 2001. And because all Survivor fans were friends with all other Survivor fans back when the show was still a phenomenon.

I love telling that story because it is a good way to put into perspective what a big deal Survivor was back in its glory years.

Okay, since I mentioned Ethan, I guess I better finally write a chapter about him. I mean, he is a pretty damn significant Survivor character. You wouldn't know it from the way that Probst and the CBS marketing team have completely crapped on the show's history throughout the years, but Ethan was (and is, he still is) right up there alongside Colby as one of the most beloved players of all time. In fact, if you put a gun to my head and asked me to decide who was more beloved in their heyday, Ethan or Colby, I would have to think about it for a while because it really is much closer than you would think. I mean, for every Colby devotee out there (like my mom) there were just as many Ethan devotees out there (like my wife Diana, and my co-worker Susan.)

In fact, for years I have referred to Ethan as the all-time single most beloved Survivor winner.

By the way, that particular category ("the most beloved winner") isn't really even all that close. Colby might have been the all-time male hero when it comes to Survivor, but last time I checked, Colby didn't win the game. Meanwhile, Ethan DID win. When it comes to the all-time most beloved Survivor winner (male or female), I don't think anyone is ever going to come close to Ethan Zohn.

And, believe me, this is going to become very important in a couple of chapters, when I talk about the ending of Africa. So just file that little tidbit away for later.

> **Side note:** Yes, I already know the arguments I am going to get over this. You are going to say that Parvati is more beloved, and you are going to say that Boston Rob is more beloved. But... no. Just no. Ethan's fan base was so much bigger than either of theirs at its peak, in fact they both really aren't even in the same ballpark. And besides, fuck returning player seasons anyway. Returning player seasons mean nothing. Ethan won Survivor the first time he played

and he will always be Survivor royalty because of that. Let us never forget that.

So anyway, Ethan was a big deal. He was a REALLY big deal. People loved him. Younger women in particular loved him. He was one of those rare players that (as T-Bird would famously point out a couple of episodes later) you just couldn't say anything bad about. I mean, right T-Bird? "What can you say that's bad about Ethan? <u>Nuthin'</u>."

Naturally, because of this, I thought there was no way in hell he was ever going to win Survivor.

Seriously, think back to the early days of Survivor, and look at who won. Richard and Tina. Two people who were nice enough to win a jury vote, but who were not necessarily nice enough that they were a slam dunk jury vote threat. I mean, Richard and Tina were likable, sure, but they still both had enemies. The Pagongs sure weren't very big fans of Richard. And Jerri absolutely HATED Tina. I am sure Amber wasn't much a fan of what Tina did to her either. So yes, Richard and Tina both won a jury vote, but neither one had been 100% jury vote unbeatable. Colby easily could have taken that win from Tina if just one vote had gone a little bit differently.

But Ethan?

Well Ethan was different.

Ethan had NO enemies in this game. Ethan was never going to have an enemy in this game. Ethan was one of those rare people in the world who you could meet for two minutes as a stranger, and you would apparently walk away liking. And believe me, that is <u>not</u> a very common trait among human beings. People with that kind of natural humble charisma are very hard to find in this world.

So here comes Ethan Zohn, and he is super likable. And he is super nice. And the females love him. Heck, <u>everyone</u> loves him. In fact, at no time at ANY point during Africa did I see somebody on the message boards write anything even remotely mean about him. And we are talking about Survivor Sucks! This is a message board where people would routinely wish for the death of Jerri Manthey. This is a message board where people would openly try to calculate the fat content of Richard Hatch. This is a message board where Erin Collins would later be called a trannie and Danielle DiLorenzo would routinely be compared to a horse.

Yet whenever Ethan would come up on Survivor Sucks? Whenever anybody on the meanest message board in the history of TV would ever talk about Ethan?

"Yeah, Ethan's cool. He won't win. But he seems like a good guy."

So no, I did not think that Ethan could ever possibly win Survivor. He was just way too popular. He was just way too well liked. He was a guy who was never ever <u>ever</u> going to have any enemies. And of course on Survivor, which is a game that is basically just a giant popularity contest (and it always has been), I figured the other players would have to be idiots to even let him get within sniffing distance of that final jury vote.

I mean, Ethan Zohn as a jury opponent? Somebody would willingly want to go up against Ethan? Heck, why not just go up against Colleen? Why not go up against the Pope? See how that strategy works out for you.

The reason I bring up Ethan as a possible winner (or not a possible winner, as most people at the time believed because of the way that Survivor worked) is because as episode six of Africa rolled around, as the aftermath of the twist reared its ugly head, and Silas and Lindsey were systematically voted out, it was clear to pretty much anyone who was paying attention that a member of Boran was probably going to win the game now.

I mean, come on. With Silas and Lindsey gone, the Mallrats were doomed. You knew that Brandon or Kim Powers were never going to win the game. That just wasn't the way that Survivor worked. And weird old quirky Frank as a Survivor winner? Puhlease. Frank Garrison was as likely to win Survivor as Kimmi Kappenberg was likely to win Survivor. That fantasy just wasn't going to happen either.

That left T-Bird (who could possibly win, because she was smart) and the Borans. And simple logic said that since Boran had the numbers, and since Boran had a strong three man alliance in Lex, Ethan, and Tom, the winner was more than likely going to be one of the Borans. No one thought the winner would be Kim Johnson. Definitely no one thought it would ever be Clarence. And the only other player left in the game, Kelly Goldsmith? Well she had a lot of fans out there, but at the time she was considered little more than a dark horse contender to win. I mean, she COULD win. In theory. But she certainly wasn't in the big Lex-Tom-Ethan alliance. And that was a problem for her.

And this is why I mention Ethan at this point in my essay.

As episodes five and six rolled around, as Silas and Lindsey were eliminated and the power of the Mallrats was basically destroyed, it was evident to EVERYONE who was watching the show that a member of Boran was probably going to win now. It turned out that the Borans were the tribe that you were supposed to be focusing your attention on.

And since Ethan was a member of Boran... and since Ethan was right there in the middle of that powerful three-man alliance... well... let's just say that he started to get a <u>lot</u> of attention right around this point in the season. All of a sudden, Ethan went from being "that cute floppy haired guy in the blue shirt who everyone likes" to "hey, do you think this guy might actually be the star of the season? Do you think it is possible that we might have our first likable Survivor winner?!?"

Like I said, I never thought that Ethan could possibly win. Never. Ever. No way in hell, no chance in a million years. I thought the Borans would be smart enough to take him out. I also thought he was way too young to ever win Survivor. Remember, Mario's Theory still said that a person under the age of 30 could never possibly win Survivor. At no time at any point during Africa did I ever consider Ethan to be the likely winner.

I thought he would get far. I thought he would be a major character. I thought he would be the sweeter and even more beloved version of Colby.

But the winner?

No, at this point I was almost certain the winner was going to be Lex.

60. Why Africa Episode Six is So Awesome

Oh, I just realized something. There are two other things I wanted to mention before we get to the Africa merge. In fact, both of the things I wanted to talk about specifically happened in episode six.

When most people think about Survivor: Africa, the things that they tend to remember about the season are the big moments. They remember the epic events. They remember Lex, Kim, and Ethan battling it out in that final immunity challenge. They remember The Twist. They remember the scene with the lions circling the boma at night, and Ethan and Kim Powers standing inside being terrified. They remember the awesome scene where Ethan gives his hacky sack to the little kids in the African village. They remember Lex delivering all the AIDS supplies to the hospital. They remember what happened to Kelly Goldsmith.

What they DON'T tend to remember are all the little funny moments.

They also don't tend to remember anything that happened in episode six.

And that is a shame, because Africa episode six has two of the all-time funniest Survivor scenes.

Africa episode six is one of those episodes that I would call "the long lost classics." This is one of those episodes that never shows up on anyone's list of the top 20 Survivor episodes (or even top 100 Survivor episodes, for that matter). Yet every time I watch it I am reminded how awesome it is. In fact, if you ask me, this is easily one of the best episodes of the entire season. And that is saying something, because like Australia and Borneo before it, Africa is just chock full of fantastic episodes. Which reminds me, by the way, don't pay any attention to the reputation that Survivor: Africa has unfairly picked up over the years. Anyone who will sit there with a straight face and tell you that Africa was a bad season simply doesn't know what the hell they are talking about.

So anyway, here we are in the middle of this great season, within a string of solid episodes back to back to back (remember, The Twist was only one episode before this), and here comes Episode Six. The long lost forgotten episode.

The hilarious one.

And right there at the start of the episode we get Clarence and the Chickens.

Oh yes, Clarence and the Chickens. Awww HELL no. One of my all-time favorite Survivor scenes.

If you are familiar with the Funny 115 (the countdown I would later put together counting down the all-time funniest Survivor moments), you will know how much I have always loved Clarence and the Chickens. It is ranked #27 on the original Funny 115, and every time I go back and I re-read my countdown I tell myself that I probably should have ranked it about ten spots higher. This is EASILY one of the top twenty funniest scenes out of the first few Survivor seasons.

I don't have a whole lot to say about Clarence and the Chickens, other than to say you will remember it if you've seen it. Although let me just point out right now how absolutely <u>perfect</u> it is in terms of editing, and how <u>perfect</u> it is in terms of the characters involved. And how the editors just absolutely nailed the comedy in the scene with the way they inserted the pauses and all of the background music. I mean, my God, that whole scene is just an A+ television comedy moment all around. Seriously, go back and watch Africa episode six, and just pay attention to the Clarence and the Chickens scene. Watch how well-crafted that whole thing was.

By the way, I should also point out that for more than a decade now I have claimed that, from an entertainment point of view, Clarence Black has always been one of the single most underrated Survivor characters. And, well, obviously, the chicken scene is Exhibit A in that particular argument. But it isn't his only funny scene in the season. Next time you watch Africa, just pay attention to Clarence and watch how many funny little moments he has. Pay attention to how funny he is if you listen to all of his little background quips.

In fact, this doesn't surprise me at all, but I just found out about a year ago that Clarence Black is actually the host of a popular radio show in Detroit now. I had no idea what ever happened to him after Survivor, he was one of those players that just seemed to have dropped off the face of the earth after he was on the show. But then in 2013 a friend of mine from Michigan pointed out to me that Clarence is now the host of a local radio show in Detroit, and he is actually a pretty big deal.

Again, when I heard this update about Clarence it didn't surprise me at all. I could have told you back in 2001 that he was one of the more entertaining players in Survivor history. The fact that he later made a career out of just being himself and just talking on the air doesn't surprise me at all. In any case, good for you Clarence. I sure hope the radio station you work for has a large budget for cherries.

Okay, so that is one of the big funny moments in episode six. Clarence and the Chickens. Featuring Kim Johnson leaning in at a 45 degree angle and doing a close-up dead-on impersonation of Clarence Black. Again, this is one of those little character scenes that I would later immortalize on the Funny 115, and with good reason. It is just perfect.

But there is ANOTHER hilarious little moment later in episode six, and it happens during the immunity challenge.

Yes, I can only be talking about Brandon and his mishap with the flaming arrow.

If you remember Brandon and the Flaming Arrow (which I also ranked as a top 30 entry on the Funny 115), I am sure I don't even have to spend much time describing it to you. You will probably be able to picture it in your head. In fact I'm sure you just did. You replayed it in your head and then you probably laughed about it.

Africa episode six featured one of my all-time favorite Survivor immunity challenges. It featured the flaming arrow competition. And it was a good one too. This is one of those challenges in Survivor history that almost nobody remembers, that almost nobody talks about, but in terms of television it was about as exciting and as well-edited as an immunity challenge can possibly get. I mean, I don't mean to keep harping on this, but go back and watch that challenge again. Watch how the editors timed every big shot to the music. Watch how epic it all was. Watch how close that challenge was at the end, and how exciting it was when Ethan nailed that final target for the win.

I mean, my goodness. THAT is what an immunity challenge on Survivor is supposed to look like. That one was as big and bold and as epic as you can possibly get.

And then right there in the middle of this awesome challenge, you have Brandon and the flaming arrow.

Honestly, there is no way I can describe this moment to you and do it justice in print. I wish I could, but I can't. You just sort of need to see it for yourself to understand. Or, at the very least, you need to see pictures.

356

Let's just say that Brandon Quinton, who was openly gay, and who was about as flamboyant and... well, queeny... as you can get, tried to shoot a flaming arrow at a target and he missed. In fact he didn't just miss, he flat out failed at everything he was trying to do altogether.

Brandon drew back his bowstring, and he accidentally pulled the arrow off of the bow. So instead of hurtling forward at the target, the arrow just unhooked itself and it fell directly down at his feet. And the minute Brandon realized he was about to impale his own foot with a flaming arrow, he let out a girly squeal and he spun dramatically backwards out of the way.

Luckily for us, the cameras caught it all on film. And it was shown in the episode.

And the other players (including Brandon) all laughed about it.

I know, I know. I'm asking for trouble making a joke about the gay guy almost shooting his own foot, and then letting out a girly little squeal because of it. I know that according to Ellen DeGeneres I am now officially bullying. But I don't care. That shit was funny. All of the other players were laughing about it. Hell, even <u>Brandon</u> was laughing about it. He knew how ridiculous it was going to look on TV. So I have no qualms with ranking it as a Top 25 moment on the Funny 115, and proclaiming it to be one of the all-time most randomly funny little Survivor character moments.

Like I said at the start of the chapter, when most people think of Survivor: Africa, they think of the big moments. They think of the epic moments. They think of the strategy moments. If they are Linda, they masturbate to the thought of Mother Africa.

When I think of Survivor: Africa, I think of the funny moments.

And, thanks to Clarence and Brandon and chickens and arrows, Africa episode six is one of my favorite Survivor episodes.

Believe me, we will talk a lot more about funny Survivor moments later on, when I get to my chapters about the Funny 115. Which is free online at funny115.com, by the way, if you have never read it before. For now, just file away in your head that Africa episode six is awesome, and that Clarence is awesome. And that Survivor: Africa is a hilarious and underrated season in general.

For now, let's get back to the merge.

Because there is a lot of interesting stuff in this season that is about to come up.

61. The Birth of The Power Rankings

As we came to the merge in Survivor: Africa, as the game whittled down to its traditional final ten players, I was racking my brain to figure out some way that I would be able to increase my readership. Because I knew that there was a market out there just waiting for the appearance of a big name Survivor internet analyst. I could feel it. There were <u>so</u> many people watching this show, there were <u>so</u> many people talking about each episode afterwards on the internet, and floating their theories about it, that there was a tremendous opportunity just sitting out there at the moment. This golden opportunity of "celebrity" was just sitting there, waiting for the right person who was sharp enough to take advantage of it.

And, well, as you can guess, I wanted to be that right person. I desperately wanted to be that right person.

The only problem was that I still didn't know what kind of a hook it was going to take to get people to notice me.

Like I said before, by this point in Survivor history I was writing recaps. I was writing weekly episode recaps at Survivor-Central.com. Which, surprisingly, considering we had only been on the internet for a couple of months, had already developed a pretty fair-sized reader base. Of course, most of our readership at that point was because we had Dr. Sean Kenniff writing for us, but hey, as a startup you don't look a gift horse in the mouth. If you're a newbie, you take your publicity any way you can get it. The readers came there for Dr. Sean, we were aware of this, and the rest of us were happy to simply latch on to that particular gravy train and try to take a slice of it for ourselves.

Of course, Survivor-Central was still nowhere near as big as some of the other big "name" Survivor websites at the time, like Survivor Sucks, or Survivor News. We were clearly one of the bigger fan run websites at the time, true, but in terms of comparing us to the big boys? We were still just a big nobody. We were in no way any sort of a go-to source if you wanted to get any sort of interesting Survivor content.

Yet.

As for the size of my own personal reader base, well, ever since I started adding my little "Mario's Notes" section at the bottom of my recaps, the number of my readers had been increasing each week. And that was good.

In fact, I was actually starting to get emails from my readers after each episode now, and that was awesome. I was having a blast responding to anyone who would take the time to actually write me an email. Heck, even if somebody wrote in and told me I was a piece of crap and that my column sucked, well hey at least that was a fan letter. And as I have always said, fan letters are always better than no fan letters.

As my readership was slowly increasing each week, it was quite obvious to me at this point that opinion pieces about Survivor were what people out there on the internet were dying to read. And this was amazing to me because, again, THERE WERE JUST NO OPINION PIECES ABOUT SURVIVOR OUT THERE AT THE TIME. I was like the only person out there doing anything like this on the internet at the time. And when I realized that I was the only one out there doing this, it just boggled my mind.

By the way, when I say that there were no opinion pieces about Survivor at the time, I am only talking about a specific type of opinion piece. I am talking about people writing about strategy. I was literally the only writer at any of the major Survivor websites at the time who was writing a column each week about what made a person good at Survivor. And about which types of people tended to do well at this game. And about who was likely to win the current season we were watching, and who was likely to lose the current season, and why.

I know this will blow your mind if you have been a fan of this show for a while, and if you have followed strategic discussion of it on the internet throughout the years (especially now, when it is practically anyone ever talks about when it comes to Survivor), but I seriously cannot stress this point enough. In the early days, **THIS WAS NOT THE WAY THAT MOST PEOPLE ON WEBSITES TENDED TO WRITE ABOUT SURVIVOR!**

If you went to any website other than Survivor-Central in the fall of 2001, this is what you would see. You would see news. You would see interviews. You would see hints and editing speculation (or sometimes, outright spoilers). You would see "Why did so and so lose?" But there was nobody other than me who was writing about the psychology of the game. There was nobody other than me who was spelling out exactly what was likely to happen next from a gameplay/strategy/sociology/psychology point of view.

Heck, this was even true on my own website. Every other column on Survivor-Central at that time (other than Dr. Sean's) was about spoilers. Every. Single. One of them. Every other column on Survivor-Central that

360

season was about Murtz's spoiler prediction of the week. Or about what the state was of all the major Survivor spoiler groups out there. Or Potato talking about which spoiler was the most popular one floating around out there, and which spoiler(s) you should probably be paying attention to.

This was the product that the websites at the time were producing for their readership. Spoilers. And I'm sorry, God bless the Survivor spoiler world for thinking they were an important part of the experience for people, but this was NOT the product that the vast majority of readers wanted when they went to a website! When people went to a Survivor website in 2001, and heck even when they go to a Survivor website now, what they want is to read something interesting about the show. They want to get into the intricacies of why this game and why this TV show have always been so damn fascinating to everyone.

What readers have always wanted when they go to a Survivor website is something like this: They want to read stuff like "If you want to do well at this game, you should never be the leader of your alliance. You should always be the #2 or #3 guy in power. Because, that way, when other people go after your alliance, you will never be their main target. And that is why Ethan and Big Tom are playing exceptionally well and they are both likely to get far. They will simply never be considered a threat to anyone because they are never the ones who are seen as being in control. Lex will always be the target."

That is word for word one of the comments I wrote in my "Mario's Notes" section at the bottom of my recaps. And stuff like that always got a HUGE reader response. I would get flooded with emails whenever I included anything that looked like any sort of a strategy discussion. It was evident to me, even just from this brief dipping of my toes into the water, that Survivor fans on the internet were simply DYING to talk about this stuff.

And right there and then, because of that response, I knew that this was where my writing style was now going to be headed.

Nobody else on the internet was writing a Survivor strategy column?

Well damnit if I wasn't going to be the first.

Once I decided that "strategy" was where all the readers were going to be, the next step after that was that I needed to figure out what was going to be my hook. After all, every big shot writer out there needs a trademark. Or a hook. You need something that makes your writing pop out and stand out compared to every other writer on the internet. Because believe me, I was not the greatest writer in the world. I have never been the greatest writer in the world. But you sure can fake being the greatest writer in the world if you have a style that people enjoy. Just ask Stephen King about that.

So this now became the big question for me. What was going to be my hook? When people thought "Mario Lanza, Survivor Writer", what was going to be the gimmick that they were going to associate with me?

Was it going to be strategy? Did I want to be known as "Mario Lanza, the Survivor Strategy Guy"?

No, not really.

I mean, I wanted to WRITE about strategy, that was the whole way I was going to draw in my readers in the first place. But I didn't want to be known as some sort of a strategy guru or anything. I mean, hell, have I ever actually even <u>played</u> Survivor? Was I actually a cast member on the show? No, of course not. So who am I to try to pass myself off as any sort of a strategy guru? Right off the bat I knew I didn't want my name floating around as any sort of a Survivor "strategy expert."

What I wanted was to be known as "the funny one." What I wanted was to be known as "the interesting one." What I wanted was for people to read my stuff and to think, "Wow this guy knows psychology and he knows how people think. This guy gets how Survivor works and he really knows his stuff. And he also makes me laugh."

But again, I needed that hook. I needed something that was simple and was catchy, and that people would remember. Mostly, I needed something that nobody else in the Survivor world was actually doing at the time.

And then, one day, finally, it hit me.

One day in late 2001 I was surfing around on the ESPN website, and I was looking for baseball scores. And right there on ESPN.com was the idea that I had been waiting for. And, it turns out, that <u>everyone</u> had been waiting for.

The Power Rankings.

ESPN had a list on their website each week of who the best teams in baseball were, from best to worst. And they listed who the hottest teams were. And they listed which teams were going up and which teams were going down.

Basically, they had a snapshot each week of what was playing out in the world of Major League Baseball, and how it was likely to continue to play out as the rest of the season developed.

And I'm sorry. But this was an idea that was just BEGGING to be stolen.

The minute I realized that nobody was doing a Power Rankings column for Survivor yet, I knew instantly that this was going to be my hook. And that it was a hook that would work. And you better believe I RAN to my keyboard and I wrote up my very first Survivor Power Rankings.

As fate would have it, that happened to be the week of the Africa merge. It was episode seven of Survivor: Africa. The episode that Clarence was voted out.

It was November 22, 2001.

This was the day that Survivor fans on the internet would finally notice me.

Clarence was voted out of the game that night. Survivor: Africa was whittled down to its final nine players. So I wrote up my episode seven recap as usual, and I included my "Mario's Notes" section at the bottom as usual too. And sure enough, I then added a special section at the very bottom of my recap that I knew that people would love. I included the very first appearance of the Survivor Power Rankings.

I even included a little explanation at the beginning of my recap talking about what a "power ranking" was, and why I was including it. Because, you know, I figured that the Survivor audience and the ESPN audience might not exactly have all that much overlap. Even back in the early days of the show, just like it is now, the Survivor internet audience was largely made up of middle aged females and younger gay males. I wanted to make sure people knew why I was including this section, what it was, and why I would be updating it each week.

So I wrote my very first Survivor Power Rankings column and I posted it at Survivor-Central. And I sat back and waited.

And I was not surprised at all that my readership went up by about 5000% that week.

Because that was it. Bam. That was the hook. That was the variable that the internet fan base had been missing from all of their weekly Survivor readings. The Power Rankings. This was the moment that I officially became "a Survivor writer."

For the next four years of my life, I would be known all over the internet as "the Survivor Power Rankings guy."

P.S. By the way, remember how I said that I never wanted to be known as any sort of a "Survivor strategy expert"? Well here is Exhibit A why I say that. The very first person I ever ranked as #1 in my Survivor Power Rankings was T-Bird Cooper.

Yeah, great work, Nostradamus. When in doubt, always predict that the most likely winner of a season is going to come from the alliance that is currently being Pagonged.

I got better at the Power Rankings later. I promise. ☺

62. Follow The Star

Okay now here is an interesting little side trip into Survivor history. If you have never heard about "Follow the Star" before, you are in for a treat.

You know how I said that I was the only person on the internet who was writing up any type of game analysis or strategy discussion around the time of Survivor: Africa? Well that is mostly true, but it is not one hundred percent true. There were definitely other people who were writing things about Survivor at the time that were more interesting than player interviews or simple spoiler updates. In fact, one of them (Follow the Star) could easily be called the single most interesting thing that anyone has ever written about Survivor.

Let me clarify here. When I say that I was the only person who was offering any sort of insight into strategy and the way that a game like Survivor will probably play out, what I mean is that I was the only person who was doing it on one of the main Survivor websites. Remember, there were still only a handful of Survivor websites that existed at the time, and most of the diehard fans back in 2001 would have read all of them on pretty much a weekly basis. So if you were doing something that was different than any other website was doing at the time (like I was with my Power Rankings), it would immediately be noticed by thousands of people (maybe even millions) and it would immediately stand out.

In other words, like I said before, it's not like I was ever the greatest writer in the world, or anything close to the world's greatest Survivor expert. I was simply the right person in the right place at the right time. I simply stumbled onto the one idea (a strategy column and weekly Power Rankings) that the audience had been waiting for before anyone else did. And I had a HUGE advantage over most other people because I happened to have a platform on one of the major Survivor websites at the time.

I will freely admit that there were people in other places on the internet who were better writers than me. And who were coming up with more interesting theories than I was.

The only problem with the other guys' stuff was that it was usually buried somewhere in an obscure thread on some hard-to-find message board. It was impossible to find unless you specifically went looking for it. So a lot of the really neat Survivor writing from this time period unfortunately never really found much of an audience.

And, well, "Follow the Star" is the best example of this. Seriously, if you can track down a copy of it through Google or the Internet Archives, go find it and read it for yourself. You will be blown away by how detailed it was.

If you have never heard of "Follow the Star" before, it was basically a theory written by a guy named Tapewatcher on the Survivor Sucks message board. His theory (which of course turned out to be true) was that Ethan Zohn was going to be the winner of Survivor: Africa. And that the editors had a whole storyline worked out in the episodes where "Ethan = Jesus." And that there were clues hinting at this Biblical storyline in each and every episode of Africa if you went and you looked for them.

Tapewatcher posted his "Follow the Star" theory on Sucks around episode four of Africa (if I remember correctly, it has been a long time). He pointed out screencaps of Ethan looking up at a star and Ethan praying with the sun behind him in episode one. He posted screencaps of Ethan doing more Jesus things in episode two. He showed how the editors portrayed Ethan doing even more Jesus things in episode three. He illustrated how Ethan carrying wood from a certain angle looked like Jesus holding up a cross. And he kept adding pictures to his thread each and every week that backed up this theory. He said that the editors were making it <u>obvious</u> that Ethan was the winner, and that Survivor editors do stuff like this in the episodes all the time. Furthermore, he pointed out that there is <u>always</u> a story hidden beneath the episodes of Survivor. The editors ALWAYS put some sort of a storyline there.

He concluded by saying that it is our job as an audience that we are supposed to be looking for it.

Now first off, this was just an amazing piece of writing. As I said before, "Follow the Star" might be the single most interesting thing that anyone has ever written about Survivor. It was YEARS ahead of its time. And what was amazing was that this wasn't the first time that Tapewatcher had actually done this. As I said about twenty-five chapters ago, he had actually done the exact same thing in Australia (to much less fanfare) when he predicted Tina Wesson's win early on through a theory that he called "The Dog That Didn't Bark."

One of the questions that people always ask me when they hear that I was on Sucks around the time of Survivor: Africa is "What did you think of Follow the Star"? Because by this point in history Tapewatcher has become a legend among people who consider themselves hardcore Survivor internet fans.

Survivor diehards are fascinated by the question of who Tapewatcher really was. Or how his theories were received at the time. Because, oh yeah I guess I forgot to mention this, Tapewatcher disappeared from the internet pretty much immediately after Africa ended. He just dropped completely off the face of the Earth. And to this day nobody in the Survivor community knows what the hell happened to him or who the hell he really was.

Basically, Tapewatcher is the D.B. Cooper of the Survivor internet world. He is the rogue scoundrel who randomly showed up for a while, gave away all the producer/editor secrets, gained a very strong cult following among the internet fan base, and then disappeared out the back of a plane and was never seen again.

In fact, to this day, a lot of people think he might have actually been one of the Survivor editors.

So to get back to the question, what did I think of Tapewatcher and "Follow the Star" at the time? Well naturally, I thought it was bullshit. I thought it was absolute complete 100% bullshit. I am embarrassed to say that now, fourteen years later, but it's the truth. At the time I remember thinking, no WAY do the editors have a fabricated storyline that they are trying to tell under the episodes. No WAY are the editors doing anything more complicated than simply whittling down the footage from the game and showing us what happened. I mean, come on. You really think the editors are shaping the raw game footage into some masterpiece of editing and theme and foreshadowing and symbolic allegory? Yeah whatever, Tapewatcher, you pretentious douche. Yes, I'm sure we are watching the Bible play out on Survivor: Africa.

At the time I remember thinking, I bet this guy Tapewatcher is probably an English major. Because this is what English majors do, they invent themes. They reach.

Oh and I also figured that Tapewatcher probably had a lot of time on his hands.

So yes, that is the sad answer to your question. Yes, I read "Follow the Star." Yes, I was aware of it just like everyone else on Survivor Sucks was aware of it (even though it was never really all that well known outside of Sucks at the time.) And yes, I thought that the whole thing was complete horse crap.

At the time, I was convinced that people who were doing storyline analysis and editing analysis (and a lot of people were indeed doing this at the time, it wasn't just Tapewatcher) were wasting a lot of time searching for storylines that simply weren't there. I believed they were astronomers who were taking three stars in the night sky and they were trying to turn them into the belt of Orion.

I had no idea that Tapewatcher was right. I had no idea that storyline analysis was right. Heck, I was so naive at the time that I didn't realize that storylines on Survivor even existed in the first place! I just thought that when we sat down to watch the episodes, we were simply watching filmed game footage.

By the way, if you are curious, Survivor storyline analysis still does exist out there, even to this very day. A friend of mine named Justin Lesniewski recently ran a group called the SSAC (The Survivor Story Analysis Commission). He and a group of friends had a website where they tried to pick out the storyline that the editors are trying to tell in every Survivor season. They tried to predict the winner of a season without the help of any spoilers whatsoever, the predictions came simply from the story that they felt was being told in the episodes. Basically, what the SSAC does is the exact same thing that Tapewatcher became famous for doing back in Australia and Africa. They play the role of editor and they try to figure out what the hidden storyline is for each Survivor season.

To sum up this chapter, storyline analysis has never really been my thing when it comes to Survivor. For me, I have always been more focused on the strategy of the game, or on the psychology. Or when all else fails, I just keep an eye out for the funny stuff. I have never really been all that into storyline analysis simply because of the fact that when somebody is really good at it (like Justin is, or like Tapewatcher was) it becomes suspiciously close to becoming spoiler info. People who are really good at storyline deduction can usually tell you who the winner is going to be after about the fourth episode. And as I have said before, I want absolutely nothing to do with knowing what is going to happen on Survivor before it happens. So as interesting as this stuff might be on paper, I tend to stay far away from this particular subset of the Survivor fan community.

Survivor storyline analysis has never really been my thing, but it is a thing. And if you are a Survivor fan on the internet at all you should probably be aware of it. It is a group of really smart people who get together and who do really smart things, and who do their best to educate the rest of the fanbase on how reality TV editing works.

Again, it's not my thing, but story analysis has long been a respected part of the online Survivor world. So check it out if you are looking to learn more about how this show works, and how the way it is presented to us means a lot more than you think it does. The guys at the SSAC (and other groups like it) have an interesting hobby, and reading their writeups will make you a smarter Survivor fan.

P.S. Tapewatcher, if you ever read this chapter, please write to me and tell me who you were. Thank you. :)

63. The Curious Case of Kelly Goldsmith

The eighth episode of Survivor: Africa (entitled "Smoking out the Snake") aired on Thursday, December 6, 2001. And in my opinion it is one of the single most interesting episodes in the history of Survivor. Because there was something that happened in this particular episode that had never happened before in an episode of Survivor. And naturally, this something was so outrageous when it happened for the first time (and it was so unfair) that it drove the Survivor fans on the internet completely insane.

Naturally, my new best friend from Santa Clara, Lex, happened to be smack dab in the middle of it.

Okay, before we get to the infamous Kelly Goldsmith incident in episode eight, let's flash back to the end of the episode before this.

Episode seven. The merge episode. The Clarence episode. Remember the end of the Clarence episode? That was the episode where Clarence received eight votes on his way out of the game, and Lex received two votes. He received one vote from Clarence, and he also received a random little mystery vote from T-Bird. Why? Who knows. Maybe T-Bird was feeling mischievous that night and she just wanted to shake up Lex's world a little bit. No one knows.

So anyway, Lex received two votes at the end of the Clarence episode. And that second mystery vote just drove him absolutely berserk. Lex saw it come up, when he had only been expecting one vote with his name on it to come up, and because he already had paranoid/anger tendencies to begin with, he completely flipped out. From here on out, from episode eight until the end of the game, it seems to me like Lex van den Berghe went a little bit psychopath.

And all because of that one little mischievous T-Bird vote.

Side note #1: By the way, I should point out right now that if you have ever read my column "The Andy Kaufman Strategy" (which I will talk about later), you will know that one of the things I advocate several times in that column is that if you really want to mess with people on Survivor, one of the fun ways to do that is to just randomly cast votes for them. In particular, you can have a lot of fun just casting throwaway votes at the more paranoid ones. And if you REALLY want to have fun while you are doing it, you can also change the handwriting on your vote to make it look girly if you are a guy (or vice versa).

These random passive aggressive shit-disturbing votes were one of the key components of my Andy Kaufman Strategy, and if you know your Survivor history you will know that I only could have come up with that idea after watching Lex and Teresa and Lex's spectacular #SurvivorBreakdown.

I hate to say this, since I am friends with the guy at all, but Lex is one of those special players who would be an awful lot of fun to mess with if you ever played Survivor against him.

Side note #2: Oh yeah, and that whole "change your handwriting if you are a guy so that your votes look like they came from a girl"? Well let's just say that a very important player named Rob Cesternino adopted that strategy a few years later because he read about it in my column. And I immediately knew he was a reader of mine because I could tell he was doing it. But more on that later. We will have a <u>lot</u> more about that later.

Okay, so Lex received that second mystery vote from T-Bird, and he completely flipped out. And when I say he flipped out, I am not exaggerating. He just completely lost it. From here on out, for the rest of the game, Lex was forever searching for enemies that he thought were trying to destroy him.

And the first enemy he got in his sights was his alliance mate Kelly.

Now, Kelly Goldsmith is an interesting figure in Survivor history. In fact, forget that, she isn't just interesting, she is downright fascinating. And the reason she is so fascinating is because there may be no player in the history of Survivor who has a bigger discrepancy between "what a big deal she was at the time" and "what a big deal she SHOULD have been at the time."

For starters, let me point out this poll to you.

At some point between Marquesas and Thailand, a poll was held on the Survivor Sucks message board to determine who was the single most popular player in Survivor history. It was an informal survey, and thousands of random Survivor internet fans wrote in to respond. And sure enough, at the end of the poll the winner was determined to be Kathy. Kathy Vavrick-O'Brien from Marquesas. Which makes sense, because Marquesas had just ended, and because of recency bias. Recent players/seasons will always win a Survivor poll like that. Oh, and of course Kathy also won because she really was a big deal and because she really WAS beloved. The fact that Kathy was named the #1 overall favorite player in Survivor history right after Marquesas ended was not surprising in the least.

And who came in at number two on that poll? Sure enough, you guessed it. Kelly Goldsmith. A relatively minor figure from Survivor: Africa.

In 2002, Kelly Goldsmith scored higher on the Survivor Sucks popularity scale than Colby Donaldson. She scored higher than Colleen. She scored higher than Boston Rob, Rudy, Ethan, Gervase, Rodger, T-Bird, or Elisabeth. And at the time I remember thinking, what the hell? Where did Kelly Goldsmith all of a sudden get this incredible fan base?

Now, I'm not gonna lie to you, this is a question that I have wrestled with in my head for years. Why is Kelly Goldsmith so fricking beloved? Because she really is. In fact, even to this day, fourteen years later, she is still considered one of the most popular Survivor contestants ever by people on the internet. People routinely rate her as one of the players they most want to see come back and play again. Or as one of the best players never to win. Or as one of the thousands and thousands of tiny females from the show who are still four inches taller than Russell (sorry, couldn't resist).

First off, let me point out that I don't dislike Kelly Goldsmith. I have nothing against her at all. In fact, I always thought she was a fun character. I was especially a fan of her sarcasm and her snark. To me, Kelly Goldsmith was one of those randomly fun background characters (like Mad Dog a season earlier) who brought a lot of fun little character moments to the season during her limited airtime. In fact, in many ways, at the time Kelly kind of reminded me of Boston Rob. Who, of course I have to point out, was not really considered a major Survivor figure at the time either, just like Kelly wasn't. Kelly Goldsmith and Rob Mariano were both fun little minor Survivor characters who weren't around all that long, but who both made the most out of their limited screen time.

And yet... that Kelly fan base. Sheesh. For more than a decade, I have never understood it.

Kelly Goldsmith developed a legion of fans almost immediately. And people on the internet just went absolutely crazy for her. There may be no player in the history of Survivor who has ever had a more dedicated fan base.

Let me share a little personal anecdote with you. This will do a good job of putting the "Kelly Goldsmith a.k.a. the second coming of Jesus" fanbase into perspective for you.

In 2002 I wrote a Survivor story called "All Star Survivor: Alaska." It was a big hit. In fact, out of all the Survivor projects I have ever done in my lifetime, that Alaska story was by far the most popular thing I have ever written. There is no question at all that, at its peak, that story probably had at least a million readers.

And naturally, since I wanted to ride the wave of Kelly Goldsmith popularity at the time, I cast Kelly as one of the characters in my Alaska story.

Now, of course the question here is, was Kelly really an All-Star? If you were casting an All-Star season right around the time of Thailand, would you really have picked Kelly Goldsmith as one of your castmembers?

Personally, I don't think you would have. If it were up to me, I would have cast Kelly in a real All-Star season about the same time that I would have cast Shii Ann in a real All-Star season. Because Shii Ann wasn't really considered an All-Star either. Except... oh... wait... never mind. I guess she was. Bad example.

So anyway, I cast Kelly and I used her in my Alaska story. And a million readers turned out to read it. And then, because of the way the story developed, I wound up with Kelly being the third person voted out. I didn't really have any say over it, I didn't <u>want</u> to vote her out of the game. That was just the way that the narrative sort of played out. Kelly was voted out of the game at the end of my third episode.

And I am not kidding when I tell you this next part.

Because I had Kelly go out third in my story, I came as close as you can to receiving death threats.

DEATH THREATS!

People were so incensed that I would dare vote Kelly out third, they were so furious that I would "give her a second chance to play", and then get rid of her so early on, that they just came down on me. Practically the entire Survivor internet fan base came down on me. And I have to say, in fifteen years of writing about this show, I have received my fair share of venom. Sure, I have had phases where Survivor fans on the internet all love me, but I have also had phases where most of the Survivor online fan base absolutely hates me and they want to rip my throat out. But at NO point has the fanbase EVER been angrier with me than they were because of that Kelly episode. That was the one moment in my life that I really questioned if I still wanted to be writing about Survivor anymore.

It was all because I dared to write a story where the other players voted out The Golden Child.

And so there you go. My Kelly Goldsmith story. You might not believe that she was (and still is) that popular, but believe me, I've felt it. I've been there. I was right there in the trenches and I was right there on the other side of it when shit went down. Her fanbase is dedicated. And they are a little bit frightening.

I mean hell, I had Kathy Vavrick-O'Brien get voted out in my Hawaii story. And Kathy was WAY more popular in real life than Kelly ever was. And I barely got any fallout over the Kathy storyline!

Okay enough of that sidetrack. Back to Africa.

So Lex received this mystery vote at the end of episode seven of Survivor: Africa. And he immediately turned his suspicions onto Kelly.

Why Kelly?

Well because Kelly Goldsmith was a sneaky little mofo, that's why. I mean, that's exactly why Lex had been using her as a secret weapon in all of his little spy missions ever since the two of them wound up on the same side of the numbers after the twist. Lex knew that Kelly was a sneak. Lex knew that she was smart and that she was observant as hell. And most importantly (this is an aspect of the Lex/Kelly incident that has sort of been forgotten over the years), Lex knew that Kelly was a gossip who liked to stir up drama and that she was a troublemaker.

Now, was Kelly guilty of casting that mystery vote for Lex? Of course not. We know for a fact that T-Bird was the one who did it, because we saw the evidence. And because she admitted it.

However, on the flip side, was Lex unreasonable to suspect that Kelly might have been the one who had done it?

I know this will be an unpopular opinion among the Jonestown Goldsmith Cult on the internet out there, but absolutely not. He was <u>not</u> unreasonable. I mean, if you were Lex, if you had the same type of paranoid observational snap judgment tendencies that he had, you would have suspected Kelly too. On paper, she is the EXACT type of player who would have done something like that to you.

Now, I know it has been become kind of a running joke over the years (especially by me) to make fun of Lex's gut. I mean, go back and watch Africa, and watch how many times Lex references following his gut. And watch how many times his gut is proven to be wrong. I mean, dang, Lex's gut is as bad at predicting Survivor as it is at digesting elephant crap. It has a terrible track record.

But in this case his gut was actually kind of right.

Okay, here's the deal. I don't care what you think about Lex, or what you think about Lex's gut. Lex's gut is a joke, ha ha I get it. But he <u>wasn't</u> just pulling a name out of a hat when he suspected that vote might have come from Kelly. Again, if you were Lex, if you were in the exact same situation that Lex had been in, you would have suspected the troublemaking snarky genius girl who didn't respect you very much too.

So Lex turned on Kelly for no reason. Well, that's how the audience saw it, anyway. Lex turned on Kelly, he turned on the sarcastic little female fan favorite who was a hit with the internet crowd, and he got her voted out of the game. And he forever cemented her image as the lovable Jesus-like little Survivor martyr. Because Kelly Goldsmith was basically now Obi-Wan Kenobi. By striking her down, Lex only made this minor Survivor nobody from Africa's legacy all that more powerful.

Now I admit, this argument (that Lex wasn't really all that wrong in his suspicions) is actually a very difficult one for me to be putting out there in a book like this. Because I know how unpopular it is going to be. And the reason I know that is because I know for a fact how unpopular Lex van den Berghe in general is among the internet Survivor crowd. Seriously, go to any Survivor message board where Survivor fans hang out, go to any Survivor website anywhere that has ever existed on the internet, and ask them about Lex. See what happens. See what they say. Chances are, you talk to 99% of online Survivor fans in the world and they will all say the exact same thing.

They will all say that Lex is a hypocrite. And that Lex is a crybaby. And that they have no respect for Lex because he is a poor sport and a sore loser and an asshole.

> **Side Note:** What's interesting about the internet reaction to Lex is the fact that most of the crap that people have slung at him over the years, they are only saying because of All Stars. The fan base hates Lex because of All Stars. But what most people don't realize (or they have simply forgotten over time) is that fans were saying the EXACT same stuff about Lex after Africa too. People were calling him a hypocrite and crybaby even way back when he was playing for the first time. And they were saying it because of the Kelly vote.

Okay, so here we go. Remember when I said that Africa episode eight is interesting because something happened in that episode that had never happened on Survivor before? Well here it is. This was the first time in Survivor history that a player was voted out specifically because of something they did. Even though the evidence was overwhelming that they did not actually in fact do it.

In pro wrestling terms, this was the very first screw job in Survivor history.

> **Side note:** Yeah, I know. People will say that Joel was voted out for something that he didn't do in Borneo. And some will still argue that Kel was voted out for having beef jerky that he didn't actually have. But I would argue again that the cow joke had nothing to do with why Joel was voted out of Pagong. I think he was going to be voted out anyway, simply because the females in Pagong (plus Greg) had the numbers advantage and Joel was taken out because he threatened their leadership. I think the "cow joke" explanation was more or less fabricated by the editors simply because it made for a more memorable TV episode.
>
> As for Kel, well I don't think beef jerky had anything to do with why he was voted out. From everything I have ever heard (from interviews, insider stuff, etc.), Kel was voted out because he was weird and selfish and because he didn't fit in with the rest of the Ogakors. Whether he had beef jerky or not on top of that

(personally I think he did) is really sort of irrelevant.

No, in my opinion, Kelly Goldsmith was the first. She was the very first Survivor screwjob. She was the first player in Survivor history who was voted out specifically because of something that she did not do.

And, understandably, the audience reacted very strongly to this.

Now, I know that this chapter is not going to make me a lot of friends. I know that 95% of the fans in the Survivor online world (yes, you!) hate Lex, and they can't stand it if anybody ever sticks up for the guy, or says anything nice about him. I get that. Survivor fans hate Lex. Survivor fans love Kelly. Survivor fans _hate_ what happened to Kelly. Believe me, I have been witnessing this particular dance for more than a decade. And like I said, I have also been smack dab in the middle of it.

And of course I also know what people are thinking when they read all of my pro-Lex propaganda. I bet a lot of people will read this chapter and they will think well duh, of course Mario is going to stick up for him. Mario and Lex are buddies because they went to the same school. And because they were email pen pals back in the day. No duh, of _course_ Mario is going to take Lex van den Berghe's side on the Kelly incident.

But I'm not really taking Lex's side. All I am doing is asking you to think about that whole Kelly Goldsmith situation from Lex's point of view for a moment.

Think of what happened with that mystery vote from T-Bird. And think how you would have felt if you had been Lex. Think of how angry you would have been. Think of how annoying that little sneak attack would have been, especially when it came from a person you thought was a friend.

Now look at the variables that were around you and were staring you right in the face.

Who would you have suspected had cast that mystery vote?

Would you have suspected Ethan? I doubt it.

Would you have suspected Frank, a military man of honor who had given you his word? Of course not.

Would you have suspected Kim Johnson? Mama Kat, the mother figure of the tribe? Um no, I don't think so either.

Would you have suspected T-Bird?

Hell no. Of <u>course</u> you wouldn't have suspected T-Bird. <u>Nobody</u> would have ever suspected T-Bird. And that is exactly why T-Bird was such an amazing Survivor player. She is like Tina Wesson in the fact that she is sneaky, she is cutthroat, she is competitive, but because she is sweet and pure and innocent and she has that cute little southern accent she can always get away with it.

If you were Lex, if you were there in that exact same situation that he had been in, with those exact same variables, I can almost guarantee you that there were only two people in Moto Maji that you wouldn't have had a lot of faith in. You wouldn't have had a lot of faith in Kelly. And you wouldn't have had a lot of faith in Tom. And if you remember Africa and you have done your homework, you will remember that Lex's distrust of Tom didn't show up until much later in the season.

Meanwhile, Kelly Goldsmith is a sneak. And Kelly Goldsmith is a genius. And Kelly Goldsmith likes to stir up trouble around camp.

And Kelly has flat out admitted to you that she is <u>good at lying,</u> she is <u>a student of psychology,</u> and she is <u>an amazing manipulator.</u>

Honestly, if you were Lex, you probably would have suspected that vote came from Kelly too.

So there you go, that was what happened. Kelly Goldsmith was voted out at the end of episode eight. And the audience HATED it. And the audience hated Lex. And the internet fan base rallied around Kelly like no Survivor player has ever been rallied around since. To this day, almost one hundred percent of the time, Kelly Goldsmith shows up on lists of the best players in Survivor history that probably would have won if they hadn't been screwed.

And meanwhile, I have always been sitting here thinking, well if she had been <u>that</u> great a player, maybe Lex wouldn't have immediately suspected her when things started to go wrong. If she had been <u>that</u> amazing at all of her little mind games, if she had been <u>that</u> great at manipulating people, maybe she would have been able to pass herself off as being not that big of a threat to Lex when she actually was.

Honestly, if Kelly had been <u>that</u> great a player, she would have been much more of a chameleon like T-Bird.

In the end, do I think that Lex was right in the way he targeted one of his own alliance members? Of course not. His gut was wrong, just like his gut is always wrong. In fact, the neverending failure of Lex's gut (seriously, pay attention to this next time) is one of the funniest storylines in Survivor: Africa.

However, I do not think that Lex's suspicions were wrong. I think that he and Kelly probably would have wound up in a head to head showdown at some point down the road anyway, because that was just where the season was headed. And they were probably headed for that big showdown very soon. Because, remember, Kelly did admit to us (on more than one occasion) that **she was planning to take Lex out the first chance she got.** What I think really happened with the Moto Maji Screwjob was that Lex got wind of Kelly's intentions before they went down, and he simply accelerated her 5150 status by a couple of days. I think he caught Kelly with her shoes untied before she was ready to have the big showdown. And more than anything, I think THAT was what she was so pissed about. Kelly was upset because she knew that she had the numbers. And she knew that she had the brains. And she knew that she could have taken down Cult Leader Super Dad in a couple of days.

And she was furious because Lex just beat her to the punch.

Remember, and this is the big lesson from this chapter. Just because you like Kelly, and you don't like Lex, that doesn't mean that she necessarily got screwed. I have always believed that she was going to be voted out of the game soon anyway. In fact, I am guessing that even if the Moto Maji screwjob hadn't happened, T-Bird <u>still</u> would have lasted longer than Kelly. Simply because T-Bird was sneaky and not in an obvious way, and Kelly wasn't. Kelly was the type of player who was so obvious about what she was doing that you always just KNEW she was trouble.

In the end, I have to go back to the old Chris Rock routine about O.J. that I quoted a couple of chapters ago, because it fits in Kelly's case too. In fact it fits her scenario even better than it fit the twist scenario. When it comes to the most popular sarcastic martyr in Survivor history, I'm not saying that Lex should have killed her. But I understand. If you were in Lex's position you probably would have killed her too.

I like Kelly Goldsmith. She was a fun character. She has always been a fun character. She has an amazing fan base.

But like most players in Survivor history, she finished exactly where she should have finished.

64. The Hacky Sack

Unfortunately, Survivor: Africa is a season that has never really been a favorite among the internet crowd. It has long been chastised by the Survivor online community as being "boring." Or "dull." Or "unmemorable." In fact, up until about five years ago, Africa was usually lumped in with Thailand as being the two all-time worst Survivor seasons. And I have always felt that this was ridiculous. Because in my personal opinion, I believe that Africa is easily the best of the first three Survivor seasons.

And believe me, that is not something that I say very lightly. Especially if you know how much I love Borneo and ~~Tina~~ Australia.

----Fun With Survivor History!-----

Have you ever seen a Zagat's restaurant review? Well if you haven't, Zagat's is one of those books where they take a bunch of reader comments and they cobble them together into one big overall restaurant review. And they put "quotes" around all the reader comments so you can see what people are saying about a particular place.

Well I thought it would be fun to come up with my own Zagat's review for each of the first three Survivor seasons. So here you go. Here is what the Survivor internet fan base generally thought about each of the first three seasons at the time they were airing on TV.

Ratings (just like all Zagat reviews) are out of 30, by the way.

Survivor: Borneo - Sixteen "every day Americans" are "stranded on an island" in a "thrilling" game show based on "a million dollar prize" and also "survival and ethics." In the end, a "fat naked fag" wins the game over "the rafting persona queen" "with a weird nose" through his "heartless" "Machiavellian tactics" and also his "shitty" "naked" "flabby" "lack of a soul." Featuring "amazing" characters like "Sitting Duck", "Derk", "The Alphabet Strategy Doofus", "The Coconut Phone Guy", "Souna", "the lazy black guy", and "B.B. Andersen", who "died repeatedly after the season." This "still amazing" season has held up "very well" over the years and will forever be known as "the grandfather of all reality T.V.", even though fans still bemoan its "terrible ending" where "four fuckhead cheaters" "stole the game" from "our beloved Pagongs." Highly recommended for fans of "strategy games", "really gay spin dancing", "superpole" and "wondering what gender Sue was." **Rating**: **30**

Survivor: The Australian Outback - Sixteen "every day Americans" are "marooned" in "what Americans think is the Australian Outback" and compete for "a million dollars" in this "thrilling" yet "sometimes tedious" sequel to "the show that cock Richard Hatch won the first time around." In the end, "Survivor 2" is won by "that bitch who went through Kel's bag" in an incredible upset over "that idiot" "whose creepy mom had the hots for him." Featuring characters that "were just as beloved as the players from the first season" and "also Mitchell." "Big moments" in this season include "that psychopath" "whose hands melted off", Kel and the "beef jerky", Jerri "going to hell and roasting in hellfire for all of eternity", "Peas proposing to carrots, or maybe the other way around", and "Lamber" Brkich, who "never shut the fuck up about food." While not as "revered" as Survivor: Borneo, "season two" was an "amazing adventure" with an "enormous fan base" that should not be "ignored like it was the lazy black guy." **Rating: 29**

Survivor: Africa - Sixteen every day Americans "led by the amazing Kelly Goldsmith" "mock the victims of 9/11" and "pretend to suffer" in an attempt to "win a million dollars" while "simultaneously shitting on America." In the end, the "winner" of "the first boring season" is "that nice young man" Ethan, whose "ethics" and "honor" and "poofy jewfro" are enough to win "the final vote" over "that grandma in the thong." Big name characters in "this shitty season" include "Big Tom", "Chip" Gaither, "the lazy black guy", "Silas" Gaither, "that Lindsey girl who needed to die in a fire", and also Lex, "who is a crybaby" and who "eats shit" and who "sucks." While nowhere as "revered" as "Australia or Borneo," "the first bad season" has "maybe a couple of good moments" and is "begrudgingly recommended" for "people who hate America", "fried chicken and mashed potato enthusiasts", "people who scream down down down faster faster faster", and "anyone who wants to learn more about Mother Africa." **Rating: 18**

Now, obviously, I have nothing bad to say about Borneo or Australia. Yeah right, like the guy who bills himself as "the Survivor Historian" is going to sit here and say anything bad about the two most important Survivor seasons. Whatever, get real. Even fifteen years later, I would still rank Borneo and

Australia as being among the top ten all-time best Survivor seasons. In fact, let's go even further than that. I think Borneo and Australia are so good that I would rank them both among the top twenty five seasons of <u>any</u> television show that I have ever watched at any point in my life.

> **Side note**: I know this is kind of a dick thing to say, but any new school Survivor fan who didn't watch Borneo or Australia at the time that they aired, and who will sit there today and tell you that both seasons were boring and unwatchable and that they are both impossible to sit through (which is an opinion you hear surprisingly often if you visit a Survivor message board these days)? Well, any person who tells you that, I'm sorry. That isn't a person that you really want to be talking Survivor with. And yes, I know how elitist that sounds. I don't care.

I am a HUGE fan of Borneo and Australia. Just like I am a HUGE fan of Africa. All three of those seasons were amazing.

But to me, Africa is the best of the three.

And why do I think Africa is even better than the first two seasons, which I hold so near and dear to my heart?

Easy. It is because of the location.

Simply put, the idea to set season three of Survivor in Kenya, in the middle of the African plains in a boma surrounded by lions, was genius. Oh sure, it might not have exactly been <u>smart</u>. At least not in a "wow this a responsible way to treat our players" way. The idea to set Survivor in a lion's den easily could have ended with one of the players actually being killed. Or, just as bad, it could have ended with the players becoming so weak and dehydrated by the end of the game that they would have grown lethargic and they would have refused to do anything for the cameras. In fact, now that I think about it, by the end of Africa that is pretty much exactly what DID happen (it happened at the end of Australia too.) So no, setting Survivor in a location as striking and as dangerous as Africa wasn't all that particularly <u>smart</u>. At least, not from a common sense point of view (or from a CBS legal department point of view) it wasn't. To this day I am still amazed that none of the players actually died out there.

But damn, did it result in some amazing TV.

The reason I say that Africa resulted in some amazing TV is because of the rewards, of course. The famous Africa rewards. The thing that nobody ever talks about when it comes to this season, yet it's the thing that I believe ranks Africa right up there with just about any other Survivor season. There is no way you can talk about season three of Survivor without talking about the kickass rewards that the players got to go on.

For starters, since we are up to episode eight now (The Kelly boot), let's talk about the reward that Ethan and Lex got to go on in this episode. To my dying day, I will always say that this could be my all-time favorite reward scene in any episode in any season at any point in Survivor history.

In episode eight of Africa, Ethan wins a reward that doesn't sound all that amazing on paper. But it's the type of cultural reward that the show was so good at featuring back in the early days of the franchise. And that of course the producers rarely, if ever, even make an effort to include on the show anymore. Which (and I will say this over and over and over) is one of the main reasons why the early seasons were so much better than the later ones.

Because he wins the reward challenge in episode eight, Ethan is awarded a pair of goats. And he wins the right to travel to the small African village of Wamba where he will get a chance to barter them.

Oh, and naturally, he gets to take his best friend Lex along on his big wacky African goat bartering adventure.

Honestly, there is no way I can describe the "Ethan and Lex barter goats in Wamba Village" scene to you and really do it justice. If you have never seen it before, you will just have to track it down on the internet and watch it for yourself. Because it really is that good. I mean, here you have these two middle class Americans, who clearly have no experience whatsoever bartering goats in an African village, and who clearly have no idea what the market price of a goat even is, let alone how you are supposed to barter one in the first place, yet they are thrown face first into the cutthroat world of goat bartering against Wambans who actually do this sort of thing for a living. And the result? Well like I said, it is just magical. This is one of those scenes that I look forward to EVERY SINGLE TIME I watch Africa, because it really is one of the greatest and funniest Survivor scenes ever. It also incorporates the culture of the location much better than the producers were ever able to do in most other seasons. I mean, Lex and Ethan are IN Africa in this scene. They are knee deep in the middle of it. They are doing African things with African people in an African way in an African village in the

384

middle of Africa. Show me any other season that ever had a reward like that.

The whole goat bartering scene with Lex and Ethan in episode eight is fun. I mean, that's it, it is just fun. This is one of those types of scenes that I used to love on Survivor, because it had nothing to do with strategy whatsoever. There was no gameplay involved in this scene at all, there was no strategy, there were no people jockeying for position in the game or looking for hidden idols, or going on a five minute monologue on what their strategy was for how they were going to split the vote tonight. No, this was just two dudes walking around rural Africa trying to get money for their goats. And naively thinking that whoever bought their goats wasn't going to just take them right over to the butcher and turn them into goat meat. Again, there is no way I can put into words just how fun this scene is. And, well, for lack of a better term, how "real" it is. Like I said before, there was no show better at showing off and working in the culture of its location than Survivor was in its early days.

So that was it. The famous goat bartering scene in episode eight of Survivor Africa. One of my all-time favorite Survivor scenes.

But wait. What's this?

This awesome reward scene isn't even over yet!

There was actually a second part to Ethan and Lex's little goat bartering adventure that a lot of people don't really seem to remember these days. And to me that is just heartbreaking, because to me this is the single biggest moment of Survivor: Africa. Seriously, if you want to understand Africa's importance to the Survivor timeline, if you want to know why in my opinion it was just as important as Borneo or Australia in the overall scheme of things, well here you go. Look no further than the second part of Ethan and Lex's little Wamba adventure.

At the end of the goat bartering trip, Ethan and Lex are given the chance to trade some of their personal items for luxuries that they can bring back to camp. So they do. Lex trades the villagers some hats. Ethan trades the villagers some shirts. Lex gives away an autographed picture of Kelly Goldsmith because he knows that will fetch a hundred trillion dollars on the internet. They do all the usual stuff.

And then, at the end of the scene, Ethan plays hacky sack with a bunch of little African boys. They just kick the bag around right there in the middle of the road. Just Ethan and a bunch of little ten year olds. It is very sweet.

And then, after the game, Ethan is so touched by his visit here to Wamba, and the experiences he is having in Africa in general, that he decides to give the kids a gift. Just as his truck is about to leave, just as he and Lex are about to be taken back into the cutthroat world of Survivor, and leave Wamba forever, he leans out of the truck and he tosses his most prized possession to one of the little boys. He throws the little African boy his hacky sack.

Then Ethan waves goodbye and he smiles at the kids. And he has a great big tear in his eye.

And my goodness, if you ever wanted to know why Ethan was such a beloved Survivor figure, well there you go.

This is something I am going to hammer at a lot in the next couple of chapters of this book. I am going to point out what a big deal it was that somebody like Ethan finally wound up winning Survivor. I am going to drive home the idea of just how universally beloved he was. And how the show desperately NEEDED an Ethan to win after two not-exactly-embraced winners in Richard and Tina. Because make no doubt about it, Ethan really was beloved. He was absolutely revered by the fan base at the time, and he still is today. Just like the famous Teresa Cooper so accurately said, there is almost nobody out there who doesn't like Ethan. And I have always said that the moment that really happened for him, the moment that Ethan went from "that cute soccer player with the floppy hair" to "the most universally beloved winner in Survivor history" was this scene. It was the hacky sack moment. The minute he tossed that kid the hacky sack in the African village, the minute the music swelled and Ethan started crying because he was so touched by the majesty of Africa, well that was the moment that America officially fell in love with Ethan Zohn. And that love would only grow stronger as the season went on, and more players were eliminated, and you realized that nice guy Ethan might actually have a legitimate shot to win this thing.

Again, much more on this later. This is a very important subject when it comes to Survivor history that I don't think ever gets discussed enough.

And so anyway, there you have it. The famous goat bartering trip with Ethan and Lex. One of the most outstanding combinations of location mixed with culture mixed with TV entertainment that Survivor has ever managed to pull off. And again, this scene is only the tip of the iceberg when it comes to the awesome rewards and the cultural inclusion that were featured all season long in Survivor: Africa. I mean, do I even have to mention the awesome reward challenge in episode two where African warriors drained blood from a cow and then the players had to drink it? Do I have to mention Brandon and Frank's "date" in episode nine where they went out to the middle of Kenya and watched "Out of Africa" together on a movie screen? Do I have to mention the scene in episode eleven, where Lex and Tom went on a hot air balloon ride, and they got to witness the migration of the wildebeests? Good lord. I mean, show me any other season that featured as much of its location as Survivor Africa did. I can't think of any other season that even comes CLOSE.

Oh yeah, and then as the cherry on top of the sundae, let's not forget the scene that hardly ANYONE ever remembers today, but was nearly as awesome as Ethan and the hacky sack. Let's talk about the reward scene in episode twelve, where Lex gets to deliver AIDS supplies to a hospital in the middle of rural Africa. And then he gets to bond with and play with all the little kids that have been stricken with HIV. I mean, my goodness. You talk about a scene that is a tear jerker.

Again, Africa was a bad season? Africa was lackluster and boring? Nothing memorable happened in Survivor: Africa?

To quote the great Jonathan Penner, "My ass!"

There was so much going on in Survivor: Africa. There was so much culture, there was so much location, there was so much love put into the production of each and every episode. I mean, there is a damn good reason why I think it is even better than Australia or Borneo.

The reason I think it is the best of the first three Survivor seasons is because it is awesome.

65. Thomas and His Fanciful Theories

By this point in my Survivor writing career, I had finally started to put together a pretty good sized reader base. Now that I was adding a commentary to each one of my weekly episode recaps, and in particular now that I had more or less invented the idea of the "Survivor Power Rankings", and I was throwing that into my weekly comments as well, this was when my readership really started to take off. This was when my career as a Survivor writer began to slowly take shape.

And of course when you develop a readership, naturally one of the things that happens is that you start to get a lot of emails from people.

One of my favorite readers back in the early days (I have mentioned him before) was a guy named Thomas. At least, that's what he told me his name was. Heck, between people being frightened of the internet, and the availability of free anonymous email accounts, and all the privacy issues floating around the news these days, and Survivor fans just pretty much being oddballs in general, who knows what his real name was. I mean, for years there was one guy who wrote me emails all the time, and I only knew him by the name "Ethan's StarPenis."

So anyway, here is this guy named Thomas who starts writing me emails about midway through Africa. And he keeps writing me emails. Sometimes daily. Some days he would write me multiple emails. He was by far the most dedicated emailer out of all of the people who made up my early reader base. And whenever he wrote me, he would always delve into what I liked to call "his fanciful theory of the day." This was where Thomas would make his predictions about how the current season of Survivor was likely to play out.

Midway through Africa, maybe the first episode after the merge, Thomas wrote to me and he made a prediction. He predicted that even though the Borans were currently up in numbers, 5-4, he believed that a member of Samburu was going to win the game. Because, he explained, "Somebody on Boran is going to realize that they are headed for fifth place, and they are going to want to switch alliances to improve their position in the game. Somebody is going to wise up and they are going to get greedy."

Thomas went on to explain that Kim Johnson was probably the lowest member on the totem pole among the Borans. So she was the most likely person to defect and team up with the Samburus.

Now, naturally, I know what you are thinking. You are sitting there reading this and you are thinking, wow that Thomas was a really sharp guy. Because he realized that players were going to start switching alliances after the merge on Survivor. Even though it hadn't actually happened in a season yet (and it really <u>wouldn't</u> happen in a game changing manner until a season later, in Marquesas), Thomas was clearly on to what was going to happen as the game of Survivor evolved. Sooner or later, the players were going to figure out that locking yourself into a five person alliance early on in the game wasn't always going to be your best long term strategy. Every once in a while, especially late in the game, it would actually be a much better move for you if you improved your position by jumping over into the minority alliance.

So here comes Thomas with his common sense theory of how Survivor should work.

He laid it out to me in a very logical, matter of fact manner.

People at the bottom of the totem pole are going to start switching alliances. They have to. Sooner or later they are going to realize that being fifth in a five person alliance is little more than putting a gun to your head and committing suicide. Because players are smart. They are going to <u>have</u> to start figuring that out.

And of course you know how I responded to him.

As the bright, insightful, clearly brilliant Survivor analyst that I always believed myself to be, I emailed Thomas and I told him he was an idiot.

There is NO way anyone is ever going to jump out of an iron clad five person alliance after the merge, I told him. They are never going to do that if they are already in the majority, because that just isn't how Survivor works. The only way to win Survivor is to get in the majority and to <u>stay</u> in the majority. You stay in the majority for as long as you can, and then when you get to the end you cross your fingers and you hope for some luck.

I was so adamant about "this is the way that Survivor works, and this is the way that Survivor will <u>always</u> work!" that for about a year and a half I pretty much openly mocked Thomas right to his face. Any time that he would dare suggest something like this in an email, and believe me, he wrote to me a LOT, our email exchange would inevitably end the exact same way. He would tell me that a Boran should start switching sides. And I would say he was delusional, that was never going to happen. A Boran was never going to switch sides. Then I would write something in my column that week about a reader of mine who loved to present his "fanciful theories" on how he thought Survivor worked. And how this guy was making the game of Survivor seem way more complicated than it actually was. Then Thomas would get his feelings hurt and he would go off and pout for a while.

And then about twenty four hours later he would present me with a new email with a brand new theory about why he thought it was in Ethan's best interest to switch sides and team up with T-Bird.

This cycle lasted for months. Months, I tell you, months! There was no escaping from it. In fact, when I think back to the second half of Africa, which was really the first time that I ever had much of a reader base, there are really only about three things that I remember from those early heady days of being a "famous internet writer." I remember being excited that a guy I knew (Lex) was probably going to win Survivor: Africa. I remember being amazed that something as simple as "The Survivor Power Rankings" would suddenly become the gimmick that everyone would associate with me. And I remember Thomas fucking writing me every fucking day, and me being annoyed because he clearly didn't know what the fuck he was talking about.

Now, of course, you might be wondering, if you were so annoyed by this guy Thomas, why even write about him fourteen years later in your Survivor book?

Ah, now that is an excellent question.

The reason I bring up Thomas is twofold.

First off, I bring him up because he was right. I mean, I hate to say it, especially more than a dozen years after the fact, but he was absolutely right. People WERE going to start switching alliances on Survivor. They were going to have to. As the seasons kept coming out, and there were more and more players and winners and strategies to watch and study and learn from, inevitably the people watching at home were going to come to the exact same conclusion that Thomas had already come to. If you locked yourself into a five person alliance very early on in the game, that meant there was a 20% chance that you were going to finish in fifth place. And sooner or later a really good player (which was basically anyone who had watched the first few seasons of Survivor and studied them and knew how the game worked) was going to realize that fifth place in a game for a million dollars would be a complete waste of time. Fifth place? In a game like this where I have sacrificed so much and I have worked so hard just to get here in the first place? Fat chance I am going to settle for fifth when it is obvious that that is where I am going to wind up.

Sooner or later the players were going to realize that there were opportunities on the other side too. In a counter alliance. Where you would have a chance to finish <u>better</u> than fifth.

It hadn't happened yet, midway through Africa, but Thomas was quite correct that the game was going to start heading in that direction one day. It had to. The players were getting smarter. There were more and more seasons now to learn from and build from. Players jumping from one alliance to another was simply just a matter of time.

So that is one reason why I bring this up in my book. I bring it up because I want to apologize to Thomas. Oh whatever his name really was. I'm sorry, dude, you were right. I'm sorry that I called them "fanciful theories" and I'm sorry that I said (or I very strongly implied) that you were an idiot. In retrospect, you were easily the smartest person who was writing me back in the day. And yes, that means you were definitely even smarter than Ethan's StarPenis.

However, there is a SECOND reason that I wanted to bring this up in my book too. And to me, this is a way more important reason.

The second reason why I think this is an essential chapter for my Survivor book is because it is a good example for newer viewers of the show to see just how different Survivor was back then compared to what Survivor is now. I mean, read my argument with Thomas above and notice what a moron I look like. Players will never switch alliances? Players will always ride their fifth place finish right up until the day they are voted out? What kind of idiot would say something like that?

But here's the deal.

AT THE TIME, I WAS RIGHT!

THROUGH THE FIRST THREE SEASONS, THAT IS EXACTLY HOW SURVIVOR WAS PLAYED!

I mean, I hate to say it, but that <u>was</u> Survivor for the first year and a half. At least ever since ~~Richard Hatch~~ Stacey Stillman invented the concept of "an alliance."

Here is how Survivor worked in the early days. You got into an alliance.

And if you were lucky it was the dominant alliance. And then you tried to get numbers at the merge. And then if you were lucky enough to have the numbers, you just rode that alliance all the way to the end until you inevitably had to turn on one another. And along the way you hoped and prayed and hoped a little more that luck would be on your side at the end, and the "cannibalism" part of your alliance would wind up with you in the final two. And then at that point you tried your best not to come off as a douchebag, so that the jurors would respect you and they would award you the win.

And there you go. The very essence of the game of Survivor. Through the first three seasons. That was how it would always play out.

My comments to Thomas might make me look like an idiot now, fourteen years later, in retrospect. But at the time I was absolutely right. And I wasn't alone. If you had presented one of Thomas's fanciful theories to anyone who really followed and understood and studied the game of Survivor at the time, which was pretty much me and about thirty million other people, any one of them would have said the exact same thing that I was saying. Uh yeah, Thomas, that's really interesting. Uh, what kind of dope have you been smoking? You honestly think that a member of the majority is going to jump out of the majority and team up with the minority? Really? Well if you really believe that, well then how about this? How about you trade your cow for this handful of magic beans? I promise they are going to make you a millionaire one day. Come on dude, let's trade. I love the alternate universe with the alternate rules that you have found yourself living in.

Again, I hate to keep saying this, but if you didn't watch the first few seasons of the show, if you didn't experience them and watch the game develop and play out and change like the original viewers all did at the time, it will be almost impossible for you to relate to anything that I am saying in this chapter. In fact, I am sure that most new viewers reading this chapter will read my comments to Thomas and they will think that I was the world's biggest idiot. Actually, I know for a fact that they will. In fact, here is a good experiment for you. Just go onto any Survivor message board these days, and read all the comments that modern fans make about the first couple of seasons of the show. Here are the kinds of comments that you will see a lot:

"None of the players knew what they were doing yet!"

"Richard only won because he was playing against a bunch of idiots!"

"There were no good strategists back then! The players were all morons!"

"There weren't any blindsides yet, the show was so boring!"

I read these comments all the time. And when I see them, they always burn me up. Because the players were <u>not</u> idiots back then, and neither were the fans. The game was just different. That's really the only way you can describe it. Through the first three seasons of Survivor, there was one way to win, and one way to win only. You got into the majority, and then you hoped for a lot of luck at the end. Why would anyone think that any other way of playing would work? Why would anyone think any other way of playing COULD work? It went against everything we knew or had ever seen on the show. Telling a Survivor fan in 2001 that alliance hopping would improve your position in the game would be like telling a man in 1852 that his great grandchild would one day own a twenty gig iPod. He would look at you like he was a dog and he saw you eating with a fork.

Yes, Thomas's theories were correct. Absolutely. But at the time they were really quite fanciful. I was correct too. At the time, Thomas's strategy resided in a Survivor universe that didn't really exist.

I mean, come on. Paschal and Neleh are going to team up with the Maraamus after the merge? They are going to switch sides and knock out all of their friends from Rotu? Yes Thomas, I am sure they are. Yes honey, I am suuuuuure we are going to have our first ever cross tribal alliance in Marquesas. I can toooooootally see that happening. You bet.

Oh, and also, please let me have some of that delicious peyote when you are done chewing on it. I bet it's amazing.

P.S. Okay I saved the best part of this chapter for the end. Do you know who Thomas turned out to be? Ten years later, he turned out to be a Survivor fan from Boston named Rob Mariano.

P.P.S. Just kidding. No he didn't. Wouldn't that have been amazing though?

66. The Temporal Junction Point

Have you ever seen the Back to the Future trilogy? Well if you have, you are aware that there is one date in history which is far more important than any other date in the entire Back to the Future universe. That date, of course, is November 12, 1955. The night of the Enchantment Under the Sea Dance. And also, the night that a lightning bolt hit and destroyed the Hill Valley Clock Tower.

Now I'm not sure how big of a science fiction nerd you are, or how big of a movie nerd you are (obviously I am a bit of both). But in the Back to the Future universe this date (11/12/55) is known as a "Temporal Junction Point." Which is just a fancy way of saying, this is the exact point on the space-time continuum that all sorts of futures and realities and alternate realities converge and can be affected and changed. In other words, this is THE moment in time that you want to play around with if you want to change history. If you really want to screw around with the characters in the Back to the Future universe, go right to the Temporal Junction Point on November 12, 1955 and start messing around with things.

Now, obviously, this isn't a book about Back to the Future. This is a book about Survivor. And you might be wondering why I bring up the concept of a Temporal Junction Point in my Survivor book.

Well rest assured. If you have never heard about this before, I am about to blow your mind. Because right in the middle of Survivor: Africa, we come to a moment in time which many people have argued is the single most important strategy decision that has ever been made in Survivor history. That's right, we are about to talk about the franchise's Temporal Junction Point. This is the one point in Survivor history that, had things played out even a little bit differently, it would have had an enormous impact on the way that the franchise played out and developed down the road.

And what's funny is that you won't even realize how important this moment was unless you stop and you think about it for a bit.

Okay, to spare you the suspense, let's get right into it. Oh yeah, and keep in mind that this "Survivor Temporal Junction Point" business isn't something that I came up with on my own. This is something that HUNDREDS of people have pointed out to me over the years. In fact, I would say that this is one of the most often-discussed subjects that comes up whenever people talk to me about Africa. Any time you meet somebody who knows their

Survivor, and who really knows their Survivor history, if you bring up Africa you will eventually come to this question. Inevitably, one of you will at some point ask, "Hey, so what do you think happens if Lex goes home instead of Kelly at the end of episode eight?"

And there you go. That is the Survivor Temporal Junction Point.

Episode eight.

Where one vote (a lone Brandon vote) was all that stood between what we know as Survivor NOW, and what would have changed just about everything we know about Survivor history forever.

Okay, let's back up for a second so we can talk about this moment. Let's talk about how a young gay bartender named Brandon Quinton affected just about everything that would happen on Survivor for the next ten years. And all because he just didn't want to be in the same alliance as the cranky old military guy.

So episode eight. Remember that one? Smoking Out The Snake. Lex thinks that Kelly has voted for him. Kelly, meanwhile, has not voted for him. So the two of them square off against one another in a battle for supremacy. Kelly gathers up her allies on one side, and Lex gathers up his allies on the other side. And then right in the middle, they both think that they have Brandon.

No matter who wins this showdown, it is going to be 5-4. It is going to be very close. It will really only come down to which one of the two sides has Brandon.

Which means that Brandon Quinton is the key swing vote for the entire season.

Now, obviously, you know what happened in the end. Anyone who is reading this book knows what happened. Lex proved to be a much better salesman than Kelly, and he persuaded Brandon to jump on board and vote along with him. So Kelly was voted out 5-4. Then Brandon was voted out next because his former allies were all pissed at him. And this of course paved the way for Ethan and Lex to rise to power, where Ethan eventually became the first fan favorite Survivor winner.

Now, just for argument's sake...

Let's take a look at what changes if that particular scenario DIDN'T happen.

Let's say, just for the sake of being a contrarian, that Kelly wound up being a better salesman than Lex. Yeah, I know, that probably never would have happened, because Lex is a force of nature who will always be the leader and who will always be the alpha male. And because Kelly Goldsmith, well, isn't. But let's say, just for the sake of argument, that Lex said something that day that annoyed Brandon. And Brandon voted for Lex out of spite. Let's say that the vote swung the other way, and Lex van den Berghe became the first juror of Africa instead of Kelly.

Let's look at everything in Survivor history that changes because of that.

Get ready.

As Samuel L. Jackson said in Jurassic Park, "hold on to your butt."

Okay, for starters, does Ethan win Survivor: Africa now? I doubt it. With Lex out of the picture, I don't think Ethan has much of a say in what is going to happen in the game anymore. At this point it is now going to be all about Kelly and the Samboohoos. And just from her jury question alone, you know that Kelly probably was never really a very big Ethan fan. So I bet Tom and Ethan are probably the next two players out of the game after Lex. And then at that point, who knows. But it's safe to say that Ethan probably doesn't win Survivor anymore. Brandon's decision to vote for Lex just took away the very first popular winner we ever had in Survivor history.

> **Side note:** In this particular scenario, my suspicion is that Teresa probably would have won the game. If only because she would have been the sharpest player out there with Lex out of the way. And, well, because T-Bird is awesome. It doesn't really have any place in this particular chapter, but if you asked me who I think would have won the game if Lex had been out of the way, I think the answer is obvious. I think that T-Bird owns everyone.

Okay so Lex and Ethan and Tom are now out of the way. The three of them are no longer factors in the endgame. The Big Three of Africa have now been removed from importance. And that is a big deal. Because there is a very pivotal immunity challenge coming up in a couple of episodes called Fallen Comrades. And, well, if you know what happened in real life during that particular challenge, you will see why I call the Brandon vote for Kelly the Survivor Temporal Junction Point.

I will get into this more in the next couple of chapters (because believe me, this is a <u>very</u> <u>big</u> <u>deal</u>), but in real life there was a problem with the Africa Fallen Comrades immunity challenge. The problem was that the producers screwed up. They had one question in the challenge that technically had more than one right answer. And the producers didn't realize that. So what happened (in real life) was that Lex was told that he lost the final four immunity challenge, when he really didn't. Had the producers not screwed up and accidentally counted one of Lex's answers as being wrong, that challenge should have ended as a tie between Lex and Kim Johnson. And it should have gone on to a tiebreaker.

Unfortunately, the producers didn't realize their mistake until the episode had already aired on TV.

They didn't realize they had screwed up until it was way too late to do anything to change it.

Again, I don't want to get into the specifics of this particular error by the producers, because I am going to do it much more comprehensively in the next couple of chapters. Trust me though, this whole thing has been very well documented throughout the years. This is not something I am just making up. This is pretty common knowledge when it comes to insider Survivor history. Lex got totally screwed by the producers because of their error in the Fallen Comrades immunity challenge.

And because Lex got screwed in real life, that meant that Tom also got screwed. After all, with Kim immune in the final four instead of Lex, that meant that Tom was now officially a sitting duck. So Tom was voted out of the game at the final four, and Kim made the final three. And all because of a producer error that likely cost either Lex or Tom the game.

And THIS is where we get back to the Temporal Junction Point.

There have been rumblings over the years that there was some sort of a payoff between the producers and Tom and Lex behind the scenes after Africa ended. Lex and Tom were allegedly paid some sort of a monetary amount because the producers admitted that they f'd up and they screwed them over. This has been talked about hundreds of times on the internet over the years. But the part about this that a lot of people DON'T know is that I have also heard rumors over the years that a <u>second</u> part of the payoff was that Lex and Tom were both also promised a spot on All-Stars. Since

CBS screwed them both so badly at the end of Africa, the allegation I have heard over the years is that CBS not only paid them to keep their mouths shut about it, they also told Tom and Lex on the sly, "Hey if we ever do an All-Star season, you guys will be in the cast for sure. It will just be our little gesture of thanks for not spilling your guts and complaining about how we screwed up the Fallen Comrades challenge."

Again, I should point out that Lex and Tom have never talked about any of this publicly. As far as I know, neither of them have ever even said a word about it. But if you are like me and you hang out around cast members and insiders all the time, you just sort of hear this sort of gossip when it comes to behind the scenes stuff. Let's put it this way. Let's just say that the story of "Lex and Tom were guaranteed a spot on All-Stars" is something I didn't make up, and that I have heard it independently from a number of people over the years. Let's just leave it at that.

Okay, so anyway, back to the Temporal Junction Point.

Without Lex and Tom in the endgame of Africa, that Fallen Comrades error doesn't happen anymore. Or, if it does, it happens to somebody else. And Lex and Tom more than likely are NOT picked to participate in Survivor: All Stars. Okay, maybe one of them MIGHT have been picked. Maybe. But it doesn't seem likely. After all, I need to remind you that Africa was NOT a very popular season at the time, and Lex was never really much of a fan favorite. You take Lex, Tom, and Ethan out of the endgame of Africa, and only one of those guys is picked as an All-Star. One of them, AT MOST. Maybe.

And here is where this all starts to blow your mind.

Let's go to All Stars now, and let's just say that Lex is not there. Let's just say that Boston Rob's best buddy in the history of the world (Lex) is not involved in All Stars. And let's say that there is no pre-game alliance between Lex and Boston Rob. Which means that there is no guarantee that the two of them will work together, and Rob has no allies over on Mogo Mogo when he needs somebody to help save his new girlfriend.

Let's just say that Amber is voted out about midway through All Stars. And that without Amber, Boston Rob no longer has his #1 ally.

Actually, wait a minute. It's even worse than that. Not only does Boston Rob not have his number one ally, he also doesn't have his number two ally. Because Big Tom isn't there either! Big Tom, who was ALSO involved in the alleged pre game alliance between Boston Rob and Lex. Now Rob is missing an entire group of his allies.

Okay, so now let's do the math here.

If Brandon Quinton changes his mind and votes for Lex instead of Kelly in episode eight of Africa, here is what happens. Lex and Tom and Ethan are likely not All Stars. Ethan doesn't win Africa. The first popular winner in Survivor history is probably T-Bird. Oh, and Boston Rob and Amber probably doesn't happen either. I mean, they still probably get married, but they don't dominate All Stars like they did in real life. Amber becomes a forgettable late season boot in All Stars, just like she was a forgettable late season boot in Australia. Boston Rob never becomes a Survivor legend. He probably never comes back for a third or a fourth season either, simply because there is no longer a reason for it.

Oh, and the winner of All-Stars is probably somebody like Jenna Lewis.

I mean, just think of all the dominoes that start falling if something like this changes.

Without Boston Rob as a Survivor legend, there is no need for Russell vs. Boston Rob season in Redemption Island. And without Boston Rob, now there is no one for Phillip Sheppard to emulate. I mean, who is the Specialist going to model himself after in this alternate universe? Is he going to model himself after T-Bird?

And speaking of her, what about T-Bird? Is she now considered the single greatest player in Survivor history? You better believe that if she had won Africa she would have turned into a much bigger deal. And you know she probably would have replaced somebody like Shii Ann in All Stars. And then after All Stars, then what? Does T-Bird become as beloved as Colleen?

Over the years, people have often asked me to get into "what if" Survivor scenarios. And I don't like doing it. Personally, I hate "what if" scenarios, because there are so many ways you can argue them, and they have the potential to just spin off into an infinite number of ridiculous directions. I mean, what if Rudy won Borneo? What then? What does that change about Survivor? What if Tina broke her leg on day two of Australia and Colby won? What then? What if Zoe worked so hard and played so hard that she won Marquesas?

I mean, who knows? What if a meteor fell out of the sky on day six and killed Elisabeth? Who cares.

In general, I don't like "what if" scenarios. In general, I find them annoying. But when you go back to the Brandon vote for Kelly in Africa, well that's different. Because like I said, this really is the Survivor Temporal Junction Point. SO MUCH Survivor history would have changed if Brandon had been feeling a little bit bitchy that day and Lex had annoyed him. All it would have taken was one wrong sentence by Lex, one wrong move, one wrong word, and Brandon essentially kills George McFly. And Biff Tannen becomes the Mayor of Hill Valley. And then everything we know as Survivor fans would have been different.

I'm sorry if this chapter was long, but think about that for a minute. Think of how significant that would have been. One vote. That's all it would have taken. One vote. By a guy who was already impulsive as it was.

I mean, man, I bet you haven't thought of Brandon Quinton in more than a decade. But you will most definitely think of him now.

His vote was the Temporal Junction Point that determined the entire Survivor franchise.

67. Preparing for the Inevitable

As the third season of Survivor started to wind down, and the field narrowed from seven down to six, and six down to five, at this point the goal as a fan was to predict who the winner was going to be. Which player from Survivor: Africa was going to join Richard Hatch and Tina Wesson as the first three luminaries in Survivor history? Whose life was going to change as a result of the million dollars (and the fame) they were about to win on this show?

And do you know what's funny?

Almost nobody at the time predicted that the winner was going to be Ethan.

I know this will be hard to believe now, since obvious winner is obvious, and since Survivor isn't necessarily known for trying to hide their winners anymore, but Ethan's win in Africa really wasn't the slam dunk inevitability that you might think it was. It really did kind of come out of nowhere during that final episode. Well, unless you were familiar with "Follow The Star", of course. But like I said before, that theory really wasn't even all that well known unless you were a regular at Survivor Sucks. And even then, there were many people out there (like me) who knew about it but who didn't think it was all that likely or credible.

No, if you had asked the online Survivor audience who the winner of Africa was going to be, the vast majority of them going into the final five would have predicted that it was going to be Lex. Or Tom. Or, if something went horribly wrong and there were some crazy immunities involved, it could possibly be T-Bird.

Kim Johnson? No way was she ever going to win. In fact, a lot of people forgot that Kim was even a part of the Boran Four Alliance at all. The fact that she would later make it into the final two (against this level of competition!) was just incredible.

And then, of course, there was the fifth player left in the game, Ethan.

Now, as I have said before, Ethan was incredibly popular at the time. The audience loved him. In fact, I would dare say that Ethan might have been even more universally loved than Colby had ever been. I know that is a difficult argument to pull off, but you have to keep in mind that for as many people out there who loved Colby, there were also a bunch of people out there who hated Colby. There were people out there in the fan base who thought he had been an arrogant douche. There were people out there in the fan base who thought he had been a creep to Jerri. There were people out there in the fan base who just hated the Texas flag and all the "I'm proud to be a Texan" stuff. So yes, while Colby Donaldson was incredibly popular and was incredibly beloved at his peak, and for good reason, there were also some very vocal people out there who would have called him a dick.

Now, with Ethan, you never really saw that.

With Ethan, the love for him might not have been as strong as it had been for Colby. And it might not have been as rabid. Rosie O'Donnell might not have gotten all moist just from riding on a motorcycle with him. But with Ethan there was almost NO backlash. There was almost <u>nobody</u> who hated Ethan. I mean, again, Teresa Cooper even said it herself, "What can you say that's bad about Ethan? Nuthin'!"

And for a player to have almost <u>no</u> detractors in the notoriously nasty and finicky online Survivor fan base? Well that's saying something.

So here you had Ethan Zohn, who was probably the first universally liked and respected player since Colleen in Borneo and Rodger in Australia, and he had just made it into the final five. And he was in the majority alliance. That kind of combination just doesn't happen very often. At this point he had a very legitimate shot to make it into the final two and just destroy everybody else in a jury vote.

Yet for some reason there was almost NOBODY out there who thought that was going to happen.

Oh they sure might have <u>wanted</u> it to happen. An Ethan Zohn win in Survivor: Africa would have made so many people happy. In fact, I don't think I have seen another player at any point in Survivor history whose win would have made more people happy. An Ethan Zohn win in 2001? The good guy winning Survivor, for the first time ever? And so soon right after 9/11? Well that is the kind of an ending that a Survivor producer must have been dreaming about.

But again, it isn't what most people thought was going to happen.

I know I keep beating you over the head with this, but what you have to keep in mind when you talk about Survivor from this era is that the producers did NOT tip their hands regarding who the winner was going to be back then. They just didn't do it. In fact, if anything, they would intentionally steer the audience in a direction <u>away</u> from the winner just so that nobody would never be able to predict it. This is a huge fundamental difference between how Survivor was "then" compared to how it is "now." There was just no effort whatsoever to try to portray the season as "the winner's story" back in the early days. And I am guessing that was because the producers were so completely terrified of spoilers at the time. Because the show was still such a big deal to so many people, and because so much revenue money was still involved with the show at this point in time, the producers knew damn well that they would be shooting themselves in the foot if the audience could figure out who the winner would be before the finale aired.

So anyway, we get to the final five of Africa, and here we have these two really big favorites to win. We have Lex and Tom. The two sharpest players in the majority. The two that are running the game. The two that are getting the superstar edits. Naturally, Lex is getting the bigger edit, since he is the favorite to win and all, but if you pay attention and watch Africa again you will notice that Tom actually got a really subtle winner edit as well. In fact, as we neared the end of the season, I actually ranked Tom as #1 in my power rankings a couple of times because I thought that he might be able to sneak out a win. As we got closer and closer to the end of the season, I believed that <u>he</u> might be the super secret Africa winner that the editors were trying to hide behind Lex.

But Ethan?

Well when it comes to Ethan, I NEVER saw him as the potential winner of Africa. Ever. Never ever. He is the only member of the Boran Three (Lex, Tom, Ethan) who I never ranked as #1 in my Africa Power Rankings at any point during the season. And do you want to know why I never saw him as the winner?

Simple.

It's because the winner of Survivor (after two seasons) was always the most cutthroat player in the bunch. Always. It was always the person who played the hardest. It was always the player who clearly wanted it the most. And I'm sorry, but gentle introvert Ethan just wasn't as cutthroat or as obsessively competitive as a Lex or a T-Bird or a Tom were. He just wasn't. As an introvert myself, I can tell you full well that's just not the nature of an introvert. There wasn't a chance that Ethan was ever going to win Survivor over all of these Type-A people.

I know this reasoning must sound odd now, so many years after the fact, but

403

trust me, I was not in the minority on this. Almost <u>nobody</u> was picking Ethan to win. Even his diehard fans weren't predicting he would win. The common belief among Ethan fans at the time was something along the lines of "Wow, I love that guy. What a great guy, it would be so cool if he won. But he is just way too big of a jury threat. I am going to be so heartbroken when Lex cuts his throat right before he gets to the end."

As the days led up to the Africa finale, my pick to win season three was Lex. I was backing my Santa Clara University buddy Lex all the way. With a sneaking suspicion that the winner was actually Tom. I thought it was going to be the funniest thing in the world when Tom Buchanan, the guy who had once stuck a feather in his ass, pulled a Survivor win out of his butt just like he pulled out that feather. And then he was going to stand up there on that winner platform next to Richard and Tina, and Richard Hatch was going to have a heart attack because this big sloppy goat farmer in the overalls was now considered his Survivor peer. That was the ending that I was expecting from Africa. And I thought it was going to be hilarious. I mean, can you imagine? Big Tom Buchanan wins Survivor, and Richard Hatch, the king of Survivor, has to go up there and raise his hand and stand next to him in victory. And meanwhile Tom would probably have a live chicken in his pants. Wouldn't that have been awesome?

I never thought that Ethan was going to win. Most people didn't think that Ethan was going to win. Heck, even people I knew who were in love with Ethan, like my wife Diana and my friend Susan at work, had resigned themselves that he probably wasn't going to win. The talk among the fan base (not all of them, of course, but certainly most of them) leading up to that final episode was generally something like this:

"I know that Lex is going to win, and I am going to hate it. I hate Lex. What I really hope is that Ethan wins."

We had never had the fan favorite win Survivor before. And it looked like we weren't going to have a fan favorite win the third time around either. It looked like the cutthroat pseudo villain was going to defeat the heroes at the end, just like we had seen happen every time on Survivor before. Even after two seasons, you could already see that the audience on the internet was preparing for it. They were lowering their expectations so that when "the wrong person won", just like the wrong person always won, they wanted to be sure that this time they were going to be ready for it.

Again, NO one was expecting that the good guy would win.

And this is exactly why the Survivor Africa finale was such a big moment for the franchise.

68. The Fallen Comrades Screw Up

Now, I already talked about how the producers screwed up at the end of Africa a couple of chapters ago. And how, because they screwed up, they probably cost Lex a win. But this was such an important event in Survivor history that I wanted to dig into it here much more extensively in it its own chapter. After all, in my opinion, you really can't discuss Africa or Africa's place in Survivor history without first knowing about the Fallen Comrades Screw Up. And knowing why it took place. And knowing what the fallout was.

Okay, so here is some backstory for you. Just so you can get into the mindset of exactly what happened and why it happened in the finale of Survivor: Africa.

We are in the final episode, and there are four members of Boran left in the game. There is Lex, the leader. There is Tom, his second in command. There is Ethan, their loyal third. And there is Kim, who... well... who is pretty much only around because her buff was the same color as theirs. And because she has never been a threat to anyone. At this point, all we have left in the game is a rock solid ironclad alliance of three. And then we also have an old lady named Kim. You have the Boran Three, and then you have some lady they live next door to and they like to bring cookies to. There you have it, the final four of Survivor: Africa.

So we get down to the final four, and naturally the immunity challenge at this point in the game is the one that the producers call "Fallen Comrades." This is the challenge where the players are asked trivia questions about each of the players who have been voted out of the game ahead of them. And the player who answers the most questions correctly (aka the person who knew their fallen comrades the best) wins immunity.

Sounds simple, right?

Well it is.

Oh, and why did the producers decide to go with Fallen Comrades at the final four? Well because this is the immunity challenge that the producers ALWAYS did at the end of the game at this point in Survivor history. By the third season of Survivor, this was already a well-known staple of the show. And it would remain a staple of the show for one more season. At least, until Vecepia Towery would break it a season later, and her mastery of it would ensure that the producers would never have any interest in ever using Fallen Comrades as a part of a Survivor season again.

Oops. Sorry, I jumped ahead there. Forget I said that. We'll talk more about Vecepia (one of the most criminally underrated players ever, and in my opinion, maybe the all-time greatest Survivor player) when we get up to her.

So anyway, where was I? Oh yeah. Fallen Comrades at the final four of Survivor: Africa. The point of the game where the Boran Three was just about done finishing off their hapless opponents from Samburu and Boran. All they had to do next was win one more immunity. And take the old lady out of the game. And then at that point it would just be the three of them left standing. Then the proverbial gloves would come off, and when there were only three of them left, may the best man win.

So here we are.

Fallen Comrades begins.

The trivia questions start coming.

And right off the bat it is pretty obvious that the winner is going to be either Lex or Kim. Lex, because he is Lex, and because Lex is awesome. And Kim, because she is smart. Kim has a good memory and she has always paid attention to things.

Lex gets a question right, and Kim gets a question right. Then Kim gets a question right, and Lex gets a question right. Down to the wire they go, it is mano a mano.

> **Side note:** Big Tom was actually tied with both of them going into the final question, but no one remembers that. However, I figured I should mention it here so that I don't get deluged with emails. Yes, I know that Big Tom had six answers correct too. But in the end it really just came down to Lex vs. Kim.

Lex has six right. And Kim has six right. They are tied going into the final question. Whoever gets the next question right will win immunity.

And then we come to one of the most infamous moments in the history of

407

Survivor.

The very last question of Fallen Comrades is **"Which female Survivor does not have anything pierced, including her ears?"**

Lex writes down his answer. Kim writes down her answer. They both know that they are correct. Then Jeff asks them to turn their answers around, to see which one of the two is going to win immunity.

"Lindsey," it says on Lex's tablet.

"Kelly," it says on Kim's tablet.

And just like that, Jeff Probst raises his arm in the air and announces that we have a winner.

"Kim," he says triumphantly, "Congratulations! Kim wins, and she is immune from being voted out tonight."

And with that, Kim Johnson has now won immunity. She has screwed up the plans of the Boran Three. She has forced them to turn on one another a vote earlier than they had originally planned to do so. In fact, she basically just did exactly what Kelly Wiglesworth did to the Tagi Three at the end of Borneo. She screwed up their plans to get rid of her by pulling out an improbable immunity win.

And that means that drama is about to go down really nastily here in Survivor: Africa. Thanks to Kim winning immunity when her back was against the wall, Lex is going to have to turn on Tom a day earlier than he was ever expecting to. Because Kim is immune, that means that shit just got real.

Now of course you know what happened next. Tom was voted out of the game in fourth place. And then Kim won a <u>second</u> improbable immunity the very next day, where she saved her butt again. At which point Lex was voted out of the game. Then Kim faced off against Ethan in the Final Tribal Council, where Ethan beat Kim like she was the proverbial red headed stepchild. And just like that, Ethan Zohn became the first beloved winner in Survivor history.

All of this was well and good. This is all documented fact. There was no controversy about it at all. This was just the ending of Africa.

No, the controversy over the Fallen Comrades Screw Up didn't rear its head until much later.

Okay, now here is what <u>really</u> happened with Fallen Comrades, in case you have never heard the details before. Pull up a seat, because this is going to be good.

It was the night of the Africa live finale. It was January 10, 2002. And, as all Survivor players do on the night of the finale, the cast of Africa were backstage in the green room at CBS Studios, watching the episode. All sixteen castmembers of Survivor: Africa were back there, watching their season of Survivor play out for the first time on TV. And with about five minutes left to go before they went out and took the stage for the live reunion show, we came to the Fallen Comrades scene.

Lex held up his answer for Lindsey, and Probst announced that it was wrong. Probst announced that Kim had won immunity. The Boran Three would be unable to finish the job, and would be unable to vote Kim out of the game tonight.

And right there in the green room behind the stage, Lindsey Richter piped up with a protest about this.

"No," she said, "That's wrong. I don't have any piercings either. Kelly and I both don't have any piercings."

Now I wasn't there in the room when she said this. So I don't know what the reaction was when Lindsey mentioned this. I can only go by what I have been told. But from what I know about Lex, and from what I know about how competitive and how intense he is, I have to believe that the minute he realized he had been screwed out of a million dollars because of a producer mistake, he probably threw a little shit fit.

I mean, put yourself in Lex's shoes. Imagine how close you came to winning Survivor. Imagine how annoying it must have been when Kim Johnson not only won immunity and screwed up your plans, but she actually did it TWICE. Then imagine how you would have felt if it turned out you actually weren't wrong in Fallen Comrades. If your answer had actually been right. And that the only reason the challenge didn't end in a tie, and you moved on to a tiebreaker, was because the producers hadn't done their research well enough.

I don't know about you, but if I were Lex van den Berghe, I would have been

PISSED.

Now, to Lex's credit, he didn't make a big deal about it during the reunion show. If you go back and you watch the Africa reunion, you will notice that Lex actually seemed pretty chill that night. He didn't seem whiny or like a crybaby, and he didn't come off as a poor sport at all. He just sat there and he answered Bryant's questions, and he put on a good face about everything. But he must have been seething. I mean, think about it. He only learned about the Fallen Comrades Screw Up about fifteen minutes before that reunion went live on the air. It could not have been any fresher in his mind. In fact, I can't see any way that it wouldn't have been the only thing he would have been thinking about. He was probably already lawyering up in his head the minute that he learned about it

Now, I know what you're probably thinking. You are probably reading this and wondering, did all that really happen? I mean, I could sit here and say that the producers screwed over my favorite player too. In fact, Mario, I could even write it in a book just like you're doing. I could say anything I wanted about what "really" happened behind the scenes on Survivor, and because most fans don't have any idea what really happens behind the scenes, nobody would ever be able to call B.S. on me. So I bet you are wondering if I am making this up. Maybe I am just inventing some sort of a Survivor conspiracy to explain why my good buddy from my college didn't win Survivor.

Well all I can say about that is this. Do a Google search. Look for "Survivor: Africa" and "Fallen Comrades." Look for "Lex" and "producer mistake" and "payoff." There is no way I am just making this up. It has been documented everywhere. It is even mentioned on the Survivor: Africa Wikipedia page!

Now I don't know exactly what happened when Lex confronted the producers about their mistake. No one really does. I have heard stories about how they paid him $100,000 to stay quiet. I have heard that they may have offered him more. I have also heard that Tom and Lex were BOTH paid $100,000 to stay quiet. And that as part of the deal of the payoff they were also both guaranteed a spot on All Stars. I have heard all of these stories over the years. And personally I don't know which one is them is the 100% God's honest truth. But I do know for a fact that Lex was given a bunch of money by the producers to make up for their mistake. And that Tom was probably paid off as well (after all, if Kim doesn't win immunity at final four, Tom very well could have won Africa too). And I have heard enough gossip over the years to believe that they were probably both guaranteed a spot on All Stars as a gesture of good faith. All of this makes total sense to me, because this is exactly what I would have done if I had been CBS. I would have paid these guys to keep their mouths shut and not make a big stink about it, because we were at a very critical point in the franchise where credibility was still everything. The very LAST thing CBS needed at this point in Survivor history was a second castaway (after Stacey) going to the media and claiming that the show wasn't fair. Had that happened so soon after the Borneo screwjob... I am not exaggerating about this... it very easily could have been the last time that there was ever a Survivor season.

Now here's the funny part. I don't remember exactly when I heard about the Fallen Comrades Screw Up for the first time. It certainly didn't come out right after Africa. In fact I don't remember <u>when</u> I first heard about it. All I remember is that Ethan won Africa, and everyone was happy about it. And then when All Stars came around about three years later, there were rumors that Lex and Tom were promised a spot because of what had happened in Africa. And then all of a sudden everyone on the internet seemed to know about the Fallen Comrades thing.

Unfortunately I can't pinpoint exactly <u>when</u> everyone knew about it. I just remember that all of a sudden, everyone knew. It was weird. One day, there were no scandals to report about Africa whatsoever. And then, the next day, the Fallen Comrades Screw Up was repeated all over the internet as if everyone knew about it. And people weren't even all that outraged about it! That was the strange part. When people talked about it, it was pretty much like this: "Well Lex got screwed at the end of the Africa, so of course he should get a second chance in All Stars. That's only fair." Word of the Fallen Comrades screw really did spread that fast. And there was hardly any outrage about the whole thing at all. It was so bizarre.

Oh, and I'm sure that you are now asking yourself this: Hey wait a minute, if Lex and Tom weren't allowed to talk about the whole thing (which is standard policy for any payoff behind the scenes of a TV show), then why does everyone on the internet seem to know about it? Why is it that you can go to any Survivor website on the internet, and people will talk about how Lex got screwed at the end of Africa and everyone knows this? Why is this such common knowledge when it really isn't supposed to be?

And do you want to know the answer to that?

I don't know!

I have no idea why there is so much info out there about the Fallen

Comrades Screw Up. I have no idea why it is as widely known and as widely reported as it is. It is one of those weird unexplained mysteries that surround the early shady years of the Survivor franchise. Lex and Tom have never really talked about it, yet everyone knows about it. Do you have any idea how that would have happened? If you do, I would like to hear about it.

In any case, YES there was a big scandal at the end of Africa, and YES it probably influenced the history of Survivor. In a very big way. And if you have never heard about it before, well now you have.

Did the Fallen Comrades Screw Up cost Lex van den Berghe a million dollars? Well there's no way to know. I mean, even if he gets that last question right he is still tied with Mama Kim. He still has to beat her in at least one more question if he wants to win immunity. And you know that Kim might not have been all that great at a lot of stuff, but she sure had a really good teacher's memory. And even if Lex DOES win immunity that night, he still has to beat Tom and Ethan in the final immunity challenge. Which would have been tough, what with his famous gut being overrun by elephant shit germs and all.

In the end, I'm not sure if the Fallen Comrades Screw Up really affected the end of Africa. But I also don't know that it didn't. No one is ever going to know. All I know for sure is that it definitely affected the casting of All Stars, and it definitely affected how All Stars would play out. Because the producers screwed up at the end of Africa, Lex was cast in All Stars, Tom was cast in All Stars, a pre-game alliance was made between Lex, Tom, and Boston Rob, and it affected just about everything that would happen in Survivor after the seventh season. So yes, I would say that the Fallen Comrades Screw Up was a pretty significant important Survivor moment.

Of course I still don't think it was as big a deal as Ethan winning was.

And I guess it is time to talk about that now.

P.S. There have been many Survivor fans over the years who have pointed out that Fallen Comrades (which was once a well-known Survivor staple) has never been used on the show since the Africa debacle. And most people will claim it was because the producers screwed up. The general belief out there is that the producers were so concerned that they might cost another player a

412

million dollars because a question might have more than one correct answer, and they wouldn't be aware of it, that they decided to move away from memory challenges and get rid of Fallen Comrades altogether. In fact, if you look around the internet, you will see that a lot of Survivor websites will report this statement as fact. They will often say "Because the producers screwed up in Africa, Fallen Comrades was never used again on the show."

Well first off, I don't necessarily agree with that. I mean, Fallen Comrades was never used again after they discovered the mistake in Africa (which, again, was only discovered when it aired on TV, which was after it had already been used and filmed in Marquesas). But it WAS used again in Marquesas. And it was in Marquesas, like I said before, where a woman named Vecepia Towery basically broke the challenge and ensured that it could never be used on Survivor again.

And how did Vecepia break Fallen Comrades?

Easy. Because she knew it was coming at the end of the game, because it always came at the end of the game, she basically spent the entire game in Marquesas preparing for it. While the other players brought less practical items to the island as their personal luxury items, Vecepia brought a pen and a journal. And she spent the entire game writing down everyone's personal details so that she could ace Fallen Comrades. And then when she got to the final four and Fallen Comrades appeared, just like it always did, guess who won? Well hey, it was aced by THE FIRST PLAYER WHO WAS SMART ENOUGH TO BRING A JOURNAL AND JUST WRITE ALL THE ANSWERS DOWN.

So anyway, if you asked ME why there is no Fallen Comrades anymore, I think that only about 20% of that is because the producers screwed up in Africa. I think the other 80% was caused by Vecepia, who basically broke the challenge and ensured that there was no way they could ever use it on Survivor anymore. Because now people would be smart enough to just write down all the answers ahead of time.

You will hear me say this many many times in the upcoming chapters on Marquesas, but this is just one of many reasons why I say Vecepia was awesome. She was so good at Survivor that she broke it.

69. Meeting My First Survivor

January 10, 2002-- the night of the Africa finale-- was a magical night. In fact, there are some who would argue that the Africa finale is maybe the most unheralded of all the great episodes of Survivor. It never makes anyone's list of The 20 Best Episodes in Survivor History, but I am one of those people who have always argued that it should. Because it really is that good. Go buy the season on DVD (or track it down on the internet) and watch the finale again for yourself some time. It is really outstanding.

It also features the huge fan favorite winning Survivor for the first time ever. Which, again, I know I have pounded on this before, is something that simply cannot be overlooked in the overall history of the franchise. Survivor desperately needed a player like Ethan to win the game the third time around. They desperately needed a fan favorite to win after the underwhelming wins (from a fan relations point of view) of Richard and Tina. They desperately needed an Ethan to come around when he did, and they were lucky that they got one.

Oh, but before we get to the importance of Ethan's win. I have a little story to share with you.

While January 10, 2002 is a very important date in the history of Survivor, it was also a very important week in my own personal history as a Survivor writer. Because that happened to be the very first day that I ever met a Survivor contestant. Yes, I know it is hard to believe, being that I was the guy who developed so many connections to Survivors over the years and I have had so many interactions with the players on a personal level. But even after writing to Nick Brown and Lex van den Berghe for the past year over snail mail and email, I still had never actually MET either of them. It wasn't until the week of the Africa finale that I ever actually met my very first Survivor contestant.

Okay, let me set the scene for you. It was the week of the Africa finale (the second week of January, 2002), and I knew that the reunion was going to be taped on Thursday, January 10th. Remember, this was back before CBS aired the finale on a Sunday. Back in the early days of the show they still showed the Survivor finale on a weekday.

The reunion that year was scheduled to be taped in Los Angeles, at CBS Studios. And because I already lived in Southern California... and because I knew that CBS usually flew the Survivor alumni and their families into L.A.

414

so they could attend the reunion... well you can see where my mind was going to go here. I figured, well if I just go out to some of the popular tourist sites around L.A. that weekend and hang out, odds are I will run into at least one Survivor alumnus. I mean, if you were flying into L.A. with your family and you had a couple of days to hang out, wouldn't you want to do all the tourist stuff? Remember, this was years before the show would only cast people who were actors and who already lived in Los Angeles. In the third season they were still casting everyday people from all over the country. Which meant that since they didn't already <u>live</u> in L.A., you were bound to find these people doing L.A. tourist stuff with their families in the days before and after the finale.

And with that thought in mind, it was decided. My wife and I had never met a Survivor player before, and we wanted to. So we looked at a map of L.A., and we tried to determine what was the most likely place somebody like Ethan or Richard or Tina would take their family if they were in town and they wanted to walk around and do tourist things.

After a little bit of deliberation, we decided on the Santa Monica Pier. After all, it was January, and most of the players who would be flying into L.A. that week would be flying in from other, much colder, parts of the country. And I figured, well if I was flying in from a place where it was thirty degrees out this time of year, and if I came to L.A., which is pretty much the only place in the country where it is eighty degrees out on Christmas, wouldn't I want to experience the novelty of going to the beach the first week of January? If you were a tourist in L.A. in January, isn't that what YOU would want to do?

And so that was what we did. We watched the Africa finale on Thursday the 10th. Ethan won, yay. All was right in the world. Then, on Saturday, January 12th, when all the alumni who had attended the reunion were still in town and probably hadn't flown back home yet, we headed out to the Santa Monica Pier. I figured, okay there is about a 50% chance that at least one of the 50+ Survivors who are in town this weekend are probably going to be out here walking around the boardwalk today.

I didn't have complete confidence in this plan, but hey, it was a plan. And I didn't have a better plan. I figured, well if nothing else, at least we can say we got a day at the beach out of the deal. At the very least I could come home with a suntan and maybe a corn dog.

My wife and I arrived at the Santa Monica Pier around 10 A.M. that Saturday. We plopped ourselves down on a bench and we decided to do a little bit of people watching.

And I kid you not. We weren't there for more than about TEN SECONDS when I spotted a Survivor walking around.

"Oh hey," I said, very casually. "There's Rudy."

Sure enough, my plan to meet my first Survivor could not have worked out any better. I have no idea which deity was smiling down upon us that day, or what kind of a lottery we had managed to win (remember, there was no such thing as a big reality charity event back in those days, there was no way a fan could interact with a Survivor unless you had very good connections through CBS, and I certainly didn't), but there he was. There was Rudy Boesch walking around the Santa Monica Pier with his wife Marge. Right there in person. Arguably the most popular out of any of the Survivors from the first three seasons, aside from maybe Colleen.

A huge celebrity.

And here he was, about thirty feet away from me.

"What should we do?" my wife asked. "Should we bother him?"

Hell yeah we should bother him. I mean, why else are we here? Screw decorum and manners and general politeness. We came here to meet a Survivor!

"HEY RUDY!" I yelled loudly. And I waved my hand at him.

Rudy looked over at me and he looked a little surprised. I don't think he was used to being recognized out in public. He raised his hand and he waved back to me.

"WE'RE BIG FANS OF YOURS!" I said.

Now unfortunately I hadn't really planned what else I was going to do if I actually met a Survivor. I would love to say that I had this all mapped out down to the last detail, how I was going to tell him that I loved the show, and how I wrote a column about it, and how I had a whole little speech prepared. And how Borneo was awesome. But unfortunately I am not a planner, and I really hadn't planned this at all. I had no idea who I was going to meet, or if I was even going to meet a Survivor at all. So I just blurted out the very first thing that came into my brain.

"RUDY, I ALSO HAVE A PROBLEM WITH QUEERS!"

Ha ha. Okay, no, I didn't actually say that. It would have been funny if I had though. Yeah I'm sure that would have gone over really well at family fun day on the Santa Monica Boardwalk. No, what I really yelled to Rudy was something stupid like this:

"GO RUDY! YOU WERE OUR FAVORITE!"

I know, I know. I'm embarrassed. But that's all I came up with. Trust me, my interactions with Survivors got a lot better after this.

Rudy (and Marge, of course) walked towards us, and we exchanged some pleasantries with him. I don't really remember what we said, but it was nothing substantial. I would like to say I got some juicy dirt out of him about how the producers had rigged Borneo, or the truth about if Kelly Wiglesworth really did sleep with a cameraman in exchange for a sandwich. But again, I was so star struck that I don't think we actually talked about anything of interest. I believe we told him we were big fans of his, and that we loved Survivor. And that we wished he would have beaten Richard. And then Rudy and I had beautiful homosexual sex right there on the pier. Actually, no, that last part probably didn't happen. I am pretty sure we just said hi, and that we loved him, and then we said goodbye because we didn't want to bother him. The whole interaction couldn't have lasted more than a minute.

But hey, I had just met my first Survivor. My plan had worked. I was on cloud nine. This was a pretty big deal.

It wasn't until about five minutes later that my wife realized the problem with what had just happened.

"Oh crap," she said, after Rudy and his wife had walked away from us and had faded back into the crowd. "We never even acknowledged his wife. We probably should have actually said hi to her."

Uh. Yeah. Oops.

Maybe that had been kind of rude.

So anyway, there you go. The very first time I ever met a Survivor. We never saw another one around the Santa Monica Pier that day, nor did we see another Survivor at any of the other places we went looking for them the

417

entire rest of the weekend. But hey, we got to see Rudy. And we even got to indirectly insult his wife. I don't know if we actually <u>did</u>, but I definitely felt bad about it. In fact the very next time I met a Survivor in person (Lex, a year later at the Thailand finale), the very first thing I did was I said hi to his wife.

See, I promise I got better at this.

70. The Importance of Being Ethan

If there is one hard and fast rule you can use to accurately describe the first two seasons of Survivor, it is this: They were amazing TV. The first two seasons of Survivor were far and away better than just about anything else that network TV had to offer between the years 2000 and 2001. This show was so much bigger and better than anything else on TV, in fact, that it pretty much dominated the world of popular culture for about a year and a half. Right down to the fact that Saturday Night Live-- the most celebrated parody TV show of the past forty years-- famously refused to ever do a parody of it. Yes, that's right. As I have mentioned before, Lorne Michaels (the producer of SNL) referenced this in an interview right around this time in 2001. He said that he would never do a parody of Survivor on his show. Why? Well because even as early as 2001 he felt that Survivor parodies and Survivor popular culture references were already all played out.

Oh, and he has STILL never done a parody of Survivor on SNL, and it is now fourteen years later. Shows you how much things haven't changed over the years.

So that was Survivor's legacy. It was the show that had completely taken over network TV. It was the show that had completely taken over pop culture. It was the show that completely changed everything about the way that TV shows were cast, the way they were marketed, and the way they were scripted. It was the show that was making a mockery out of traditional scripted television.

And all this, despite the fact that it hadn't actually produced a popular winner yet.

Yes, and now here we are. The skeleton in the closet of Survivor history. The red headed stepchild in Survivor's legacy, if you will. The fact that a huge chunk of the Survivor fan base wasn't very happy with the two people who had won so far.

To me, this has always been one of the most fascinating aspects of Survivor history. I mean, think about this for a second. Survivor was making history left and right. It was the show that followed the Super Bowl. It was the show that smacked down Friends and kept it from becoming the biggest and only juggernaut show of its era. It was the show that was so popular, it was so goddamn popular, that it actually got Colleen Haskell (who had no acting experience whatsoever!) the lead role in a major motion picture. I mean, you laugh at The Animal now, but that was a major movie starring a pretty big comedy star at the time. That was an A list movie. And Survivor was such a big deal at the time that they cast a completely untested, completely underqualified Survivor alum as their female lead. Tell me another TV show that could have had that kind of impact on pop culture in America.

So yes, Survivor was huge. Survivor was everywhere. Survivor was as popular as it would ever be. And this is amazing when you take into account the fact that SURVIVOR HAD YET TO ACTUALLY PRODUCE A SATISFYING ENDING YET!

Again, just think about that for a second. Think of how big Survivor would have been if America hadn't hated Richard. Think of how big Survivor would have been if people hadn't been meh about Tina. Or hadn't been actively calling her a c-word all over the internet, like they were doing in 2001 on lot of the nastier message boards. Imagine if Colleen or Rudy had won Borneo. Imagine if Colby or Rodger or Elisabeth had won Australia. I mean, if Elisabeth Filarski had won Australia they might as well have put her right up there on Mount Rushmore. Had the endings of Borneo or Australia been even <u>slightly</u> satisfying, Survivor would have reached heights that would have been even more staggering than the ones that we saw. And that is saying something.

But they had not been satisfying. Richard and Tina had not been popular winners. Neither one became much of a celebrity at all. And this was a huuuuge black eye if you were a fan of the franchise.

After two seasons, Survivor's legacy was already shaping up to be "that show that was bigger than anything else on TV, where people were stranded on an island and they had to vote each other out. And then at the end, all the good people were gone and the best of the worst got the money pretty much by default."

I know that will be a little jarring to read if you aren't familiar with Survivor history, but it is totally the truth. Most of the audience in 2000 considered Richard to be a cowardly asshole who had lied and cheated. A good chunk of the audience in 2001 (especially on the internet) considered Tina to be the bitch who had gone through Kel's bag and who was faker than crap. I didn't happen to agree with either one of those descriptions, I have always been a big fan of both Richard AND Tina. But I knew full well that I was in the minority among the general fan base at the time. Trust me, no one knows what Richard and Tina's reputations were like in 2000 and 2001 better than a guy who spent 50% of my time back then trying to defend them. And being repeatedly made fun of and crapped on and shot down because I would defend such terrible people.

So that was the legacy of seasons one and two. Oh, it would change over time. Over the years Richard and Tina would eventually be seen as the elder statesmen of Survivor. The two who had invented the game. Two of the most deserving and most respected winners in Survivor history.

But at the time?

At the time they were Machiabelly the embarrassing fat naked guy. And Tina, the fake bitch who only won because Colby had mommy issues.

Survivor was desperate to crown a winner that the audience actually liked. Survivor was desperate to prove that they could finish a season strong, with an ending that actually satisfied everyone. At this point in time, it was that one all important variable that still eluded the franchise. It was the one all important variable that many people (including me) thought might be impossible to get. In fact, I was actually starting to worry by the third season that Survivor was going to run out of steam very quickly if it got three unpopular winners in a row. There was a very real chance that if it happened a third consecutive time, the audience might start to think "Well screw this, this is annoying" and they might give up on the franchise and turn their attention elsewhere. After all, it's not like America (after 9/11) wasn't already starting to turn their back on reality TV. If it had happened a third straight time to Survivor, the timing could have been disastrous.

> **Side note #1:** How sure was I that Ethan wasn't going to win Survivor: Africa? Well as the season went along, and I started to add more and more commentary to my Power Rankings at the bottom of my recaps, (I have mentioned this before) I came up with a theory that explained who I believed could and who never could win Survivor. My theory was called "Mario's Theory." And, well, in retrospect it is a little embarrassing. However, I stood behind my theory 100% at the time, because I really did believe it would predict the future of Survivor.
>
> What was Mario's Theory? What was the formula that I touted so heavily in my early Survivor recaps, and which blew up really badly in my face about six weeks later? Well Mario's Theory simply stated that **no one younger than 30 would ever win Survivor**. At the time, I just didn't believe that a young person would ever have the

patience or the foresight or the single minded focus and determination necessary to be able to outlast all of the older people. After Richard (39) and Tina (40) won the game, and after Colby (26) chose ethics over dominance, I was pretty sure that you had to be over 30 to ever be able to finish a win all the way to the end. And that is why I was 100% behind Lex going into that Africa finale. Or, to be more specific, it is why I was 100% behind the winner being anyone but Ethan. Shows how much I know.

Side note #2: Oh and before anyone accuses me of ageism, I wasn't just some crusty old man when I came up with Mario's Theory. I was 27 years old. I didn't think I could have ever won Survivor either.

Okay, so Mario's Theory didn't work out for me. Here I was, in my very first season as a Survivor writer, and my very first theory that I had been hyping for weeks completely blew up in my face. And it made me look like an idiot. But I didn't care. Because Ethan won. Ethan won. Good God Almighty, we are free at least, we are free not to eat ham at last, a good guy had won. How awesome was that?

Seriously, there is no way I can relate to you in writing what a big deal it was that Ethan won Survivor: Africa. This is one of those moments that NEVER gets mentioned as one of the all-time great Survivor moments, but for me it is right up there. It has to be up there. It was such a big deal. I mean, Lex was no more popular among the fan base than Tina had been. Not after what he did to Kelly, he wasn't. And if Lex had been the third Survivor winner? Right after a hated winner, and then a meh winner, and then 9/11, and then America completely turning its back on Survivor? Well even if you weren't there at the time I am sure you can imagine what a blow that would have been to the franchise. And believe me, I am a Lex fan. I am one of the biggest Lex fans. Dude went to Santa Clara. His dad was my French teacher. Yet I was right up there next to my wife, cheering and pumping my fist in the air when Ethan won Africa.

There is really not much more I can say about it. The good guy won. The nice guy won. For the first time ever in Survivor history, the fan favorite won. This was a really big deal.

There are so many little moments that happened during the early years of Survivor, where you can look at them and think "Well if x had happened a

422

different way", or "if y had been voted out instead of the person who wound up being voted out", it would have altered the franchise. Certainly the Temporal Junction Point at Brandon's decision in Africa was a really big deal. And of course Mike falling into the fire had been a really big deal too. And so was Colby choosing Tina at the end of Australia, and Greg winning immunity and ensuring that Gretchen would be the first person voted out after the merge in Borneo. And of course the Tagis ~~being persuaded by the producers~~ choosing on their own to vote out Stacey instead of Rudy. All of these were really big moments that clearly impacted the future of Survivor.

But nobody EVER mentions Ethan winning as one of those moments. Nobody EVER mentions that the first really popular winner in Survivor history was a pretty big deal. Nobody EVER mentions that, for a long time, Ethan Zohn was right up there along with Colby and Rudy as the three most popular male Survivor players ever.

People have asked me this question a lot over the last couple of months. They ask me, Mario, why do you feel the need to write a Survivor book? I mean, what is there about Survivor history that you want to talk about that hasn't already been written about by dozens of other people? What could you possibly say about Survivor history that hasn't already been documented at least a thousand times before?

Well now you know. Here is one of things that I wanted to write about.

I want to point out that Ethan winning Survivor was a big deal. It was a really big deal. And it happened right at the time when the franchise needed a popular winner. They <u>desperately</u> needed somebody like Ethan to finally win Survivor, just to prove to the skeptics that they could actually pull it off. Because believe me, I was NOT the only one out there who doubted that Survivor would ever be able to do it. I was just as sure as 99% of the audience at the time that Survivor would always be this great and wonderful and fantastic example of a new type of game show... that in the end would always produce a winner that would (at best) divide the audience.

But Ethan did not divide the audience. Ethan was the ultimate Survivor good guy. And that was a significant accomplishment for a show that had never actually had one before.

It is time he finally gets some credit for what an important player he was.

423

71. Africa's Legacy

So, in the end, what is the legacy of Survivor: Africa?

Well for starters, it is a season that was NOT popular at the time. I mean, take away the euphoria of Ethan winning, take away the awesome fall of Silas and the fall of the Samburu Mallrats, and you have a season that would have been universally considered the worst season of Survivor until about season nine. In fact, even with those two awesome variables (Ethan and the fall of Silas), it was still considered the worst overall season of Survivor for a very long time. Yes, you heard me right. For years, a lot of fans on the internet would have even ranked it behind even Thailand and Vanuatu. And trust me, those were two seasons (at the time) that were just completely and universally crapped on. Unjustly crapped on, I might add, but we will talk more about them later.

So yes, Africa was not a very popular season at the time. Due to a combination of bad timing airing right after 9/11, a TV watching populace that was just sort of burnt out on reality TV in general, a dry dusty location where the players were clearly miserable and were not having very much fun, and... I hate to say this, but it's true... a lot of fans who just really didn't like Lex, it was never really embraced the way that Australia and Borneo had been. And to me that is a huge shame. Because if you ask me, Africa is clearly the best of the first three Survivor seasons. I just think it had everything. But it was never really embraced at the time. And if Ethan hadn't won, wow, I can't even imagine how reviled it would have been. In fact I don't even want to imagine a scenario where Ethan didn't win the third season of Survivor. Let's just move on and talk about something else.

The good news, of course, is that for as reviled as Africa was at the time (and it really was, I am not making this up), its reputation seems to have done a complete 180 as the years have passed. There have been very few seasons over the years who have had their reputations change as drastically as Africa's has. Nowadays, if you go and you ask people on the internet about the early days of Survivor, you are just as likely to hear people say that they love Africa as you are to hear them say that Africa sucks. And that is very heartwarming to me. In fact, in the informal poll I took among people who I would consider Survivor "history experts" a couple of weeks ago, I asked one hundred people what they thought of Survivor: Africa. And 91 out of 100 of them said it was a fantastic season. 91 out of 100! I mean, my God. If that isn't the sign of a season with a magnificent turnaround, I don't know what is. These days Africa is as popular as it has ever been. And yes, I know that isn't saying much. But still, a turnaround is a turnaround. In fact, that would be the most dramatic Survivor season reputation turnaround I have ever seen if there hadn't been a season called Survivor: Vanuatu.

Yes, I promise we will talk about Vanuatu later. I promise. Lord knows I have more to say about that season than about just about any of them. Just trust me on this.

So anyway, that is the first part of Survivor: Africa's legacy. It is the season that was completely crapped on at the time, yet somehow turned it around and eventually became beloved by the fan base. Not by everyone, of course. I know for a fact that about 20% of the people who are reading this chapter are probably shaking their heads right now and saying that I am an idiot. And that Africa still sucks. But meh, whatever. Who cares. Africa is an awesome season and you Stiffly Stiffersons out there can't crap all over it anymore. I wish I could take the high road on this, but I can't. Nyah nyah nyah nyah nyah. Africa won.

> **Side note:** At the end of the book I will write an addendum where I rank my top ten favorite seasons. I think you will be surprised where I rank Africa. In fact, I am pretty sure there is almost nobody out there who thinks as highly about Survivor: Africa as I do. Except for maybe Ethan's mom I guess.

Okay, and now we come to the second part of Survivor: Africa's legacy. And to me, this is the bigger one.

Ready for this?

To me, Survivor: Africa will be remembered as the season where the producers simply went too far. It is the season where they came the closest to almost killing someone. I mean, go back and rewatch Africa sometime, and look at how bleak those conditions were. Look at how hot it was every day. Look at how isolated it was. Look at how little water the players were allowed to have. Look at how close to danger those players were every single minute of the day. Do you remember that scene where the players were walking around outside their fence and they came face to face with a cape buffalo? Do you remember those scenes where all a lion had to do was hop over the boma at night and it could have eaten Ethan and Little Kim for dinner? Do you know that the producers had very little security in place that would have been able to stop that? That was some real shit those players were facing in Africa. That was as hardcore as Survivor ever got. I mean, my God, the players drank water that was saturated with elephant crap. Do you know how dangerous that is?? When Lex came home from Survivor: Africa, he had so many parasites living in his body that he was on antibiotics for a looooong time. And I am not making that up. Read an old interview with Lex some time, read how messed up his body was when he came back from Africa. The producers came so close to killing somebody that season that it is amazing that they didn't actually do it. Again, think back to that scene where Lindsey got so dehydrated that she had a kidney attack in the middle of a 200 degree workday. Africa was so hardcore that they might as well have named a WWE belt after it.

I know I am exaggerating a little bit but... actually no... no, I'm not. Playing Survivor in Africa was no joke. Those players' bodies very nearly shut down out there. And coming right after Australia, which was also hardcore and which ALSO very nearly had contestants' bodies shut down and go into shock? In fact I have heard rumors that Elisabeth actually did start to shut down. Rodger Bingham once told me she came much closer to dying than we actually saw on TV. He told me her body literally started the process of beginning to die.

After the escalating harshness of Borneo to Australia to Africa, if Survivor had continued on the homicide mission that it seemed to be going on, we probably would have seen some very bad things happen to the players around season four or five. If Survivor had tried to up the ante after what they did to the players in Africa, I imagine we might still all be talking about the season four lawsuit today.

However, luckily for us (and very luckily for the players in season four), that isn't what happened. Survivor four didn't turn out to be the most intense and the harshest season of them all. No, Survivor four went back to the beach. The producers made a very specific effort to make the conditions less harsh starting in season four, because I think they knew as well as anyone how lucky they had gotten in Africa. They had played a very dangerous game of Russian Roulette with sixteen lives out in the middle of Kenya. And I think if you asked any Survivor producer still working today what they thought of that third season, I think they would probably tell you the same thing that I just said. I think they would probably admit, "Yeah, that was the season that we went too far. That was the season that we really got lucky."

Side note: Of course we can't give the producers 100% credit for their decision to go "less harsh" starting in season four. Obviously, a lot of that was caused by 9/11, and because the producers had to make an emergency decision to not set the season in Jordan anymore. And because Tahiti was the only backup location they had that they could use. So let's not say the producers were that benevolent in this particular case. "Survivor 4: Back to the Beach" was only thrown together because it was easy to do.

So those are the biggest things when it comes to Africa's legacy. It was the first season that was unpopular at the time. It was also the season that had one of the biggest reputation turnarounds over time. It was also the harshest that Survivor ever got, and in my opinion it was the season where the producers finally crossed the line and they went too far. After Africa, after Lex nearly died from ingesting thirty consecutive days' worth of elephant crap, Survivor would never be that brutal again.

On the flip side, Survivor: Africa was the season with the first popular winner. It was also the season with the very first Twist. Which, like it or not, really infused a lot of new energy into the show. That Twist episode (Africa, episode five) is one that people were talking about the time, and it is an episode that Survivor fans still talk about enthusiastically today. In my opinion, it is one of the single most important Survivor episodes of all time.

And hey, there is some more important legacy stuff when it comes to Survivor: Africa too. It was the first Survivor season that I ever wrote about!

As the season wrapped up, as I prepared to put down my pen (okay, my keyboard) for the season and wrap up my very first season as a Survivor columnist, I was proud that I was starting to make a name for myself in the Survivor fan community. Oh, I certainly wasn't as well-known as I would be in about six months. And I was nowhere near as popular as I would be in about a year and a half. But still, it was something. If you would later become a fan of the Funny 115, or my Fallen Comrades Parodies, or my All Star Stories, or of the Survivor Historians podcast, or of any of my Survivor writings whatsoever, well it all started here. It all started because I was the first guy on the internet to do something called the Survivor Power Rankings.

And so that was that. Survivor: Africa was in the books, and we were prepared to move on to the fourth season. One that would turn out to be amazing. One that would feature an episode midway through the season that would completely change everything that fans thought they knew about the

427

game of Survivor.

Marquesas (season four) would turn out to be the game changer.

Honestly, I wish I could sit here and write about fifty more chapters about Marquesas. I wish I could do that, because I think it is maybe the most important Survivor season. It is also one of my two favorite Survivor seasons. Yet, sadly, it is a season that I think most Survivor fans have not really ever learned to appreciate yet.

I wish I could write about fifty more chapters, but I can't.

Because my Marquesas love will have to wait until the next book.

P.S. I know I have mentioned this before, but since we are wrapping up Africa for good I better mention it one last time. If you are a fan of comedy, you have to go back and rewatch Africa. And you have to pay attention to one the greatest season-long storylines of all time, the story of Lex's gut. Watch what a big role Lex's gut plays throughout the course of the season. Watch how many decisions he makes based on what his gut is telling him. And watch how many times his gut turns out to be wrong. Watch how Lex's gut figuratively (and literally) costs him the game of Survivor. Oh, and then just to drive the point home, watch the final episode of the season where he loses the final three challenge and he winds up being voted out of the game.

Remember why Lex lost that challenge?

Well he lost because he drank too much elephant crap the night before. He lost because he got amoebic dysentery.

When most people think of Lex getting amoebic dysentery in Africa, the very first thing they think of is "Ha! Lex warned us about amoebic dysentery way back in episode one! He foreshadowed his defeat way back in his very first confessional. Ha ha, the editors were so hilarious in the way that they foreshadowed that!"

But when I think of Lex's defeat in Africa, I think of it a different way. I think of it as, "Well Lex's gut cost him all game. I guess it might as well have cost him in the end too. Lex's gut was the biggest game changer this side of Russell Hantz. It literally shit away his chances during that final immunity challenge."

I know, I'm sorry. I'm sure Lex hates me now. But come on, that is one of the single greatest Survivor story arcs of all time. You have to appreciate that.

P.P.S. Okay I gotta say this. It has been bugging me for years. It drives me crazy that Ethan Zohn's only legacy over the last couple of years has been "the guy who fought cancer."

Yes, Ethan has been valiantly fighting lymphoma. Yes, he is an amazing survival story. Yes, he is tremendously inspirational. But it drives me crazy that THAT is the only thing that people remember about him when it comes to Survivor. I mean, come on people, Ethan was the FIRST POPULAR WINNER IN SURVIVOR HISTORY. Why isn't that a bigger deal? That should be a HUGE deal when it comes to his Survivor legacy. But no, no one ever seems to remember that. No one seems to remember that he was once as big a deal as Colby was. Or Rupert was. People only remember him as the guy who got sick. And I'm sorry, but if I was Ethan I would be a little bit pissed about that.

I know Ethan is too polite to ever come right out and say it, so I guess I will be the guy who has to say it. Ethan is a major, major figure in Survivor history, and it is a shame that no one seems to ever treat him like that. I mean, look at what that guy did with his winnings. He started a soccer foundation for at-risk kids in Africa. He put his money where his mouth was. He took all his Survivor winnings and he invested them in charity, just like he said he was going to do. He went out and he actually made a difference. Tell me how many other Survivor winners have actually done that over the years. Ethan is so far up the "great guys in history" scale compared to just about any other Survivor winner that it isn't even funny.

Is it a big story that Ethan got cancer? Of course. Am I a huge Ethan fan? Of course, and I have been for years. Is it inspirational, how he has fought cancer? Absolutely. The guy has gone through a hell that few of us will ever

429

experience. He is amazing, and he deserves all the respect that he gets.

All I am saying is, let's put this guy up on a pedestal where he belongs, right up there next to Hatch and Boston Rob and Rupert and Parvati. As a player. As a big deal. As a first ballot Survivor Hall of Famer. As a guy who means (and who has always meant) an awful lot to the Survivor franchise.

I am tired of the only thing you ever hear about Ethan being "What a sad story, he got sick." Don't you think he deserves to be remembered for a little bit more than that?

72. Bonus Chapter: FAQ about Survivor: Arabia

I wasn't really going to delve too much into Survivor: Arabia (the mythical fourth season that was later changed to Survivor: Marquesas), but it crossed my mind right before I published this book that there were a bunch of questions people might have about it that I don't feel like answering over and over again in emails. So here is what I know to be true about Survivor: Arabia, and how much of the other stuff out there is B.S.

Question #1: Was an official logo ever designed for Survivor: Arabia?

Answer: I don't know. I have heard mixed responses about this. If you look around the internet, especially on Survivor Sucks, and you do a search for Survivor: Arabia, you will find all sorts of logos floating around out there. Some of them even look pretty legit. However, it is my opinion that every logo I have ever seen has probably been created by a fan. I don't personally think CBS and Burnett ever came up with an official logo, I think Arabia was canceled long before it could actually get to that stage. Again, I could be wrong about this, but at this point who really knows. There are logos that have been floating around the internet for more than a decade that have routinely been referred to as "the official logo." Were they really the official logo? Who knows. Even back in 2002 I don't think anyone knew.

> **Side note:** I actually got a little more clarification about this question right before I published this book. According to a person who would know this stuff, some sort of a logo for Survivor: Arabia WAS created by the Art Department, but it was never actually approved by SEG or CBS. So no formal logo (or informal logo) for Survivor: Arabia was never released. Anything you have ever seen on the internet is simply fan-made.

Question #2: When did the fans learn about Survivor: Arabia? Was it well known when Marquesas was airing?

Answer: This is one of those questions that I can only answer from personal experience. I can only say when I personally first heard about it. And I don't remember hearing about it during season four. I only remember hearing about it a little while later, during Thailand. So for me that is my answer. I could be wrong about that, but I only remember hearing that Marquesas was supposed to be set in Jordan a little while after the fact. I remember Burnett casually mentioned it during some interview at some point in late 2002. He mentioned, "Oh yeah, by the way, we came <u>this</u> close to filming in the Middle East but we had to cancel it because of 9/11." And when I heard that, in the immortal words of Sandra Diaz-Twine, when I heard it I was like ohhhhhh shit.

Question #3: Is it true that Survivor was becoming too harsh, and they only canceled Jordan because they were afraid that somebody was going to die out there?

Answer: No. I mean sure that might have been their thought process at the time (it certainly is my thought process now. Survivor in a desert? Are you nuts??). But I have never heard any explanation for the switch other than "We were going to film there, but because of 9/11 and all the tensions in the region, we decided it would be a bad idea."

Now, personally, as weird as it is to say this, I think 9/11 was actually good for Survivor because it forced the producers to stop focusing on the harshness of the environment, and it forced them to focus on fun and the adventure and the excitement again like they had done with Borneo. If 9/11 hadn't happened I honestly think they would have kept ramping up the location intensity until they had managed to hospitalize (or literally kill) one of their players. But was Jordan canceled because the seasons were getting too harsh? No. This is maybe the only thing you can say in American history that 9/11 was actually good for. It made the Survivor producers focus back on the fun again.

Also, just as an aside, most of the Survivor fans at the time had no idea that Africa and Australia had been so harsh on the players. I mean, we knew about Mike falling in the fire, obviously, but a lot of the other extreme medical issues (such as with Elisabeth and Lex) had been hidden from the public. So while it was true that seasons 2 and 3 WERE getting way too harsh for the players, most Survivor fans at the time wouldn't have been aware of that.

Question #4: I heard that Jordan was canceled because fans weren't happy with the dry bleak setting in Africa. Because Africa sucked the producers wanted to go back to the water and get the fan base back on their side again.

Answer: Well there is probably some truth to that answer. The fans really didn't like Africa at the time. But that had nothing to do with why Jordan changed to Marquesas. Again, it was only because of 9/11. Remember, Survivor was as much a travel porn show as it was a strategy game back in the early days. Half the fun of the show back then was seeing what amazing exotic locations the producers came up with that the players would be thrown out into the middle of. Africa might not have been a very well loved season, true, but it certainly wasn't because of the location. The location was awesome. And Jordan would have been a pretty kickass location too. At least, up until the point that a player actually died, of course.

Question #5: Hey Mario, you're from Seattle. I love when Jordan took apart the Seattle Supersonics and killed you guys in the '96 NBA playoffs. That was awesome. Do you think Seattle will ever get an NBA team again?

Answer: *gives you the middle finger*

Epilogue

Well that's it. My first ever book about Survivor. I hope you enjoyed it. Over the past seventy plus chapters, we've shared some wonderful memories about the first three seasons of Survivor. We laughed. We cried. We talked about the legend of badass Tina. We delved into how Richard Hatch really wasn't a villain at all, if anything Kelly was the villain. We learned how to finally appreciate Ethan. We learned that Colby's decision to take Tina really wasn't that stupid when you look at it in context. We talked about how the players in Borneo really weren't clueless at all, they were simply playing the ethics/perception game instead of the "win at all costs" game. We discussed that you should never ever refer to Elisabeth as "Lis" because that wasn't her fucking name. And, most importantly, we learned that Survivor was already an amazing franchise with amazing characters and an amazing rich history years before anyone had ever heard of that idiot Russell. I hope you enjoyed reading it as much as I enjoyed writing it.

Will there be a sequel to this book? Where I get to write about Marquesas through Pearl Islands? Will there be more books after that? Well at this point I suppose that is all up to you. When I first sat down to hammer out of the details of this book, the publisher I was working with was worried that it would be catering to a market that is a little too niche and a little too specific for its own good. So this first volume (seasons 1 through 3) was more or less a test to see if there would actually be a market for a Survivor history book like this.

I guess what I am saying here is that if this book sells well, there will be another. And another. And probably another. Because believe me, when it comes to Survivor, I have a lot to say about it. At the time, I was right there in the trenches as an "insider" as much as any Survivor fan has ever been allowed to be an insider. And I really want to write about Marquesas through Pearl Islands, because those were definitely my peak years as a Survivor writer. I mean, I had a million readers per week right there in the middle of some of the all-time greatest Survivor seasons. I am DYING for people to want a sequel to this book.

In any case, like I said, I guess it is up to you now. If you liked this book, if you want to see a sequel to it, please tell me about it. Just drop me a line at MLanza1974@aol.com or on my website at funny115.com. And by all means, if you liked it, please pass the word along to your friends. And please write me a positive review on Amazon. That's the kind of thing that will really help.

435

I hope you enjoyed reading my Survivor book. I had a lot of fun writing it. In the words of 98% of my friends when I told them Survivor was coming out with a fourth season in 2002, and it was going to be set in Marquesas, "Oh wow, that show is still on? What the hell, are they going to just beat the concept into the ground? Why don't they just let the whole thing die already?"

I should point out that, at the time of this writing, that was 26 seasons ago.

Mario Lanza
May 25th, 2015

Addendum #1: Did All The Winners Deserve To Win?

Did Richard Hatch, Tina Wesson, and Ethan Zohn deserve to win Survivor?

Does any player _ever_ really deserve to win Survivor?

These are questions that have been asked a countless number of times over the past fifteen years. In fact, if you look around the internet, you will notice that they continue to be asked right up to this very day. Survivor fans on the internet _love_ to ask debate questions like "did so and so deserve to win?" just to provoke a discussion out of everyone. Or to debate who the all-time greatest Survivor winners were. Did Richard Hatch deserve to win? Did Tina Wesson deserve to win? Did Ethan ~~Zorn~~ Zohn deserve to win? Or was there a more deserving winner in each of their seasons?

Well let me make this chapter very short and sweet. Because if there is one thing that I cannot stand about the online Survivor fan base, it has always been the "did so and so really deserve to win Survivor?" debate. This aspect of the Survivor fan base has gotten under my skin for years.

So here we go.

Did Richard deserve to win Borneo? Yes, because he won Borneo.

Did Tina deserve to win Australia? Yes, because she won Australia.

Did Ethan deserve to win Africa? Yes, because he won Africa.

There. Done. Questions answered.

All Survivor winners deserved to win.

The moral of the story here? Nobody likes a winner basher on the internet. So please stop doing it. All Survivor winners deserved to win, and they always will. They deserved to win the game because they won. And besides, who the hell are we to say that they WEREN'T deserving? Especially considering that, as fans, we only see about one percent of one percent of everything that actually went down out there when the game was being played.

Remember, when we watch Survivor, we are simply viewers at home. That's it. We aren't players. We are spectators. And we will never be players. All

<u>we</u> see when we watch Survivor are the edited highlights that create the storyline that the producers want us to follow on their TV show. That's it. To think that we have any "knowledge" of how a season should have ended, and that the jury who was actually there and who actually made that decision, <u>didn't</u> have that knowledge, well I don't think I need to point out to you how ridiculous that is.

All winners deserve to win. A Survivor winner will always deserve to win.

Don't be that guy who says that they weren't deserving.

It's annoying.

Addendum #2: My Top Ten Survivor Seasons

Obviously I haven't had a chance to write about most of these seasons yet. But since I know that a ton of people will email me this question after my book comes out, I figured I better get it out of the way now so that you will know where I stand. So here are my top ten all-time favorite Survivor seasons. From top to bottom, entertainment, characters, comedy, strategy, location, awesomeness, these are the seasons that hold up really well (and actually get better and better) over multiple viewings. Because they pretty much have everything.

Mario's Top Ten Survivor Seasons

#1. Survivor: Pearl Islands - season 7

Pearl Islands is the crown jewel of Survivor seasons. No other season will ever be able to top it. There is so much going on in this season, with so many amazing A+ characters, and such an amazingly well thought out and well produced theme, that it is just an embarrassment of riches that no other season should ever have to try to compare to. I mean, let's put it this way. Sandra is one of my all-time favorite Survivor characters, and she probably isn't even one of the top three best characters in Pearl Islands. Try finding a season that can top that.

#2. Survivor: Marquesas - season 4

If they ever have an entry for what "Survivor" was in an encyclopedia a hundred years from now, Marquesas is the season that I think they should use. Because it is the perfect example of a fantastic Survivor season. It just has big characters and great scenes and great moments all over the place. In fact, the only reason I wouldn't rank Marquesas as my #1 favorite season is because Pearl Islands is so over the top that it is almost like a cartoon. Marquesas is much more gritty than Pearl Islands is, and it is without question an A+ all around masterpiece of a Survivor season. It also has my all-time favorite Survivor theme song.

#3. Survivor: Africa - season 3

Supremely underrated, killer location, amazingly awesome. This is the crown jewel of the first three Survivor seasons. Even Mother Africa would approve of this season.

#4. Survivor: Vanuatu - season 9

I have an incredibly personal connection to this season because Chris Daugherty is maybe my all-time favorite Survivor winner (arguably, and if so, sorry Tina). Chris also has the most amazing storyline of any Survivor winner ever. Seriously, there is <u>no</u> season that improves on a rewatch more than Vanuatu does. Go watch it again sometime and just follow Chris's storyline. It is so good that I have actually flip-flopped Africa and Vanuatu as my #3 season from time to time. Simply because I love them both so much.

#5. Survivor: Amazon - season 6

There has never been a Survivor season that was as "fun" as Amazon. From the first minute of the game to the minute they crowned a winner, Amazon was just light hearted fun and over the top goofiness from start to finish. It is one of those rare seasons that is universally loved by just about everyone, and for good reason. It deserves every bit of praise that it gets.

#6. Survivor: China - season 15

I am not really a fan of anything that CBS and Jeff Probst have done to Survivor since about season eleven. Yes, if you don't know that about me already, I better get that out of the way now so that it won't surprise you. I can't stand about 90% of what has happened to Survivor since they started going to hidden immunity idols and (yuck) a final three and (gag) returning players all the time. I am as old school a Survivor fan as you can possibly get. However, there is ONE season in the modern era that I think is just outstanding, and that is China. The fact that a modern season can almost make my top five? Well that should tell you how outstanding I think China is. To me this is the Survivor: Amazon of the modern era. Just fun, fun, fun, characters, goofiness, and theme. Oh, and also Amanda is there too. It is incredible.

#7. Survivor: The Australian Outback - season 2

Um, Tina won. As if I would ever rank Australian Outback anywhere outside my top ten. And no, I don't care how dull the last two or three episodes were. Tina Wesson won the season, and Tina Wesson is a badass. Also, let's never forget that season two was the biggest that Survivor ever got, and from a historical perspective that is a pretty big damn deal. Oh, and also, Australia episode six (the Mike episode) is maybe the all-time single greatest Survivor episode. This certainly wasn't the best season that Survivor ever put out, but the highlights of Australia were really, really good. It had a ceiling that was much higher than just about any other Survivor season.

#8. Survivor: Thailand - season 5

Underrated, underrated, underrated. You think Africa was underrated and it got crapped on a lot at the time? Wow. Just wait until I get to write about Thailand. By the way, quick note from the guy who wrote the Funny 115: Thailand is maybe the all-time funniest Survivor season, and it never really gets enough credit for that. And just wait until I get a chance to write about Brian Heidik, who was maybe the single greatest (and easily one of the most interesting) Survivor players of all time. Thailand is one of those quietly great early seasons that is just sitting there on DVD, waiting for the fan base to rediscover it and fall in love with it. It is only a matter of time. It really is one of the better Survivor seasons.

#9. Survivor: Borneo - season 1

The original. And in many peoples' eyes, still the best. I don't PERSONALLY think it is the best, since Australia did everything Borneo did, and it did it bigger and better. But still, this season was the grandfather of them all, and you could tell just by watching it that there was so much love put into it. By the way, normally I refuse to include Borneo when I rank my favorite Survivor seasons, because it is really more of a documentary, while the rest of the other seasons are really just homages to Borneo (or just flat out strategy games.) But because I don't want any more modern seasons to make it into my top ten here in my book, I am reinstating Borneo into my rankings just as sort of a one-time special. But really, you can't compare Borneo to any of the other Survivor seasons. It is impossible because they are two completely different types of shows. Borneo was different than the others and it was one of a kind. I will always hold a special place in my heart for it.

#10. Survivor: Samoa - season 19

Samoa is the dark horse on my list, and it is a season that people who know me will probably be very surprised to see in my top ten. Because it really isn't a season that has very many fans out there. But I am telling you right now, watch it again. And watch it this time knowing that Russell loses. Watch it from the perspective of the players OTHER than Russell. When you watch it that way, trust me, it turns out to be a really fun season. The Galus are one of the most underrated Survivor tribes of all time, nearly every single one of them is a hoot. And hey, if watching it that way fails, if you still don't appreciate the Galus after a rewatch, just watch Samoa again knowing that Russell loses and because lol Russell. If nothing else, his warm salty tears should be enough to vault Samoa up onto anyone's list of the most awesome Survivor seasons.

P.S. Yes, I know you have a favorite season, and I know that I didn't include it in my top ten. I know. But it would have been my #11 favorite season. I promise!

Addendum #3: The Underrateds

This is a special section where I want to pay tribute to some of the more underrated characters in Survivor history. You never hear these people mentioned when you talk about "the all-time Survivor greats", but had things gone just a little bit differently, had one vote gone just a slightly different way at a crucial point in the franchise, these are the players you would think of when you think of the big name Survivor legends.

For the first installment of The Underrateds, I would like to shine the spotlight on:

* Stacey Stillman, Borneo
Comments: This one is easy. Stacey was the first player in Survivor history to put together some sort of a voting bloc (it wasn't Richard who invented alliances, it was Stacey), and she was also the one player out of all of the Tagis that Richard was frightened of. Again, let me repeat that. Richard Hatch, the King of Survivor, was an intellectual snob and an elitist of the highest order. He thought that NOBODY was ever in his league when it came to Survivor strategy. Well, except for Stacey. Richard was scared to death of Stacey because he could tell how cunning she was. Stacey was THE most dangerous player early on in Borneo, and Mark Burnett writes about this in great detail in his book. And it is about time she finally gets credit for being the person who invented the Survivor alliance.

* Joel Klug, Borneo
Comments: Joel was the best strategist on Pagong, and he was easily the Pagong equivalent of Richard Hatch. He was the ONE guy on that tribe who knew that if they stuck together and they all voted as a group, that they could take the game and they could run with it all the way to the end. Now, obviously, it didn't really work out for him in the end, since he was on a tribe that was voting based on ethics and not based on numbers. But you can't blame Joel for that. He KNEW that Pagong needed alliances. He knew it. He tried to explain it to them. Hell, just like Dr. Sam Loomis in Halloween, he tried to warn them until he was blue in the face. Had that season worked out just a little bit differently, had the alliance thing just worked out a little bit better, Joel becomes the original Colby and he becomes the first young male

star of the franchise. As he should have been. Also, Joel had nothing to do with the cow joke. That entire episode where he was voted out was complete bullshit.

* Rodger Bingham, Australia

Comments: Kentucky Joe is a great person to have on an underrated list. Why? Well because if you ask the cast of Australia who the sneakiest player was in their season, they will almost always give the exact same name. Almost to a man they will say "Rodger." And why do they always say that? Well because, unbeknownst to anyone in that cast, Rodger was once THE CEO OF AN EFFING BANK. He wasn't just some simple farmer who drove around on a tractor all day and spent his time figuring out crop yield. Nope. Don't you remember the Australia finale, where the rest of players learned that Rodger had a master's degree? Nobody knew that. Not even Elisabeth knew that. Not even his BFF best friend in the world knew that he had a very advanced education. And I can guarantee that no one for damn sure knew that he had been the CEO of a bank for more than a decade, and that he had probably participated in things as nasty as asset liquidations and mortgage defaults and hostile business takeovers. Oh I'm sorry, I'm Kentucky Joe. Did I forget to mention that I once worked in the most cutthroat industry in America? Gee, I'm sorry, I reckon I forgot to tell that to all y'all. And this wasn't the only thing that Rodger was sneaky about. According to interviews that came out after the season, he was constantly trying to undercut people and he was always pulling some sort of mindgame shenanigans when he was playing out there. Heck, this is a guy who the other players considered even sneakier than Jeff Varner. There is no player on Earth who has ever been more underrated than Rodger Bingham. The more I have learned about him over the years, the more I realize how fascinating and unique he was. And you thought Tina was good at hiding behind that cute little country accent.

* Clarence Black, Africa

Comments: Clarence is without question one of the most underrated characters in Survivor history. Just go back and watch Africa again, and this time only pay attention to Clarence. Watch how funny he is. Watch how funny he is in every scene. He is one of those rare Survivor characters (like Sandra) who can make any scene better, simply because he is just one of the bit players in the background. Very few players have ever been able to pull that off over the years, and it is time that Clarence finally starts to get some credit for this. Oh and also, those chickens laid the smallest egg possible. Aw helllllllll no.

* Frank Garrison, Africa

Comments: I love Frank. He was such an endearing weirdo. Seriously, name one other character in Survivor history who was as awkward and who was as out of touch with what normal human beings do as Frank Garrison was. He just sort of existed in his own little alternate universe, and that alone makes him a slam dunk for any sort of a Survivor underrated characters list. Frank was the very definition of memorable and he was one of a kind. And seriously, he really needs to get better at those tell-all sex games.

* Teresa Cooper, Africa

Comments: Just from a player point of view, T-Bird is pretty much the queen of the underrateds. I mean, if ONE little break had gone her way during Africa, she wins that season. She wins and she becomes the new and improved version of Tina. And then everyone worships her. And this is amazing when you realize that T-Bird was never a part of the majority at any point during the entire season of Survivor: Africa. She was ALWAYS a part of the outside, just looking in. Yet everyone loved her, everyone respected her, she had ties to everyone, and she made it all the way to the final five. She even managed to mess Lex up and cause him to go into a tailspin along the way. And all this on top of the fact that the producers tried to sabotage her at the beginning of the game because she was so similar to Tina that they absolutely did not want her to win! I mean, please find me another player from the early seasons who was more underrated than T-Bird. I dare you. It is a travesty that she never got any consideration to come back for All Stars. It is even MORE of a travesty that the fans decided not to vote her back for Second Chances more than ten years later. Come on, Survivor fans, I really expected more from you guys than that. It's too bad this book didn't come out a couple of months prior to the voting for Second Chances, maybe I could have done something to help out poor T-Bird.

* Lindsey Richter, Africa

Comments: Lindsey was once as big a female villain as Jerri, yet for some reason no one in the Survivor fan base ever seems to remember that. But I remember it. Lindsey, I'm sure you hated being a villain at the time, but I know what a big deal you were. I will always remember. And I will never forget how much energy you brought to this franchise. I'll be damned if I let people forget how much the internet talked about you at the time. Even if, yes, you were nowhere near as annoying as Flo was.

Addendum #4: The Real Survivor Hall of Fame

There has been a lot of talk on the internet lately about "The Survivor Hall of Fame." This is a website where the public gets to log in and vote on who they think the most significant players in Survivor history were.

Naturally, I think the Survivor Hall of Fame is a complete load of crap. You should never let the general public vote on anything. Fans have terrible memories.

Here is the Survivor Hall of Fame that I have come up with, which I am ever so diplomatically calling "The Real Survivor Hall of Fame."

Just ignore the other one. The other one sucks. Here are the players (through the first three seasons) that should never be forgotten because of how significant they were to the overall Survivor franchise.

The Real Survivor Hall of Fame
Seasons 1-3

1. **Richard Hatch, Borneo**
2. **Colleen Haskell, Borneo**
3. **Rudy Boesch, Borneo**
4. **Susan Hawk, Borneo**
5. **Gretchen Cordy, Borneo**
6. **Gervase Peterson, Borneo**
7. **Dr. Sean Kenniff, Borneo**
8. **Greg Buis, Borneo**

Borneo comments: The first four people I am electing (Richard, Colleen, Rudy, and Sue) are no brainers, because you really can't even discuss having a Survivor Hall of Fame without beginning with those four. And I also strongly believe that Gretchen is a no brainer. Simply because her vote off (and her importance to the season as a whole) was such a big deal at the time. The fact that Gretchen was voted out, at the time she was voted out, in the

447

manner she was voted out, basically just turned her into the ultimate Survivor martyr. Her vote off moment in Borneo was really where "Survivor" began.

After those five I think you can make a good case for just about any of the other members of Rattana who made the merge. Borneo really <u>was</u> that significant a season. But in the interest of not overwhelming the Real Hall of Fame with Borneo players I will only pick three of them.

Gervase Peterson was one of the biggest Survivor fan favorites at the time, and when it comes to him being a castmember in the first season, that makes him a really big deal. Yes, I know he came back later, and he sucked when he played the second time, but that really doesn't matter to me. Borneo should have the largest representation out of all the players in the Real Hall of Fame, and Gervase was right there behind Colleen as the second most popular Pagong member.

I pick Dr. Sean as my seventh member of the Real Hall of Fame just because his storyline (as infuriating as it was) was so integral to the season. I mean, seriously, try imagining Survivor: Borneo without Dr. Sean always mucking things up. You can't do it.

And Greg? Well I pick Greg Buis because he was weird and because he talked about having sex with sister and because everyone remembers him. And I also do it for the Rebel Alliance.

So these are my eight Borneo Real Hall of Fame members.

Half the cast makes it into the Hall of Fame? Sure, why not. Borneo was huge and Borneo deserves it. No other season will get eight. In fact you are lucky I didn't say we should just include all sixteen.

Kelly Wiglesworth and Jenna Lewis, you were close but sorry, no cigar.

9. Tina Wesson, Australia
10. Colby Donaldson, Australia
11. Jerri Manthey, Australia
12. Michael Skupin, Australia
13. Elisabeth Filarski, Australia
14. Rodger Bingham, Australia
15. Alicia Calaway, Australia

Australia comments: Since Australia was almost as big a deal as Borneo was (in fact, some would argue it was even a bigger deal), I felt it was appropriate that I select seven members from Australia to go along with Borneo's eight. And again, the first three names are total no brainers. Any Survivor Hall of Fame without Tina, Colby, and Jerri is a complete joke.

After those three, I think that Mike is a pretty easy choice to make it in too, simply because his episode (Australia episode six) is without question one of the single greatest Survivor episodes of all time. Not to mention maybe the all-time most memorable one. And again, I don't care if Mike came back and he played again later. I am only going by Australia, and in Australia (especially because of his accident) he was a mega star.

After Mike, I am also including Elisabeth and Rodger, simply because they were both hugely popular characters at the time and they both had an enormous fan base. Plus, Rodger is maybe the one player in Survivor history who I have never heard anyone (fans or players) ever say anything bad about.

For the last slot, I am making a slightly controversial decision and I am going to go with Alicia. Why Alicia? Well because I am tired of hearing people on the internet say "Alicia shouldn't have been on All Stars. Alicia was never a big Survivor character." Um, yes she was. Name one other female Survivor from that era who was so tough and who was so strong (and who was so angry) that she easily could have killed you with her bare hands. Seriously, name one another female that all the males were frightened of. Alicia was a BIG Survivor character. You might not believe me when I say that, but how about this? She starred in a Reebok commercial with Tina right after the season ended. That is what a big character she was. There was no Survivor in the early days who was even slightly comparable to her. Oh yes, Alicia Calaway did absolutely deserve that All Star spot.

Oh, and my apologies to Amber. We can vote her in when we get up to All Stars, I guess.

P.S. Although again, lol that Amber was an All Star.

16. Ethan Zohn, Africa
17. Lex van den Berghe, Africa
18. Tom Buchanan, Africa

19. ~~Chip~~ Silas Gaither, Africa
20. Lindsey Richter, Africa
21. Teresa "T-Bird" Cooper, Africa

Africa comments: The first two seasons were really "the big ones" when it comes to Survivor, so once we get to Africa we can drop down to six inductees. But Africa definitely had some slam dunk Hall of Famers in its cast too. I mean, Ethan, Lex, and Tom, those three have to be in there. And I won't even hear of a Survivor Hall of Fame without Silas Gaither in it. If you care anything about Survivor history at all, the Chipster has to be a member of your Hall of Fame. In fact, that guy was so important he should get his own wing.

I would actually make the exact same argument to include Lindsey Richter, who again, was at one point nearly as big a Survivor villain as Jerri was. You have to reward that kind of impact on the franchise. Like her or not, Lindsey has to be in there. Oh, and people forget that she also had a fantastic boot episode.

That makes five, and after thinking about it long and hard, I have decided that I would like my last Africa Hall of Fame spot to go to T-Bird. Simply because nobody ever remembers T-Bird, and because T-Bird was awesome. And because screw all of you who didn't vote for T-Bird for Second Chances. In the immortal words of Sue Hawk, you guys sucked on that game.

Those are my Africa six, and it breaks my heart that I couldn't include Frank or Brandon or yes even the ever-beloved Ms. Kelly Goldsmith. Even her. But they just miss the cut, simply because I think Africa should have less inductees than the first two seasons.

About the Author

Mario Lanza lives in Southern California with his wife and two children. Over the past fifteen years, he has written way too much about Survivor.

You can read more of Mario's work at funny115.com, and you can also listen to him on his podcast The Survivor Historians, which is available for free over at iTunes.

Mario's future plans are to write a third installment of The Funny 115, and to also write a sequel to this book, which would hopefully go from seasons four through seven.

He also plans to work hard and play hard like Zoe from Marquesas.